Herndon on Lincoln

HERNDON ON LINCOLN

Letters

William H. Herndon

Edited by
Douglas L. Wilson
and Rodney O. Davis

Published by
the Knox College Lincoln Studies Center
and the University of Illinois Press
Urbana, Chicago, and Springfield

Frontispiece: William Henry Herndon (1818–1891)

Library of Congress Cataloging-in-Publication Data
Names: Herndon, William Henry, 1818–1891, author. | Wilson,
    Douglas L. (Douglas Lawson), editor. | Davis, Rodney O.,
    editor. | Knox College (Galesburg, Ill.). Lincoln Studies Center.
Title: Herndon on Lincoln / William H. Herndon ; edited by
    Douglas L. Wilson and Rodney O. Davis.
Description: Urbana : University of Illinois Press, 2016. | Series:
    The Knox College Lincoln Studies Center series | Includes
    bibliographical references and index.
Identifiers: LCCN 2015026551 | ISBN 9780252039812 (hardcover :
    alk. paper) | ISBN 9780252097928 (e-book)
Subjects: LCSH: Lincoln, Abraham, 1809-1865. | Presidents—
    United States—Biography. | Herndon, William Henry,
    1818–1891—Correspondence.
Classification: LCC E457 .H579 2016 | DDC 973.7092—dc23
    LC record available at http://lccn.loc.gov/2015026551

Contents

Preface

The Lincoln Studies Center at Knox College has been engaged in a long-standing project to make accessible the many contributions of William H. Herndon to the study of his law partner, Abraham Lincoln. The impetus for the project was the editors' concern that a great many of the letters and interviews about Lincoln that Herndon had collected from others were either still unpublished or available only in poorly edited and unreliable texts. The effort to compile and edit all these informant materials culminated in the publication in 1998 of *Herndon's Informants: Letters, Interviews, and Statements about Abraham Lincoln*. Drawing on what had been learned in this process about Herndon's efforts as a collector of information and his subsequent collaboration with Jesse W. Weik, the editors next produced an annotated edition of Herndon and Weik's influential biography, *Herndon's Lincoln* (2006).

The present volume is the first of a two-volume work, *Herndon on Lincoln*, that will form the conclusion to the series; it is drawn exclusively from letters written by Herndon himself. The second volume will include Herndon's lectures and other writing about Lincoln. Together, these two volumes will make available the very substantial body of writing, much of it scattered or previously unpublished, that constitutes what Herndon had to say about his law partner beyond the precincts of the famous biography.

As Herndon was a prolific letter writer, and his law partner a frequent subject, the number of Herndon's letters that make some *mention* of Lincoln is quite large, but the Herndon letters and portions thereof included in the present volume constitute a more circumscribed collection, having been selected because they are believed to convey, with few exceptions, something actually indicative about Abraham Lincoln, whether information, anecdote, opinion, or speculation.

As Herndon typically wrote lengthy letters that often address a range of topics, the editors have opted to include here only those portions that concern Lincoln. Admittedly, this raises questions about whether Herndon's remarks appear out of context, and while the editors have attempted to guard against this possibility, the reader is cautioned accordingly. The reader should also note that while the number of letters from Herndon to his collaborator, Jesse W. Weik, relating to work on their joint biography is large enough to fill a substantial book, only those portions that, in the editors' judgment, impart information or opinion about Lincoln are included. As will be apparent, such a distinction can prove difficult to make, and the editors are willing to concede that, in some cases, there may well be reasonable grounds for disagreement as to what has been included or left out.

Many of the letters in this volume are published for the first time, but the collection is by no means exhaustive. While the editors performed a national search of repositories and consequently turned up many previously unknown documents, they found references also to others that could not be located but probably still exist. For example, Herndon wrote a good many letters to newspapers, and not all of those that he himself mentions have been located.

Many of Herndon's letters that have already appeared—such as those in Emmanuel Hertz's *The Hidden Lincoln* (1938)—are presented here for the first time in a carefully edited text.[1] While *The Hidden Lincoln* performed a valuable service in making Lincoln students aware of a great many revealing documents, it is no secret that its editor struggled with the challenge of deciphering Herndon's often difficult handwriting and was insufficiently versed in the details of Lincoln's life. Noting these problems, Paul M. Angle concluded: "A compilation that could have been enormously valuable to the general reading public is actually often misleading except to the relatively small number of students who are themselves capable of correcting its many errors."[2] A less-recognized problem is Hertz's failure to maintain the leaves of the assembled manuscripts in their correct order, with the result that the texts of different letters are sometimes intermingled. For example, a letter to Herndon's collaborator, Jesse W. Weik, dated January 15, 1889, several months prior to publication of their biography, includes references to expected prepublication activity such as preparing an index, but it also contains references to postpublication concerns about the distribution of profits, and concludes with references to the high rate of sales and to the overall character of the reviews.[3] Not surprisingly, Hertz's text of this letter proves to be an amalgamation of four pages from three different letters: the first page from January 1889, the second and third from July 1890, and the fourth from December 1889. This intermingling is still evident in the assemblage of photostats Hertz apparently worked from, which is now in the University of Illinois Library.[4]

Perhaps because Hertz proclaimed in his introduction, "Here at last is Herndon's complete evidence," the idea took root among scholars and other students of Lincoln that *The Hidden Lincoln* had pretty well exhausted the field. When complete, the contents of *Herndon on Lincoln*, especially when combined with that of *Herndon's Informants*, will demonstrate the magnitude of Hertz's miscalculation.

---

1. Hertz.
2. Angle, 97.
3. Hertz, 237–38.
4. The editors are indebted to John M. Hoffman for information about Hertz's materials and their acquisition by the University of Illinois.

Introduction

William H. Herndon was Abraham Lincoln's law partner for sixteen years before Lincoln was elected president in 1860. Nine years younger than Lincoln, Herndon had worked as a student-clerk at the law office where Lincoln was junior partner to Stephen T. Logan in the 1840s. Logan and Lincoln dissolved their partnership in 1844 near the time their clerk was about to be licensed to practice law, and to Herndon's great astonishment, Lincoln proposed that they become partners.[1] Why Lincoln, who was already a rising star in politics as well as at the bar, picked the inexperienced clerk for a partner was a mystery to all, including Herndon. Asked the question late in life, Herndon replied: "I don't know and no one else does."[2] But part of the answer is perhaps suggested in what Herndon remembered Lincoln saying to him at the time: "Billy, I can trust you, if you can trust me."[3]

The two men were very different, but they worked well together, and their new firm prospered. Although they divided their fees equally, Lincoln was clearly the senior partner in most other ways. He had been practicing law since 1837 and had already served four terms in the state legislature, where he had gained stature as a leader of the "Long Nine," the Sangamon County legislators responsible for bringing the state capital to Springfield in 1839. His statewide reputation as a leader in the Whig party was growing, and he would be elected to Congress two years later in 1846. Herndon was then young and untried, but he would prove himself a sound and energetic lawyer who was content to be, as he once described himself, the "runt of the firm." In the same letter, he described his partner as a "hoss," and while admitting that he himself was not, he added, "Yet I suppose will pass among the crowd as a Liberty lover—a fool and a Reformer."[4]

By the time he wrote this in 1857, a reformer and liberty lover he certainly was. Unlike his partner, Herndon became an abolitionist, which was a decidedly radical stance in his part of the world and evidence that he was his own man. His views were quoted approvingly by William Lloyd Garrison in the *Liberator*, and he corresponded regularly with other leading spokesmen for abolition, such as Wendell Phillips and Theodore Parker.[5] He was also a diligent reformer at the local level

---

1. Donald, 18–19. WHH more than once remembered the year he formed his partnership with AL as 1843.
2. WHH to JWW, February 24, 1887, §190.
3. *Herndon's Lincoln*, 168.
4. WHH to Wendell Phillips, May 12, 1857, §4.
5. See Donald, 84. Letters to Parker and Phillips that mention AL are included in the present volume, but they represent only a small fraction of the total.

and was sufficiently respected to have been elected mayor of Springfield in 1854. As his biographer has shown, Herndon was a reform mayor and an active one.[6] In an age when there was much talk about the social problems created by alcohol but little actually done about it, he succeeded in getting a local ban on the sale of liquor, in spite of (or perhaps in part, because of) his own susceptibility to binge drinking. His most notable achievement as mayor was in starting Springfield's first public school system. Always active in politics, his acknowledged stature in this field is indicated by his prominent role in the founding of the Republican Party of Illinois in 1856.

From that time on, Herndon was tireless in his support of his partner's political ventures in the new Republican Party, ventures that would raise Lincoln to national recognition and, eventually, the presidency. Yet among the group of Lincoln's closest associates and supporters, Herndon was one of the few who did not seek or expect a presidential appointment in return. Apart from corresponding occasionally about their law business and local developments, and a brief trip to Washington to lobby for a government office for his prospective brother-in-law, Herndon seems to have had little meaningful contact with his by-then-famous law partner. Like many other radicals, Herndon criticized Lincoln for what he saw as the tardiness and timidity of his presidential dealing with slavery, but the news of Lincoln's assassination, he told a correspondent, "struck me dumb . . . [and] incomprehensible, leaving a misty distant doubt of its truth."[7]

Lincoln's death and his immediate status as a martyred national hero dramatically changed Herndon's life. Almost at once he was besieged by reporters, prospective biographers, and others for firsthand information about his law partner, while at the same time he was urged by friends and associates to compile his own personal recollections of Lincoln. Little more than a month after the assassination, Herndon began gathering information for an intended work that he described as "a short little thing" that would present "the subjective . . . 'The inner life' of Mr L."[8] But this effort brought Herndon such interesting new information about Lincoln, especially about the years before Herndon knew him, that the quest took on a life of its own. New information brought new questions to be investigated and new leads to develop, and these would quickly involve Herndon in a prodigious amount of research. Neglecting his law practice, he spent a great deal of time interviewing people who had known Lincoln in the early phases of his life, corresponding with others, and traveling to places where Lincoln had lived before coming to Springfield. He ransacked newspaper archives for texts of Lincoln's speeches and accounts of his activities in the state legislature. He seems to have been utterly consumed by this project, which took much of his time for more than two years.[9]

Realizing the historical importance of this material, Herndon hired a scribe in 1866 to make copies of everything he had collected—an archive he called his "Lincoln Record." Keeping the originals in his own possession, he had the tran-

---

6. Donald, 67–71.

7. WHH to Caroline Healey Dall, May 26, 1865, §29.

8. WHH to Josiah G. Holland, May 26, 1865, §28.

9. For a fuller account of his investigations and the fruits of his research, see *Herndon's Informants*, xiii–xxiv.

scribed copies bound into three large volumes and deposited in a bank vault for safekeeping. His stated intention was to write his projected biographical account of his law partner in 1867, but for a variety of reasons this did not happen. For one thing, he could not resolve the ambiguities in the evidence he had collected about certain delicate matters, such as Lincoln's paternity. Having boldly committed himself to telling the truth, he understandably wanted to be reasonably certain he knew what the truth was. He had probably underestimated the difficulties that attend the apparently straightforward task of writing a coherent and readable narrative, as time would prove that this was not his forte. Another problem was that Herndon had inherited a farm at his father's death in 1867, and, losing interest in the law, he was eager to move to the country and set up a family farming operation. As he attempted to deal with these crosscurrents, Herndon put his Lincoln biography on hold.

By 1869, Herndon's enthusiasm for writing his partner's biography had cooled, and, needing money, he sold the copies of his "Lincoln Record"—the three bound volumes, not the originals—to Ward Hill Lamon, a friend of Lincoln's from the Eighth Circuit. Lamon turned Herndon's "Lincoln Record" over to his partner and ghostwriter, Chauncey F. Black, a member of a prominent Democratic family. The book published under Lamon's name in 1872 was largely based on Herndon's materials, but its rank treatment of Lincoln's background and early life was widely considered in bad taste and too sensational for the biography of a martyred president.[10] Josiah G. Holland, whose earlier biography lacked the richness of detail that Herndon's research had provided, nonetheless denounced it: "The violent and reckless prejudice, and the utter want of delicacy and even of decency by which the book is characterized will more than counterbalance the value of its new material."[11] Nor was it just Victorian prudery that made the book objectionable. In 1948, David Donald would charge: "It combined ruthless revelation and flippant cynicism to give a devastating caricature of Lincoln."[12] Roundly condemned by reviewers, Lamon's book fell dead from the press, but it effectively made public a substantial portion of the eyewitness testimony and personal information Herndon had collected. Many of those who disapproved of its revelations, like Robert Todd Lincoln, the president's son, tended to hold Herndon personally responsible for their disclosure.

One of the things in Lamon's biography that rankled Lincoln's admirers was its treatment of the skeptical attitude Lincoln held in his youth toward orthodox Christian beliefs. Without permission and against Herndon's advice, Lamon and his ghostwriter used testimony Herndon had gathered from prominent Springfield citizens about Lincoln's outspoken religious skepticism in his early years. When Rev. James Reed, a Springfield clergyman, approached the embarrassed witnesses about their testimony, they issued canny denials, which Reed promptly featured in an 1873 lecture defending Lincoln's religious orthodoxy "in his later years."

---

10. Lamon.

11. Quoted in Donald, 269. The valuable testimony Holland collected, often overlooked, is presented in Allen C. Guelzo, "Holland's Informants: The Construction of Josiah Holland's 'Life of Abraham Lincoln,'" *Journal of the Abraham Lincoln Association* 23:1 (Winter 2002), 1–53.

12. Donald, 268.

Subsequently published in *Scribner's Monthly*, Reed's lecture attacked Herndon personally, and this, together with the urging of his wife and close friends, convinced Herndon to respond with a public lecture of his own on "Lincoln's Religion."[13]

The lecture was printed in a Springfield paper, the Democratic *Illinois State Register*, and widely reprinted across the nation. Herndon's combative stance and his stout insistence that Abraham Lincoln had "died an unbeliever" earned him nationwide hostility. The affair even took on political significance, as the Republican Party and its newspapers reacted strongly to anything that threatened to undermine Lincoln's stature as a great national hero. Mindful that Herndon had recently left the Republican ranks and supported Democrats, Republican editors approvingly reprinted an editorial from the *New York Tribune* that denounced him as a "Judas in Springfield."[14] This public furor was compounded by Herndon's use in his lecture of testimony he had taken in an interview with President Lincoln's wife, in which she allowed that her husband had not been a "technical Christian." When an angry Mary Todd Lincoln disingenuously issued a flat denial, Herndon published an open letter that recounted her entire testimony, in which she had admitted that Lincoln had never joined a church and that he "had no hope and no faith in the usual acceptation of these words."[15]

As a result of these public forays and the damning implication that he was a willful purveyor of unbecoming, if not libelous, stories about Lincoln, Herndon found himself the object of widespread enmity. In 1882 he characterized in a public letter the cloud he had been under since his controversy with Reed:

> Soon thereafter, say from 1874 to 1882, I saw floating around in the newspaper literature, such charges as "Herndon is in the lunatic asylum, well chained," "Herndon is a pauper," "Herndon is a drunkard," "Herndon is a vile infidel and a knave, a liar and a drunkard," and the like. I have contradicted all these things under my own hand often, except as to my so-called infidelity, liberalism, free religious opinions or what-not."[16]

An example is a brief exchange that appeared in the *New York Tribune* in September 1877: "Mr. W. H. Herndon, once the law-partner of Abraham Lincoln, attempted to commit suicide at Springfield, Ill., last Saturday by taking laudanum. He is very ill in consequence." Two weeks later, the paper printed Herndon's answer: "I never attempted to commit suicide, never took laudanum; am well, happy, hearty, doing well, and hope to live just one hundred years, and to do good to my fellow-man to the end."[17]

It is probably not a mere coincidence that Herndon's reemergence in 1882 as a public spokesman on the subject of Abraham Lincoln followed the death that

---

13. Published in the *Illinois State Register* (Springfield, Ill.), December 13, 1873.

14. Donald, 279. See Donald, 279–82, for evidence of widespread Republican defensiveness at Herndon's revelations.

15. WHH to Editor, *Daily State Journal*, January 12, 1874, §103.

16. WHH to Editor, *Truth Seeker*, November 20, 1882.

17. *New-York Semiweekly Tribune*, September 14 and 28, 1877.

year of Mary Todd Lincoln. Offering himself as public lecturer on his former law partner, he had only a few takers, but he continued his practice of answering inquiries from all comers. A few years later he attempted to set down in a memorandum the kind and extent of his activities over the years as a provider of information on Lincoln.

When men—writers—biographers—correspondents asked information about Lincoln I freely gave it—did so to all interviewers—all men in short. Never sold a letter of Lincoln—gave them away—never received a dollar from man nor woman for what I wrote, except for a lecture which I delivered in Petersburg in 1887-2(1882) and except for a lecture delivered in Pekin in this State in 1882–3. I have helped all people to facts—characteristics—qualities &c. &c of Lincoln and never charged a cent, except as above. And except an article for North Am Review for 1886–7[18]

I have helped Doctr Holland to some of the facts of Lincolns life—many new facts.[19] I have helped Arnold to facts for both of his works on Lincoln[20]— gave him a list of Lincoln's Speeches when and where to find them—. . . I have tried to accommodate all persons when they have asked for facts—opinions &c &c—have talked freely to all persons and it is quite likely have been misunderstood and misrepresented, but I stand on the record . . . I have tried in all that I have said or written to be truthful and impartial. I felt it my religious duty to tell all that I know about Lincoln—facts—opinions—attributes— characteristics—qualities &c.[21]

In 1885 Herndon began an informal collaboration with Jesse W. Weik, a young man from Greencastle, Indiana. The son of a German immigrant and graduate of what would become DePauw University, Weik was hoping to begin a career as a writer, and the subject that most appealed to him was his idol, Abraham Lincoln. Herndon agreed to help by sending him little known facts and stories, which he did through a series of almost-daily letters that were, in the words of David Donald, "chock-full of information and anecdote about Lincoln."[22] Before another year was out, Herndon and Weik had drawn up a contract as collaborators on a biography of Lincoln, for which Herndon was to provide most of the substance and Weik was to do the organization, editing, and composition. Accordingly, Herndon transferred his archive of original materials into Weik's keeping, and, after a great many ups and downs, the partnership produced a landmark biography that was published in 1889 as *Herndon's Lincoln: The True Story of a Great Life.*[23]

---

18. This article, whose subject was Lincoln's domestic life, was apparently submitted but never published. See pp. 157, 165, and 229–30.

19. Josiah G. Holland, who wrote the first extensive biography after Lincoln's assassination. See Holland.

20. See Arnold (1) and Arnold (2).

21. "A Statement—Memoranda By Wm. H. Herndon," January 8, 1886. LC: HW3253–57; Exp 4:9:1910– 19.

22. Donald, 299.

23. For information on the travails of the partnership in writing and publishing the biography, see Donald, 296–342; and *Herndon's Lincoln*, xxiii–xxxv.

To the authors' dismay, their publisher printed only fifteen hundred copies of the biography, precisely the number for which their contract specified that they would receive no royalties, and promptly went bankrupt. By the time the publishers were able to emerge from bankruptcy and print additional copies the following year, demand for the work had all but lapsed, and the authors received nothing for their four-year effort. Before another publisher could be secured and a revised edition issued, Herndon died on March 18, 1891.

Except for his wife, Abraham Lincoln had no associate with whom he worked more closely over a longer period than William H. Herndon. Herndon thus had an ideal opportunity to observe Lincoln at close range, to acquire a basic familiarity with his characteristic attitudes and behavior, to be privy to some of his confidential thoughts, and to act as a sounding board for a man who tended to keep his personal views and intentions to himself. Herndon has been justly criticized for recklessly claiming, on occasion, to have known Lincoln better than the man knew himself, which is, of course, hyperbole. But as the reader of these letters will discover, what he usually imparted in this regard was something quite different—that he was more often frustrated by his inability to penetrate Lincoln's habitual reserve.[24]

Another reason Herndon's letters about Lincoln are valuable is that Herndon, having carried on an ambitious project to collect information about his law partner's life and career, frequently offers revealing circumstances about his sources of information, including his doubts or misgivings about particular informants or their testimony. Surprisingly, this even included his own. For example, the printed text of his joint biography has him saying about Lincoln's humiliating treatment in the famous Manny reaper trial: "He [Lincoln] told me that he had been 'roughly handled by that man Stanton'; that he overheard the latter from an adjoining room, while the door was slightly ajar, referring to Lincoln, inquire of another, 'Where did that long-armed creature come from, and what can he expect to do in this case?'"[25] In reading proof on this passage before publication, Herndon protested in a letter to his collaborator: "Heaven's sake do not forget to erase the words—'*Lincoln told me so*' in the long armed ape Stanton story. I cannot swear at this late date where I got the story—I want to be on the safe side."[26] But characteristically at this stage of their project, his collaborator ignored Herndon's plea, with the result that many writers since have cited this quotation in the biography without benefit of Herndon's own reservations.

This incident points to another important consideration, for unlike the text of his joint biography, *Herndon's Lincoln*, these letters were written by Herndon himself, in his own voice and idiosyncratic style of presentation. Although the first-person narration of the biography appears to be coming directly from Hern-

---

24. See, for example, WHH's open letter to the public, November 9, 1882, §115; to _____, November 24, 1882, §116; to Fowler, October 30, 1888, §232; to Remsburg, September 10, 1887, §205.
25. *Herndon's Lincoln*, 220.
26. WHH to JWW, January 15, 1889, §245.

don, the composition of the biography can be shown to have been almost exclusively the work of his collaborator, Jesse W. Weik.[27] Using the information in the letters Herndon had sent him and the material in Herndon's "Lincoln Record" (frequently quoted by way of Lamon's biography), Weik crafted a presentation whose principal feature was an appealing, first-person narration. While this narrative voice was suitably convincing for the purposes of the biography, it is very different from the authentic one on display in Herndon's letters. This is also the case with the content thereof, which is why David Donald issued this cautionary note: "To understand Herndon's own rather peculiar approach to Lincoln biography, one must go back to his letters."[28]

One important aspect of his "peculiar approach" has to do with Herndon's early determination not to suppress what he deemed "necessary truths" about Lincoln. "Necessary truths" he once described in his singular manner as "those facts—truths, & principles which illustrate—show and boldly develop Mr Lincoln's mind, nature—constitution of body, as well as of mind—the qualities of mind—heart—soul—feelings—education, aspirations—modifications of mind &c. &c."[29] Such an approach to biography meant including revelations that would have been considered in Herndon's day too private or embarrassing or otherwise inappropriate for inclusion in a published biography, especially where the subject was a martyred national hero. Effectively, this meant that Herndon intended to defy the accepted Victorian prohibitions on discussion of such things as illegitimacy, unorthodox religious views, and marital discord, to name a few. He argued that this was "necessary" because all were contributing factors to Lincoln's distinctive makeup and development, which in turn gave rise to his emergence as an exceptional leader and one of the world's greatest men.

The arguments and issues surrounding Herndon's early commitment to "necessary truths" are a notable dimension of his biographical efforts, and they can be fully accessed only through his letters. Ironically, the letters reveal not only the character of Herndon's original intention, his rationale, and his determination to carry it through but also his eventual willingness to censor his disclosures to some degree, so as not to offend informants or alienate prospective readers.[30]

As this implies, over the long course of Herndon's biographical enterprise he disclosed and discussed many things pertaining to Lincoln in his letters that never made it into his lectures or published writings. Many of these had to do with Herndon's constant attempt to humanize his partner in the face of overwhelming public pressure to portray him as a hallowed saint. His young collaborator, Jesse W. Weik, grew up idolizing the martyred president and tended to picture him in ideal terms. Accordingly, Herndon wrote him at an early stage of their association:

---

27. Donald, 318; *Herndon's Lincoln*, xxviii–xxxii.

28. Ibid., 301.

29. WHH to Mr. Hickman, December 6, 1866, §62. See Douglas L. Wilson, "William H. Herndon and the 'Necessary Truth,'" *Lincoln before Washington: New Perspectives on the Illinois Years* (Urbana: University of Illinois Press, 1997), 37–52.

30. See, for example, WHH to JWW, October 10, 1888, §229.

"Sometimes he [Lincoln] fell short of his own ideal, as he has often told me: he has told me facts of his life that were not Lincoln's but poor human nature's *in* Lincoln. I shall never tell them to mortal man and of this be sure. Lincoln *as a whole* was really a most noble man."[31] Like his partner, Herndon did not always live up to his own ideals either, for letters written near the end of his life show that he eventually did reveal some of the very things that he had previously intended to keep to himself.

A prime example of such a revelation was that, as a young man, Lincoln had visited prostitutes. While not included in his biography and not revealed publicly until many years after his death, this revelation is precisely the kind of thing that triggered strong resentment from Lincoln's admirers. Such resentment helped to engender mistrust of Herndon as a reliable witness, even though the sources he cited in this case were confidential disclosures from Joshua Speed, Lincoln's closest friend, and from Lincoln himself.[32] Doubts about Herndon personally, as well as about his methods and disclosures, seriously clouded his reputation with his contemporaries, but in the twentieth century his standing as a source of reliable information would suffer a period of drastic eclipse.[33] Whereas his contemporaries had reprehended his candor and indiscretion, his twentieth-century critics charged him with bias and a calculated *lack* of candor. Some would go further and see his unwelcome disclosures as evidence of malice and a wish to demean his famous partner.[34] The editors of the present volume have not attempted here to sort out or assess these issues, a process that is far from settled, but there can be little doubt that his letters about Lincoln constitute an important source for testing the aptness and validity of the biographical offenses Herndon has been charged with over the years.

Both Herndon's virtues and his shortcomings as a biographer are on display in these letters. For most readers, they tend to convey an impression of honesty and sincerity, which is partly created by his willingness to share his own foibles and naiveté. He admits, for example, that he did not record many of the things he was told about Lincoln by his informants. "In fact I did not, many times, see the importance of the information imparted to me till long after it was told me. Never saw the importance of much—many things till they rounded up as a whole."[35] Acknowledging this afterward as a fault effectively exhibits one of his virtues.

In his letters generally, his intention to be truthful in what he relates about his partner rings clear, but as his biographer David Donald has observed, "to tell the truth one must first be able to recognize that rare article."[36] Herndon's difficulty

---

31. WHH to JWW, November 21, 1885, §137.

32. See WHH to JWW, January 1891, §278, and WHH to JWW, January 5, 1889, §242.

33. See John Y. Simon, "Abraham Lincoln and Ann Rutledge," *Journal of the Abraham Lincoln Association* 11 (1990): 13–33; and Douglas L. Wilson, "Herndon's Legacy," *Lincoln before Washington*, 21–36. See also *Herndon's Informants*, xx–xxiii.

34. See, for example, Ruth Painter Randall, *Mary Lincoln: Biography of a Marriage* (Boston: Little, Brown); and John J. Duff, *A. Lincoln: Prairie Lawyer* (New York: Rinehart, 1960).

35. WHH to JWW, October 20, 1888, §230.

36. *Lincoln's Herndon*, 348.

in differentiating fact from opinion was apparently real and is sometimes blatantly evident in his letters. For example, he once described for his collaborator Lincoln's public posture on the secession crisis during the period between his election and his presidential inauguration: "You will perceive in one of [his speeches before his inauguration] that Mr Lincoln pleads for patience & to put all restraints on our passion—ill temper—hot acts &c. Strange as it may appear to you it is nevertheless a fact, *in my opinion*, that Mr Lincoln never fully comprehended the situation; he talks of patience when treason has done its work; he should have talked of, 'to arms' or kept his silence."[37]

Here Herndon reports what he acknowledges to be his own *opinion* as a *fact*, which perhaps sheds light on a basic problem in distinguishing one from the other. Part of the difficulty is, of course, one of terminology. What Herndon firmly believed to be true—either because well-attested or self-evident from the circumstances—he was inclined to call a *fact*. Thus the stories he collected from Lincoln's former friends and neighbors in New Salem were leading him to "the *facts & thruths* of Lincoln's life—not fictions—not fables—not floating rumors, but *facts—solid facts & well attested truths.*"[38] How authentic facts were to be sorted out from fables and fictions is not made clear. Nor is it clear that all things he calls "facts" are necessarily factual. For example, "All these facts, if facts they are I received from different persons at different times and places."[39]

Herndon's understanding of the difference between "fact" and "opinion" takes on an interesting coloration as applied to his thinking about his own Lincoln biography. On more than one occasion, he urged his collaborator that they should confine themselves to reporting only the "facts."[40] After the book's publication, he wrote a correspondent "In my 'Life of Lincoln' I tried to stick to facts without giving my opinions about them or the man, leaving each person to form his own opinions."[41] Even if he was using "opinions" to mean "analysis" or "interpretation," as may well have been the case, the most casual reader of *Herndon's Lincoln* will encounter "opinion" and "analysis" and "interpretation" in profusion. Biographers can hardly avoid such things and still do what is expected of them, since facts are often neither self-evident nor self-explanatory. In Herndon's defense, one should note that he lived at a time when Abraham Lincoln was still a subject of controversy, North as well as South, and he probably felt sincerely that he had tried to present the incidents of Lincoln's life straightforwardly and without the customary polemics, which is to say, factually.

It is worth noting in conclusion that Herndon, who sometimes despaired of ever producing a formal biography of his law partner, nonetheless took consolation from the circumstance that, in having assembled and preserved his massive "Lincoln Record," he had undoubtedly performed an important service for future

---

37. WHH to JWW, August 8, 1890, §268.
38. WHH to J. S. Holland, June 8, 1865, §30.
39. WHH to JWW, January 19, 1886, §160.
40. For example, WHH to JWW, January 2, 1887, §174.
41. WHH to Cyrus O. Poole, March 14, [1890], §259.

generations. A few weeks after delivering a much-criticized lecture, he wrote to a friend: "I don't care whether men like this or not—nor whether they like my Lectures or not. My day is to-morrow—not to-day, and to to-morrow I appeal."[42] Nearly 150 years later, for all its faults and unrealized intentions, his overall contribution to the study of Abraham Lincoln far exceeds that of any other and remains indispensible.

---

42. WHH to Charles Hart, November 28, 1866, §58.

Editorial Note

The selections in this volume are all drawn from letters written by William H. Herndon, a substantial number being excerpts, as noted in the preface. The text is presented as written, with spellings and punctuation as found. Words inadvertently repeated have been omitted. Words inadvertently dropped are not editorially supplied. In cases where there is uncertainty as to the identity of the word or the spelling, the word is followed by a question mark and shown in square brackets.

The difference between a capital and a lowercase letter, though clear and potentially meaningful in print, can be very difficult to discern in a handwritten text, and the reader is advised that this is especially true for Herndon's handwriting. Marks clearly intended as punctuation are sometimes ambiguous and might, for example, be taken as representing either a period or a comma. In such cases, the mark is here given a conventional interpretation, so that a mark at the end of a sentence that might be either a comma or a period is rendered in the text as a period.

The doubled dash, which resembles an equal sign, is here rendered as a regular dash; the double underline is treated the same as a single underline, with the words rendered in italic type. Raised letters are lowered to the normal position. Words that have been stricken by the writer are not usually shown, but where strikeouts are considered possibly significant, they are either shown in the text or pointed out in the notes.

In addition to what was described above, square brackets are used to present material absent from the text or unable to be transcribed. When enclosing matter in roman type, square brackets indicate words or letters that the editors believe were originally in the document but have since been obliterated through stain or mutilation. Bracketed material in italic type (such as [*illegible*] for illegible matter) represents an editorial insertion.

In the interest of a consistent format, certain elements of the documents are always treated in the same way. The place and date of the document, where present, are given at the beginning of the text flush right, regardless of where they appear in the document itself. Place and date are given as written, although the county, where superfluous, is ignored. Letters bearing the same date are given sequential numbers within brackets after the date. The salutation is always given flush left on the next line. Redundant salutations ("Mr. Parker / Dear Sir") are reduced ("Dear Sir") to conserve space. The closing line, such as "Yours truly," and the signature are always printed at the end of the text. The inside address, if any, is omitted, as is docketing, unless it is the source of the date or is cited in the notes.

A substantial majority of the documents presented here are reproduced from original manuscripts in the Herndon-Weik Collection at the Library of Congress. These are marked at the end of the entry by the designation LC, followed by HW and the foliation, or mounting, numbers: for example, *LC: HW2991–94.* Researchers are cautioned that the current foliation numbers were added after the microfilm was created, so that documents depicted in microfilm may bear an earlier number. As an aid to the many researchers working from the Library of Congress microfilm of the Herndon-Weik Collection, the editors have, where possible, listed the document's group, reel, and exposure numbers, so that the source notation *Exp 4:7:447–48* indicates that the document will be found in group 4, reel 7, exposure numbers 447–48.

Documents found in other locations are identified by repository and, where possible, collection. Where the repository of the original manuscript is unknown, the copy or printed source is given.

The dated entries appear in chronological order. For undated documents, a conjectural date is given in italics within square brackets. The presence of a question mark indicates a degree of uncertainty about the dating; its absence implies the contrary. Placement of the undated documents is conjectural, based on available evidence. Documents for which there is evidence only of the year are ranked after dated documents from that year. Where there is only evidence of the chronological range of the document, it is ranked after the dated documents in the latest year of the range. Where there is no indication as to when the document was written, it is placed in the "date unknown" section at the end of the volume.

Short Citations and Abbreviations

AL	Abraham Lincoln
ALPL	Abraham Lincoln Presidential Library
Angle	Paul M. Angle, *A Shelf of Lincoln Books: A Critical Selective Bibliography of Lincolniana* (New Brunswick, N.J.: Rutgers University Press, 1946)
Arnold (1)	Isaac N. Arnold, *The History of Abraham Lincoln, and the Overthrow of Slavery* (Chicago: Clarke, 1866)
Arnold (2)	Isaac N. Arnold, *The Life of Abraham Lincoln* (Chicago: Jansen, McClurg, 1885)
Barrett	Joseph H. Barrett, *Life of Abraham Lincoln* (Richmond, Va.: Loomis National Library Association, 1888)
BPL	Boston Public Library
Brown	John Hay Library, Brown University
Carpenter	F. B. Carpenter, *Six Months at the White House with Abraham Lincoln: The Story of a Picture* (New York: Hurd and Houghton, 1866)
CHM	Chicago History Museum
Collected Works	Roy P. Basler et al., eds., *The Collected Works of Abraham Lincoln,* 9 vols. (New Brunswick, N. J.: Rutgers University Press, 1953)
Columbia	Columbia University Library
Concerning Mr. Lincoln	Harry E. Pratt, ed., *Concerning Mr. Lincoln* (Springfield, Ill.: Abraham Lincoln Association, 1944)
Cornell	Division of Rare and Manuscript Collections, Carl A. Kroch Library, Cornell University
Donald	David Donald, *Lincoln's Herndon* (New York: Da Capo, 1989 [1948])
Every-Day Life	Francis F. Browne, ed. *The Every-Day Life of Abraham Lincoln* (New York: Thompson, 1887)
Exp	Microfilm exposure number
Fehrenbacher	Don E. Fehrenbacher and Virginia Fehrenbacher, comp., *Recollected Words of Abraham Lincoln* (Stanford, Calif.: Stanford University Press, 1996)

Ford
Thomas Ford, *A History of Illinois*, edited by Rodney O. Davis (Urbana: University of Illinois Press, 1995 [1854])

Herndon's Informants
Douglas L. Wilson and Rodney O. Davis, eds., *Herndon's Informants: Letters, Interviews, and Statements about Abraham Lincoln* (Urbana: University of Illinois Press, 1998)

Herndon's Lincoln
William H. Herndon and Jesse W. Weik, *Herndon's Lincoln*, edited by Douglas L. Wilson and Rodney O. Davis (Urbana: University of Illinois Press, 2006)

Hildene
Hildene: The Lincoln Family Home. Former home of Robert Todd Lincoln, Manchester, Vermont

HL
Huntington Library

Holland
J. G. Holland, *The Life of Abraham Lincoln* (Springfield, Mass.: Gurdon Bill, 1866)

Houghton
Houghton Library, Harvard University

HSP
Historical Society of Pennsylvania

HW
Herndon-Weik Collection

Illinois
University of Illinois Library

Iowa
University of Iowa Library

JWW
Jesse W. Weik

Lamon
Ward H. Lamon, *The Life of Abraham Lincoln: From His Birth to His Inauguration* (Boston: Osgood, 1872)

LC
Library of Congress

Lincoln-Douglas Debates
Rodney O. Davis and Douglas L. Wilson, eds., *The Lincoln-Douglas Debates: The Lincoln Studies Center Edition* (Urbana: University of Illinois Press, 2008)

LMU
Lincoln Memorial University

MHS
Massachusetts Historical Society

Nicolay and Hay
John G. Nicolay and John Hay, *Abraham Lincoln: A History*, 10 vols. (New York: Century, 1890)

NYHS
New York Historical Society

NYPL
New York Public Library

Oldroyd
Osborn H. Oldroyd, ed., *The Lincoln Memorial: Album-Immortelles; Original Life Pictures, with Autographs, from the Hands and Hearts of Eminent Americans and Europeans, Contemporaries of the Great Martyr to Liberty, Abraham Lincoln; Together with Extracts from His Speeches, Letters and Sayings* (New York: Carleton, 1882)

Oral History
Michael Burlingame, ed., *An Oral History of Abraham Lincoln: John G. Nicolay's Interviews and Essays* (Carbondale: Southern Illinois University Press, 1996)

Rail-Splitter	*The Rail Splitter: A Journal for the Lincoln Collector*, available at http://railsplitter.com/?page_id=248; accessed September 18, 2012
Six Historic Americans	John E. Remsburg, *Six Historic Americans: Paine, Jefferson, Washington, Franklin, Lincoln, Grant: The Fathers and Saviors of Our Republic, Freethinkers* (New York: Truth Seeker, 1906)
Speeches and Writings I	*Abraham Lincoln, Speeches and Writings 1832–1858: Speeches, Letters, and Miscellaneous Writings / The Lincoln-Douglas Debates* (New York: Library of America, 1989)
Temple	Wayne C. Temple, "Lincoln the Lecturer, Part I," *Lincoln Herald* 101 (Fall 1999): 94–110; "Part II," *Lincoln Herald* 102 (Winter 1999): 146–63
Warren	Louis Warren, *Lincoln's Youth* (Indianapolis: Indiana Historical Society, 1959)
WHH	William H. Herndon
Yale	Yale University Library
Yates and Pickering	Richard Yates and Catherine Yates Pickering, *Richard Yates Civil War Governor*, edited by John H. Krenkel (Danville, Ill.: Interstate, 1966)

Herndon on Lincoln

1. To John J. Hardin

Springfield Ills Feby 12th 1844

Dear Sir

When I was in Jacksonville I promised to write to you. I now will fulfill my promise. You in return promised me you would send me some *whig* documents, but I have never had the pleasure of seeing one from you.[1] I do not accuse you of carelessness by any means, but shall impute it all together to forgetfullness or to a slip of the memory. Now about politics in general. We have had several whig meetings in Springfield lately and they seem to have carried enthusiasm to its highest pitch and every feeling seems to be strained toward one common centre and that common centre is *Henry Clay*. You may talk about enthusiasm for Gov Harrison, but this far excells the feeling of 1840. We are forming "Clay Clubs" in every precinct in the county and at this minute E. D. Baker[2] is in Mechanicsburg addressing a "Clay Club" there and friend Hardin if nothing happen between this and november Henry Clay will get *One Thousand majority in Sangamon County*; that is permitted M. Van Buren and Henry Clay are the respective candidates of the two parties. Van Buren's name is cold and icy to the people feelings, but Clay's name is a spark of fire thrown into a magazine. You may think this is exageration, but when you return home you will find the statement true in letter and in spirit. At these "Clay Clubs" we sing good old songs for "Gallant Harry" and this with eloquent speaking from Logan[3] Lincoln and Baker You may well imagine the effect. I will not describe all these meetings to you, but suffice it to say we have a meeting once or twice in a week and we intend to keep them up till November and it is by these means that we intend to beat our neighbor, Morgan County, at least 500—We intend to print a small paper Called the "Olive Branch" here till January 1845 or at least till after the election in *november 1844*. Subscriptions are coming in very fast and we also intend to print a Dutch paper to continue perhaps longer, to this also subscriptions are Coming and "Still the cry is they Come they come" If we cannot carry Illinois in November 1844 for Gallant Hal, by singing, speaking truths, [tatling?] facts and publishing documentary evidence we then intend giving her up to hardness of heart. I do not hear of such movement as there is in Morgan County, but hope and pray that her good citizens are doing their duty

---

1. Hardin was in Washington serving in Congress, whose members were expected to send politically useful government documents to supporters for distribution.
2. Edward D. Baker was AL's Whig rival to replace Hardin in Congress.
3. Judge Stephen T. Logan was another Whig politician and AL's current law partner.

and in fact I feel well assured that they will do it for the good of the whigs- whig cause and Henry Clay. I hope that You are sending whig documents in Morgan to enable the whigs there to be armed and equiped in this coming revolution of 1844. You know that truth is the armor of our cause and by sending documents you doubly ensure them for the approaching contest. I have collected some $20 or 30 to send on for the lives of Clay and political documents which are needed by the whigs of Sangamon.

I know that if you were in Morgan all would go well but I fear that the people of Morgan have lost what they are not able to replace.[4] I know how this goes if Baker or Lincoln is missing at our meetings. It seems that something is lost. Hardin I do not make a business of flattering any persons and I do most heartily despise a flatterer, but let me tell you, that the speech you made and sent on here is well spoken of and were I to tell you more than this you might think that I was playing the part of a despicable flatterer. The people of Sangamon are *astonished*, yes *astonished* how our Locofo[5] friends in congress can possibly go for internal improvements by the general government, but always wind up in their conversations, by saying that Locofocos have no doctrines in common or that every principle is cirscumscribed by a small section of the country. This is true as "holy writ" You know it. The North and South disagree upon a Tariff and the East and West disagree upon all locofo doctrines. So there is no principle in common. I am happy to learn this you at your post at Washington are doing [battle?] for the [Whig?] cause and Henry Clay and it is my individual opinion that you can do more good there than if you were in Morgan. The influence which you there exert and that in some little measure from the position, will more than fill up the vacuum in Morgan. This I can consciensiously say. Lincoln is going down in Cass on the 22nd of this month, I believe to Virginia,[6] to make a good Clay whig speech to the boys there. they are anxious to hear him.

One or two more words before I close this. There is a good deal of talk here about an abolition Candidate for the *Presidency*. Burney from Ohio is the man of whom So much is said.[7] If he be the abolition candidate we may "hang our harps on the willows" in despair for Illinois. I have talked with several of these *enthusiastic* _____ and all seem bent, blindly bent, upon running a candidate for the Presidency. If this be done I fear the result over the Whole Union. The abolitionists are generally intelligent men and generally our own way of thinking as regards politics. Heaven forefend the result!! If I had any influence with these leading enthusiastic _____ I would implore them to hold on till the next campaign, for it now is my beleif, candid beleif, that this premature move will ruin Clays prospects. Enough of this. There is nothing new from Morgan and it is believed that Hodge[8]

---

4. Hardin was from Jacksonville, the seat of Morgan County.
5. Locofoco: derogatory Whig term for Jacksonian Democrats.
6. The town of Virginia in Cass County, Illinois.
7. James G. Birney. WHH also considered himself an abolitionist, but a Clay Whig in electoral politics.
8. William Hodge, a strongly partisan Whig editor.

will have to wind up his paper on account of the death of Gov. Duncan.[9] I wish he could get a situation in this place with a good paper. He could do us much good. Since this Congress has been in session Gen. Jackson's fine[10] has employed a considerable time and the people hope generally that something will be finally done with it and tell Douglas[11] not to make such a "grand flourish" any more. By the by give Douglas my best respects and tell him to send me some documents. Do not forget it, if you please. Our Supreme Court has adjourned. It adjourned on Saturday—One question was decided about which much anxiety was felt. That is the *tax titles*. They decided that *tax titles* were good.

If McDuffe's report can be got on the National Bank will you please send one to me. I hardly expect that one can be got.[12] If you can conveniently get hold of the January number of O. A Brownsons Democratic Review send it likewise. These two Democratic—Ajax Telemons—Reviews hold doctrines as diverse, in sentiment and feeling, as the poles.[13] Send me an almanac—whig almanac and all other things which will be of any service to me, provided it do not put you to too much trouble. I do not want you to put yourself to any expenses at all and to but little trouble. Please excuse the length of this and believe me

Your friend
Wm. H. Herndon

CHM: Hardin Family Papers

2. To Lyman Trumbull

Springfield Ills May 20 1856

Friend Trumbull,

I saw a letter from you, written to Wm Jayne,—a few days since, in which you speak as if our friend Bissell[1] were disheartened. This I am sorry to see as I feel, or see it in others, and this too when there is no Earthly necessity for the *gloom*. Let me say to you that yesterday, Sunday as it was, Lincoln and myself had a long talk in reference to affairs, and I have never seen him so sanguine of success, as in this election—*he is warm*. I gathered this from him,—recollect he has been round our Judicial Circuit—, that the people are warm and full of feeling on this

---

9. Former Whig Governor Joseph Duncan.

10. Congress was then in the process of remitting a fine of $1,000 that Andrew Jackson had paid in 1815 for defying a court order at the time of the battle of New Orleans.

11. Stephen A. Douglas, also an Illinois member of Congress.

12. South Carolinian George McDuffie authored a congressional report in 1830 favoring the rechartering of the Bank of the United States.

13. Orestes Brownson, who had previously edited the *Democratic Review,* had just begun editing the pro-Catholic *Brownson's Quarterly Review.* "Ajax Telamon"—an expression here meaning "number one" or "leading light."

---

1. William Bissell, a former Democrat who would be nominated for Governor of Illinois as a Republican that year and would win.

question—this great and mighty issue. They have moved more since Bissell wrote you than in the past year—never saw so much *"dogged determination"* to fight it out;—that Democrats are coming to us daily—best in the State, and if you will look over our papers you will see that Lincoln is correct. He says this—that some few corrupt old line whigs who are [grasping?] for office in and about towns, and going with the nigger driving Gentlemen, but that the whigs & Democrats in the country are all right on the question, and are becoming more so every day—riper and riper they grow for Freedom the longer the time is extended. There is no doubt of this I have been in several counties, and have spoken as I have once or twice since to you I can speak the same Sentiment—idea, opinion. Friend no use of getting gloomy. The South are just commencing to move. Look at Coles—hundreds of names to the call The *"school master is abroad"*[2]

I see this—that the nigger-extension boys are passing resolutions *"right lately"* as in Alton & other places, that they are opposed to slavery Extension—can you not see where the shoe pinches.

If words are left out in this letter fill, for I am just going to make an address out in country.

Yours
W. H Herndon

LC: Lyman Trumbull Papers

3. To Richard Yates

Springfield Ills July: 28 1856

Friend Yates

I this day arrived at home, finding yours of the 24th inst. You know I am punctual in this matter; and absence must be my Excuse to you. Will you take that Excuse?

Mr. Palmer[1] has not *officially*, or publicly, declined the nomination; but suppose he will before long. I think it would be prudent for him to do so, when it is remembered that his nomination is not liked by the K. Ns or Fillmore men.[2] These are curious boys;— honesty I suppose is the ruling power: "honesty my lord":— precisely so friend Yates. This is a great world. The *vice* of my political life, is and has been *unsuspiciousness*; and my political *virtue* hereafter shall be a steady watchfulness to the End of things. It is not too late to commence is it? I hope not. You ask me if I would not run. I answer Never—Never. I have seen Lincoln; and have

---

2. WHH describes the collapse of Illinois's two-party system, which would lead to the organization of the state's Republican Party on May 29, 1856.

---

1. A recently converted Republican, John M. Palmer eventually refused the nomination for Illinois's Sixth District congressional seat.

2. That is, Know-Nothings, or members of the nativist American Party, whose presidential candidate in 1856 was Millard Fillmore.

talked over the matter; but he knows no more than you & I do—not so much. He is not, and never was, and never can be a wire puller:— he can drive a nail—*with power*, if a man will hold the nail and give its point the cunning direction.[3]

They say Mr Thornton—the Gen, made a Buchanan speech a few days since. This came to town on Sunday—do not know how this is—

Can you not run? The boys say you must and shall run yet, *unalterable*—Eh? Dick you did not write that word Who put that in your letter.?

We have had a small split here; but it seems to draw together—ligaments have reached over their nerve hooks; and drawn together the lips of the wound—Easily done this. I made a speech at Middletown in Logan Co. on Saturday—tolerably good one, I think We think we shall have no trouble here—all will agree to things except the Presidency—disagree on this badly

Yours
Bill Herndon

Rail-Splitter

4. To Wendell Phillips[1]

Springfield Ills. May 12, 1857

Mr. Philips

. . . I am now in my office writing this letter, with a good hickory fire in the stove and several good jolly fellows keeping it warm. Lincoln—the joker—the funny man—is cracking his jokes:—he beats Hale to death *in that line*. By the by—Do you know Lincoln? as we say out west he is a *"hoss"* I am the runt of the firm and no "hoss", yet I suppose will pass among the crowd as a Liberty lover—a fool and a Reformer. This is a happy position—is it not? . . .

Your friend
W.H. Herndon

Houghton: Wendell Phillips Papers

5. To Elihu B. Washburne

Springfield Ills. April 21d/58

Dear Sir

I this moment recd yours of the 15th inst, and for which I am much obliged. I did not, I hope, say anything from which you infered that my charges—assertions or what not were directd to any of our Ills delegation. This, friend, was not my intention, for I Expressly underscored, *the point* to which I wanted to direct

---

3. For similar doubts as to AL's political capacity in the 1850's, see §6.

1. Since 1854, WHH had conducted a correspondence with this radical abolitionist on such issues as Illinois politics and their mutual opposition to slavery.

your attention. If my memory serves me right I Expressly said "*in the East*"; and to *underscore it to avoid misconstruction*. It is true that such things have been said, often & often to Mr Lincoln & Myself; but both of us have turned a deaf Ear to all such insinuations, having rather a desire to stop it there to arrest the lie.[1]

We will have a sweet time to-day[2]

Your Friend

W. H. Herndon

Lincoln is just in—read your letter—did him *good*, and he sends back his best respects and says—all is right

LC: Elihu B. Washburne Papers

6. To Lyman Trumbull

Springfield Ills. June 24th/58

Dear Sir:

. . .

Mr. Lincoln wrote to you on yesterday, and read it to me. I adopt all he said, and do not Know of any contract with either wing of the Democracy Either Express or implied, directly or indirectly. I know of no such Contract finished—commenced or in embryo—.[1] I think I would know it, if any body did—probably sooner and better than Lincoln, for you know he does not know the details of how we get along. I do, but he does not. That kind of thing does not suit his tastes, nor does it suit me, yet I am compelled to do it—do it because I cannot get rid of it. Doug's & Buck's forces may take Care of themselves; and the Republicans *will* most emphatically take care of themselves. We have no understanding with Either faction of the so-called Democracy as to What shall be done or what shall be left undone Either directly or indirectly, and upon this you may depend.[2]

Your Friend

W. H. Herndon

LC: Lyman Trumbull Papers

---

1. Washburne had written to assure WHH that he supported AL, not Douglas.
2. Both of the warring Democrat factions—those backing Douglas and the National (Buchanan) Democrats—were holding their state convention in Springfield on this date.

---

1. Presumably a reference to the rumor that the Republicans were secretly in league with the National Democrats in a coordinated campaign to defeat Douglas.
2. To the gratification of Illinois Republicans, the state's Democratic Party was dividing into pro-Douglas and pro-Buchanan or National Democracy wings ("Doug's and Buck's forces") as the 1858 Senatorial campaign began. The split originated in Douglas's opposition to the Lecompton Constitution in Kansas Territory, beginning the previous December. Archer G. Herndon, WHH's father, and Elliott Herndon, his brother, were operatives in the pro-Buchanan camp.

7. To Theodore Parker

Springfield Ills. July 8, 1858

Dear Friend

I thank you for yours of July 1st, and agree with you that Douglas has blundered. We feel that he has Committed great faults, and Cannot Ever recover therefrom. He is dead. Had we a fair apportionment in this state we Republicans could beat him 20 on first ballot;[1] but as it is, the apportionment having been made when we were very young & wild—not so densely populated as now—*he may* defeat us. These are some complications, which it would take too long to Explain that hinder us. Some old Senators hold on—Elected long ago—and where Districts are wholy revolutionized: they belong to the Republicans, but there is no way of reaching the Evil. Time will set us right, and give us our Rights. Our State ticket will be Elected without much trouble; but as to Lincoln there may be some doubts. These doubts will Energize us—fire us—move us.

Mr. Lincoln's Speech is quite compact—nervous—Eloquent: it is the best Executive Expression of the ideas of politics—Republicanism, as at present organized, that I have seen.[2] Stump orators will take higher and more lofty grounds. Prudence is written all o'er the political world, and we Cannot help it—Do not blame us for not jumping higher just now. Remember *your* great Law of the historic continuity of the Development of ideas and then you will say—*"All is right."*

. . .

Your Friend
W. H. Herndon

Iowa: Theodore Parker Papers (microfilm)

8. To Lyman Trumbull

Springfield Ills. July 8, 1858

Dear Sir,

Yours of the 30th June Came to hand a day or so since, and to which let me say, we are getting along admirably well. Mr Lincoln was here a moment or so since, and he told me that he had just seen Col Dougherty,[1] and had a conversation with him. He told Lincoln that the National Democracy intended "to run in every County and District a National Democrat for each and every office"—Lincoln replied to this by saying—"If you do this the thing is settled—the battle is fought".[2]

1. Senators were elected by the state senate, not by popular vote.
2. WHH refers to AL's "House Divided" speech of June 16, 1858, *Speeches and Writings 1832–1858*, 426–34.

1. A leader of the Illinois National Democrats, John Dougherty was also a candidate for state treasurer.
2. AL's meaning apparently is that concerted efforts of the National Democrats, as described by Dougherty, would make the defeat of Stephen A. Douglas a certainty.

This you may depend upon. The National Democrats are fighting *in the Still*—on the sly, as we say west. Mr Lincoln told me at the same time that he had just seen *Shutt*.[3] Shutt told Lincoln that the Chicago Times was injuring the Democracy, because it took too high abolition grounds: that the Democracy could not defend it in its assaults on the South; and that the Times was otherwise doing them harm. What he meant of this last expression I do not know.

There is to be a National Democratic paper Started here in a few days, and it is said by those who ought to know that it will be conducted with Energy and ability. The Administration Democracy are fighting hard and still *on the sly*. They Know that it is life or death with them—. Elliott Herndon McWilliams—Gibson & others talk this way to me: they make "no bones" in telling me what they are going to do. They are in dead Earnest—Sincere. The Split widens & deepens daily: there can be no mistake in this at all; *it is dead Shot*. The National Democracy Seem to be making Every preparation—*I Know*—to fight it out. My position—remember where my father and Bro stand—is such that I Know what I am talking about.[4]

Every thing looks well and Unless we are deceived we are to be victorious. Lincoln is very certain as to Millers & Bateman's election,[5] but is gloomy—rather uncertain, about his own success. This is natural. His friends seem to be in good Spirits—have high hopes.

Douglas is to be in Chicago on the 9th inst, and Lincoln told me he should be on hand and hear what the giant had to Say. This is, I think, prudent. Foes face to face and Eye to Eye put on some restraints: it prepares them to Engage in the Encounter when it does Come. They then know the strong and weak points of their adversaries and their cause.

. . .

Your Friend
W. H. Herndon

LC: Lyman Trumbull Papers

9. To Lyman Trumbull

Springfield Ills. July 22nd 1858

Dear Sir

. . . Douglas' reception here was not good—well planned or Enthusiastic: it did not go off—did not blaze up, as it should have done or rather as intended and supposed by the Democracy.[1] I was on the ground and suppose there were *really*

---

3. George W. Shutt was a Springfield attorney and Republican activist.

4. WHH further describes the plans of the pro-Buchanan "National Democrats" in Illinois, and the tacit encouragement given them by Republicans, including AL. See also §6, n. 2.

5. James Miller and Newton Bateman were Republican candidates for state treasurer and superintendent of public instruction, respectively.

---

1. Douglas and AL both gave major speeches in Springfield on July 17, 1858.

about 2 or 3 thousand people—no more and there was [no?] deep long hearty Cheering: it was *really* cold. The ground preparations and the manifestations did not correspond; things fell flat. Douglas Spoke in Edwards' Grove, and from thence he was escorted into Town. Mr. Lincoln spoke in the City on the Same Evening to a Crowded house: he spoke in the House of Representatives; it was as full as it could be and all was Enthusiasm. It was a most Enthusiastic gathering of the intellect, and heart, and Soul of our Town. Lincoln made a most excellent Speech indeed: the Speech of Lincoln was as we say here a "whaler". It gave great satisfaction to his friends. Lincoln made no special Converts, nor did Douglas.

. . .

There is nothing new here. We are waxing warm—hot and now the fight goes bravely on. I received a letter from Horace Greely in Which he uses this Expression—"Now, Herndon, I am going to do all I reasonably can to Elect Lincoln." From this letter I judge that Horace is with us and soon will be *hearth* & *homed*.

Your Friend
W. H. Herndon

LC: Lyman Trumbull Papers

10. To Theodore Parker

Springfield Ills July 24 1858

Dear Sir:

. . .

We are now approaching a very animated—warm—Energetic Canvass; and if it do not get into personalities it will be a great, and, I think, a grand canvass. I fear that personalities will creep into the debate. Mr Lincoln takes broader & deeper grounds *now* than he did in his Springfield Speech. I told you the Speakers would do so, and Even Lincoln had to follow. The canvass opens deep & rich; but we Republicans have a clever villain to Combat. Douglas is an ambitious and an unscrupulous man; he is the greatest liar in All America; he misrepresents Lincoln throughout, and our people *generally* are not logical Enough to see the precise manner, point & issue of deception. Douglas holds up his glaring letters "Squatter Sovreignty", which *he knows* is dead and buried beneath the Dred Scott case. It suits Douglas' purposes however, and he fiddles on it quite cunningly and shrewdly. Politics is a great game and delusion is its greatest power. The politician who knows the game and can use that delusion the Cunningest is the greatest man. Hurrah for politics—bah!

. . .

Your Friend
W. H. Herndon

Iowa: Theodore Parker Papers (microfilm)

11. *To Theodore Parker*

Springfield Ills Aug 23rd 1858

Dear Sir

. . .

Now for politics in Ills. Mr. Lincoln spoke at Ottawa on Saturday. Mr Douglas also spoke there: this was their first place of meeting. We have not heard from others, but we Republicans know how the debate Ended, if Lincoln was well. Lincoln will deliver a speech there that will do himself credit. He is too much of a Kentucky gentleman to debate with Douglas; ie, he will not condescend to Lie: he will not bend to Exposing; he will not bring Shame, and so he labors under a disadvantage in this State; Yet he will take hold of Douglas and prove the Conspiracy to Enslave America on him. He has got the documents and will shoot the charge home. Judge Trumbull made a very fine speech at Chicago, a week or so since, which you have seen, doubtless: it was what we call out west a *clincher,* or what you call a *crusher.* Politics is getting hot—angry, and somewhat furious here. We are determined to Kill off Douglas, if we can by honest—fair, & manly means. We will resort to no wrong—no business—no demagoguism—no trickery or "trappery". We have charged Douglas with a conspiracy to Enslave America, and we think the proof incontestable—incontrovertible. The whole free, as well as Slave States look on Ills battle, we suppose, with a good deal of interest. How is it? This state is being fired up from Cairo to Chicago, & from Paris to Quincy—from Center to Circumference. Our Republican friends take high and Elevated grounds for Freedom—as high as our People will bear just now. What we may do in the future I Cannot Say. You know the undercurrents as well as I do—better than I dare dream

. . .

Your Friend,
W. H. Herndon

Iowa: Theodore Parker Papers (microfilm)

12. *To Richard Yates*

Springfield Ills. Aug. 26, 1858

Dear Sir:

. . . The fight between Douglas & Lincoln goes bravely on, and if my private letters are to be relied on, and I think they are, Lincoln whipped Douglas badly—very badly, Douglas' forgery hurts him: The Chicago Times—Douglas' paper, has confessed the error![1] It is done over it—So is the democracy generally. This fraud—this base forgery would kill "*Hell,*" but it will not hurt Douglas, I

---

1. Douglas's purported "forgery" of radical anti-slavery resolutions, allegedly adopted at a Republican state convention in Springfield in 1854. It was quickly determined that those resolutions had been adopted without AL's knowledge at a *district* convention in Northern Illinois.

am afraid. Carpenter[2] has found him a liar: he acts the liar and *blackguard* on the stump: Lincoln favors the conspiracy & Trumbull clinches it, and yet Douglas hold his head up & looks gentlemen in the face—Good Heavens!

. . .

Your Friend
W. H. Herndon

Yates and Pickering, 133

13. *To Theodore Parker*

Springfield Ills Aug 31st 1858

Dear Sir

I have but a moment to spare, and I propose to devote it to you. I am now—not this instant—out on the Stump, doing all the good I can for Republicanism;—namely—Liberty. The politics now in our State are in the blue-hot condition: it has ceased to Sparkle but now it burns. Mr. Lincoln and Sen Douglas have had two *"hitches"*—2 debates and it is the opinion of good Sensible men that so far Lincoln has the decided advantage.

In their late debate at Freeport Douglas took the stand that *at present* we needed no more territory. You remember I told you that Douglas told me, at Washington, that he would oppose the acquisition of [Cuba,?] Central America &c—: he seems as good as his word. You know what I told you he said about the passage of Lecompton: it turned out as he said, and doubtless you recollect other pledges he made me, and which I told you when in Boston—. When I once told you by letter, that if I could once "look Douglas in the Eye" I could tell what he intended, you supposed doubtless, that I was quite arrogant, did you not? By the by—Do you remember what I told you about friend Greely—i E; that the Republican platform was too "hifalutin"—too abstract, in his opinion, and that it ought to be *lowered*—"Slid down"? What *is now unfortunately* taking place? I fear that the Republican platform will get deeper in the "Hell"—direction than the old whig platform of *measures*. I hope you will continue to remember my conversation with you, not because I said it; but because what was said was uttered by greater men. I always tell you the truth—never dodge.

If you remember our State is a peculiar one politically—. First, we have a north which is all *intelligence*—all for Freedom,—2nd we have a south, people from the sand hills of the south, poor white folks: these are pro-slavery and *ignorant* up to the hilt; And 3rdly we have a belt of land, say 75 miles in width, running from the west Bank of the Mississippi to the Wabash—To Indiana; and running from—north—Bloomington to Alton. In or upon this strip or belt of land this "great battle" between Lincoln and Douglas is to be fought and victory won. On this belt are three Classes of individuals—first *Yankees*—2nd intelligent Southerners, and

---

2. R. B. Carpenter of Chicago was a spokesman for the National Democrats.

thirdly—poor whites. [*In margin:* These poor whites are Chivalrous good open hearted men.] I now speak *Sectionally*—. Again: on this belt are 4 political shades of party politics—First Republicans—Second American—old whigs—thirdly Douglas Democrats, and 4thly National Democrats—Buchanan men. "Quite a mess."

Two of these parties are acting *as one*: they are the Republicans and the Filmore men: they have a majority over both factions of the Democracy. The materials we have to struggle against are voting Buffalo—Catholic Irish backed and guided by corrupt and villainous Douglas.: they can do no good to the Douglas Democracy in the North: they will be run down here *on pretence of getting a job*, and so in the closely contested fight, they will carry *we fear*, the uncertain Counties. These "Hell-doomed" Irish are all for Douglas, and opposed, *here*, to the National administration.

I hope you can understand this complication. I give it to you as my opinion, and the opinion of good honest Republicans that we will crush out Douglas—pro-Slaveryism. I give it *now* as my *present* opinion that Lincoln will be the next U. S. Senate for Ills. *[Private?] Except to Special [friends?]*

Your Friend
W. H. Herndon

Iowa: Theodore Parker Papers (microfilm)

14. To John J. Crittenden

Springfield Ills Novr 1—1858

Dear Sir

Your letter to my partner was this minute received and opened by me. This is our usual custom in the firm. The notices going the rounds of the papers is wholy unauthorized by Mr Lincoln. I speak from Knowledge. I am the only person in the world who Knows that you wrote Lincoln, and outside of us—you, Lincoln, & myself no person Knows any thing about the matter. In the Sangamon Journal or *Ills State Journal* a letter was spoken of in an Editorial, as being in Town and from you: but nothing was Said, as to when the letter was written, in that paper. The papers took it up at once—those outside of the State and *thought* it was from you to Lincoln, and so said, but the allusion of the Journal was to an other letter that was said to be in Town.

Again: What the Journal *really did say*, as I understand it was this—that you were thought to have said ~~that~~ you hoped that the opposition would unite and Crush out *the Democracy*—but *not Douglas*. When the news got to St. Louis it was telegraphed to you that the Journal said ~~that~~ you wanted *Douglas* crushed out.

This I think is the way the thing has happened—. Mr Lincoln does not doubt your manliness or honor: he Knows that *you did not authorize or sanction* a word, that is said; and I Know he does not—What is out has been guessed at.

When Mr Lincoln comes home he will write to you a satisfactory letter.

Your Friend
W. H. Herndon

LC: John J. Crittenden Papers

15. To William H. Seward

Springfield Ills. Decr 28 1858

Dear Sir:—

I have one or two moments to give away, and know of no one to whom I would rather give them than to you, and so I propose to trouble you one moment with a letter. Mr. Lincoln and yourself have both given Expression to ideas that are true in the abstract—true in the concrete—true philisophically—true in fact—Eternally so in history, through its long Sweep from India to America; namely, that two *absolute* Antagonsims cannot Co-Exist permanently on the same Soil; and that one or the other *must perish* from the forest of human actualities.[1] The N. Y. Herald and such mud-material sheets call that truth the *"bloody issue."*

. . .

Your Friend
W.H. Herndon

NYHS: William H. Seward Papers

16. To Lyman Trumbull

Springfield, Ills. June 19th 1860

Dear Sir

. . .

We are all very busy here; we are organizing as we never organized before, and shall carry Sangamon Co, if truth—industry—organization—eloquence, &c Can Carry it—so with Morgan & the Centre Generally. Almost all the old line whigs are with us *now*;—Some are yet on the fence, *leaning* Republicanwards. Matheny has taken an open—bold—loud—open mouthed stand for Lincoln and he will do us some good—. Remember, I do not say that he is actuated by patriotism. Many men are now with us who see the *[illegible]* of our *[illegible]*—our rule—our success, and our *Loaves* and *Fishes*. Matheny is, however, not for these, I think, but others are.

. . .

Lincoln is well and is doing well—has [thousands of?] letters daily—many visitors Every hour from all sections.[1] He is bored—*bored* badly—Good gracious, I would not have his place and be bored as he is—I could not Endure it.

. . .

Your Friend
W. H. Herndon.

LC: Lyman Trumbull Papers

---

1. WHH refers to AL's "House Divided" speech of June 16, 1858, and to Seward's Rochester speech of October 28, 1858, both of which asserted that the Union could not remain half slave and half free.

---

1. AL had received the Republican nomination for president a month before.

17. To Sydney Howard Gay

Private
Springfield Ills. Aug 10th 1860

Dear Sir:

Your very kind letter, dated the 4th inst, is at hand and should have been answered sooner: but a press of very important business prevented. I read Mr. Phillipps' article first in the Liberator—your reply in the Trib, and Mr. Phillips rejoinder. Mr. Phillip's statement of Lincoln's *intentions* was wrong, and yours was right.[1] You are familiar—too familiar with legislative business not to know that among all Classes of men, some highly developed and others holding antagonistic ideas logically settled, that no one man can possibly get his own ideas put into any statute—any Law, or any Constitution. The whole affair is Concession—Compromise or what not. When Mr Lincoln was in Congress this state of affairs Existed: he was then a strong Anti-Slavery man and is now the same. This I know, though he wishes and will act under the Constitution: he is radical in heart, but in action he must ~~somewhat~~ Conform to Law & Constitution as Construed in good old times. Believing the above to be generally correct the Conclusion follows that Mr Lincoln, in reference to the Bill about which Mr. Phillipps wrote his articles, was actuated by Anti-Slavery sentiments alone, and not to advance Slavery or Slavery power or influence but to somewhat crush it. In doing this he had to consult his friend's feelings and ideas—his enemies feelings and ideas or he could do nothing; and so his bill was drawn up with reference to all the aforesaid Conditions—conflicting sentiments & ideas—: and when the final voting Come on some proposition springing out of his bill he voted against the prohibition of the slave trade in the District, and for this reason—the bill and its parts when finally fixed so as to suit some Southerners it did not suit him; because he wanted a more radical measure—and as he could not get something for the slave—justice and the Country he abandoned the bill entirely. Mr Lincoln wanted the Slave trade in the District of Columbia cut up by the roots and Slavery gradually abolished as substantially stated in your answer to Mr. Phillips. Mr Lincoln's sentiments—intentions—ideas were then Anti-Slavery—not so much as Mr. Phillps as a matter of course, yet were anti-slavery and are so now. His heart is better than his platform—his sentiments as good as any man's. This I know. You state correctly that if Mr. Phillip's had taken the course pointed out in your letter to me it would have been—hard—extremely hard to answer. Phillips went off half "cocked", as we say west.

. . .

Your Friend
W H Herndon

Columbia: Sydney Howard Gay Collection

---

1. Always hostile to AL, Wendell Phillips accused him in *The Liberator* of having moved to replace the portion of a bill abolishing the slave trade in Washington with the fugitive slave provision, for which he deserved to be considered "the slave hound of Illinois." Gay, managing editor of the *New York Tribune*, rebutted Phillips vigorously, undertaking to clarify AL's intentions and accusing Phillips of misrepresenting them. See *The Liberator* (Boston), June 22 and July 13, 1860; *New York Tribune*, July 4 and July 18, 1860.

18. To Wendell Phillips

Springfield Ills. Decr. 28th 1860

Dear Sir:

Your short letter is this moment received. You need not fear concession, nor secession. Neither will take place during your life time. To be mild but firm is not concession, nor do bluster—threats, & whiskey make secession. You do not give the Republicans credit for anything. You forget that a young vital courageous civilization has burst up behind "old Whiggery", commanding it—"onwards & upwards": Republicanism must obey or perish.

Lincoln is "Jackson redivivus" and though you may not believe it, I say to you, that Mr Lincoln has a superior will—good common sense, and moral, as well as physical courage. He will in my opinion, judging from his nature, make a grave yard of the South, if rebellion or treason lifts its head: he will execute the laws, as against Treason & Rebellion. If I had your private ear close to my lips I could tell you much that bears on the present crisis.

Your Truly
W H Herndon

Houghton: Wendell Phillips Papers

19. To Wendell Phillips

Springfield Ills Jany 12th 1861

Dear Sir:

Your very kind letter from Boston, dated the 2d inst., was duly received a day or so since. I am sorry I did you injustice: it was not the heart that did it; it was the flash of the *pen*—ugly rough iron pen. So I am right, ain't I? Sometimes you flash out such—throw out such granite stones, rough edged, at the Republicans, that I get angry and fling back.

Mr Phillips I always make it a point to speak the truth, & what I told you of Mr Lincoln is *the truth*. I know him as well as he does himself; and I say to you, that he is a man of broad deep good heartedness: but he has a *will* of his own. On questions of *economy—policy—calculations* over *mud* & *dollars* you can rule him: but on the questions of Justice—Right—Liberty he rules himself. Mark what I say to you, and bear it in mind. If he ever fails here I am mistaken.

Your Friend
W H Herndon

. . .

Houghton: Wendell Phillips Papers

20. To Lyman Trumbull

Springfield Ills. Jany 27th 1861

Dear Sir:

. . .

Lincoln is in a fix. Cameron's appointment to an office in his Cabinet bothers him. If Lincoln do appoint Cameron he gets a fight on his hands, and if he do not he gets a quarrel deep—abiding, & lasting.[1] What a world we live in! The game of Politics is a pure game, full of honesty and [over] deep gratitude. Three fourths of the political world—those who lead Especially—are corrupt—fish—dollar—Power seekers—mad hunters—scoundrels. So this political world wags—Poor Lincoln! God help him! Pshaw what a scramble for office! What angry looks & growls for bones that have fat & meat on them. Dogs fight away!

Lincoln will start for Washington about the 6th or 8th of Feby. See him landed safe, and all will go right hereafter. Lincoln is as firm as a rock yet—opposed to all concessions that yield an iota of principle.

Your Friend
W H Herndon

LC: Lyman Trumbull Papers

21. To [Samuel E.?] Sewall

Springfield, Ill, Feb. 1, 1861

Dear Sir

. . .

Mr. Lincoln yet remains firm as a rock: he is true game & is strong in the faith of Justice, Right, Liberty, Man & God. He has told me, not only once, but often & often, that rather than back down—rather than concede to traitors, his soul might go back to God from the wings of the Capitol.[1] I believe it. He & I have been partners in law for 13 years & I know him. Say to the Mass. boys "Stand firm—keep your convictions true to your soul."

Yours Truly
W. H. Herndon

BPL: copy

---

1. By offering a cabinet post to the controversial Simon Cameron on December 30, 1860, then withdrawing the offer a few days later at the behest of Cameron's political adversaries, AL further exacerbated Republican factional warfare in Pennsylvania.

---

1. Another close Springfield associate, William Jayne, wrote at about the same time: "Lincoln said that he would rather be hung by the neck till he was dead on the steps of the Capitol, before he would buy or beg a peaceful inauguration." Jayne to Sen. Lyman Trumbull, January 28, 1861, in *Concerning Mr. Lincoln*, 47.

22. To Wendell Phillips

Springfield Ills. Feby 1st 1861.

Dear Sir:

. . .

Lincoln is still true—as firm in his convictions of Justice—Right—Liberty as the rocks of Gibralter. He has been approached here for compromises—Crittenden's—border state one—Douglas &c. &c.; but he says—"Away—off—begone!"[1] In substance he said—"If the Nation wants to back down let it—not I". I will, I hope, see you eye to eye, and then I'll tell you to whom this nation is somewhat indebted for some of Lincoln's courage—for some brave words spoken by Lincoln—& for some of his brave acts—This sentence—the last few words are private *now*. So keep them housed till the right time comes.

. . .

Yours Truly
W H Herndon

Houghton: Wendell Phillips Papers

23. To Edward L. Pierce

Springfield Ills, Feby 18th, 1861

Dear Sir:

Your very kind letter, dated the 9th inst., is this moment at hand. Let me say—I have had no correspondence with Govr Andrew; but it is true I have had with others, who have doubtless shown him my letters. What I write therein was & *is*, to-day, true to the letter and to the spirit. Mr. Lincoln—the Prest Elect—is true to the living spirit of this age—is a good—firm—progressive Republican, standing on the Constitution—the Laws, & the Chicago platform as his ideal—his best ideal of *the now* practical application of justice in the affairs of men, under government. If men could govern themselves on a higher platform Lincoln would be there—the first—the firmest. The Republicans *may rest in perfect Confidence*, that Lincoln will never betray them or the Cause they have trusted to his hands. I know him well—long and I may say intimately. I say to the Republicans—fear not—stand firm. If Lincoln's Cabinet do not make base Concessions—and compromises the President will stand as solid—as firm—as fixed as the granite hills of New-England. The very last words he said to me when I took leave of him were in substance—"I am decided—my course is fixed—my path is blazed, the Union—& the Constitution shall be preserved, and the Laws Enforced at every & at all hazards—. I expect the People to sustain me. They have never yet forsaken any true man".

---

1. Senators John J. Crittenden of Kentucky and Stephen A. Douglas of Illinois. AL resisted all proposed compromises on the extension of slavery, saying "the tug has to come, & better now, than at any time hereafter." AL to Lyman Trumbull, December 10, 1860, *Collected Works*, 4:150.

I have no fears of Prest Lincoln—none in the least, but my fear is *otherwards*. Mr Lincoln will in 30 days after he is sworn in and gets firmly seated in his Chair, order Gen Scott to retake all Forts &c. &c. The South will have a sweet time in Disunion—on paper.

I am happy to be informed that you were at Chicago & were an original friend of Mr Lincoln. Sen Seward is a good man—a great man, but Frank Blair said right—namely—that to throw off the odor he would bend low. This is always the Law of those who are ~~Expected~~ accused or suspected of unpopular tendencies . . .

Yours Truly
W H Herndon

Houghton: Edward L. Pierce Papers

24. To Edward L. Pierce

Springfield Ills, March 4th, 1861

Dear Sir:

Your kind note, dated the 24th Feby., is at hand; and for which please accept my most hearty thanks. I almost regret having sent you my letter, as it was written hurriedly from my Court desk, having no time to think or to re-write it, but so it is, and so let it go. You speak very candidly and highly of Mr Lincoln; and now let me assure you, that you are not mistaken. I know Lincoln better than he knows himself. He has got the finest—most *womanly* heart I Ever knew. His judgment is most Excellent—not Keen & subtle—but broad, & deep, & comprehensive. He is somewhat intuitive—though not spiritually intense. Lincoln's Conscience is his ruling attribute—power or what not; and loving man he will be as true to Justice—to Right—to Liberty and Humanity as it is possible for his peculiar attributes—his nature to be. They guarantee, *a priori*—high hopes in the future—, or rather high hopes now of the future. I Know of no man now living whom I would sooner trust than him. . . .

Your Friend
W. H. Herndon

Houghton: Edward L. Pierce Papers

25. To Caroline Healey Dall

Springfield *Ills*. Novr 10th 1861

My Dear Friend

. . .

As to my friend & partner, "Abraham," he is not acting as rigorously as I could wish. I think he Erred in modifying Freemont's proclamation.[1] This People has got to meet this negro question face to face now or at Some future time. God writes *this* in the instincts of the race—in the intuitions of the great. There can be no freedom where there is slavery. Heaven or Hell must rule.

. . .

Your Friend
W H Herndon

MHS: Caroline Healey Dall Collection

26. To Lyman Trumbull

Springfield Ills Nov 20th 1861

Dear Sir:

. . .

What is Lincoln doing? Does he suppose he can Crush—squelch out this huge rebellion by pop guns filled with rose water. He ought to hang somebody and get up a name for will or decisiveness of character. Let him hang somebody, Child or woman, if he has not Courage to hang a *man*. This Union must be preserved. The question is—Shall the Union go under—or shall Slavery go out of sight. If this be correct whatever is necessary to save the Union let him do—1stly abolishing slavery, and 2ndly arming them if necessary. The issue must be met sooner or later—dodge it as we may. Good God! if I were Lincoln I would have my name deeply Empressed on the worlds great [Minds] and to do this I would declare that all slaves shall be free and stand Emancipated. *I would be this ages [great] hero.* What—does Lincoln suppose he Can squelch out this rebellion whilst he and the South in Common are fighting for the Status of Slavery? Good Heavens! What say you?

If you see Sumner give him my best respects—and old Abe too & you may say to him for me what I say to you if you wish. I have no Concealments on this question.

Your Friend.
W. H. Herndon

LC: Lyman Trumbull Papers

---

1. AL had revoked General John C. Fremont's order freeing the slaves of Confederates in Missouri.

27. To Caroline Healey Dall

Springfield Ills. Jany 28th 1862

My Dear Friend:

. . .

I was in Washington some days since and saw all. Mrs Lincoln is a very curious—Excentric—*wicked* woman. Poor Lincoln! He is domestically a desolate man—has been for years to my own knowledge.[1]

Your Friend

W H Herndon

MHS: Caroline Healey Dall Collection

28. To Josiah G. Holland

Springfield Ills May 26th 1865

My Dear Sir:

Inclosed you will please find a true copy of Mr Lincoln's letter to me dated in 1847 when he was in Washington, he then being a member of Congress from this, the Capitol District.[1] One word of explanation you will allow. It is this—several influential gentlemen of this City were applicants for the Receiver's office—a branch of the land office. I think I took pains to write to Mr L, & urged him to appoint Mr Davis,[2] but stated that Davis was publicly asserting that he was to get the Post office, thus putting Mr L wrongly on the record, he having promised an other man *that* office. Subsequently he gave—had Davis appointed Receiver of the land office. The letter is a good one—quite—*thoroughly* characteristic of the good great man now gone, yet still among us. The influential men, Lincoln's friends, were passed over and Davis Lincoln's partial enemy, appointed for the reasons specified in the letter. Now the letter speaks for itself. I send it to you. You may use your own good discretion in its suppression or publication. It never has been made public. I have, since I saw you, received several good letters from various friends giving me information—copies of which I shall send you soon.

When you were in my office I casually informed you that it was my intention to write & publish the *subjective* Mr Lincoln—"the inner life" of Mr L. What I mean by that expression is this—I am writing Mr L's life—a short little thing—giving him in his passions—appetites—& affections—perceptions—memories—judgements—understanding—will, acting under & by motives, *just* as he lived,

---

1. Seeking a Federal appointment for a prospective brother-in-law, WHH visited AL in the White House in January of 1862, where he was invited to dinner. His remarks about MTL may have been prompted by reports circulating in Washington about her unseemly conduct. See Michael Burlingame, "Mary Todd Lincoln's Unethical Conduct as First Lady," in *At Lincoln's Side: John Hay's Civil War Correspondence and Selected Writings* (Carbondale: Southern Illinois University Press, 2000), 185–203.

---

1. Probably AL to WHH, January 5, 1849, *Collected Works*, 2:18–19.
2. Walter Davis was a Springfield mechanic and Whig activist.

breathed—ate & laughed in this world, clothed in flesh & sinew—bone & nerve. He was not God—was man: he was not perfect—had some defects & a few positive faults: he was a good man—an honest man—a loving, true & noble man—such as the world scarcely, if ever saw. It is my intention to write out this *Life* of Mr L honestly fairly—impartially if I can, though mankind curse or bless me. It matters not to me. The world does not begin to understand the grand full orb of Lincoln, as it swung amid the heavens of men. My purpose is to *try* to make it understood. This age and all future ages demand the truth. This is my purpose & motive.

I regret that you could not have been with me 8 or 10 days consecutively. I think I could lead you to the dawn of his great light. One more word—: I shall not make my *little thing* of more than 50 or 75 pages, pamphlet form. I am too poor to set down & write voluminously. I have not got the capacity to write much at best and not that much well

Truly Your Friend
W H Herndon

NYPL: Holland Papers

29. *To Caroline Healy Dall*

Springfield Ills May 26th 1865

My Dear Friend

Your kind note, dated the 16th inst, was duly received. An answer has been delayed til this late day, for the reason that I did not feel like doing any business— Even answering good letters from kind friends. Please excuse me, therefore. My good friend—*is gone*—yet is with us in *Spirit*. The news of his going Struck me dumb, the deed being so infernally wicked—so monstrous—So huge in Consequences, that it was too large to Enter my brain. Hence it was incomprehensible, leaving a misty distant doubt of it's truth. It yet does not appear like a worldly reality. It is Sad—grievously Sad to think of—one so good—so kind—so loving—so honest—so manly, & So *great*, taken off at the bloody murderous hand of an assassin. So it is however. I am writing a short life of Mr L's inner—subjective life, & will send it to you when printed. You make a request: it is, that I may send you some little thing, as a memorial of the good great man—Abraham Lincoln. I cannot *just now* do it, but will remember you when I distribute what is left behind. I have long since, beginning as Early as 1860, given away all my little remembrances—letters—ink[stands?] pencils, &c. &c. &c. I promise you that you shall be remembered. God bless you.

Truly Your Friend
W H Herndon

MHS: Caroline Healey Dall Collection

30. To Josiah G. Holland

Springfield Ills June 8th 1865

Dear Sir:

Since I saw you last, since I wrote to you some days since, I have been search-ing for the *facts* & *thruths* of Lincoln's life—not fictions—not fables—not float-ing rumors, but *facts*—*solid facts* & *well attested truths*. I have "been down" to Menard County where Mr L first landed and where he first made his home in Old Sangamon. I have been with the People—ate with them—slept with them, & thought with them—cried with them too. From such an investigation—from records—from friends—old deeds & surveys &c &c I am satisfied, in connection with my own knowledge of Mr L. for 30 years, that Mr L's whole early life *remains to be written*. All the stories we hear floating about are more or less untrue in part or as a whole.

I wish to make on correction, & it is this—Mr Douglas promised Mr Lincoln that if he would go home and not speak any more in 1854 he—Douglas would not speak more. I think on reflection, not modifying anything else I told you, that the understanding & obligations between them at Peoria were mutual—not one sided.[1]

Again—when I told you the words which Lincoln told Douglas about his [impertinent?] criticisms—the Republicans sat down cool & calm, satisfied that Lincoln had Douglas: they had felt uneasy at Douglas' interruptions, & L posi-tion—the Democracy had seen it, but now the Republicans were happy &c— Probably this will put the point in the story—It shows the confidence the people had in Lincoln's honor & power[2]

Again—: In Lincoln's letter to me, a copy of which I sent you I forgot to state that I had informed him—L, that his friends here were loudly & bitterly complaining against him for appointing Davis—a man not very popular. That is probably apparent in the letter, but if it is not it puts the point—one point to these letter.[3]

. . .

Truly Your Friend
W H Herndon

Will you have the [goodness?] all my sayings—Lincoln's short remarks to me & to others which I gave you—[notice?] this—I have found some old memoranda [touching?] the same things. When I saw you I put myself in place of Lincoln &c and then I was fresh &c. I can now mend and better it, when I get my expressions

---

1. Holland's account in his biography as to whether AL and Douglas had a truce about speaking in public after their meeting at Peoria in 1854, what the truce may have consisted of, and whether either one or the other did speak later became an obsessive personal issue with WHH. See §43, §66, and §223.

2. For other versions of WHH's account of Douglas's interruptions to AL's October 4, 1854, speech, see §270 and §275. Holland included this anecdote in his biography (137–38) accompanied by some excerpts from WHH's October 10, 1854, article in the *Illinois Journal*.

3. See §28.

to you and when I put them side by side with my memoranda &c—I will when I fix them up—talk to friends & get Lincolns exact words as near as possible and then will send you true & exact copies. Please accommodate me & I'll pay in return &c.

Hurriedly
Your Friend

NYPL: Holland Papers

31. *To Ward Hill Lamon*

Springfield Ills June, 12th 1865

Dear Sir:

I want to ask of you a favor. Please send me the wall paper life of Lincoln that O. M. Hatch loaned you. I am authorized to ask this. Don't fail to send it. I am writing the life of Mr Lincoln Especially in his younger days. Again—Please sit down & tell me what Mr Lincoln loved to Eat—what 3 or 4 things he loved best—How he acted about the *White House*—his habits, customs—Modes—Manners & times of doing what he did—privately—socially & politically &c. &c.[1] Again—Did Mr Lincoln change his religious views since he left the City of Springfield—did he rave & rant & whine religiously as represented in News Papers & speeches—&c. &c. *Come*—sit down and tell me all you know, Especially in Washington—, about Mr Lincoln—his thoughts—ideas—Expressions—acts—customs habits—modes—manners & times of acting &c. &c. Don't be short—crusty—snappy & crabbed. Give me a good long letter. Again—go to some news paper office and cut me out 4 or five slips—letters—pieces & scraps of information that you *know to be true and correct* to the letter, at least substantially so, in reference to any of the above topics—themes &c. &c. I want truth—facts—not fictions & falsehoods. I know I can rely on you. Please answer this letter minutely—fully and correctly. *Soon*

Your Friend
W H Herndon

HL: Ward Hill Lamon Papers LN341

32. *To Caroline Healey Dall*

Springfield Ills. June 23d 1865

Mrs C. Dall

I, a few days since, received your most excellent letter, Expressing your feelings—acts—and history of them upon receiving the sad news of Mr Lincoln's assassination. This deed has shocked the Civilized world. But Providence will Strengthen the connections of mankind thereby in this—The whole race will now *Everywhere* strike to destroy all forms & kinds of despotism. I think the argument producing

---

1. For Lamon's testimony on these topics, see *Herndon's Informants*, 466.

this connection was the bullet of Booth—figuratively Speaking—Crushing through the life of the great dead martyr. I am some what Enthusiastic—fanatical in my beliefs—philosophy &c and you had better not pay any attention to what I say.

The best *Portrait* of Mr Lincoln is now in the possession of J. F. Speed of Louisville Ky. Mr S slept with Mr L. for 5 ys—and says that his picture is the best one in Existence—It has the humor—laugh—good nature—sweetness which Mr Ln *occasionally* had, playing & romping all over it as if inspired by semi-Omnip-otent happiness—great great human happiness. Mr S is a good judge—has been at Washington for 3 or 4 ys with Mr Ln as his Special friend in the border State business. You may rely on his judgement.

Your Friend
W H Herndon

MHS: Caroline Healey Dall Collection

33. To George U. Miles

Springfield Ills Decr. 1st 1865

Mr Miles

It is said in one of Mr Lincolns biographies that he attended a debating society in New Salem? Was there such a society & did Lincoln ever speak in it? Get all the facts & write to me.[1] It is said that Mr Lincoln when elected to the Legislature in 1834–36—& 1838 went to Vandalia a foot? Is this true? Get all the facts—See Carman—Bails and others.

Henry McHenry[2] once had a suit here and Lincoln could not attend to it because McHenry was in the wrong.—That Mc got mad—said much to Mr Lincoln—That Mc went & got another lawyer and gained his case. See McHenry & get the facts—

If you ever see Mrs Armstrong[3] please get out of her all the facts in reference to Mr Lincolns life when in Menard—what he did—what he said—when he said it and where he said it—before whom—How he lived—his manners—cus-toms—habits—spirits, frolic—fun—his sadness—his wit, his humor. What he read—when he read it—How he read—and what & who he loved &c. &c. and in short all she may know about him in mind—heart—soul—body. You need go to no expense—nor trouble.

Your Friend
W H Herndon

LC: HW2393, Exp 4:7:447–48

---

1. This correspondent, WHH's father-in-law, subsequently interviewed friends and acquaintances of AL in Menard County, Illinois, for WHH's biographical project. See *Herndon's Informants*, 66, 236–37, 143–44, 368, 472, 534–37.

2. Caleb Carman, Esther and Hardin Bale, and Henry McHenry were all early associates of AL in New Salem.

3. Hannah Armstrong was the widow of AL's New Salem friend Jack Armstrong.

34. To Lyman Trumbull

Spgfd Ills Jany 4th 1866

My Dear Sir:

Your very kind and flattering letter, dated the 27th Decr., is this moment rcd, and for which I thank You. I did not have my lectures published—only condensed parts got up by partial friends.[1] I am too lazy a man to do what I ought to do. I felt it my duty, my friend, to place Mr Lincoln on his true stand point, and if I have pointed out where the world may find the true greatness of the man I am Content. The Eulogies delivered by men on Mr Lincoln's Character &c make me sick sometimes. I sent you a day or so since an abstract—Condensed report of my 2 Lecture, leaving off his domestic—social—Religious—& other characteristics.[2] Please accept my thanks for your letter.

Your Friend

W H Herndon

LC: Lyman Trumbull Papers

35. To Charles H. Hart

Springfield Ills Jany 8th 1866

My Dear Sir:

I have not published my 2 lectures. My friends got up condensed things—report of them. I am an extremely lazy man and have to be kicked to act. It took 3 hours to read them, and hence you have only seen mere extracts. Many things were left out, & not noticed, because time & space, Especially Space in the Papers forbade a longer notice of them.[1] I was just & truthful in the lectures—made no humbug statements, & fussy flourishes. I dearly loved—and now reverence the memory of my good dead friend. I wrote the lectures *soley* for the purpose of putting him where he in fact and truth & justice belongs. I have not any autograph letters of Mr Lincoln now—gave all away—am sorry I cannot accommodate you.

Yours Truly

W H Herndon

HL: Charles H. Hart Papers HM23569

---

1. Trumbull, U. S. Senator from Illinois, had written to compliment WHH on a newspaper report of his Dec. 12 public lecture on AL: "It is the best analysis of his character I have seen. The wonderful events which transpired during his administration, & the manner of his taking off were such as to blind most men to everything except the bright sides of his character. You have taken a more dispassionate view of the man, & presented him more as he really was." For the abbreviated report that Trumbull read, see the *Missouri Democrat*, December 23, 1865; for a transcription of the manuscript text of the lecture, see "Analysis of the Character of Abraham Lincoln," *Abraham Lincoln Quarterly* 1, no. 7 (September, 1941): 343–83.

2. The "condensed report" of his second lecture sent by WHH was most likely either a broadside titled "Abraham Lincoln Concluded" (HL 151264) or the brief summary that appeared in the *Daily Illinois State Journal* (Springfield), December 27, 1865.

---

1. For the condensed report of WHH's first lecture (December 12, 1865) that Hart probably saw, see the *Philadelphia Press*, December 27, 1865.

36. To Richard J. Oglesby

Spgfd Ills Jany 8th 1866

My Dear Friend:

I recd your kind and considerate letter, written after reading the condensed Reports of my 2 Lectures: it took 3¼ hours to read them and you can well judge from what you have read, *how much you have got of them.*[1] I am glad to know that you agree with me in the main, and thank you kindly for your notice of them. In the writing of these lectures I was moved to do it from a sense of Truth—Justice & Affection. The writers on Mr Lincoln, in my humble judgement, make him a feeble ass—a soft fool, and this I could not stand. Lincoln was great *headed*—having a great calm clear Conscience and a tender heart. I loved my friend when living and now that he is no more, I reverence him. Some things in those lectures may seem harsh, yet I am justified for various reason—and *among* them is this one. The Ears of the world could not be hailed unless I had thrown out the pure white flag of peace—Truth. I am now satisfied from many letters from Washington, and New York, and Philadelphia &c &c, that I *caught the Ears of men:* again—I could not lie and hence let out the whole truth, as I understand it

I am extremely obliged to you for your suggestion, and shall gratefully follow all such truthful and *manly*—honest suggestions. Govr I now appreciate you more than Ever. I think you feel that I want to be honest and truthful. I could not put all things in: 2 lectures. Hence excuse imperfections. I think your suggestions are good ones—truthful ones and let me assure you that I shall follow them. You get eloquent yourself in your letter. The reason why I say appreciate &c is, because you make to a friend a friendly criticisms. D——n a two faced man. Bless a true friend.

Your Friend
W H Herndon

I will publish sometime, if I don't get too lazy.

ALPL: Oglesby Family Papers

37. To Lyman Trumbull

Spgfld Ills Jany 11th 1866

My Dear Sir:

I sent you a few days since a little Condensed report of only a part of my 2 Lecture on Mr Lincoln. It took me 3¼ hours to read both. I did not get up the Reports.[1]

---

1. For Oglesby's letter, see *Herndon's Informants*, 152–53. Condensed reports of WHH's first two lectures on AL were widely reprinted and extracted.

---

1. See §34, n. 2.

Judge—I wish to Know questions—1st What were the *Strong* points of Mr Lincoln's character as a *statesman* & *Executive*: 2dly What were the *weak* points of Mr Lincoln's Character as to his *Statesmanship* & Executive, including the Exact abilities of both. *Please* give me your opinion—the opinion of a majority of senators on these 2 questions. Weigh your words & sentences and answer as soon as you can conveniently do so—I need it. Your letters shall be *sacredly private.*[2]

Your Friend
W H Herndon

LC: Lyman Trumbull Papers

38. To David Davis

Spgfd Ills. Jany 11th 1866

My Dear Sir

I have often heard it said that Mr. Lincoln was *Kicked*, from external & internal fear into the issuing of the Proclamation of Emancipation. How is this, Judge? Is it true or false? *Please* ask Hon S. P. Chase, if proper so to do, what the truth is. My own opinion was, at one time, that there was a *shadow* of truth in the allegation, but now I think otherwise.

Please, answer the following questions—What were the strong points of Mr Lincoln's Executive ability and his ability as a statesman, if you think prudent so to do. I can trust you. Remember I only ask for his *strong* points. I should like to hear further, but I leave this subject to your goodness and Common Sense. Your letter shall be *Sacredly private. Answer Soon.*

Your Friend
W H Herndon

ALPL: David Davis Papers

39. To John J. Hall

Springfield Ills January 22d 1866

Friend Hall—

Will you have the kindness to Copy Mr Lincoln's bond to Johnson or your father, which I saw when I was down to see you.[1] Copy every word—figure, and name *Carefully* from top to bottom, and send to me, if you *please*. Don't fail. I want it to defend Lincoln's memory.

---

2. Trumbull apparently did not reply, but see his candid assessment of AL printed in Horace White, *The Life of Lyman Trumbull* (Boston: Houghton Mifflin, 1913), 426–31.

1. Hall was the son of Matilda Johnston Hall, whose mother was the second wife of AL's father, Thomas Lincoln. The phrase "Johnson or your father" refers to John D. Johnston, Matilda's brother, and Squire Hall, her husband.

Please write to me at any time you may think of any thing that is *good or bad* of Mr Lincoln, truthfully just as it happened and took place. Were any of you boys applicants for any office made to Mr Lincoln while he was President?

Hall—What is your honest opinion—come *honest* opinion—in reference to Mr Lincoln's love for his kin and relations generally. *Please*—friend—accommodate me

Your Friend
W H Herndon

Private collection: Bob G. Field

40. To Edward McPherson

Spgfld Ills. Feby 4th 1866

My Dear Sir:

Your kind note, dated the 29th ult, is this moment handed to me and for which I thank you. I sent you my 2d lecture because some of your friends here wished me to: they wanted the 1st one, but I did not have it.[1] I did not make out the abstracts—Reports of any one of my lectures. I have delivered the 3d one.[2] I thank you for your appreciation of the Lectures. The condensed Reports are *timid*. If I ever get time I will write out fully and publish.

Mr Lincoln's Religion is too well known to me to allow of *even a shadow of a doubt*; he is or was a Theist—& a Rationalist, denying all extraordinary—Supernatural Inspiration or Revelational. At one time in his life, to say the least, he was an elevated Pantheist doubting the *immortality of the Soul* as the Christian world understand that term. He believed that the Soul lost its identity and was immortal as a *force*. Subsequent to this he rose to the belief of a God, and this is all the change he ever underwent. I speak knowing what I say. He was a noble man—a good great man for all this. My own ideas of God—His attributes—man, his destiny, & the relations of the two are tinged with Mr Lincoln's Religion. I cannot, for the poor life of me, see why men dodge the Sacred truth of things. In my poor Lectures I *stick* to the truth and bide my time.

I love Mr Lincoln dearly—almost worship him, but that can't blind me. He's the purest politician I ever saw, and the justest man. I am scribbling—that's the word—away on a life of Mr Lincoln—gathering *known—authentic* & *true facts* of him.

. . .

Yours Truly
W H Herndon

Private collection: Joseph Rembusch

---

1. For newspaper abstracts or reports of WHH's second lecture on AL, see §34, n. 2.

2. WHH's third lecture on AL, "Facts Illustrative of Mr. Lincoln's Patriotism and Statesmanship," was delivered in Springfield on January 23, 1866; a transcription of the manuscript text is published in the *Abraham Lincoln Quarterly* 3, no. 4 (December, 1944): 178–203.

41. To Zebina Eastman

Springfield Ills Feby 6th 1866

My Dear Sir:

Your kind letter from England, dated the 2d ult, is at hand, and for which I am much obliged. Your letter has called up old and pleasant associations—ideas, & thoughts. I well remember the first moment you ever put your foot in our office. I think it was in 1854—probably in 1855 early. However I did not know *why* you came. I now know and thank the stars I did not deceive you. I was true to Freedom and to the negro—knew that Lincoln *wanted* to be—knew he could be trusted. Hence I always told the Anti-Slavery men to have *faith* in Mr Lincoln: he and I, figuratively speaking, had many silent closet prayers over this question. I was at an early day—don't know when an Anti-Slavery—nay an Abolitionist and hence it was my policy to *educate* Lincoln up to *action*. I took your paper—The Anti-Slavery Standard—had Channing's and Theo. Parker's etc. and used to read to Lincoln what was *hot*—pointed and good. Mr Lincoln was naturally & constitutionally an abolitionist yet he was tender footed—cautious—timid I may almost say. I spurred him less. He had great *faith* in my intuition—none in my reason for he had that to the brim. He conversed with me *out of that side of my nature*. I *forged* his name to the Document that got him to go to Bloomington.[1] Whiggery & Know nothingism tried to hold him, but they couldn't. The world will never know what influence I had in making Lincoln *out & out* an abolitionist. I worked hard & I think well for two years with my "Student" He was educable and thank God the good and great and faithful student & man among students and men

What a change since I first saw you! Four million slaves Free men to day. America a scoff and *[law?]* now the great of the nations of the world—the guide—teacher—the Ideal nation of the world—So God weaves his purposes in the destinies of things. America Free! Lincoln the constant figure of the *good* and *great* dead—mankind going upward & onward from America's impulse!! What a change! Wonderful Providences!

Lincoln once my true living friend—now dead, shall live forever, and I am glad you saw & knew him. I *[illegible]* him *in truth*: he was the purest minded politician I ever saw or expect to see: his was a kind—true—noble soul. As you are aware I have delivered 3 lectures here on his characteristics 2 of which have been published and have gone the rounds of this land. The 3d is not published and will not be. I want it as a chapter in my life of Lincoln. The lectures are faithful to the man and to truth. I am writing Ls life leisurely.

I am glad you have the position you occupy[2]—hope you will keep it and grow rich—am glad you told me one thing—namely—, that Lincoln loved to pay true, old, faithful abolitionists for the sacrifices they gave to *Justice—to man*, *to Liberty*, and *to God*.—glad you told me this—will use it to show how he felt and how he acted

---

1. This was a call for a local meeting to send delegates to the founding convention of the Illinois Republican party at Bloomington on May 29, 1856. For an account of his "forgery," see §71.

2. Eastman had been appointed U. S. Consul in Bristol, England, by AL.

I am still a radical—don't want reconstruction till justice is done the negro everywhere under our flag. The battle is deep—finely radical yet. The end is not yet. Would to God it were! I have faith in the sense of justice that fills the American heart. That Heart says—"Justice and fair play to all mankind".

. . .

Your Friend

W H Herndon

CHM: Zebina Eastman Collection

42. To Joseph Gillespie

Spgfd Ills Feby 20th 1866

My Dear Friend

Your excellent and well thoughted letter is at hand and has been read: it is the very best letter, except one, if not better than that too, that I have recd.[1] You know Mr Lincoln better than I thought you did. Your letter is quite discriminating and I know of nothing that you and I disagree about. Lincoln *ran smoothly* in Society—complaining of no immorality—no intemperance—no vice—no tobacco chewing &c. Lincoln had no appetites, but *women* must get out of his way. Lincoln never worked nor toiled for friends—unless they represented a principle and then he did not toil for them—only the principle. Lincolns *quiet* judgements—his intuitive insight was slow. Lincoln's great good common sense came to him not through his judgements, but through his reasoning—his logical faculty. A woman & some men get their Common Sense, as it were, by inspiration—catch it by lightning intuition—not so Lincoln. Lincoln's Common Sense came through his *brain* and not through his soul. This is the reason why some now Contend that Mr Ln had not good Common sense, and literally this is do—Still it is only a discussion of ideas—terms.

Your letter shall be preserved quoted—used, and then it shall go down to posterity. I speak this frankly and candidly. I am under many—many obligations to you and should I think of any questions I shall avail myself of your kind offer. *We all* owe this to Lincoln. Hurriedly

Your Friend

W H Herndon

CHM: Joseph Gillespie Collection

---

1. See Gillespie to WHH, January 31, 1866, *Herndon's Informants,* 180–88.

43. To Josiah G. Holland

Springfield Ills Feby 24th 1866

My Dear Sir:

Your more than kind letter, dated the 19th inst, is this moment handed to me, & for which I am much obliged. When I wrote you my last letter I confess I was angry.[1] My friends, who were more angry than myself, kept at me till I did write; and now if you will *burn* my letter I will withdraw all that was said that was offensive to you. What I told you in every-thing I *know* to be true. But suppose I was mistaken, *you should have written to me* requesting me to look up the matter &c. and explain before you denied what I said, leaving me on the record in *rather an unpleasant* fix. I assure you: it stings. I know well what Mr L said to me; & now after much trouble in finding out *persons* & dates I know I am absolutely correct. I hunted for 4 mo for men who heard what I heard They are good honest men—have given their statement of the matter in writing &c. and know what I know. Remember the Peoria debate was on the 16th & 17th day of Oct *1854.* Mr Lincoln was here writing out his Speech some week or more after the Peoria debate. This I know, because I assisted him to gather facts. The speech is published in the weekly Journal—date 21 & 29th *concluded.*[2]

I have no disposition to drive you or any gentleman to do anything—not even a Right thing. I have no disposition to urge you to make statements that you do not *know* to be true, and hence take your own time; and if you think my request is too hard simply make the correction in your own paper and write to me a letter, so that I shall *feel* cleared at all events.

Mr Holland—I am a cautious man and never state a thing that I doubt or do not know. Mr Lincoln had no idea of Christianity—did not believe in it—was not a Christian—couldn't be from his very nature—: he had no more religious emotion than an angel an [undivided?] emotion. Lincoln ~~denied~~ doubted the *immortality* of the soul—was a perfect *fatalist*—: he bordered on Pantheism—wrote a book against the Bible—: it was snatched out of his hands and burned by his friends. Bateman is a good man, but a mistaken one. He is the only man in the world who stands committed to such assertions &c. &c.[3] When he Lincoln threw his arms around some ministers shoulders *as said*, when his little Willie's death was mentioned & in reference to Willie's immortality &c. he said *inquiringly* to the minister who asserted his immortality—*"Do you really think so"* is enough for us who knew him. The *Infidel* world don't care about this matter one way or the other, as I suppose: it would not have disliked Lincoln had he been a christian—would

---

1. WHH's anger arose mainly from Holland's account in his biography of the "Peoria truce" following Lincoln and Douglas's debate at Peoria on October 16, 1854, which WHH regarded as personally offensive. See §66, n. 3.

2. WHH is here mistaken in stating that AL remained in Springfield during the week in which his speech was appearing in installments in the *Journal.* See §66, n. 1.

3. According to biographer Holland, Bateman asserted that AL, though admitting not to be a Christian, said to him that "God knows I would be one," and that by opposing injustice and slavery, he was doing the work that God had intended for him. See Holland, 236–37.

have loved him better for it. Hence there was no use in his concealment &c. &c. I'll put this question beyond dispute: it is due Mr Lincoln—mankind and truth. No man will be made Christian by forcing Mr L into false positions, & no man will be made infidel by putting him in his true Relations. Religion—Christianity needs no such props—Hurriedly

Yours Truly
W H Herndon

NYPL: Holland Papers

44. To Charles H. Hart

Springfield Ills. June. 29th 1866

My Dear Sir:

. . .

I hope to write a correct Biog when it can be done. I shall make it truthful or not at all, and men shall intuitively feel that the Biog is true—correct & fair. The trouble is very *very* great, I assure you. Thousands of floating rumors—assertions & theories &c. &c have to be hunted down—dug out—inspected—Criticised &c. &c. before I can write. I can't Scribble on a sentence without knowing what I am doing—. Between you & I, I as busily Engaged to-day in Collecting materials—times—places &c. &c as ever—am going to Ky in July—in search of new & important facts.[1]

. . .

Your Friend
W H Herndon

HL: Charles H. Hart Papers HM23581

45. To Charles H. Hart

Springfield Ills. July 22d 1866

My Dear Sir:

. . .

You can finish your "B" when you wish.[1] A year will do me. So take your own time. My professional business disturbs me—takes me off—divides my mind and I "can't go fast". I have many old relics of Mr L which I wish you could see, and among them is a love letter which he wrote to his sweetheart at the age of 23.[2]

---

1. WHH's contemplated trip to Kentucky never came about.

---

1. This refers to a bibliography Hart was compiling of sermons and eulogies on AL, which WHH considered publishing in his biography of AL.

2. A reference to one of the letters AL wrote in 1836–37, which WHH had received the previous month from the recipient, Mary Owens Vineyard. See *Herndon's Informants*, 248.

Honor "sticks out" in it as in all his after life. I have a leaf of Mr L's old Copy book made in 1824—when 15 years of age. I wish you could see it: it is neat—clean and Exact in what is done—one of his characteristics. Mr L's life is a sweet—clear—clean—manly noble life. The more I study it the more I like it. I sometimes thought that some of his peculiarities were things drawn on for Effect, but letters to friends—his youth—boyhood—manhood, through all Stations, positions & conditions are identical—one and the same—ever honest, & simple, & sincere. His is a primitive type of character that the young must admire and over whom it must exercise in all coming time a vast influence. You once said to me that you thought I somewhat exaggerated. In some particulars I may have done so. Will you please tell me where—*in what*, I rose above the truth in your opinion. I shall be obliged to you. I want to be exactly correct in my estimate of Mr L. Please say to me what you think and I promise you to mend my mistake. Come—be candid. I'll admire you the more for it.

. . .

> Your Friend
> *W H Herndon*

HL: Charles H. Hart Papers HM23583

46. To Lyman Trumbull

Springfield Ills Aug 19th 1866

Dear Sir:

Now that the U. S. S is adjourned and you are more or less idle I wish you to assist me *a little* in making up Some part of Lincoln's life. What I want to know just now is—How did Mr Lincoln treat his Cabinet ministers—ie did he have frequent or infrequent Cabinet meetings as often or oftner and *like other Presdts*—. It is said that he scarcely Ever had Cabinet meetings—letting Each department run itself by its own head of office, he the Presdt paying no attention to any Except the War department &c. &c. Please tell me how this is. Give me your opinion of the above questions—ideas &c. &c and what is suggested by them.

I hate to trouble you, but can't avoid it and you must grin and bear it for a friend who is desirous to Know and who wishes to Speak truthfully in and on what he does Say.

I promise to get [through] asking you questions in about 3 answers.

> Your Friend
> W H Herndon

Your letters shall be Kept *sacredly* private
W H H

LC: Lyman Trumbull Papers

47. To Robert Todd Lincoln

[Prior to August 28, 1866]

Rob't—I want to give a sketch—a short life of your mother in my biography up to her marriage to your father—or say up to 1846 or 1858. I wish to do her justice fully—so that the world will understand things better. You understand me. Will she see me.[1]

LC: HW3774, Exp 4:11, 2917

48. To County Clerk, Hardin County, Kentucky

Springfield Ills. Octr. 4th 1866

Mr. Clerk

Will you have the kindness to look over the marriage Records, and tell me when Sarah Bush married her first husband. I may not get the name—Bush—right, but I mean the woman who married Mr *Thos Lincoln*—she being Mr Thos. Lincoln's 2d wife & he being her 2d husband. What day & month & year did she marry her *first* husband. If you told me this once before I have lost your letter. *Please*—accommodate me.

Truly yours.
W H Herndon

[*In another hand:*] Sarah Bush & Daniel Johnston were married on 13th Mar 1806 Would have written you before but have been very busy
V. Hewitt[1]

LC: HW2092; Exp 4:7:26

49. To Caroline Healy Dall

Oct. 28th 1866

Mrs Dall

You are authorized to state that I never knew Mr Lincoln to do a mean thing—nor a dirty trick—in any walk of life—You can say that Mr Lincoln & myself never had a cross word—quarrel nor any misunderstanding—however small—you can state that he & I never kept books or accounts against Each other. Kept moneys of each other as told you—I know I was never wronged by the man in one cent

---

1. Presumably clipped from a letter he had sent to Robert Todd Lincoln, this manuscript fragment was subsequently returned to WHH in a letter from Robert's mother, Mary Lincoln, dated August 28, [1866]. Her letter is a friendly invitation to meet her in Springfield for a long conversation and contains this reference to the enclosed fragment: "You will excuse me enclosing you this sentences of yours & asking its meaning." For a full text of Mary Lincoln's letter, see *Herndon's Informants*, 326–27.

---

1. Virgil Hewitt was County Clerk of Hardin County, Kentucky.

of money. You may say that Mr Lincoln was the best & truest friend I ever had outside of my own family—always Excepting my mother. Mr Lincoln when he did attach himself to man or woman he was *[illegible]* warmly wrapt in the man or woman—nothing but demonstration of dishonesty or vice could shake him. You may state that in Elections & in Electionary proceedings—he—Lincoln invariably refused to give money as corrupting funds directly or indirectly. I know this because I have seen him refuse—heard him over and over. Mr Lincoln was intensely honest—religious in the true sense and philosophy of that term. What I have told you or shall tell you is literally true—

[*In margin:*] You are welcome to make anything public I tell you except his love letters—his love scrapes—his women or Mr Lincoln's domestic relations at his home &c with Mrs Lincoln. These things are *Sacredly private*—yet.

W H Herndon

MHS: Caroline Healey Dall Collection

50. To Chauncey Goodrich

Springfield Ills. Novr 17th 1866

My Dear Sir:

Your kind and suggestive letter, dated the 13th, is at hand, and for which I give you my thanks, truly.[1] I do not know of anything in the life—public or private of Mr Lincoln that would lessen your estimate of him. I never heard of his doing a mean thing. I never knew him do a dirty thing. He was a noble—high minded—liberal souled, and tolerant man. He had less vice & more virtue than any man I ever knew, or expect to know. He was true to himself—his Country, and his God—as he saw Him. I loved the man when living, & reverence him, now that he is dead. I do not think you will ever hear anything about the man's acts—thoughts—opinions or views that ought to diminish your love for the man. I thank you, my dear Sir for your letter.

Truly Yours
W H Herndon

Cornell

---

1. Goodrich had written to WHH a few days earlier to urge that he not write anything that would "belittle" AL.

51. To Isaac N. Arnold[1]

Springfield Ills. Nov. 20th 1866.

Friend Arnold:

I wrote you a hasty note on Saturday, and now propose to finish my defence.[2] You ask me if Mr. Lincoln was ever crazy in Menard County—was insane in 1835; and in answer to which I say—he was, as the People in that region understand craziness or insanity; and I *fear* much worse than I painted it, though I told the story as my reason and evidences make it—show it, and see it. You ask me if Mr. Lincoln *in fact* made the Identical Speech which I put in his mouth. He did not make that speech in words, though he did in substance and spirit—just as I have told them.

Again—did you know that Mr. Lincoln wrote a work—a book on *Infidelity*, and that his friends *say* they burnt it up. Beware that some leaf is not slumbering—to be sprung on you, when we are dead and gone, and no defence being made—he—L.—will go down all time as a writer on Infidelity—atheism &c—! How are you going to meet this? Don't scold and suspicion even by shadowy vision indirectly your true friend—your co-laborer, till you know all—know it as I do, and as time *will have it* and make it irrespective of you and myself. My own present opinion is that *that* book was written in 1835 and 6 written through the spirit of his misery—through the thought and idea that God had forsaken him: and through the echoes of Lincoln's mental condition—suffering—a burst of wild despair.[3] The dates as I have them make *the book* before the crazy spell but my knowledge of Lincoln and my reason tell me that the book was written in 1836. I am now in search of *the facts*—the true, and exact facts as to time, place and persons. Men place the book before the spell *and I after it*. I will write you my final conclusions about the facts. Let me alone—(smiling and good humoredly), I have my own work and mission. I may here say as I have said before to *you*, that I worship—reverence Lincoln—his memory and fame. I loved him while living and reverence him, that he is now dead and gone; he was the best friend I ever had excepting my own wife and my mother; he was the best friend I ever expect to have—save Mother and wife; and I repeat *to you* that I think Mr. Lincoln was the best man—the kindest—tenderest—noblest—loveliest *since Christ*. He was better and purer than Washington; and in my mind he stands incomparable, grandly looming up. He is now the great central figure of American History. God bless Abraham Lincoln!

Again—did you know that Mr. Lincoln was "*as crazy as a loon*" *in this city in 1841*; that he did not sit—did not attend to the Legislature, but in part, if any— (special session of 1841); that he was then deranged? Did you know that he was

---

1. The recipient's copy of this letter has been lost, but WHH retained a copy, an indication that he considered it an important record. This copy was included in a letter to Charles H. Hart on November 26, 1866 (§56).

2. The "hasty note" not located. The "defence" refers to his justification of a controversial lecture he delivered in Springfield on November 16 that related AL's tragic love affair with Ann Rutledge.

3. AL's grief following the death of Ann Rutledge.

forcibly arrested by his Special friends here at that time; that they had to remove all razors—knives—pistols &c—from his room and presence, that he might not commit suicide? Did you know that his crazy [bout?]—was partly caused by *that old original Love* coming in conflict with *new relations about to be assumed*—his fidelity to it *was sublime*. Did you know that all Lincoln's struggles—dificulties &c. between himself and wife were partly, if not wholy, caused by Mrs. L's cognition that Lincoln did not love her and *did love an other*. Lincoln told his wife that he did not love her—did so before he was married to her; she was cognizant of the fact that Lincoln loved an other. Did you know that the *Hell* through which Lincoln passed was caused by these things? Mrs. Lincoln's knowledge that Lincoln did not love her and did love another caused much trouble between them. I say, Lincoln told her *he did not love her*. The world does not know her, Mrs. L's sufferings—her trials—and the causes of things. Sympathize with her. I shall never rob Mrs. Lincoln of her justice—Justice due her. Poor woman! She will yet have her rewards. All these facts are not to go into my biography *now*, and yet the world will know all in spite of your wish or my desire, or any man's will. Do you not know—you ought to know that the Chicago Times and some mean men have these facts stowed away in their malicious brains and desks and a purpose and will meet the facts face to face and modify where I cannot truthfully deny. Justice to the dead and to all mankind demands it now when it can be done. Poor man! the world knows ye not and who shall defend thee and set thee right before the world; *and chain and rivet the* deep—eternal, and forever abiding sympathy of mankind to thee? My dear Sir, What makes Europe and America love Christ It is our sympathy that is at the root; and *shall I* strip Abraham of his crown and cross? It is criminal to do so.

Did you know that Mr. Lincoln was informed of *some facts* that took place in Kentucky *about the time he was born*—(was told so in his youth), that eat into his nature, and as it were, crushed him, and yet clung to him like his shadow,—like a fiery shirt around his noble spirit.[4] Lincoln for more than 50 long years walk through *his* furnace—had his cross and crown. Friend—What's the cause of his sadness—his gloom—his *sometimes* terrible nature. What made him so tender—so good—so honest—so just—so noble—so pure—so exalted—so liberal—so tolerant—so divine, as it were? It was the fiery furnace through which God rolled him, and yet the world must not know it—eh! Good heavens! shut out all light—freeze up all human sympathy from *this sacred man!* Never, No Never. All that I know of Mr. Lincoln only exalts him—brightens, and sublimes him, and will endlessly draw the sympathies of all mankind to him. Kind man—good man—noble man—who knows thy sufferings but one man, and God? God bless thee thou incomparable man!

Would you have Mr. Lincoln a sham—a reality or what—a symbol of an unreality? Would you cheat mankind into a belief of a falsehood by defrauding their judgements? Mr. Lincoln must stand on truth or not stand at all. This age

---

4. See §67.

is remorseless in its pitiless pursuit of facts, and do you suppose you and I can escape the honest judgments of mankind? Mr. Lincoln always admitted facts, and avoided them if he could. He never told a lie by suggestion or suppression; he thought it criminal; and shall I by suggestion or suppression lie? The man that dares *now* tell the truth—all and every necessary truth in reference to Lincoln, mankind will bless, and curse him that lies. *Mark my words friend.* All truths are *necessary* that show—explain, or throw light on Mr Lincoln's mind—nature— quality—characterstics—thoughts—acts, and deeds, because he guided the Rebellion—rather suppressed it, and guided the grandest of Revolutions through its grand consummation.

We have had a great Rebellion—ending in a magnificent Revolution. Mr. Lincoln guided it. Mankind will know the causes—facts and the relations of things, if the truth is told, and they will not if a lie is told. Cheat and delude mankind into a false philosophy ending in ruin! My duty is to the ever living man—and to God—not forgetting my own poor self—before the memory of the dead that hears not and cares—it may be, not. Truth is due mankind; and would you prefer a false Ideal character that you make by suggestion or suppression through pen and paint above the real that God has made? The age of blind Hero worship, thank God, has gone, and the worship of the Truth is coming. My duty is to truth—man, and God. My mind is made up, and nothing but facts—experiences run and purified through reason shall ever change my course.

My dear friend all that is said is kindly said, but firmly said.

Your Friend

P.S.

Since I began to gather *facts* nearly two years I have undergone various shades of opinion and belief and after two years reflection on the facts—beliefs and opinions of others, you now have my own opinion of the man and the spirit of my book. You may show this to as many men as you choose—the more the better opinion—idea &c you will have.

HL: Charles H. Hart Papers HM23594 (copy)

52. To Mr. Main

Springfield Ills Novr. 22d 1866

My Dear Sir:

Your note requesting a letter from Presdt Lincoln. Your kind voice touches me. Enclosed is a letter from Presdt Lincoln to me, dated the 8th Jany 1848.[1] I hate to part with the letter—yet—I must not be selfish. You love my friend: he was a kind—tender—strong man—a man of great [fidelity?]—integrity and honor: he is to me the noblest—the loveliest character that America has yet borne. He was

---

1. See *Collected Works*, 1:430–31.

the best—purest, and noblest man I ever knew or expect to know: he was above meanness, loving justice: he never did a dirty deed, remembering his general honor. I lived *closely* with him for more than 20 years & I can honestly say to you that I never knew him to do a mean thing: he couldn't do it. He is a lofty souled man and time will only prove the whisperings now of Common Consciousness.

Yours Truly
W H Herndon

Source not recorded[2]

53. To Mr. Smith

Springfield Ills Nov 22d 1866

My Dear Sir:

Enclosed you have a letter of Mr Lincoln, dated the 20 Nov. 1858., written to some excellent merchants by the name—the firm name of S. C. Davis & Co. This is the very best I can do for you—at least for the present. Anything from that good—tender—manly—noble—the very loveliest of men, I presume will do you some good. Mr Lincoln was a man of great honor, integrity, and general character: he was full of fidelity—full of candor, and sincerity. He was tolerant, liberal, and *broad minded to all human frailties*. He harbored no malice; and I think he is the finest American character yet born. He is the best & purest man I ever knew, or expect to know—yet he was human, having his weak sides

Yours Truly
W H Herndon

Brown

54. To Charles H. Hart

Springfield Ills. Nov 23d 1866

Friend Hart—

Your kind letter is just handed to me—am on my way to Chicago—must go—go to get facts & information generally. I published 500 of my Lectures. I can defend that Lecture to the end of the world.[1] I have a method—plan—and

---

2. The editors regret that their source for the photocopy of this letter has been lost.

---

1. Refers to WHH's lecture "Abraham Lincoln, Miss Ann Rutledge, New Salem, Pioneering, and THE Poem," delivered on November 16, 1866, in Springfield. Public reaction was harsh and widespread. See Donald, 229–30.

am guided alone by the *Love* of *Justice* & *Truth*—myself and my Creator. Don't you form a hasty opinion against that Lecture. I know what I'm doing and I know what Lincoln needs.

Hurriedly

Your Friend
W H Herndon

HL: Charles H. Hart Papers HM23592

55. To Mr. Kline

Springfield Ills Novr. 25th 1866

My Dear Sir:

To-day, as per request, I send you my 4th Lecture on Presdt Lincoln. The first two were the attempted analysis of Mr L's mind—; the third was in *some facts* showing his Patriotism & Statesmanship; and the 4th one is an attempt to show the modifications of his natural mind—the mind that God created uninfluenced by surroundings. Nature outside of man assists in making—modifying and developing it &c. The 5th Lecture will be on his education—the process—means—methods—manners of education, and the development of his mind &c. I will send you a copy if I deliver it—the poor thing. I never publish any of the 3d and the 1st & 2d were *in part* stenographed and given to the world in the winter of 1865 & 6, part of which you possibly saw at the time. See Carpenters 6 mo at White House toward the end for part of the first one.

My poor lectures somehow get a greater run than they are entitled to. The popularity is solely due I know to Mr Lincoln's fame &c

Yours Truly
W H Herndon

CHM: William Henry Herndon Collection

56. To Charles H. Hart[1]

Springfield Ills., Nov. 26th 1866.

My Dear Sir:

I have just returned from Chicago; and now wish to say a word or two to you. Enclosed is a copy of a letter which I wrote to the Hon. I. N. Arnold of Chicago, who is writing a life of Mr. Lincoln.[2] He is a good man, but I don't think he is a man of much nerve; he is an honest man, yet I think he is a timid man. Now first

---

1. In top margin: "You may show these letters to as many men as you please. The word suspicion does Mr. Arnold injustice. The word is *fear*. Don't publish. Any one may copy, though not to be published.—Herndon"

2. See §51.

as to the programme or, class of things; My first two Lectures, as you are aware, were attempts to analyze Mr. Lincoln's mind. My third Lecture was to show his Patriotism, and Statesmanship. My second and third Lectures were attempts to show the *practical application of that mind* to things &c. while I analyze it &c—. My 4th Lecture is an attempt to show external influences on it—material—and mental—matter and mind on mind. My 5th Lecture *is to be* on his infant and Boy*hood* education—the *means*—*methods* and *struggles* of it—his mind—to know and to develope itself.[3] When these things shall be done—corrected—annotated &c., I think I shall have rendered mankind some 5 cents worth of service. Possibly they will so hold. When these things are done mankind could spare me well, I giving them the Record which I have made of the man *worth one million of dollars* to the race.

So much for an Introduction. After having read Arnold's letter—my letter to him, you will prick up your ears. However—you will now begin to detect a purpose in my 4*th* late, Lecture, not guessed at before; and it is this: Mrs. Lincoln must be put properly before the world. She hates me yet *I can* and *will do* her justice; she hates me on the same grounds that a thief hates a policeman, who knows a dangerous secret, about him. *Mrs. Lincoln's domestic quarrels in my opinion sprang from a woman's revenge which she was not strong enough to resist.* Poor woman! The world has no charity for her, and yet justice must be done her—being careful not to *Injure* her husband. All that I know enobles both and their difficulties sprang from human nature—a philosophy, if you please. You must have faith in me. I am willing to live by, and to die by my letter to Arnold. The composition I care nothing about—in its artistic beauty, but the substance and Spirit I do care for.

Mr. Arnold is *afraid* that is the word—that I shall drop some *necessary* truth that Lincoln's enemies will use to unholy purposes. I am not responsible for the misapplication—misappropriation, or other wrong use of a *great necessary truth in Mr. Lincoln's life.* I have a sublime faith in the triumph and eternity of truth—of humanity—man and God; they will put Arnold—you, and myself just where we belong. Is any man so *Insane* as to suppose that any truth concerning Lincoln, or in relation to his thoughts—acts and deeds, will be hid and buried out of human view? Pshaw! Folly! The best way is to tell the whole truth, and let it by its very presence and eternity crush and burn up all lies. Let it "burn to ashes what it lights to death".

I propose as one of Mr. Lincoln's friends to meet the slumbering facts—deny them where I can; and modify where I cannot absolutely deny them. In my judgment, and I appeal to mankind in the future, is that if the matter is talked over *now* that the subject will be dropt in a hundred years or *less* from to day. My judgment is—poor as it may be, that if these facts are concealed from mankind by his—L's—biographers now, that they will grow and develope into a huge ever—discussed lie, bothering and fretting mankind forever. I know human nature; hide a mouse in a crack, and shade it, it will in the minds of men—grow and expand

---

3. This lecture was never published and possibly never finished.

into an elephant. So curious is the human mind. Glut its desires and turn away a perpetual howl. This is my judgment; and I'll risk it during all coming time. I think I know what I am doing. The friends of Mr. Lincoln had better sift the questions *now and here* while there are living witnesses on the Globe and living friends ready and willing to see and to have fair play.

Mr. Lincoln can stand unstaggeringly up beneath all *necessary* or other truths. Timid men would rob Mr. Lincoln of his crown and cross, and steal the opinions—the philosophy—the reasons of mankind by the robbery of their judgment and logical faculty through a suggestion of falsehood or the suppression of the *necessary* facts of a great man's history.

Please keep these letters safe till I go hence

W H Herndon

Your friend

P.S.

If you will change the programme a little of the publication of my Lectures you will see 1st The Education of the infant mind & its development—2d External influences—mind & matter in it—3d The analysis of the man's mind; & 4th The practical workings of that mind

Herndon

HL: Charles H. Hart Papers HM23593

57. *To Caroline Healy Dall*

Springfield Ills Novr. 27th 1866

My Friend—

I wish today one word—Enclosed is a part of the letter of a friend—L. L. Cist of St. Louis Mo, proving to you that I have had Lincoln's letters stolen in the mail—not only one but 3 or 4. If you ever see a letter from A Lincoln addressed to me from Washington in 1848 or 9, & in which Mr Lincoln speaks of a pretty girl—If you ever see a conversation between Cushing—Douglas & an other *in Mr Lincoln's hand writing*—: If you ever see a letter from Mr Lincoln written to _____ of the Central Rail Road about a case in the Supreme Court &c -; and if you ever see a letter written by Mr L to me about his vote on "Zach Taylor" in 1848, explaining his Course, *please* let me know. I dare not publish because destruction would end the letters; & I rather they should go down all time than to be destroyed. Respects to all

Your Friend

W H Herndon

Our P. Master here was arrested and Indicted about the time I sent you and others various things. I'll keep an eye out.

MHS: Caroline Healey Dall Collection

58. To Charles H. Hart

Springfield Ills. Nov. 28th 1866

My Dear Sir:

. . .

One more word—I have never informed you of my plan and this may leave you in the dark. My *first* Lecture was purely analytic—analytic of Mr Lincolns mind: the *second* Lecture was partly so, and yet partly practical—ie—it showed in part abstract mind in practical application on things & their relations in life. The *third* one was abstract mind applied—Mr. Lincoln's mind working on Love of Country & Statesmanship. My *fourth* Lecture was an attempt to show the force—influence, & power of mud flowers, & mind *on mind*—Lincoln's mind: My fifth Lecture will be—*is to be* on Mr Lincoln's infant mind—his boyhood's & manhood's mind—its nature—tending—power—growth—desires—longings—aspirations—development and general Evolution &c.; and when all this shall be done—all re-read—Corrected—annotated &c possibly I have done the race of man 5 cents worth of service; and possibly I will get paid &c. I have not published all this—the programe, plan &c. to defend myself. I never will stoop to a defence when I know that I am right

The reason why I chose—made the programe of publication that I did, was *because* the Analysis of Mr Lincoln's pure abstract mind *was an absolute necessity*—The 2d Lecture of like, but of inferior necessity—less value &c., and so on in the order of publication. I don't care whether men like this or not—nor whether they like my Lectures or not. My day is to-morrow—not to-day, and to to-morrow I appeal. Men have not my Lincoln record to read—to know & to study. Hence they do not know what is wise—what is policy &c. &c. with necessity included. I rest easy—calm & cool. It is hard to beat a man when the game stands 3 & 3, if that man has high-low-jack, and the game in his own hands.—So I laugh and grow fat when I see men fretting themselves over what I Say.

Now you are informed fully of my present plan, as to the 5 Lectures.

Your Friend
W H Herndon

HL: Charles H. Hart Papers HM23595

59. To Caroline Healy Dall

Springfield Ills. Nov. 30th 1866

My Dear Friend:

. . .

My wife tells me you read some of my memoranda, "which is all right"; and yet I wish to say a word about it for *your* sake.[1] Some facts in those little books need

---

1. While staying in WHH's home a month before this letter, Dall examined his research materials on AL, including two small memorandum books in which he kept highly sensitive information and testimony.

explanation—others are false—perverted & maliciously colored. Again—some of my conclusions, made at an early day when I commenced gathering facts, have since then changed, or been modified—: So if you want any particular idea you got from those memoranda explained, denied &c. you had better write to me, saying what you wish &c. &c; and if it is possible to do so I will explain. You must remember that I am not responsible for what others say, and which I note down. Be Careful in what you say, because you might be contradicted. Please send me what you write & print on Mr Lincoln—would be glad to see it after the facts are run through your good woman's mind You are a sharp observer,—an accute seer. What I said to you at my house on any and all questions I substantally affirm. The Cane & school house wood &c. &c I gave you are genuine and no fraud—You may swear by them—*pray* by them, and rest easy in their presence. They are just what I said & nothing else.

. . .

I am still gathering facts about Mr Lincoln, and expect so to do all my life. I want one great man—*the* good man—the noble man—His Story—true lovely man—the gentle & kind man—the *noblest*—loveliest character, on the whole; *Since Christ* well understood. I do not say that Mr Lincoln was a perfect man and a part of the *Godhead*; he had his faults & weak points, as all men have ever had and always will have—ie—man will never become *absolutely perfect*.

Give my best respects to all my friends in Boston *generally*.

Your Friend
W H Herndon

P.S.

I have the best—largest & truest record of Mr Lincoln in the world—will continually increase & perfect it. *WHH*

MHS: Caroline Healey Dall Collection

60. To Isaac N. Arnold[1]

Springfield Novr. 30th 1866

Friend Arnold—

I was sick in Chicago or would have called to see you on Saturday, according to my conditional promise. On arriving home I found your two letters, dated on the 22 & 23d Novr., and to which I wish to make a reply. I know you wrote as a friend and do not doubt that. In your letter of the 22d you say—"I do not fear the *truth*, as his L's friend. What I did fear—what I still fear, is that now, that he has gone & cannot himself explain, the bringing before the public—facts which he left to obscurity & silence may be perverted, especially, if given to the public now, while there are so many North as well as South, who yet hate him for his triumph

---

1. Because WHH added a sizeable insert to this letter (HW2821–23; Exp 4:8:1164–66), he had a fair copy made, to be sent to Arnold, as attested on the final page of the retained copy.

over slavery and rebellion". I presume I may say—I am Lincoln's friend and "do not fear the truth as his friend". I hope and believe that two men may in nature be the friend of an other third man. This is no unusual thing: it may be you are a better friend to Mr Lincoln's fame than I am or dare be. This depends on circumstances which I will not now & here discuss. What you do fear is that some fact, left unexplained by Mr Lincoln, and which he left in silence &c will be uttered by me. Did you weigh that sentence? If you dread that you had better burn up your books; *because* all Mr Lincoln's life is such a slate of facts—conditions—silence &c, as is every other man's life. No man explains all he does—nay not one tenth of what he does: these he leaves to silence and to the grave. Possibly—probably—nay *truthfully* all the good things an honest man does he himself leaves to the silences and to the graves; and shall we not build up a man's fame on these; and lift these great thoughts—ideas, & deeds out of the silences and the graves, where the good and honest man left them—to life & light? Some men—"do not wish to blow their own horns"; and where they are good—noble & vital men leaving in silence & the grave their great & good deeds, let us blow their horns for them; and snatch from the silences & the graves these great deeds, that they may not perish. Mr Lincoln was an ambitious man—struggled for the Presidency—reached it, & yet he has left his motives—his purposes, and plans in the dread silences; and shall we not talk about them; simply because Mr Lincoln was too modest, and too sensible to "blow his own horn": he made his great house-divided-against-itself speech, and yet he never explained to mortal man why he did it—wholy so: he came to Ills—he married—begot a family—studied & practiced law—loved man— Liberty—God; and yet you will find no record of explanations. Friend—good humoredly—smiling—burn your book—which I know & hope you will not do—though on every page it violates—rudely violates your own philosophy, and caution to me. Mr Lincoln cannot come from the grave and explain. You and I are left for that very duty, and let us manfully—truthfully, and corageously do it. Have no *fears!* Lincoln's reputation does not rest in my hands—nor *excluively* in yours. If Mr Lincoln has left *facts* in *obscurity*—and *silence:* his whole life is so— nearly so—i e, as to *his* explanations of what he did—said, & thought; and these facts—things—thoughts—&, deeds, you have talked about on every page of your good book, I hope & believe. Shall you cease to talk about them and give sagacious & philisophic opinion on them. Excuse your *opinions* where Mr Lincoln has left to obscurity and silence the holy purposes & intents—his ideas & motives. Erase all facts from your book that Mr Lincoln has left to obscurity and silence. Do so simply *because* some scoundrel—some enemy, North or South, because Mr Lincoln set free the African race and squelched the rebellion, still hates him—Mr L—and will pervert—misappropriate—misapply—forge—distort a great sacred *necessary* truth in relation to Mr Lincoln's life,—will you! Then erase all you have written or will write about Mr Lincoln. Great necessary truths—facts—and thoughts of Jesus have even been misapplied—misappropriated—falsely and wickedly changed, and otherwise infamously used by His enemies, North & South, because he struck the fetters from mankind, and triumphed in time over Rebellion. Was He responsible for all this—? *Is He now?* Jesus was not and is not responsible for such wicked things. I am not responsible for mean men's mean and malicious acts, North or South, now nor in the future—in reference to Lincoln—other men or subjects or things.

I am satisfied you will do what is right and I will risk your judgement on *your own* materials; and I hope you have the same faith in me on *my own* materials— Good humoredly—kindly I do not deal in "gossip", and will not. I take all you say kindly as coming from a friend, and will you be as liberal & just to me.

The Philosophy you would teach me amounts to this at least in tendency—all vice—infamy—wrong—injustice—meanness & deviltry which a man does in this life; and which the actor & doer, as he thinks, has left to the silences—the graves and obscurities, must not be snatched from the grave and held up to mankind as warning. Your philosophy would teach me, that if a man becomes great he may live any life of wrong—vice, and crime—be tyrant, murderer & despot, his memory will be glossed over for his sake, cheating the future into a lie. You would hold out to mankind, the corrupt politician, tyrant—& traitor, and criminal the guarantee—"Do what you please and what you have left to silence and obscurity shall never be dragged from the grave or other hiding place." You hold out that kind of invitation—inducement, and guarantee to vile hated men and deeds in tendency at least. I say it is an obligation high as heaven and as deep as hell—wide and universal as man to drag such things & men to light and expose them to all mankind forever. I hold out this inducement—this invitation—this guarantee to the mean vile wicked man—"Do as you will—do wrong—do injustice—be corrupt—be unjust—oppress the poor—act or *think* wrong—if the thought escapes your lips, though you are great & rich, and powerful—your acts—deeds—thoughts, which you have left unexplained to silence & obscurity—being dead or alive, explained or not explained—, shall be snatched from the deep eternal silences—obscurities, and the graves; and held up every nerve—cell & fibre of your life laid bare & exposed to human view, as warning." I tell the politician, live nobly & act justly—to all men live honestly and uprightly before man & God, or you shall be exposed. Mr Arnold, let us vow this—let men now, and *henceforward & forever* understand, that they cannot live famously—, after a life of vice & wrong, except *infamously*. Begin now. Lincoln is above reproach & is almost spotless thank God; and let the world understand from this time that all things—all necessary truths, shall be brought to clear clean broad day light.

There are now in America two civilizations as I said to you at your house— one North, & one South. These civilizations have their representatives, North as well as South. The North will attempt to build up for Lincoln a super human fame—will make Lincoln a perfect—unblemished—spotless angel of God a part of the Godhead. The South will make and paint him a perfect helion—a high criminal—a tyrant—despot—a child of the Devil. This is the tendency of North & South; and had these men their way mankind would be divided to the end of time, [groping?] and debating the question as to the existence—nature and character of Lincoln forever. If the future detect us the end we wish—Lincoln's glorious immortality and the justest & noblest fame, will be lost. *Mark my words.* Tell truthfully—honestly—heroically all necessary truths, and all doubts will die forever or rather they never will exist. I have run this through my poor brain for two years; and you have my conclusions as to what *I* shall do.

One more word: I have delivered 4 Lectures on Mr Lincoln's mind—characteristics, and intend to deliver the 5th. They will stand—*first* Mr Lincoln's infant mind—his boyhood & manhood mind—its nature as God made it—its tendencies—aspirations—growth, and struggles, and general development. The *second* the one you have just read is an *attempt* to show the power & influence of mud—scenery—flowers; and mind on mind—Lincoln's mind. The *third* is purely analytic of Mr Lincoln's manhood mind. The *fourth* is a practical application of that abstract idea, mind—Lincoln's spirit to the things of this world and their relations; & the *fifth* will be on Mr Lincoln's Patriotism & Statesmanship—mind practically at work in Country & Government—; and it is possible you may like them. I hope you will.

I hope your book will be out by the first day of Jany next and it is my sincere wish that it may be a complete success. I believe it will from what I know of its gentlemanly and talented author.

In all kindness Your Friend
W H Herndon

LC: *HW2816–19, 2821–23, 2819–20; Exp 4:8:1158–62, 1164–66, 1162–63*

61. To David L. Cronyn[1]

Springfield Ills, Dec. 3d, 1866.

My Dear Sir:

Some few days since I wrote you a short note on the question of Mr. Lincoln's Religion.[2] I did this at your request, and as so short a letter as that is Calculated to convey any Idea, or no idea, I propose at your request to state Explicitly what I know of Mr. L's Religion. I sent you a Lecture of mine delivered a week or so since; which I wish you to consider while reading this.[3] You will perceive by that Lecture that Mr. Lincoln's mind was shocked—shattered by Miss Ann Rutledge's death. I told you in my letter that Mr Lincoln once wrote a work on Infidelity, so-called. This was, and *is* true. Mr Lincoln was told when a boy some *asserted* facts—facts that somewhat disgraced some of his dear relatives. This story clung to him during all his life—a fire shirt, schorching him; he suffered that one suffering till 1835, when his love's death duplicated his suffering. The *facts*, as I can get them, are that he wrote the book on Infidelity before 1835. But from what I know of Mr. Lincoln,

---

1. WHH later misremembered this correspondent's last name as "Cronyer," "Conyer," and "Conger."

2. Not found.

3. "Abraham Lincoln, Miss Ann Rutledge, New Salem, Pioneering, and THE Poem," delivered on November 16, 1866, in Springfield.

and his double cross I aver that that book was a burst of despair. The book was a lofty criticism—a high spiritual rationalistic criticism, like, as I understand the various Evidences, my own knowledge of Mr. Lincoln included, Bishop Colenso's Conclusions.[4] There was no sneer—scoff, or ridicule of the Bible, but a noble looking into it, and a charitable telling of his conclusions of fallibility and plenary inspiration. Lincoln wrote under the Idea that God had cursed and crushed him Especially. It is possible that he was severer on the Bible than I state. I give you my opinion, and that is mine from what I know of Mr. Lincoln's own ideas than from what others state. Some men do think that Mr. Lincoln did scoff and sneer at the Bible. This is not so: he had no scoff—nor sneer, for even a Sacred Error; he had charity for all and Every thing. God rolled Mr. Lincoln through His fiery furnace *specialy*—that he might be his instrument *in the future*. This purifying process gave Mr Lincoln Charity—liberality—kindness—tenderness—toleration—a sublime faith, if you please, in the purposes and Ends of his Maker.

Mr. Lincoln as he has often told the world had faith in the People and God; he has told you—the People that Providence rules the universe of matter & substance—mind & spirit. That a law Enwraps the universe and that all things—beings—minds were moving to their appointed end. Hence Mr Lincoln could not believe, as a rational man—a logical minded one too—a very logical minded one, that the Bible was the *peculiar—only* and *special* Revelation of God, as the theologic Christian world understands it: ie, as they preach it. He did not believe that a few chosen men were *particularly—specially*—Excluding all other men, *inspired*, as the theologic Christian world understands it—ie as they preach it. It was *impossible*—his mind was so organized—for him to see or believe in such doctrines. Mr Lincoln did not believe in the Miraculous Conception of Jesus, as the theologic Christian world understands that question—subject. I say to you he believed in a universal and an unvarying Eternal Law of things. He holds this up to you, and flares it always and Everywhere in the faces of the people. I say to you that Mr Lincoln was liberal—tolerant, having Charity for all. Mr Lincoln had no conception of forms—rules—formulas, and technical dogmas in science—Law or Religion. He really was deficient in this particular as I think. Mr Lincoln Could not Endure a discussion of such things: he could not read them: he never visited wrangles of this kind.

While all this is true—yet he had a high respect for any mans Sacred liberal or other opinion: he believed in the absolute necessity of some form of *Christianity*, and never did after reflection attempt to disturb any man's opinion—obtrusively so at least: he loved the *broad* Christian philosophy—maxims—*sayings* and *moral* of Christianity—not because any particular man said them, but because they were and are great—grand leading truths of human Consciousness—the highest and loftiest inductions—deductions, if you please of human reason or intuitions of the human soul.

---

4. Anglican bishop John William Colenso concluded that important portions of the Old Testament could not be historically true.

Mr Lincoln's mind was severely Logical; he did in some moods, I think doubt immortality: the Evidence before me is plain, & to that Effect, and yet he generally believed in immortality: his doubts on this question were as follows—he doubted his precise identity individuality, and Earthly Consciousness, with all his [illegible]: he has said to me—"That would be a terrible thing." I mean to say he said this substantially, and yet I say he believed—had faith in immortality. This I know is denied by some men here: ie—some men *think* that Mr Lincoln thought the soul a mere *spirit* force—a mere *animo-spirit* force. I mean by that word a *vital* force. This is not true, for he himself says to a brother—about his dying father—this—"I sincerely hope father may yet recover his health; but at all events tell him to remember to call upon and confide in one[5] *great*—*one good* & Merciful Maker, who will not turn away from him in any extremity. He *notes* the *fall* of a *Sparrow*, and *numbers* the *hairs* of our heads; and He will not forget the dying man, who puts his trust in Him. Say to him that if we could meet now it is doubtful whether it would not be more painful than pleasant, and that if it be his lot to go now he will soon have *a joyous meeting with many loved ones gone before; and where the rest of us through* the help of God, hope ere long to join them
affectionately A. Lincoln"
This letter—the original one written by Mr L to his step brother John D. Johnston, dated the 12th 1851, *is now in my hands.*[6] I copied the above sentences—all there is on that subject, from the letter—my wife and I comparing—

This letter of Mr Lincoln's liberally read—& interpreted proves all I say or nearly so. The *underscored* words are not so *Italicised* in the original. I must be fair. From what I have said—from what Mr Lincoln has said at various times, and places and on various occasions, you *must* not believe all you hear. Mr Lincoln, in justice to him, never said—while speaking to the loyal Colored People of Baltimore, of the Bible or New Testament—This "But for *that Book* we could *not* know right from wrong."[7]

Mr Lincoln in my opinion—according to my recollection thought all Evil—*apparent* Evil—in the end, *not* absolute Evil: he thought pain in the world educa*tive*, and he positively denied all punishments as punishment in the future world, if he did not totally & entirely positively deny all such punishment for any purposes or ends. You now have my opinion, and best rememberance of Mr Lincoln's *Religion.* I am not afraid that this letter will ever be contradicted. Mr Lincoln belonged to no church & believed in none. Mr Lincoln was an intensely sincere and honest man, and as Judge Davis said of him—: "When he was convinced on any Question—when he believed he was right he *acted*, and the terrors of mob opinions had no terrors for him." I quote Judge Davis substantially. I agree to this opinion of Judge Davis; and now do you for an instant suppose, My Dear Sir; that if Mr

---

5. In margin: "The word one should be 'our.' Corrected by letter to Mr Conyer by letter Decr 17th or 18—letting him to notify—&c / WHH"

6. *Collected Works*, 2:96–97.

7. See "Reply to Loyal Colored People of Baltimore upon Presentation of a Bible" *Collected Works*, 7:542–43.

Lincoln was really a converted man to the faith of three Gods—Revelation—Inspiration—Miraculous Conception, and their necessity &c as some of the Christian world pretend to believe of Mr Lincoln, *that he would not have boldly said so and so acted like a deeply sincere man and an honest one fearlessly of that mob furor*. I know what I am saying, I think. I have evidences to support me. This letter is written with some little thought & care, I confess; and it is at your service. Do with it as you please—except its present publication. Read it to as many as you please and allow any one to take copies or send copies to whom you please—

Truly Yours

W H Herndon

P.S

Mr Lincoln never to my knowledge repudiated his original little book: he never said he was a universalist—unitarian—Rationalist—Theist or what not, & I dare not say what he was *technically*. I will write you again on Holland—Bateman, & such like men, sayings, and things—will give you a history of Holland's & Batemant's statements &c, while things are fresh & I am living. Such Speeches as recorded in Mr Carpenter's Book page 199 I deem a farse.[8] Mr Lincoln was a hypocrit or such things *are false*

W H Herndon

LC: HW2834–40; Exp 4:8:1193–99 (copy)[9]

62. To Mr. Hickman

Springfield Ills Decr. 6th 1866

My Dear Sir:

Your kind note, dated the ___ ult, is at hand; and for which please accept my thanks. I am willing to listen and learn from all men; and am especially willing to hear advice made good naturedly. I have assumed a heavy responsibility in attempting to write the life of Mr Lincoln; and yet I do not feel greatly alarmed. I know one thing, and that is, I can tell the truth, as I see it. Blind bat eyed hero worshipers—timid creatures, orthodox theologians, and other frigid souled men who cluster around form and color—never touching substance will oppose all I do or say. From such men—truth—Exact truth being my guide—Justice—Exact Justice to all men being my aim, I expect no greater: their hate—their coldness—their universal meanness—their threats—their attacks, & their gold, I care nothing for. What would such men give if they could only catch me in one broad radical mistake? Thousands! An Ideal man so created out of falsehood's & lies by suggestion & suppression is the gloating desire of millions of men & women. Such an Ideal is a sham—a lie—a fraud & a cheat. In other words it is a great lie that is worshiped, and men want me to aid in erecting such an image. Mr Lincoln would—does

---

8. A reference to AL's reply to the loyal colored people of Baltimore.
9. WHH's retained copy, docketed "D. L. Cronyn."

in heaven censure—scorn all such dishonest appliances: he would say—does say by his whole life—"Write my life truthfully as I, in my bones, blood & flesh, on Earth *thought it*, & *acted it out*. Come, no shams. I didn't live by lies & cant stand on them—either by suggestion or suppression."

All truths which are *necessary* to be told about Mr Lincoln should be boldly & truthfully told. Necessary truths are those facts—truths, & principles which illustrate—show and boldly develop Mr Lincoln's mind, nature—constitution of body, as well as of mind—the qualities of mind—heart—soul—feelings—education, aspirations—modifications of mind &c. &c—because as Ideas—Thoughts & Acts are the results of mind, as well as body helping, so his mind should be thoroughly understood. The day *will* come when body & mind will be thoroughly studied and somewhat understood. The day *will* come when to know these is to know the man. Every modification of original nature should be noted. The reading world is entitled to all necessary truths in order to understand his administration and his acts. You need not suppose, my Dear Sir, that the world will not hunt up—run down and dig out all these things though ten thousand timids should howl against the search & pursuit. This age is a persevering boring—digging—inquiring—sifting age, and wo to him that lies—wo to him who does not tell all necessary truths. Sacred lies will not protect us. Hence as Mr Lincoln's friend I propose to sink and cut a counter mine. I propose to throw overboard in other words all things now & avoid the whale & the shark. This philosophy—this policy will avoid what *you* probably *bristle* at. Suppose all these things—Lincoln's faults magnified by time through a want of the exact truth at the right moment—mankind in time & during the ages could magnify them—swell them out to imense dimensions, and pray—who would be at fault—you—Lincoln's friends or who? Why Lincoln's friends, who knew the truth & told it not. Mr Lincoln has bitter enemies—bitter deeply & thoroughly malicious ones and they are I know biding their time. I propose to cut and clip that by telling how all things are so that no future lie will have any effect on mankind.

I wish to address you as a man of good judgement—good taste and philosophy. Mr Lincoln to my own knowledge as it were has for *fifty* years been rolled by God through a firey furnace heated white hot & blue clouded: by this purifying process of God Lincoln has been broadened—widened and deepened in his sympathy & love for man—has been made more liberal—more feeling—more sympathetic—more tolerant, more kind & tender—more noble—more lovely—the noblest & loveliest character since Christ. The statement here of qualities—characteristics were developed, if not caused by the firey furnace travel, and yet timid men—false friends would rob him of his crown and cross to keep up a fancied Ideal in their own little minds. I shall not aid that crime by the robbery of the Tomb & Fame of Mr Lincoln. Mr Lincoln can never stand on the greatness of mind like Shakespear—Burke—Webster: Christ binds the worlds love & sympathies to him with cords of invisible power—namely—by their feelings & sympathies for his suffering. I want & intend to have this from all good men and woman in the world. Sympathy helped to carry him high & elevated in this world, and I do not propose to break the Power. Some one has said "let me write the People's songs and I'll rule". I say—"let me have the People's sympathies and I'll rule—govern and go heavenward, growing & expanding in the ages—a God."

Men—some men say that Mr Lincoln was a tender man &c; and yet do not wish to know or learn how he was so made. He was President of the United States, and yet men do not want to know what made him Presdt. I say to you that sympathy aided—strongly and visibly aided to make him the Ruler of a great free People. Why did he sympathise with the black man—the low born and oppressed? God's firey furnace and yet you will not hear of it. Mr Lincoln was God's chosen one—his special one—his great particular man for America & her Times: God tested him by rolling him through the firey furnace

I have thought about all these things—have analyzed myself—what I know & the facts and have determined my *general* course. I am willing to hear advice and reasons as to my course. Hence you may *freely* write to me on any & all ideas—courses—determinations, if good naturedly done. I know you will not do otherwise.

Now if you will take my Lectures, and this, and my last letter to you[1] you can well understand my opinion—my judgements of Mr Lincoln—my plans—purposes & general course.

   . . .

Your Friend
W H Herndon

LC: HW2849–52; Exp 4:8:1215–20[2]

63. To Francis B. Carpenter

Springfield Ills. Decr. 11th 1866

My Dear Sir:

   I duly received your kind—pointed, & excellent letter, dated the 4th instant, and for which please accept my thanks. You interpret me correctly. I am a pre-Raphaelite—ie a lover and worshiper of exact truth and nature; and religiously believe they should be followed—the former more than the latter. I think it eminently proper in artists when they are about to embody their thoughts into form, enwrapped in matter, to Idealize the *idea*—the *abstract Idea*; and so far you and I agree. But when you wish to paint a *thing*—a *scene*—a *man* then follow nature. Here you and I differ The difference lies in the *Idea*, and the *Thing*. Your letter is manly & honest; and in my estimation you are lifted higher than before it was written. I admire your style of a man in this; and now let me say a few words in self defense. I know—did know Mr Lincoln well—knew his sorrows and aspi-

---

1. Not found.
2. A note below the signature indicates that WHH employed a scribe to make a fair copy to send to the recipient, retaining this, his composition draft.

rations—his thoughts & history. I know—I feel—that for, say fifty years God rolled Abraham Lincoln through His fiery furnace. He did it to try Abraham and to purify the man for His purposes. One of the things the agonies I shall not name & the other is the death of Ann Rutledge. This purifying process—this fiery birth made Mr Lincoln *humble—tender—forebearing—liberal—sympathetic to suffering—kind—sensitive, tolerant, broadening—deepening,* and *widening his whole nature, making him noble & lovely—the noblest & loveliest character since Christ.* I can and have trailed the child—boy, & man day by day since the 12th Feby 1809. And now shall the world be shut out of this temple of intelligence,—prohibited from seeing and knowing what I see & know?

We—America—the People of America have just passed through the greatest Rebellion the world ever saw—*ending in a sublime Revolution.* The future should know the facts & law of it. They can only know them by being told truthfully what they are. Mr Lincoln was Presdt—guided the ship of state over the Rebellion that was planned & planted for thirty years to wreck it. His ideas—thoughts—methods—plans—means & programme formed a part of the means—methods &c. of its suppression. His thoughts shot into acts are his administration. To know the man well by nature—as made by nature, and modified by accidents—surroundings—& conditions, including men, is to know his thoughts and to a certain extent the causes of them and their motives. Philosophy is marching that way: history will soon follow—so will biography. The tendency—nay it is a fact that the age moves to a higher and grander individuality through a higher and grander development of the man. The tendency—nay it is a visible fact that this individuality, through development, approximates—is ever approximating to absolute truth. In proportion as this march is made, so dies blind bat eyed hero worship. We are marching to the worship of Truth—absolute Truth Right, & Justice.

Three things enter into my ideas—1st Self respect—2dy Respect for the dead; and 3dly *the People.* The whole truth will erect the true man's true Ideal. Shall I suppress or suggest falsehood in order to build up a false Ideal that the reading world may worship. I have two plans in view—one is to burn up my Lincoln record—*the finest in the world or ever will be*—or to write the exact truth as I see it. The great keen, shrewd, boring, patient philisophic—critical, & remorselessly searching world will find out all things, and bring them to light—; and the question is now—who shall do that—a man's friends or his enemies? Shall it be done *now* or left for the future world to wrangle over, and yet forever debate. "Close this door," experience cries. The very existence of Christ is denied because he had no good truthful Biographers. You have done much for Mr Lincoln's memory—and yet I see a blank I would gladly fill. I want, and intend to have the generous broad and deep sympathies of the universal heart for good & noble Abraham. You see, it will all come right. Trust God and the People.

What I said about Mr Lincoln is true, and we cannot dodge it. Experience says—"Meet it, and modify the idea that *will grow to be*". My philosophy is to sink a counter mine, and blow up my enemies—Lincoln's future traducers—and I do it for him, and the People, who build their Philosophy of human history out of human thoughts—acts, & deeds. Other Philosophy now is, my friend, a crime. I acknowledge that what I said is calculated to create a twinge of nerve. I have weighed results—fully—fully; and I bide my time. However what I said is no more than if I had said that Mr Lincoln was momentarily made crazed by laughing gas taken from a physician—not a bit; and you will live to see the day you will say so.

Mr Lincoln was the best friend I ever had or expect to ever to have except my wife & mother. I think he is the noblest & loveliest man since Christ—so you perceive that my *motives* are good whatever may be my judgements. I *know* I shall have to appeal to Time. I cannot argue with a sacred feeling: it is deaf, dumb, blind, and holy. It must argue with itself. Hence I want time.

We exist in the midst of two civilizations—one in the South and one in the North—. The one will try & make Mr Lincoln a perfect being—a supernatural man, and the other will say he is a devil; and so he will travel down all time mis-apprehended—not understood and pray whose fault will it be? Lincoln's friends. The middle man is needed. Hence I have two things in view—first *sympathy* for Lincoln and 2dy solidity for his memory. Appeals will be made to my record. My Lincoln's life is only *a record*. No man can now write an artistic life of Lincoln. Your life—*sayings* & doings of Lincoln will outlast all the lives of Lincoln written during this age. *Mark that.*

I am happy to know your portrait of Mr Lincoln by your friend Halpin[1] is soon to be out. If you know me right well you will know that I speak the truth when I say—I hope you entire success, and I believe you will get it—*catch it.* I shall, my dear Sir—let me say *friend*, be happy to see your "proof sheets," and will at your special request study it closely and long "till it does grow". I wish all men working in my line, & path well—in fact the whole world well, but I must say especially all who wish to build up for Lincoln a fame—a name—a monument that Time will itself consecrate. I will, after having studied your proof impression sufficiently long, give you my poor opinion. You know I am no artist—wish nature had made me so: it has given me a desire without the faculty of use.

. . .

One other word—you pay me a high compliment in mentioning my analytic Lecture, the one you refer to in your book, and for which I thank you. My 4th Lecture, as Douglas once said of some event—"set me back." My 4th Lecture is a miscellaneous one—and of necessity it is in the telling disjointed: its incoherence lies not in the idea but the matter and so far your criticism is correct.[2] When you come to read L's Biography and see him move in and about New Salem, book under arm—pale from excess of study—or see him running his compass for points, courses, & distances with an eye ever on bread, you will, I think, lift your criticism from the incoherency to the idea of unity that underfloats the lecture. Have faith and I'll move forward a little again in my 5th Lecture, which I shall send you, if I

---

1. Engraver Frederick Halpin had produced a rendering of Carpenter's portrait of AL and his cabinet.
2. See §54, n. 1.

get time to write it out & print it. So goodby. I hope this will reach you Saturday
night in order that you may rise early Sunday morning and finish it by "Tea". Will
you my dear friend—excuse me? If you have a wife & little one kiss them for me;
and I'll do ditto here for you.

Your Friend

W H Herndon

Copied & sent.

    LC: HW2885–87; Exp 4:8:1276–81 (copy)

64. To Charles H. Hart

Springfield Ills. Decr. 12th 1866

My Dear Sir:

Your kind and cheering note, 'mid the incongruous notes of many curses &c,
dated the 10th inst is this instant handed to me, and for which I thank you. I
am censured by some who do not & cannot know what I am at. It takes a cool
philosophy to bear to be misrepresented & to be misunderstood when one has in
his own hands Evidence—proofs that would instantly allay all—and from that
same censuring throng would come—"God bless you—you are right—go on." I
think I can bear it [*illegible*]—cooly. Would to God the world knew what I ~~did~~
do, and save me the necessity of being the man to open and Explain all clear as
the noon day sun. Mrs Lincoln will scold me—poor woman, without knowing I
am her friend, determined to put her right before the world for all time. She too
has borne her cross; and she shall have justice if I live. Would that I could but
talk to you one hour. Mr & Mrs Lincoln's marriage was an unfortunate one, and
I say to you that what *I know* and shall tell only ennobles both—that is to say it
will show that Mrs L has had cause to suffer, and be almost crazed, while Lincoln
self sacrificed himself rather than to be charged with dishonor. Such a man the
world never saw—& never will see again. God bless him—so pure—so tender—so
good—so honorable—so noble—so lovely—the very noblest & loveliest man since
this orb began to spin. Mrs Lincoln was shoved through her furnace, but poor
woman she rebelled! Lincoln suffered as it were by crucifixion for 45 or 50 years;
and *that process caused his glory*, and yet the world don't, it seems want to know
it. You have perceived that I am not a very *orthodox* Christian & yet I believe that
Lincoln was God's chosen one.

As to my lectures—I am to publish the 5 [by?] themselves—as *analytic* of Mr
L.: the remainder of the life will be *a record* of the facts of L—his thoughts—acts
&c. &c—. This was my first idea, and it remains unchanged. I may however
modify my plan—Scheme or what not—. Can't now tell. Probably I shall publish
the *analysis* this winter—, spring, or summer coming. I do love Lincoln and do
respect Mrs Lincoln, and yet I suppose there are men in the world who think, &
probably say that I am actuated by malice—revenge &c. Let me say to you that

Mr Lincoln did tender me an office—a *rich* one, but I refused it, *because* I did not want it.[1] The last letter he ever wrote to me contains this expression—"*God bless you says your friend*—A. Lincoln." and I echo back the same to him.[2] Now you have an other idea, and yet all this must not make me a coward, and a liar.

If you will promise me as a friend and gentleman that you will never reveal to mortal man or woman what I shall write you in reference to a hint in the Arnold letter, and in yours of the 10th inst—now before me, and being answered, I'll tell you—conditioned on an other fact, that you will burn up the letter. I have told but one other man in the world and made him do as I require of you. I hope you will not take this offensively for nothing is intended other than what I say.

I fear—*suspicion*—that I have wounded beyond heal—beyond cure my good friend Chas. G. Leland.[3] The Lecture did it, I suppose, for I have been as kind to him as I know how to be to any man. I appreciate his genius and his character, but if such things must be, so be it. I cannot be *liar*—I must be brave; and keep my own self respect, or sink. I don't propose to do that yet.

By the by—I have had my Record of Mr Lincoln taken to the Book Bindery. It *is* bound in Excellent heavy leather—spring back—strongly done &c. The record makes three vols, each the size of Webster['s] dictionary on legal cap. It has cost me 2 years hard labor with all my advantages; and they were not small. The record costs in money actually paid out about $1536. The original is at my house and a copy of the same is bound, and in Bank vaults beyond fire.[4] If I should die the Record is safe: it explains all fully, each assertion backed by written vouchers—evidences of good men & women in Ky, Indiana, Ills, and other places—men and women whom I know. I have say 200 or more of L's letters—in the Record &c. Pardon me.

Your Friend
W H Herndon

HL: *Charles H. Hart Papers HM23599*

---

1. The only documented offer of an office from AL to WHH is a minor assignment of a month's duration, which would have paid five dollars a day. See AL to WHH, February 19, 1863, *Collected Works*, 6:111.

2. AL to WHH, February 3, 1862, *Collected Works*, 5:118.

3. A prominent Philadelphia journalist WHH had been corresponding with.

4. The three-volume Lincoln Record is the work of copyist John G. Springer, who transcribed therein the letters, interviews, newspaper articles, and other artifacts WHH collected in the course of his Lincoln research. WHH sold these copied materials to Ward Hill Lamon in 1869 (see §84), and they are now part of the Ward Hill Lamon Papers in HL. The originals were retained by WHH and eventually transferred to the custody of JWW, who retained possession after WHH's death. Most of these are now in the Herndon-Weik Collection of the Library of Congress; a much smaller portion is in the Jesse W. Weik Papers at ALPL.

65. To Francis B. Carpenter

Springfield Ills. Dec. 19th 1866

My Dear Sir:

To-day I send you a precious present—one of *infinite* value to me; and to those who loved Lincoln. The world will probably say—[about?] *two cents*. I say the value to me and to you is incalculatble

[*one line illegible*]

al economy. The book *is Mr Lincoln's old Byron*, given to him by his bro-in-law, N W Edwards, in 1839–40. You can see Lincoln's own hand writing in it, and his own columns of figures.[1] I aver this—know it. Mr Lincoln read this old book year in and year out for a long time—till Shakespear—& Euclid swallowed up all other books.[2] The letter is truly a truly Representative one, written to me by Mr Lincoln himself while he was at Washington.[3] The letter Explains itself. It is a good one—an honest one, and a Representative one. I hope you will like the book and I know you will the letter—it's a treasure, is it not?

—— Some time in Jany or Feby 1861 Mr Lincoln sent me to my private residence a box ful of his books—mostly political—such as patent office Rep—Congressional Globes &c—, and among them some valuable literary works—Byron—Goldsmith—Locke—Gibbon &c—. The Byron I present to you freely—only asking that you keep it in your home forever—the forever of Books.

Your Friend
W H Herndon

Hildene

66. Open Letter, Illinois Daily State Journal

December 28, 1866

LINCOLN AND DOUGLAS

The Peoria Debates and Lincoln's Power

The writer of this has been placed wrongly on a particular record. The work to which allusion is made is a Biography of Mr. Lincoln written and published in Springfield, Mass. I have hitherto abstained from exposing the mistake, first because I thought it might injure the sale of the Biography, and second, because

---

1. Inscription in AL's hand on a blank page: "A. . Lincoln—/ Presented by / his friend, N. W. Edwards—" On the opposite page, in addition to an inscription to Carpenter by WHH, there are two columns of figures, presumably in AL's hand. This book is now the possession of Hildene.

2. For other books AL read on the circuit, see *Herndon's Informants*, 519.

3. Not identified.

I knew the people would soon see the error. It is now time to speak. The facts are both interesting and important; they show Douglas' opinion of the strength of Mr. Lincoln; they show the goodness of Mr. Lincoln, and they explain an event of interest. Hence I assert that the facts are interesting and important, and should therefore be known, in justice to all.

Now for the facts. Senator Douglas made a speech in the city of Springfield, Illinois, in 1854. It was delivered to a large and intelligent audience in the Hall of the House of Representatives, October 4th, 1854; it was made in the day time and during the State Fair. Mr. Lincoln was present at the speech, heard it attentively, took notes, and prepared himself to answer it the next day. The next day—say at one o'clock P.M. Mr. Lincoln made his appearance in the same hall and then and there spoke to a similar audience—equal in number and intelligence.—Senator Douglas spoke for about two and one half hours the day before. Mr. Lincoln spoke on the 5th of October about three and one half hours. Much enthusiasm prevailed at the time of these speeches. Senator Douglas replied to Mr. Lincoln on the same day and to the same audience. Douglas in reply spoke eloquently and energetically for about one hour. Senator Douglas at that time had a published list of appointments—say commencing at Springfield, October the 4th, at Peoria, October the 16th, at Lacon on the 17th, at Princeton on the 18th, and at Aurora on the 19th. Mr. Lincoln's friends asked—nay actually petitioned Mr. Lincoln, praying that he would follow Douglas and answer him whenever and wherever he spoke. Douglas did go to Peoria to fill his appointments: he spoke in Peoria according to published notice on the 16th of October 1854.—Mr. Lincoln did follow Senator Douglas to Peoria and did hear him speak—did take notes—did arrange them, and did answer Senator Douglas, say at 7 o'clock in the evening of that day in the same house. Senator Douglas I presume was present. Senator Douglas replied, as at the Hall of the House of Representatives in Springfield he, concluding both debates. It was the fixed determination of Mr. Lincoln to follow Senator Douglas to his appointments, and to the end. He had made full preparations to go to Lacon, Princeton and Aurora, as well as elsewhere.

After the debate was over Senator Douglas, probably on October the 17th, sent for Mr. Lincoln at Peoria or on the way to Lacon. Mr. Lincoln did go and see Senator Douglas: they had a private conversation about the speeches that were to be made. Senator Douglas at that meeting said to Mr. Lincoln substantially, if not in words, this: "Mr. Lincoln, you have made me more trouble on this Territorial question, and the facts and laws of their organization, with intents and purposes, in the government, since its organization than all the members of the Senate of the United States. You know what trouble they have given me. You have given me more trouble than all the opposition. I now propose this to you: If you will go home, and make no more speeches at my appointments I will go to no more of my published places of speaking, and remain silent. I can make nothing off you, and you can't off me." "Your will be done, Senator Douglas; I don't wish to crowd you," replied Mr. Lincoln. Douglas' remaining published places were Lacon, Princeton and Aurora. Senator Douglas did go to Lacon. Lincoln did follow.

Senator Douglas made some excuse to his friends at this place that his throat was sore. Mr. Lincoln said he would take no advantage of Senator Douglas' situation.

The two great men then understood each other, and Lincoln in kindness and nobleness never insinuated what was the matter, nor did he crowd Senator Douglas. Mr. Lincoln made his promises in good faith, and really kept them to the end, inviolate in fact and spirit. Mr. Lincoln returned to his home in the city of Springfield, Illinois, about the 19th of October 1854. He remained in this city till the election was over, making no more speeches, I say, during that canvass. Several of Mr. Lincoln's friends met him in his office some days after the 19th day of October. Some of these men were the original petitioners spoken of before. These men, or some of them are as follows: Peyton L. Harrison, Ben'j F. Irwin—a petitioner—Isaac Cogdall, and myself. Mr. Irwin probably asked him why he did not follow Senator Douglas, as he had promised to do as understood. This placed Mr. Lincoln in a dilemma; his word was out to follow and answer Senator Douglas and the petitioner asked him why he did not follow. Mr. Lincoln after a few moments' reflection then told the reasons, enjoining privacy on all as above given; he good naturedly said in mitigation or excuse: "Senator Douglas flattered me into the arrangement, and you must not blame me."[1]

A few months—say one or two months—after Mr. Lincoln's assassination, a gentleman from Springfield, Mass., came into my office and presented me with a letter of introduction from a friend in Chicago, as my memory serves me. Probably the letter was from my friend Horace White, of the Chicago *Tribune*. The New England gentleman—a member of the Massachusetts Historical Society—was informed probably at Chicago that I was writing an analytical life of Mr. Lincoln: he was so informed in this city. He made known his business, and asked me several questions—none of which did I object to—was really desirous of helping the gentleman, and so told him. I answered the questions quickly, frankly and truthfully; he was with me taking notes for parts of two days. I told him many things, without being asked, it may be. I quit my business, dropped my professional duties for those parts of days, in order to accommodate and assist the man. He got from me what I think valuable; he evidently thought so, because he used it in the Biography, with Mr. Lincoln's strong, gnarly sentence toned down, in some instances, to suit an over-refined, distorted taste, as I think. The *Massachusetts* gentleman goes back to his home in the East, sits down in his office, and pens the following lines, at pages 141 and 142, speaking of the Peoria debate and what I told him:

"At the close of the debate, the two combatants held a conference, the result of which has been variously reported. *One* authority * (* William H. Herndon, in a foot note,) states that Mr. Douglas sent for Mr. Lincoln and told him that if would speak no more during *the campaign*, he (Douglas) would go home and

---

1. WHH's investigation of AL's speaking engagements at the period in question was either faulty or incomplete, for the newspaper record shows that AL, like Douglas, spoke several times after their meeting in Peoria. WHH relied on his own recollection, and that of the friends he names, that AL made an agreement with Douglas not to speak. See n. 3.

remain silent during the same period, and that this arrangement was agreed upon, and its terms fulfilled. That there *was* a conference on the subjects sought, there is *no* doubt, and there is *no* doubt that Mr. Lincoln promised not to challenge him again to debate during the canvass, *but abundant evidence exists that Mr. Lincoln did not leave the field at all*, but spoke in various parts of the State."[2]

I am not objecting to the manner of his statement, though that is not correct. I am not raising any objection on that issue. Let it stand as it is. I have *italicised* some words which are not so in the original. Here is a direct assertion, on my part, that Mr. Lincoln said as above stated by me. I did make the assertion as I state it. Here in the book, in the sentence quoted, is a denial of what I said, and now repeat. Would it not have been quite gentlemanly for the man to have given me a chance to correct the error, by informing me of it by letter, or otherwise? If he did not choose so to do, would it not have been quite gentlemanly to have left my name out, as the author of the story, or even a part of it? There is an allegation that after the 16th day of October, 1854, and after Mr. Lincoln's agreement with Senator Douglas, that Mr. Lincoln, during the canvass of that year, did on various occasions and places address the people of Illinois on the questions of the day. One of *three* things is true: First, I told a lie; second, that Mr. Lincoln acted in bad faith—broke his sacred honor by addressing the people after the 16th of October; or *third*, that the gentleman has no abundant evidence to prove that Mr. Lincoln, after that 16th day, did speak "in various parts of the State." But suppose that Mr. Lincoln and myself are correct, *then what?* Let me state a fact here, by way of note, as it were. It is said to me, on what I consider good authority, that Senator Douglas did speak at Princeton, on the 18th day of October, contrary to his agreement with Mr. Lincoln. I regret to learn this, and leave an explanation to come from Senator Douglas' friends, who should, for his credit, investigate the matter, thoroughly and well. Senator Douglas may have been driven to this by the people—the Democrats and Republicans at that place and time; or he may have been bantered into it by the Republicans, who had then and there an eloquent champion on the spot, ready and anxious to answer Senator Douglas. The gentleman here spoken of, or alluded to, was the Hon Owen Lovejoy. There is some excuse, some explanation, some probable cause why Senator Douglas spoke at Princeton, somewhere, and it can be found out.

Now, as to that abundant evidence, let us see. Mr. Lincoln returned to his home in this city about the 19th day of October—three days after the Peoria debate; he sat down and here commenced writing out, as rapidly as he could, his Peoria speech, which in substance is the Springfield speech, with the fire died out, made October the 5th; he was a candidate for the State Legislature at that time, probably against his will. The Sangamon Circuit Court was coming on apace, and he must turn some of his attention to these things. The first part of Mr. Lincoln's speech appears in the Illinois *Daily Journal*—now called—October 21st. The en-

---

2. Holland, 141–12. The dropped word "he" in this passage is present in Holland, but none of the italicizations is.

tire speech runs through *seven* numbers of the *Daily Journal*. Mr. Lincoln was at home, writing out and correcting the proof sheets of his speech. I well know, well remember this. I so assert this now. The full speech, as written out by Mr. Lincoln, first appeared as it now stands in the *Weekly Journal*, Nov. the 2d, 1854, No. 1,213. The November election, by the Constitution and laws of the State of Illinois, took place—came off, on the 7th day of November, 1854. There are *five* days between the 2d of November and the 7th. Will some gentleman show, procure that abundant evidence spoken of? Will some good man show that Mr. Lincoln made, after the 16th of October, various speeches to the people of Illinois, during the canvass of that year? Will some searching, inquiring mind show *any* evidence by the *record* that Mr. Lincoln spoke at all after the day agreed upon between Senator Douglas and himself? I aver that there is no such abundant evidence of record, nor other well authenticated evidence anywhere. No man can show that Mr. Lincoln violated his sacred honor. No man can show that Mr. Lincoln ever addressed the people after his promise. I aver that he told me—rather told Benj. F. Irwin, Peyton L. Harrison, Isaac Cogdall and myself, that he made the agreement with Senator Douglas substantially as I state it. Men may carelessly, loosely say that Lincoln did violate his honor, by saying that he did speak contrary to the above agreement. For Mr. Lincoln's sake, and for my own sake, I appeal to, and ask for the record, or any other valid, reliable evidence. If I assert, as I do, these things, I wilfully tell a falsehood; and I ought to have no quarter, and *because* of that I ask for none.[3]

Feeling that I have been badly treated, and misplaced, as it were, wantonly, on the record, I am compelled in self-defense to publish this letter. It is probable that the Biographer would, in another edition of the work, correct the error, but I know of no law compelling me to wait for that contingency. The publication of this letter cannot now injure the sale of his life of Mr. Lincoln.

Truly yours,

W. H. HERNDON

Daily Illinois State Journal (Springfield, Ill.), December 28, 1866

67. To Charles H. Hart

Springfield Ills Decr. 28th 1866

Friend Hart—

Your kind & encouraging letter, dated the 24th inst, is recd, and for which please accept my most sincere thanks. I have not *determined* absolutely on publishing my 5 lectures by themselves—am doubtful of the propriety of such a

---

3. WHH's memory here misled him, for AL actually returned to the circuit before all the installments of his Peoria speech had been published and in time to make an anti-Nebraska speech at Urbana on October 24. Before the election on November 7, he spoke again at Chicago, Quincy, and possibly Carlinville. See *The Lincoln Log* at http://www.thelincolnlog.org and *Collected Works*, 2:283, 285.

course myself. I will walk cautiously—talk to friends &c. I am really *happy* to hear that friend Leland is as ever. Say to him for me—"Leland, success to your new undertaking." I shall be very glad to hear F. W. Smith's statement about the case of Smith & Bros. In reference to collecting Lincoln's letters—speeches—state papers &c—&c, I have really thought about it and suggested it to Judge Davis who said—"I'll think about the matter & tell you what to do."

Mr Lincoln is hard to get at—ie it will take so much talk—explanation &c to get him properly before the world, that I almost despair. He's a good—great—noble man—the great *unknown* just now. He is the finest character made since the world began to spin—at least one of the very finest. Don't think me Crazy.

Now as to what you desire. Mr Lincoln is a sad—sad—*melancholy* man: this is so organically—or *functionally*, caused by conditions &c—It is partly organic & partly functional caused by conditions. In the first place his grand mother was a halfway *prostitute*—not a common one, as I understand the facts. I say this is *truth*, for Mr Lincoln told me so Mr Lincoln's mother was an *illegitimate*. This is *truth* for Mr L told me so. As a matter of course Mr L knew this: it *saddened* his own mother, & it *saddened* Lincoln—sadness more or less has been stamped on him. Again—and what is worse, Mrs Lincoln—A Lincoln's mother *fell*—*fell* in Ky about 1805—*fell* when an unmarried—*fell* afterward. Thomas Lincoln left Ky on *that* account; and for no other as I understand the story. There can be not much doubt of this, as I now think, and *yet there is room for mistake* I am going to Ky to search this whole matter to the bottom, & if false I shall scare some wicked men, I assure you. I must get *absolutely* Right myself before I dare open. Mr Lincoln was informed of all this—probably it was thrown up to him in Ind and—don't know it—have heard so. As a matter of course on so sensitive a soul as Lincoln's it burned its way and left him a withered melancholy man. Good heavens! what a world? Poor—patient—suffering—cross bearing, sublime Lincoln! Did not God roll him through His furnace? Take all this, and the Ann Rutledge Scrape—Condition; and you will perceive that Lincoln's work on Infidelity—burnt up by friends, was a blast, Job like, of despair. Now does not melancholy drip from the poor man? Mrs Lincoln Lincoln's wife I think, knew much of this.—think Lincoln revealed it to her; & hence in part *Hell—Hell*. Good Lord—will the world have a wide—a sublime charity for all! Do you not see Lincoln's, Christ like, charity—liberality—toleration loom up & blossom above all. Who could have survived but Lincoln—the great good—strong—noble, *God loved man*. This is no disgrace to Lincoln: he is the *creator* of the House of Lincoln—the architect of the Lincoln fame world wide & eternal. What an honor! Democratic Institutions—what a Justice—what a Right—what a Power & Glory they are! Now open your eloquence on the power of the Individual man to rise above conditions & of Democratic Institutions as guardians of fair play in the Eternal Right. I wish I were an inspired man—even an eloquent man, but I am dumb in presence of the sublimity of Right.

Please hide this *away* or *burn it*—keep it a dead secret—I think the Eds & Devils of the *Chicago Times* have the bad side of these facts and intend to flash them on mankind when we are dead and gone: That Paper said about 8 mo since—"Be ware, you Lincoln men! I'll spoil your Hero." You have now the Philosophy of my drifting—my counter minds &c. &c. When you hear men scolding me *please* say to them—"Do you know what you are talking about? Have faith in the only man who knows what to do to hedge—dodge—Explain—modify, or deny &c—" Excuse this.

Your Friend
W H Herndon

HL: Charles H. Hart Papers HM23600

68. *To John A. Andrew*

Springfield Ills. Decr. 29th 1866

My Dear Sir:

You have revealed yourself by letter to me, dated the 24th inst. The pamphlets outstript your letter, and that is the cause why I addressed you as I did. I have carefully read your excellent Special Message to the Legislature of Mass—referred to in your kind & suggestive letter. May I say to you that I endorse every word you say in that message—probably excepting "cheerful"—and probably one or two other words. I say to you as a friend that I hold Mr Lincoln to be the tenderest—kindest—the most honest—liberal—tolerant—strongest—best—loveliest, and noblest man the world ever had since it began to spin. It is probable I go farther in my admiration than you do. I never saw—so good—so strong—so great—so *Religious* a soul in my life. I never knew one so pure minded. I know Mr Lincoln from head to foot—from the cradle to the grave, and I say to you—*Knowingly* say to you, that he has not a blot on his character—I say *no* blot, and no man—no truthful man dare say otherwise. Remember, I am not *guessing*. I have *trailed* Mr Lincoln as no man has ever been trailed, and I again consciously, reflectingly say Mr Lincoln stands alone in the moral world among the great so called. His mind is greater than men now think: his intellect is *sunk* in his Honor & martyrdom. The time will come when his mind will rise and assert its position. Mark what I say.

While I assert all this to you, do not understand me as asserting that Mr Lincoln was a perfect man—a kind of a supernatural Being above men. He was greater than other men in this—he had less positive defects than they in all that constitutes a good & *great* man. If you have taken up any ideas different from this in relation to myself & the humble Biography which I am slowly preparing of Mr Lincoln, *please*, my good Sir, change them at once. I have a complicated work to do—a delicate one too, and I shall do it in *honor*—not *dishon* of my friend, Mr Lincoln. I know somethings that are necessary to be done, and you do not know. I speak kindly—tenderly, and friendly to you. You must not misconstrue me. When the proper times comes I shall reveal myself as the friend—the defender; & if you please the honest worshipper of *Abraham Lincoln*. Have faith; my dear Sir.

One more word—Governor,: I shall always listen to my friends here—*Boston*—Philadelphia, as well as elsewhere. I want to seize the universal heart, and ask—nay pray for advice and instruction from all quarters, & sections; and now let me sincerely thank you for yours, by way of suggestion given to me. This letter expresses my real feelings—ideas, & purposes; and you may make such use of it as you choose, excepting its publication. I never stoop to defend my motives—purposes, & plans, and never authorized others so to do—*never*; and will not. Others may do as they please. I read Mrs Dalls letter; it is excellent—substantially true—except when she speaks of my abilities &c. which she has overstated.[1] I speak frankly.

Believe me your Friend
W H Herndon

I may write to you again explaining &c.

MHS: Governor John A. Andrew Collection

69. *To Caroline Healy Dall*

Springfield Ills Dec. 30th 1866

My Dear Friend:

Your letter, dated the 23d 1866, inst, is just at hand; and in reply to your questions let me say—1st The Bloomington Convention was held, *I think*, on the 29th day of May *1856*—2dly Mr Lincoln first noticed me in 1834 *possibly* in 1836—caught me, a mere lad defending him—3dly He came to me in the Spring or summer of *1844*, and said—"Billy do you want to enter into partnership with me in the law business" Reply—"Mr Lincoln this is something unexpected by me—it is an undeserved honor; and yet I say I will gladly & thankfully accept the kind and generous offer". I read with Mess. Logan & Lincoln: he had watched me I suppose and formed a good opinion &c—4thly Messrs *Logan* & *Lincoln* were partners from about 1839—to 1844. The cause of the disolution of their firm was *ostensibly* this—Judge Logan had a son who wished to enter into partnership with his father—Judge Logan. *Private*—The true reason was—as I *think*—Judge Logan wanted to run for Congress and didn't wish to do so while Lincoln was his partner—wanted to be free—so did Lincoln—both watching each other and glad of some move. 5thly The original *Pioneer* now bears to the population of the state—Ills & Indiana one in ten thousand—speaking on an average. The farther we go to the South in Indiana & Ills. the greater the proportion—& in the North less.—6thly *Jno* T. Stuart was Lincoln's partner from about 1837 to 1840—7thly I do not think that Harrison—Douglas—Polk—&c. are pioneers strictly speaking in the sense I am a pioneer—ie my farther & mother are. Harrison was sent to Ohio in old times as Govr. & not as poor struggling pioneer—Douglas came here in 1835—or 6 when the State of Ills was subdued—& finely cultivated &c.

---

1. Caroline Healey Dall published a letter defending WHH's Ann Rutledge lecture in the *Boston Advertiser* on December 15, 1866.

Polk was about ditto in Tennessee and as to Jackson I cannot answer more than to say—I think he was a pioneer—Lincoln was truly a pioneer from *Ky* into *Indiana*. Indiana in 1820 had a population of 147,178 & Ills had 55,211. Your Excellent letter—truly Eloquent is going through the union &c[1]

Your Friend

W H Herndon

MHS: Caroline Healey Dall Collection

70. To Theodore F. Dwight

Springfield Illinois Decr. 30th 1866

My Dear Sir:

I send you enclosed a letter—printed matter, which I somewhat grieved to publish, but I couldn't avoid it. Are you not the son *of the Theo Dwight* that wrote a severe criticism of Jefferson? It was an excellent book.[1] I bought it—read it, and handed it to Lincoln to read: he did read it; and it had a powerful impression on his mind, as it did on mine. Mr Lincoln never liked Jeffersons moral character after that reading.

Truly Yours

Wm H Herndon

MHS: Theodore F. Dwight Collection

71. To Caroline Healy Dall

Private

Springfield Ills. Jany 3 1866 [1867]

Mrs Dall—

You wrote something to me about the Bloomington Convention. It may be interesting to you to know what *means* got him Mr Lincoln there. I thought the time had come in which *he should show his hands*. He was a natural anti-slavery man— but as I thought & Still think a timid one. Not cowardly—only *timid*—cautious. Mr Lincoln happened to be from home. Some few mens hearts were burning for Justice & Liberty—So I drew up the papers enclosed herein in response *to a general* feeling—among the very first suggestions—probably not the first suggestions in this state. I say Mr Lincoln was not at home—knew how he felt—drew up the Petition— signed Mr Lincoln's name to it without authority wilfully *forged* it if you please and

---

1. Refers to letter by Caroline Healey Dall in the *Boston Advertiser*, December 15, 1866, defending WHH.

---

1. Theodore Dwight, *The Character of Thomas Jefferson, as Exhibited in His Own Writings* (Boston: Weeks, Jordan, 1839). Dwight was a Federalist editor and former member of Congress, whose book was sharply critical of Jefferson's character and conduct. It was advertised for sale in Springfield in *Illinois Weekly State Journal*, April 10, 1840, p. 3.

so Mr Lincoln had to repudiate or walk square: he like a good true man squared himself to the [*illegible*].[1] Mr Lincoln was babtised an abolitionist at Bloomington. What preceded this—for two years—is nescessary to know. The Anti-Slavery men of Chicago—the whole north of this state knew me Early as an abolitionist. Hence trusted me—Sent down a committe to see me and enquired—"Can Mr Lincoln be trusted"? I made this reply—"You *do* trust me by your very act now through what you say ando—*I say Trust*. I pledge you my personal honor that at the proper time he *shall* be with us." Hence my forgery—my plans purposes & Conduct &c in getting Mr Lincoln to Bloomington &c. This letter I thought your due. It is *wholy—Sacredly private*. You may rest assured that every word is correct. You know me. Use the facts as you please: they may assist you

Your Friend
W H Herndon

MHS: *Caroline Healey Dall Collection*

72. To Caroline Healy Dall

Springfield Ills. Jany. 8th 1867

My Dear Friend:

Enclosed you will find according to promise a photogram of Mrs Lincoln.— Abrm's step mother. Let me assure you, knowing—personally knowing the good woman as I do, that she is a Lady—a kind, tender, loving mother—was a noble woman—a considerate & attentive mother of Mr Lincoln. He is indebted to her more than to all the world for his kindness—amiability &c. Mr Lincoln all his life acknowledged this to me and to others

Your Friend
W H Herndon

MHS: *Caroline Healey Dall Collection*

73. To Charles H. Hart

Springfield Ills Jany 12th 1867

My Dear Sir:

Your kind letter, dated the 7th inst, is just handed to me. I regret to hear of your sickness, but glad you are recovering. Quit hard licks—go to play—and cease your wear and tear of soul. No man knows how to reply to what I told you—except this—"It's all a lie," saving what Lincoln told me. I am going to Ky myself and look into the eyes of men & women—watch their features, investigate their motives—Enquire into their characters, opportunities—veracity &c &c thoroughly—will—to the bottom & below the bottom, if I can go below. There

---

1. See §41, n. 1.

is some mistake as to identity—or something, and I'll find it out and expose those engaged in it—I am decided on this cost what it may—even life. I feel that there is a wrong somewhere, but can't tell you now. The Chicago Times has got what I tell you and *has* said—"Beware how you Lincoln worshipers blow your man.— we'll sink him." This is true. I never tell you anything that is not ditto—. I hated to say what I did of Holland but he treated me so shabbily that I couldn't help it. I am "cussed" a good deal by men, little things, that can't understand me, and prefer *that* to opening to the world just now my plans. I am the only man in the world who knows how to defend Lincoln and yet I am "cussed" by those who are his friends. I can bear it all and look up to *time*. So far as I am concerned I don't care how Lincoln came into the world—the lower he was created, the higher and grander looking at all thing he is to me. I am a broad liberal tolerant man. God bless Abraham anyhow.

When I spoke of making these revelations to the world I did not intend to tell what I wrote you—only a part of it in very indirect language—by hints—saying that some of the near and dear relatives of L so acted as to crush the soul of Abm. This was all. I intended boldy to deny all insinuations not told me by Lincoln— not saying or hinting where I got the information. I will get it all right—so that I can swear to it and then expose all concerned. Have faith. Please note on my letter—the last one to you so that I may not be misunderstood that Herndon does [*letter cut off*] &c.

Your Friend

W H Herndon

Mrs. Catherine H. Dall is the author of the letter you speak about.[1] I did not see it till published—should rather she had said nothing, letting time make my defense. However it is all substantially true and correct.

HL: Charles H. Hart Papers HM23601

74. To Charles H. Hart

Springfield Ills. Mch. 2d 1867

My Dear Sir:

. . .

The letter from this city to N Y Tribune sometime since was written by a Mr Townsend of the Trib office, as I understand.[1] The gentleman Lectured here; and suppose he wrote the letter—don't *know* it. People must be hard run "to run up

---

1. See §69, n. 1.

---

1. George Alfred Townsend, or "Gath" published an account of a two-day interview with WHH in the New York *Tribune*, February 15, 1867. It was later republished as a pamphlet: "The Real Life of Abraham Lincoln." *A Talk with Mr. Herndon, His Late Law Partner* (1867).

against" an anonymous letter! The letter contains a sentence, which surprises you. Mr. Lincoln's own mother was a woman of a very strong mind: it was not only strong but it was quick: she was a child of some *high blood rake* in virginia—not from a common man. When Lincoln spoke to me as he did he had reference to his mother's *mind*—nothing else; and it was thus I told it—. Letter Writers are not particular—catch an idea by halves and then open. It is a fact that Nancy Hanks—Lincoln's mother was a superior woman *in mind*. There is no doubt of this; and it was to that phase of Mrs Lincoln that her son spoke to me; and the evidence before me is overwhelming on that special phase. As to morals—that is an other question.

. . .

Your Friend
W H Herndon

HL: *Charles H. Hart Papers HM23602*

75. To David Davis[1]

Springfield Ills. Mch. 20th 1867

My Dear Sir:

Some friends as well as strangers to Mr Lincoln's history have construed a portion of my third published Lecture[2] on Mr Lincoln's life & character, as reflecting on his affection for his wife & family.[3] I beg leave through you—his old intimate & tried friend to state explicitly & truthfully that I did not intend that a shadow of an implication—or inference should be drawn directly or indirectly by any sane person that Mr Lincoln did not love his wife and family—Nor did I intend that a shadow of an inference should be directly or indirectly drawn by any person that Mr & Mrs Lincoln did not live happily together as husband and wife: nor that their domestic relations were not pleasant and agreeable through life. I had no such intents and regret the Construction placed on it by some. Any inferences thus drawn are unauthorized—illogical and despicably mean, if persisted in by any intelligent person. I know that Mr Lincoln—on the other hand—loved his family most affectionately and tenderly. I think his love for his wife & family[4] was most devoted[5] and intense: I have never stated otherwise—1st because it would have been false & 2dy I regard the family—the dead & living too highly to so state to the world. I deeply regret the unauthorized Construction and send this to you in order that you may know the truth of my intentions in this matter. You have been

---

1. Davis seems to have passed this letter on to Lincoln's son Robert, among whose papers it was found.
2. This phrase was almost certainly intended to refer to his fourth lecture, which described AL's love for Ann Rutledge in a way that implied he had not loved his wife.
3. The phrase "wife &" is a later insertion.
4. The phrase "wife &" is a later insertion.
5. The word "devoted" is written over the initial word "sincere."

with Mr Lincoln too many years & too intimately not to know that any charge
that Mr Lincoln did not love his family would be untrue.

Your Friend
W H Herndon

Illinois: Illinois History and Lincoln Collections

76. To Charles H. Hart

Springfield Ills. Feby 10th 1868

Friend Hart—

 . . . I once *intimated* to you that Mrs Lincoln was at peculiar times & under
peculiar conditions partially insane. What I said then is true. I have now no time
to fully explain any more of Mrs Lincoln's conduct—attributes—temper &c—will
sometime

 . . .

Your Friend
W H Herndon

HL: Charles H. Hart Papers HM23604

77. To Willard C. Flagg

Springfield, Ill., Decr 22d 1868

Friend Flagg—

 . . .

 I had the pleasure of knowing the great Theo Parker—corresponded with
him—He was in Lincoln's & my office once—pleased Lincoln to death—was
witty, social, broad—liberal—loving, having a great head & greater heart. You
knew Mr Parker, did you not?

Your Friend
W H Herndon

ALPL: William H. Herndon Papers

78. To Ward Hill Lamon

Springfield Ills. Feby 17th 1869

My Dear Sir:

 When you spoke to me about my Records—Facts & manuscripts of Mr Lincoln
I was not prepared to speak. In fact was taken aback. However I am glad that I
could not then Speak; because I do not think you know the amount—value &
importance of the Records—facts—&c of Mr Lincoln's life, got up—collected

& transcribed by me. I have been about 3 years in Collecting—Comparing & analyzing the facts of Mr L's life. I have paid for the facts on visits—trips &c in Illinois & Indiana and in various Counties of both States more than a thousand dollars. The facts & opinions—statements &c in reference to Mr Lincoln have been got from gentlemen & Ladies of undoubted veracity in Kentucky—Indiana—& Illinois—not omiting Virginia. My records—facts &c are broad—sweeping & critical, looking at good sides—& bad ones—perfect sides & imperfect ones. I took facts—not fancies—took truth as my guide—not falsehoods as suggested by Hero worshipers or Hero Haters. I have got the undoubted facts of his boyhood— in fact—his infancy included—have got his manhood history as it was acted by Mr Lincoln. I had advantages over all other men in knowing the facts of Mr L's life—knew where to go—who to see—what to get out of each woman & man; & what string to pull. I have got Mr Lincoln's love letters written to a lady now living in Mo[1]—written soon after the death of the loved Ann Rutledge. I think—in fact I know that my Records—facts—manuscripts &c of Mr Lincoln are the most perfect on record. He who writes a biography of Mr Lincoln from my facts writes the only true life of the good & great man that can by any possibility be written now or in the future. There is a fortune in the Records &c when put in the shape of a biography. I keep the originals at my own *private house* under lock & key. I keep Copies put up in bound vols in the 1st National Bank for safety. I have three large bound vols, besides other matter—probably enough to make an other smaller vol—say 1/2 or 1/3 the size of the larger ones. I have written some 4 lectures on Mr Lincoln—some went to Europe &c though never fully published—Simply stenografted in in part—have various notes—memoranda &c including some pictures of the customs—habits &c of the west—ie pen sketches of our People & customs—habits &c. All these are at your disposal—use &c if you and I can come to some conclusion as to terms &c. I will sell out to you—agreeing to write nothing about Mr Lincoln for 10 years—probably reserving a right to deliver a lecture or two on Mr Lincoln to our own people here—not elsewhere. Ward—there is fame in this—there is money too my good friend

Though this letter is private you may *show* it to whom you please—nothing further, remember. I shall write to you again—am now busy in court—

Your Friend

W H Herndon

HL: Ward Hill Lamon Papers LN342

---

1. Mary Owens Vineyard. For AL's letters, see *Collected Works*, 1:54–55, 78–79, 94–95.

79. To David Davis

Springfield Ills. Feby 20th 1869

My Dear Friend:

This morning I saw Ward Lamon. He wishes to get, on some conditions, my manuscripts of the Life of Presdt Lincoln. I wish to ask your advice—. You know more about the matter of the Book trade &c than I do. I have spent more than 3 years & more than a thousand Dollars in getting *the facts* of Mr Lincoln's life. I have got three or four bound vols of facts—the originals being at my house, and the bound copies in Bank for *Safe Keeping*. I had advantages that no other man had or ever can have in reference to the facts of Mr L's life—Knew where to go—to whom to go—what strings to pull &c. I took no facts—no assertions for granted—fully investigated everything critically and I think I have—in fact I know I have the *only* collection of *facts* of Mr L's life up to 1860. I have his love letters to a lady—as it were hooked them: they are not to Ann Rutledge—written soon after her death.[1] I have got my information from men & women in Ky—Indiana & Illinois of undoubted veracity, & who knew where of they said. I think in time—as well as now, that the manuscripts are of incalculable value to any man who may wish to write a biography of Mr Lincoln—no true biography can be written without them. I shall finish my biography in a year or so if I live—ie unless I sell out my manuscripts & my right to write a life &c. Now what I wish to ask is this—What are my manuscripts worth—agreeing never to write an other line about Mr Lincoln for the next 20 years? Ward Lamon wants them &c.—What ought he to pay? Please answer[2]

Your Friend
W H Herndon

ALPL: David Davis Papers

80. To Charles H. Hart

Springfield Ills. Feby 24th 1869

My Dear Friend:

. . . Some few days since a gentleman from Washington came into my office and wished to purchase my manuscripts—notes—memoranda, & facts in relation to Lincolns life—the contemplated one. I have been gathering facts &c for 3 years—have spent about 18 hundred in travelling to Indiana—parts of Ills. &c gathering up the facts; and I think I may say to you that no man can write a lasting Life—a good standard Biography of Presdt Lincoln without my memoranda &c. As you are aware I had, fortunately, superior advantages over most men in knowing facts & where to go, and to whom to go. &c. Now what I wish is this—Give me your opinion—after consulting friends—book makers & sellers among others, as

---

1. See §78, n. 1.
2. Marked at bottom by Davis: "Read & ansd / Feby 21 '69."

to the value of the memoranda—what a man ought to pay for them or the use of them. Fame & money are the rewards of him who writes a standard Biography of Presdt Lincoln

I may not sell—may finish the life myself—can't tell.

. . .

Your Friend

W H Herndon

HL: *Charles H. Hart Papers HM23607*

81. To Ward Hill Lamon

Spfgd Ills. Feby 26th 1869

My Dear Sir:

Your letter, dated the 23d inst, is this moment handed to me. There is one expression in your letter which I wish to correct, & its is this—I have no biography as yet of Mr Lincoln—only sketches—manuscripts—Lectures—facts—opinions &c. I wish to correct your idea at the start that I have a biography. I have written some few things for my own pleasure, and the pleasure of my friends—no connected history—. My record—manuscripts—facts &c come in in their proper place, order, & time. For instance the Virginia facts come first in the Record—then the Kentucky facts—then the Indiana facts—then the New Salem facts & then the Springfield facts—the Illinois facts generally. As I had the facts gathered I had a clerk to transcribe them in order in a bound volume written on our clerk's paper—say this record is between 3 & 4 reams of paper large-size. The Biographer has all the facts before him in order in the Record before him. All he has to do is to take my records & open them and read—know—analyze & recombine the facts &c &c. & write—. That is all he has to do. I think there is perfect order & arrangement. Possibly—*probably* I had better say that some few facts—papers are out of order—few—very few if any is out of order I may say. I'll make the world pay for these records sometime: they are the most perfect of any living or any dead man—probably Johnsons Biography by Bozwell excepted. Since you have mentioned this subject to me I ought to say to you as a friend that I had a proposition once to buy my records—have the same proposition now before me. This much I thought due you and I so state it. If you do not buy I probably shall finish my biography in a year or so—can do it—wish to do it. Lamon strange as it may appear to you let me say—I do not covet Fame or Wealth—! Hence I am in no hurry to complete the Biography—I need kicking—scolding—"kussing" &c in order to make me trot along briskly with head up and tail up, gaily snorting along the great road of life. I should like to see your Biog when finished—like to read 'em very much. I guess your facts of Mr Lincoln since 1860 is full & complete—my facts of Mr Lincoln from the womb to landing at Washington "as the gal says" is more so. Lamon, I should prefer to sell out horse foot &c than to do otherwise. I want money—money—Still if you have no money you can have without money on time making me safe &c &c. & paying down some few dimes—so that I can pay my debts—: Am in Court writing under calls from clients—amidst Edwards' speech before the jury—on a criminal case. How he howls Morals & religion—Bah!

Your Friend
W H Herndon

HL: Ward Hill Lamon Papers LN355

82. To Ward Hill Lamon

Springfield, Ill., Mch. 17 1869

My Dear Sir:

After consulting with friends in New York—Philad, & at home I have come to the conclusion to make you an offer: it is this—I will take four thousand dolls for my facts—memoranda—manuscripts &c—that is to say *their use* till you finish your biography. Give me two thousand dolls down & secure the other two thousand dolls in one & two years, drawing 10 per ct per anum from date till paid. I worked three years—did hard work at that—lost time in going to Indiana & other places—spent about $1800; and lost my office business during this lost time &c—hired a copyist to record what I gathered—paid book binders to bind the volumes &c. I may say to you that *the Records* will be worth Ten thousand dolls to you, or any man who writes Mr Lincoln's biography. If you conclude to take them you may *publish to the world* that you have purchased the use of my records of the great Presdt. This will give you force—give your biography value &c. &c. Again—: I want it understood that no word is to be erased—changed—no leaf torn—no mutiations—no alterations—interlineations &c of the records—want them returned to me when you are done with them in the exact order & condition you receive them, wear & tear in their careful use only excepted. They shall stand as your vouchers to the end of time. May I say to you that since I have been talking &c advising &c about this business that others will take the records if you do not want them.

Your Friend
W. H. Herndon

HL: Ward Hill Lamon Papers LN354

83. To Frederick F. Hanks[1]

Springfield, Ill., March 27, 1869

My Dear Sir:

Your note, addressed to the P. M of this city, dated the 17th inst, is handed me to answer. The Lincoln family as far as we can trace them is a Southern family.

---

1. Recipient's name and address ("Gurleysville / Tollan & Co / Conn") on original envelope.

However it is probable they came from Pennsylvania about the year 1680, and settled in the Shenandoa Vally in Virginia. The grandfather of the Presdt came to Kentucky about 1780. Mr Lincoln's father came to Indiana in 1819, and to Illinois in 1830. Mr Lincoln's mother was named Nancy Hanks. She came from Virginia—say about 1800 & is of Southern Blood. She died in 1819 in Indiana. It is said that the Lincolns were originally Quakers & from England.

Yours Truly
W H Herndon

Indiana Historical Society

84. Receipt for Ward Hill Lamon

Springfield Ills. Septr. 17th 1869

I have this day sold to W H Lamon of Washington D C my Lincoln Records in three vols. for the consideraton of Four thousand Dollars cash in hand paid. He is now the sole owner and possessor of said Records and is Empowered and authorized by me to sell—publish—use or dispose of said Records as he wishes or will.[1] Lamon promises to use discretion & good judgement as to what shall be published—Sold—or made public at the present time—

W H Herndon

HL: Ward Hill Lamon Papers LN2349

85. To Ward Hill Lamon

Springfield Ills. Decr 6th 1869

Friend Lamon—

Enclosed you will please find a plat or map of the town of New Salem—now in Menard County—once in Sangamon.[1] It is the *old home* of Lincoln—was from 1831 to 1837—. Have it engraved or what not & put it in your life of Lincoln. You will likewise find a part of my 2d Lectures on Mr Lincoln's mind.[2] Use such part as you wish or the whole of it if you wish. You will find a letter of Mine too, hitting Holland a rap[3]—use it or so much of it as you wish—will send you things of importance, as I think, from time to time as I get time to do so—am yet in Court and God knows when I can get out.

Believe me your friend
W H Herndon

HL: Ward Hill Lamon Papers LN2375

---

1. For descriptions of WHH's "Lincoln Records," see §64, n. 4; and §78.

---

1. For this map, see Lamon, 86–87.
2. Presumably refers to the broadside "Abraham Lincoln. Concluded."
3. §66.

86. To Ward Hill Lamon
Springfield Ills Decr 16th 1869

Friend Lamon—

I shall start you on tomorrow my 3 Lectures &c. &c on Mr Lincoln. I think they are all you need to finish your life, as all other things are Recorded in your records. I have cut out of my original papers 2 unpublished letters of Mr Lincoln—not having time to copy them. If you do not use them please send them back to me. I likewise send you two note books containing some *secreat* and *private* things which I would let no other man have even a sight at. These are not copied in your Record, nor any part of them. Look over them and use what you wish.[1] Preserve every thing I send you. I will send you other things from time to time. By the by—Do you see any thing in your Record about Mr Lincoln's duel with Gen Shields? If you have nothing in your Record in reference to the duel send me word & I'll send you the orginals as published &c in the Journal. On Mr Lincoln's Religion—his religious views be bold. Tell the truth—that Mr Lincoln was an infidel—a Deist—wrote a book in 1835 or about that time in favor of Infidelity &c.—that sometimes—in his fits of melancholy he was an atheist—&c He never believed that Jesus Christ was the truly & only begotten son of God as the Christian world contends & understands. He did not believe in a Special Revelation—Special Inspiration &c &c. He believed in *Laws*—universal Laws by which all things were governed. He held in contempt the idea of God's Special Interference &c &c. He believed in no Devil & no Hell worse than man & his heart &c. I know whereof I speak and so do you. Tell the truth and shame "*old Nick*"—

Your Friend
W H Herndon

HL: *Ward Hill Lamon Papers LN345*

87. To Ward Hill Lamon
Springfield, Ill., Decr. 18th 1867 [1869]

Friend Lamon[1]

To-day I send you my three lectures. None was ever published—only stenographed *in part* by friends. The one on Lincoln's patriotism &c was never *in any part* published—or stenographled—so is new to you. I send other things as promised—more too than promised. To day I send 2 letters of Lincoln which I forgot to send in the other bundle. Publish them in your biography. The *"Lincoln*

---

1. In response to complaints and threats from Lamon, who was dissatisfied that he had been sold copies of WHH's documents rather than the originals, WHH sent Lamon a number of additional items not included in their purchase agreement. Whether these additional items were offered as loans or gifts would eventually be disputed. For the two notebooks, see §59. For WHH's regret about sending these memorandum books, see §279.

---

1. [*In margin:*] I sent this to Washington Decr. 18th and it has been returned. I have sent you per mail several things lately. Please say what you recd W H H

Shields duel" will now—after reading what I send you, be plain & clear. Give it fully. Monday I will send you some briefs of Mr. Lincoln on some important suits in the Supm Court & Sangamon Circuit Court. They are good. No legal Speeches ever made by Mr Lincoln were ever published that I now recollect of—will send if I find out any in my rambles through old musty papers—speeches & Records—will send you every thing I think worthy &c. With the papers sent to-day are 2 little memorandum books: hold them secret & sacredly private except to you & "Corps" of literary friends[2]—The same with much of the Records. Be careful & judicious in all things. I hold my self responsible to you for the truthfulness of my record & to the extent that the copies are true—faithful & genuine—made out from the originals. You judge among the Conflict of things who tells the truth—I do not guarantee nor say—nor assert that every man or woman in that Record tells the truth. Reconcile all if you can. Follow your own good judgements

Your Friend
W H Herndon

HL: Ward Hill Lamon Papers

88. To Andrew Boyd

Springfield, Ill., Decr 29th 1869

My Dear Sir

. . .

Speaking about the "old cog in the wheel" let me say there is a philosophy in the kick—namely—Mr Lincoln went to mill—hitched in his old mare to the shaft—she was walking round & round grinding out the corn too slowly to suit Lincoln—: He fixed his mind on saying—"Get up you old devil;" and when he had uttered—"Get up—" he struck the old mare with a switch, and at the striking she kicked Lincoln: he was struck or kicked badly on the head—fell off the beam—lay senseless for some time—was taken up and sent home still senseless—lay so for some hours, & when he awoke to consciousness—he finished the sentence—say-ing—*"You old devil."* Can you explain? If so send it to me. Why did he finish the sentence *just* then or at all?

Your Friend
W H Herndon

Illinois: Illinois History and Lincoln Collections

---

2. See §86, n. 1.

89. To Francis E. Abbot[1]

SPRINGFIELD, ILL., Feb. 18, 1870

ABRAHAM LINCOLN'S RELIGION.

Mr. Abbot:

Some time since I promised you that I would send a letter in relation to Mr. Lincoln's religion. I do so now. Before entering on that question, one or two preliminary remarks will help us to understand why he disagreed with the Christian world in its principles, as well as in its theology. In the first place, Mr. Lincoln's mind was a purely logical mind; secondly, Mr. Lincoln was purely a practical man. He had no fancy or imagination, and not much emotion. He was a realist as opposed to an idealist. As a general rule, it is true that a purely logical mind has not much hope, if it ever has *faith in the unseen and the unknown*. Mr. Lincoln had not much hope and no faith in things that lie outside of the domain of demonstration: he was so constituted—so organized—that he could believe nothing unless his senses or logic could reach it. I have often read to him a law point, a decision, of something I fancied; he could not understand it till he took the book out of my hand, and read the thing for himself. He was terribly, vexatiously skeptical. He could scarcely understand anything, unless he had time and place fixed in his mind.

I became acquainted with Mr. Lincoln in 1834, and I think I knew him well to the day of his death. His mind, when a boy in Kentucky, showed a certain gloom, an unsocial nature, a peculiar abstractedness, a bold and daring skepticism. In Indiana, from 1817 to 1830, it manifested the same qualities or attributes as in Kentucky; it only intensified, developed itself along those lines, in Indiana. He came to Illinois in 1830, and, after some little roving, settled in New Salem, now in Menard county and State of Illinois. This village lies about twenty miles northwest of this city. It was here that Mr. Lincoln became acquainted with a class of men the world never saw the like of before or since. *They were large men—large in body and large in mind*; hard to whip, and never to be fooled. They were a bold, daring, and reckless set of men; they were men of their own minds—believed what was demonstrable—were men of great common sense. With these men Mr. Lincoln was thrown; with them he lived, and with them he moved, and almost had his being. They were skeptics all—scoffers some. These scoffers were good men, and their scoffs were protests against theology—loud protests against the follies of Christianity; they had never heard of Theism and the newer and better religious thoughts of this age. Hence, being natural skeptics, and being bold, brave men, they uttered their thoughts freely. They declared that Jesus was an illegitimate child. I know these men well and have felt for them,—have done my little best when

---

1. Taking the form of a letter to the editor of the freethought journal *The Index* WHH's first public statement about his partner's religion was widely reprinted.

occasion offered, to educate them up to higher thoughts. These men could not conceive it possible that three could be in one, nor one in three Gods; *they could not believe that the Father ruined one of his own lovely children.* This was monstrous to them. They were on all occasions, when opportunity offered, debating the various questions of Christianity among themselves; they took their stand on common sense and on their own souls; and though their arguments were rude and rough, no man could overthrow their homely logic. They riddled all divines, and not unfrequently made them skeptics—disbelievers as bad as themselves. They were a jovial, healthful, generous, social, true, and manly set of people.

It was here, and among these people, that Mr. Lincoln was thrown. About the year 1834, he chanced to come across Volney's "Ruins," and some of Paine's theological works. He at once seized hold of them, and assimilated them into his own being. Volney and Paine became a part of Mr. Lincoln from 1834 to the end of his life. In 1835, he wrote out a small work on "Infidelity" and intended to have it published. The book was an attack upon the whole grounds of Christianity, and especially was it an attack upon the idea that Jesus was *the Christ,* the true and only begotten Son of God, as the Christian world contends. Mr. Lincoln was at that time in New Salem, keeping store for Mr. Samuel Hill, a merchant and Postmaster of that place. Lincoln and Hill were very friendly. Hill, I think, was a skeptic at that time. Lincoln, one day after the book was finished, read it to Mr. Hill—his good friend. Hill tried to persuade him not to make it public—not to publish it. Hill at that time saw in Mr. Lincoln a rising man, and wished him success. Lincoln refused to destroy it—said it should be published. Hill swore it should never see the light of day. He had an eye on Lincoln's popularity—his present and future success; and believing that, if the book were published, it would kill Lincoln forever, he snatched it from Lincoln's hand, when Lincoln was not expecting it, and ran it into an old-fashioned ten-plate stove, heated as hot as a furnace; and so Lincoln's book went up to the clouds in smoke. It is confessed by all who heard parts of it, that it was at once able and eloquent; and if I may judge of it from Mr. Lincoln's subsequent ideas and opinions, often expressed to me and to others in my presence, it was able, strong, plain and fair. His argument was grounded on the internal mistakes of the Old and New Testaments, and on reason, and on the experiences and observations of men. The criticisms from internal defects were sharp, strong, and manly.

Mr. Lincoln moved to this city in 1837, and here he became acquainted with various men of his own way of thinking. At that time they called themselves *free thinkers* or *free thinking men.* I remember all these things distinctly, for I was with them, heard them, and was one of them. Mr. Lincoln here found other works, Hume, Gibbon, and others, and drank them in; he made no secret of his views, no concealment of his religion. He boldly avowed himself an infidel. When Mr. Lincoln was a candidate for our Legislature, he was accused of being an infidel, and of having said that Jesus Christ was an illegitimate child; he never denied his opinions, nor flinched from his religious views; he was a true man, and yet it may be truthfully said that in 1837 his religion was low indeed. In his moments of

gloom he would doubt, *if he did not sometimes deny, God*. He made me once erase
the name of God from a speech which I was about to make in 1854, and he did
this in the city of Washington to one of his friends. I cannot now name the man
nor the place he occupied in Washington; it will be known sometime. I have the
evidence and intend to keep it.

Mr. Lincoln ran for Congress against the Rev. Peter Cartwright, in the year 1847
or 1848.[2] In that contest he was accused of being an infidel, if not an atheist; he
never denied the charge—would not—*"would die first:"* in the first place because
he knew it could and would be proved on him; and in the second place he was
too true to his own convictions, to his own soul, to deny it.[3] From what I *know*
of Mr. Lincoln, and from what I have heard and verily believe, I can say:—first,
that he *did not* believe in a special creation, his idea being that all creation was
an evolution under law; secondly, he *did not* believe that the Bible was a special
revelation from God, as the Christian world contends; thirdly, he *did not* believe
in miracles, as understood by the Christian world; fourthly, *he believed in uni-*
versal inspiration and miracles under law; fifthly, he *did not* believe that Jesus was
the Christ, the Son of God, as the Christian world contends; sixthly, *he believed*
that all things, both matter and mind, were governed by laws, universal, absolute,
and eternal. All his speeches and remarks in Washington conclusively prove this.
Law was to Lincoln *everything*—and special interferences, shams and delusions.
I know whereof I speak. I used to loan him Theodore Parker's works; I loaned
him Emerson sometimes and other writers, and he would sometimes read and
sometimes would not, as I suppose—nay, know.

When Mr. Lincoln left this city for Washington, I know he had undergone
no change in his religious opinions or views. He held many of the Christian ideas
in abhorrence, and among them there was this one, namely, that God would
forgive the sinner for a violation of his laws. Lincoln maintained that God could
not forgive; that punishment has to follow the sin; that Christianity was wrong in
teaching forgiveness; that it tended to make man sin in the hope that God would
excuse, and so forth. Lincoln contended that the minister should teach that God
has affixed punishment to sin, and that no repentance could bribe him to remit
it. In one sense of the word Mr. Lincoln was a Universalist, and in another sense
he was a Unitarian; but he was a Theist, as we now understand that word; he was
so fully, freely, unequivocally, boldly, and openly, when asked for his views.[4] Mr.
Lincoln was supposed, by many people in this city, to be an atheist, and some still
believe it. I can put that supposition at rest forever. I hold a letter of Mr. Lincoln
in my hand, addressed to his step-brother, John D. Johnson, and dated the 12th

2. 1846.
3. WHH either did not recall or was not aware that late in AL's 1846 congressional campaign against the Methodist preacher, Peter Cartwright, he issued a somewhat evasive statement in the form of a handbill that sought to answer the charge that he was "an open scoffer at Christianity." See *Speeches and Writings*, 1:139–40.
4. A Universalist believes that all humans will finally be saved. A Unitarian asserts that God is one being, thus denying the doctrine of the Trinity. To a Theist, one God created and rules the universe.

day of January, 1851. He had heard from Johnson that his father, Thomas Lincoln, was sick, and that no hopes of his recovery were entertained. Mr. Lincoln wrote back to Mr. Johnson these words: —

"I sincerely hope that Father may yet recover his health; but at all events tell him to remember to call upon and confide in One great and good and merciful Maker, who will not turn away from him in any extremity. He notes the fall of a sparrow, and numbers the hairs of our heads; and he will not forget the dying man who puts his trust in Him. Say to him that, if we could meet now, it is doubtful whether it would not be more painful than pleasant; but that if it be his lot to go now, he will soon have a joyous meeting with many loved ones gone before, and where the rest of us, through the help of God, hope ere long to join them.

"A. Lincoln"

So it seems that Mr. Lincoln believed in God and in immortality, as well as heaven—a place. He believed in no hell and no punishment in the future world. It has been said to me that Mr. Lincoln wrote the above letter to an old man simply to cheer him up in his last moments; and that the writer did not believe what he said. The question is—was Mr. Lincoln an honest and truthful man? If he was, he wrote that letter honestly, believing it; it has to me the sound, the ring, of an honest utterance. I admit that Mr. Lincoln, in his moments of melancholy and terrible gloom, was living on the border land between theism and atheism,—sometime quite wholly dwelling in atheism. In his happier moments he would swing back to theism, and dwell lovingly there. It is possible that Mr. Lincoln was not always responsible for what he said or thought, so deep—so intense—so terrible was his melancholy. I send you a lecture of mine which will help you to see what I mean.[5] I maintain that Mr. Lincoln was a deeply religious man at all times and places, in spite of his *transient doubts*.

Soon after Mr. Lincoln was assassinated, Mr. Holland came into my office, and made some inquiries about him, stating to me his purpose of writing his life. I freely told him what he asked, and much more. He then asked me what I thought about Mr. Lincoln's religion, meaning his views of Christianity. I replied, *"the less said, the better."* Mr. Holland has recorded my expression to him, (see Holland's *Life of Lincoln*, page 241). I cannot say what Mr. Holland said to me, as that was private. It appears that he then went and saw Mr. Newton Bateman, Superintendent of Public Instruction in this State. It appears that Mr. Bateman told Mr. Holland many things, if he is correctly represented in Holland's *Life of Lincoln* (pages 236 to 241 inclusive). I doubt whether Mr. Bateman said in full what is recorded there. I doubt a great deal of it. I know the whole story is untrue—untrue in substance— untrue in fact and spirit. As soon as the *Life of Lincoln* was out, on reading that

5. Doubtless his Ann Rutledge lecture, which was the only one he had printed copies of.

part here referred to,[6] I instantly sought Mr. Bateman, and found him in his office. I spoke to him politely and kindly, and he spoke to me in the same manner. I said substantially to him that Mr. Holland, in order to make Mr. Lincoln a technical Christian, made him a hypocrite; and so his *Life of Lincoln* quite plainly says. I loved Mr. Lincoln, and was mortified, if not angry, to see him made a hypocrite. I cannot now detail what Mr. Bateman said, as it was a private conversation, and I am forbidden to make use of it in public. If some good gentleman can only get the seal of secrecy removed, I can show what was said and done. On my word the world may take it for granted that Holland is wrong, that he does not state Mr. Lincoln's views correctly. Mr. Bateman, if correctly represented in Holland's *Life of Lincoln*, is the only man, the sole and only man, who dare say that Mr. Lincoln believed in Jesus as *the Christ of God*, as the Christian world represents. This is not a pleasant situation for Mr. Bateman. I have notes and dates of our conversation, and the world will sometime know who is truthful and who is otherwise. I doubt whether Bateman is correctly represented by Holland. My notes bear date Dec. 3, 12, and 28, 1866. Some of our conversations were in the Spring of 1866, and the Fall of 1865.

I do not remember ever seeing the words *Jesus* or *Christ* in print, as uttered by Mr. Lincoln. If he has used these words, they can be found. He uses the word *God* but seldom. I never heard him use the name of Christ or Jesus, but to confute the idea that he was *the* Christ, the only and truly begotten Son of God, as the Christian world understands it. The idea that Mr. Lincoln carried the New Testament or Bible in his bosom or boots, to draw on his opponent in debate, is ridiculous. If Christianity cannot live without falsehood, the sooner it dies, the better for mankind. Every great man that dies,—infidel, pantheist, theist or atheist,—is instantly dragged into the folds of the church, and transformed through falsehood into the great defender of the faith, unless his opinions are too well known to allow it. Is Christianity in dread or fear? What is the matter with it? Is it sick, and does it dream of its doom? Would that it would shake itself free from its follies, and still live till all mankind outgrow it!

My dear sir, I now have given you my knowledge, speaking from my own remembrance of my own experience, of Mr. Lincoln's religious views. I speak likewise from the evidences, carefully gathered, of his religious opinions. I likewise speak from the ears and mouths of many in this city; and after all careful examination, I declare to your numerous readers that Mr. Lincoln is correctly represented here, so far as I know what truth is, and how it should be investigated.

Yours Truly,

W. H. HERNDON.

The Index (Toledo, Ohio), April 2, 1870.

---

6. Holland's account of what Bateman told him (Holland, 236–39) is reprinted on pp. 2–3 of the issue of the magazine *The Index* in which this letter appeared.

90. To Ward Hill Lamon

Springfield, Ill., Feby 19 1870

Friend Lamon—

Enclosed you will find a short account of what I said to Lincoln in reference to his house-divided-against-itself speech.[1] Holland at page 161 of his life of Lincoln represents me correctly, so far as it goes. Though I told Mr Lincoln that I doubted the propriety &c yet I urged him—begged—dogged him to utter it &c. If you will take Holland & what I say there at page 161 and my Lecture on Mr Lincoln's patriotism &c where I speak of Dubois & the said Speech—the house divided one, and what I send you to-day you can get an exact idea of the whole thing just as it was & is. Lincoln & I had one or two sittings over his speech—corrections were made &c. &c. and after all corrections were made then it was I begged Lincoln to utter & publish. You can use what I say if you wish to do so.

Your Friend

W H Herndon

HL: Ward Hill Lamon Papers LN347

91. To Ward Hill Lamon

Springfield Ills. Feby 24th 1869 [1870]

Friend Lamon—

Judge Logan has just handed to me your letter in which you make certain requests &c. I shall answer it in full as soon as I get time. You may use such parts of my lectures in your book as you please, giving me credit &c if you wish. I think I said so to you verbally, and I stick to what I say. I have no confidence in Dennis Hanks—Bill Green & some others. [*In margin:* "Green is not a liar, but a *blow*—a 'hifalutin'—exagerator &c—good clever fellow for all that"] They may be correct or may not. The other Hanks—Jno—I believe in—think him a good man & a truthful one, *but does not always know.*[1] He is interested in covering up the generally *leachery* of the Hanks & Lincoln family—. Mr Lincoln told me himself that his mother was a bastard—a child of a Virginia nabob—. Mr Lincoln's mother was a Hanks who had the Child—Mrs Lincoln—Abraham Lincoln's mother.

I have no promises to any one but to Miss Owen—you can give her maiden name, though not the married name. As to Bateman, he says I must not publish anything he said. I will send you a letter on Lincolns religion in a day or so. I do not recollect just now of any more promises than herein stated, but may think of some. If I do I will write to you.

---

1. WHH's interview with John Armstrong, *Herndon's Informants*, 574–75. For the speech in question, see *Speeches and Writings*, 1:426–34.

---

1. Dennis and John Hanks were first cousins to AL's mother, Nancy Hanks Lincoln. William Greene knew AL well in New Salem.

Your Publisher is—well—well—very anxious for something that will do him—
nor you any good. I have in my opinion sent you all that can do you any good &
more that I thought I ever should—*still* I will send you all the original papers &
you can pick out & scan them for yourself.

I withdrew a letter from the Revd Mr Conger[2] because there was a mistake
in it. Lincoln's letter reads "*our*" and I put it—"one" God by mistake and hence
withdrew the letter.

Your Friend
W H Herndon

HL: Ward Hill Lamon Papers LN343

92. To Ward Hill Lamon

Springfield Ills Feby 25th 1870

Friend Lamon

I have always been averse to the use of my evidence in the world of matter or
of man—hate to see my name stuck up or used in any way—instinctively shrink
from publicity—notice or flattery. But as you demand my information I shall give
you from time to time some facts & some information. I sent you some days since
more at the request of Jno Armstrong than of myself a short account of what I
had to say on Lincoln's house divided against itself speech—should not have sent
it for the same reason that I have refused—failed to say more—write more to
you—namely I do not wish to be considered a blow—boast—or fool who wishes
to be noticed &c. &c.[1] In answer to your various queries let me say—1st. You say
some of my notes are interpelated &c. Sometimes I did this for various reasons.
I had some of the papers with me in Indiana & thought I might loose them, and
hence I stated things to avoid the consequences of the loss—that is I didn't want
people to know everything—*nor the exact truth at all times.* 2dly Sometimes—as
it is with all men—I believed one way, & *when I heard further evidence believed an
other way.* In the matter of Lincoln's legitimacy at one time I thought the world
lied on him, when it stated that he was a bastard. On further investigation I now
& have for years believed him the son of Enloe.[2] My opinions are formed from
the evidence *before you,* and *in a thousand other things*—some of which I heard
from Lincoln—others are inferences springing from his acts—from what he said,
and from what *he didn't* say—In the first place Lincoln himself told me that his
mother was a bastard:—that she was an intellectual woman—a heroic woman—
that his mind he got from his mother &c. This was told me about 1852—3 miles

---

2. This refers to a copy of a letter *to,* not *from,* Rev. David Cronyn that WHH withheld from the ones
he sent to Lamon. See §61, n. 5.

---

1. See §90, n. 1.

2. Abraham Enlow (or Enloe or Inlow) was the most prominent of several Kentuckians put forward to
WHH as the actual father of Abraham Lincoln. WHH never shared this belief publicly.

west of this city on our way to Court in Petersburg—Menard County & state of
Illinois: he told me about Dennis Hanks bastardy: he told me that his relations
were *lascivious—leacherous*—not to be trusted. Again—. It is a fact that Thomas
Lincoln had children when in Ky, & when he went to Indiana he had none ceased
to have any. If you remember—Mr Thomas Lincoln courted his *second wife* when
a girl—that she rejected him—that she subsequently married an other man—that
Thos Lincoln married—both Lincoln's mother & Lincolns step mother by their
husbands had children—that Lincoln's *second wife was prolific* when her husband
lived—that in the prime of life she married Thomas Lincoln and ceased suddenly
to be prolific—when she was so with her 1st husband—*It is true* that Thomas
Lincoln had a fight with Enloe, as said because he caught Enloe with his wife—*It
is true* that Lincoln left Ky & why I was informed to take her away from Enloe
and general surrounding bad influences. I may not have recorded this, but I have
been told so and it looks to me to be prima facia true. *It is true* that Lincoln was
incapable of getting a child; *because he had the mumps* &c. Lincoln was in Indiana
in 1844 I think—your records will tell you when—and that he put up no tomb
stone to his mother's grave; and I forget whether he ever went to see her grave—.
Your records will state the truth exactly. For these reasons and for others floating in
my mind I am convinced that the weight of evidence is that Mr Lincoln was an
illegitimate. *The evidence is not conclusive*, but men have been hung on less evidence. From what Lincoln has casually and indirectly said, I was convinced that
his illegitimacy was thrown up to him when a boy. I *think* he was told of the fight
between his father & Enloe, *and the cause of it.* I got this as I remember it in Casual
Conversations in Indiana. I did not reduce every thing to writing—not at that
time deeming it of importance. Now I know better. I left out nothing important
to the understanding of Lincoln, *standing by himself.* That is all right. As to Mr
Lincoln's melancholy—it is partly organic and partly historic. Mr Lincoln was
of a low physical organization—good digestion—slow circulation—slow func-
tions—blood not hot—not impulsive—cold flesh—liver had no action—bowels
slow—costive—sometimes feverish—sometimes cold—*had not a strong life, but
a tenacious one*—would have lived a 100 years—had no haste—no impulse—had
no wear and tear of cellular tissue—muscle—or nerve. He took life easy—had no
haste—no spontaneous emotion—no impulse—*was sympathetic & emotional in
presence of the object.* I know Lincoln better than I know myself: he was so good
& so odd a man, how in the hell could I help study him. Mr Lincoln's poverty—a
sense of his origin—the origin & chastity of his near & dear relations—his father's
cold & inhuman treatment of him sometimes—the death of Ann Rutledge—his
intense Ambition, & society not energetically recognising his greatness &c. &c.
intensified his organic melancholy.

One word here about his intense popularity in Menard County in 1834: he
was popular in that County; *because for a local reason:* he advocated a canal from
the Sangamon river some few miles below Petersburg down the bluffs—being
lower there than near the Illinois river, to Beardstown—thus putting New Salem

& Beardstown in nearer contact. See his letter copied in your Records.[3] This gave Lincoln a popularity—not otherwise got: I have no time to be more particular—can't write a history. When I am wrong your records will correct me. I appeal to them, putting my own remembrance of things alongside.

As to Mr. Lincoln's religious views *he was in short an infidel*—was a universalist—was a Unitarian—a Theist. He did not believe that Jesus was God nor the Son of God &c.—was a fatalist—denied the freedom of the will—wrote a book in *1834 or 5—just after the death of Ann Rutledge*, as I remember the facts *as to time*. He then became more melancholy—a little crazed—&c—was always skeptical—read Volney in New Salem and other books. Samuel Hill of Menard was the man who burned up Lincoln's little infidel book. Lincoln told me a thousand times that he did not believe that the Bible &c were revelations of God, as the Christian world contends &c—will send you a printed letter soon on this subject.[4] You have Jno Hill's Statement as well as Bails', which see—see A. Y. Ellis & J H Matheny's testimony in your possession. The points that Mr Lincoln tried to demonstrate run 1st That the Bible was not God's revelation—; & 2dly that Jesus was not the Son of God. I assert this on my own knowledge and on my own veracity—honor or what not—Your own father-in-law[5]—Jno. T. Stuart—Jas H Matheny &c &c will tell you the truth. I say they will confirm what I say with this Exception—they will all make it blacker than I remember it. Joshua F. Speed of Louisville I think will tell you the same thing. I think this book of Lincoln was written in *1834 or 5, just after the death of Ann Rutledge—I know it was after that sad event*.

I never completed my 5th lecture—was and am too lazy—the notes of it &c now lie in my drawer. If you discover any grammatical errors &c in my lectures which you wish to quote correct them—as I paid no close attention *to the paper* when I delivered them—was hurried when I penned them. A lawyer can't scarcely snatch time to eat, as you well know. The wonder is that I could get time to think about any thing—Except—Except—*whisky*. You can have my draft &c. &c. of the 5th Lincoln lecture. You will find much loose Evidence in the Records as to Mr Lincoln's boyhood & life. You must weigh the evidence as a lawyer does. It has been weighed by me and you can have the benefit of it if you will ask me for it—putting your questions sharp & close—& clear.

I cannot frame a geneological tree of the Lincoln family for three generations, other than you find in your records.

What I Stated to Arnold was & is true. Mr Lincoln loved Ann Rutledge to the death—no mistake: he next courted Miss Owen & next *Mary Todd* & while so doing he lit on Miss Edwards' face.[6] Lincoln never loved—*ie* dearly loved his

3. "Communication to the People of Sangamon County," March 9, 1832, *Collected Works*, 1:5–9. See also "Amendment to an Act to Incorporate the Beardstown and Sangamon Canal Company" [December 12, 1835], *Collected Works*, 1:40.

4. See §89.

5. Stephen T. Logan.

6. Matilda Edwards.

"Mary"—he was engaged to her when Miss Edwards ran across his path—His vow
to Ann Rutledge's love & death—his promise to his *Mary* & their engagement, &
Miss Edwards flitting across the path &c. made Lincoln crazy *the second time*—see
Judge Logan's—in a little book I last sent you—see Stuart's—Mrs Edwards &
other testimony in your records.[7] *You must read over & over again the Records.* If
any thing is proved what I say to Arnold is proved. I know many if not all the facts
myself. Lincoln—Speed, & I slept together for 2 or 3 years—ie slept in the same
house, I being Speed's clk; & Lincoln sleeping with Speed. I have heard Lincoln
talk about the matter, & from what I know & from what I have been told by
others in whom I have implicit confidence & trust, I say if what I told Arnold is
not proved, *nothing can be proved.* You may reduce the Elements of causation this
way—say that Lincolns honor was pledged to Miss Todd—that he saw & loved
an other woman—Miss Edwards and that he desired to break away from Miss
Todd & to join Miss Edwards, and that the struggle caused the 2 crazed spell and
yet I know that the Ann Rutledge element entered as strong as any Element. His
vow to her or her memory &c was as strong as his honor at any other time—Do
you see? Read over your records again & again: it will save you much trouble &
me too. The two suppositions of which you speak as not Co-Existing do Co-Exist
nevertheless. The 2d insanity Springs from his old love of Ann Rutledge—his
engagements with his "Sweet" "*Mary*" & his determination to break that Engagement off; & to marry Miss Edwards if he could, I repeat, was the cause of his 2d
insanity. These facts do co-exist and were the sole cause of his 2d insanity. I hate
to differ from you, but I can't avoid it—nor see the difficulty you do. Excuse me.
Read your records closely again & again.

The stars in Judge Davis' evidence were put there by my clerk who could not
read my handwriting, & so was left to fill up, which I forgot to do. That is all of
that and no more nor no less.

In the matter of the geneology &c character—&c Chastity &c of the Hanks—
Lincoln & Sparrow family, I am satisfied that John Hanks—nor Dennis Hanks
know much about it—upon the same principle that I don't know any thing of
my relations chastity &c because it is kept a Secret from me. I am the last man
in the world that knows the bad phases of my relations: they may play with their
tails & I am the last man in the world to know it. Again—Jno & Dennis Hanks
were very young when they left *Ky* & Indiana especially. Jno Hanks would state
the exact truth *if he knew it.* Dennis Hanks would go a mile out of his way to lie.
Bill Green is a good man but a *blow*—an *exagerator.* In his dealing &c he is called
"*Slippery Bill*".[8] All this is true & yet I like the man. I do not now remember any
one whom I would necessarily suspect, & yet I did watch all—criticised all—
weighed all, which I want you to do toward me. Simply give me a fair chance to
put myself right on the Record.

7. See §51, pp. 36–37. For AL's infatuation with Matilda Edwards after his engagement to Mary Todd, see
Douglas L. Wilson, *Honor's Voice: The Transformation of Abraham Lincoln* (New York: Knopf, 1998), 221–38.
8. For Dennis Hanks, John Hanks, and William Greene, see §91.

I have now answered in a running & rambling way all your questions, and as I am tired out I'll say no more. Will write you again. Do you think you & Black[15] & friends can *translate* this? I have not corrected it & wouldn't for ten Dollars & wouldn't write it for $50. You know I am spontaneous—quick—off handed—rough & ready, and hate a quill—hate the mechanics of "the pen, like hell—so I do".

Correct errors—Give Mr Black my best respects &c.

Your Friend
W H Herndon

Had you not better come out to Illinois, bringing your records and making notes—questions &c in writing before starting—I hate to write so terribly? Possibly I might come to Washington in May. Keep all my letters &c

W H Herndon

HL: Ward Hill Lamon Papers LN367

93. *To Ward Hill Lamon*[1]

Springfield March 1st 1870

Friend Lamon

I promised you some days since that I would send you information from time to time and when it comes too thick & too fast "hallo-stop" as I am not anxious to write I'll quickly stop.

About the year—*Sometime before I was born*—I was an abolitionist in mind—heart & soul, though I worked & toiled in the Whig harness. I felt in 1846 or 1848 that a good time was coming. In 1850 things died—all felt it and in 1854 the new times were born. I kept my eye on Lincoln & was his friend and preceded him in all ideas of freedom and Educated him slyly & discretely as I think: he had great respect for my intuitions—instincts. I think he watched the age in me. Pardon this. In April 1856 I drew up a paper praying for a call of all radicals—those who wished to bring back the government &c to the ideas of the Fathers to meet at Bloomington. See the Paper in your records & its date &c. Mr Lincoln was then backward—sorter dodgey—*sorter so & not so*. I was determined to make him take a stand, if he would not do it willingly which he might have done as he was naturally inclined abolitionward. Lincoln was absent when the call was signed &

---

15. Chauncey F. Black wrote almost all of the 1872 biography of AL, which was largely based on the informant sources provided by WHH. The sole authorship of that book was claimed by Ward Hill Lamon, who had purchased WHH's Lincoln Records and whose name was on the title page.

---

1. Note in left margin: "Lamon—you are an odd chicken—you have never written me on receipt of [anything?]—you never say good—bad or indifferent—Can't tell whether you get [anything?]. Will you sit down and look over what I have sent you and [acknowledge?], giving date—no of pages—subjects &c &c so that I can know what you [have g?]ot / W H Herndon"

circulated here. I signed Mr Lincoln's name without authority—had it published in the Journal—Jno. T. Stuart was keeping his eye on Lincoln with the view of keeping on his side—the totally dead Conservative side. Jno. T. Stuart saw the published call and grew mad—rushed in my office—seemed mad—horrified and said to me—"Sir, did Mr Lincoln sign that abolition call which is published this morning". I remarked—"Mr Lincoln did not sign the call"—"Did Lincoln authorize you to sign it" said Jno T. Stuart. "No he never authorized me to sign it" I said. "Then do you know that you have ruined Mr Lincoln," remarked Mr Stuart; and to which I said, "I did not know that I had ruined Lincoln—did not intend to do so—thought he was a made man by it—that the time had come when Conservatism was a crime and a blunder." "You then take the responsibility of your acts do you" said Mr Stuart and to which I said—I do most Emphatically". However I instantly sat down and wrote to Mr Lincoln who was then in Pekin or Tremont—possibly at court. He received my letter, and instantly replied—either by telegraph or letter—more likely by letter—that he adopted in toto what I had done and promised to meet the radicals—Lovejoy & such like men among us.[2] On the day that the Bloomington was to meet and did meet in persuance to the call Lincoln did appear and was then and there born an abolitionist. He made the best speech then & there he ever made; he was a new born Convert—full of zeal & fire: his shut soul opened and the smothered fire burst out lighting up all around a fire beauty & a power. I have heard Lincoln make pretty much all his speeches, but this one Excelled them all: it had emotion & fire in it: it was more imaginative & eloquent than any of his former Efforts &c.[3]

Soon after this convention—say in five days after Mr Lincoln & I got up a Call for this City the object of which was to ratify the Bloomington Convention. We got out large posters—had bands of music employed to drum up a crowd &c. The Court house was the place of meeting. As the hour drew near I lit up the Court with many blazes & many lights—blowed horns and rang bells, &c.; and now the time had come say 7 O'cl and—what do you think the number of the People was—? How many? Three persons—namely John Pain—W H Herndon & A Lincoln. When Lincoln came into the Court room he came in with a sadness & a sense of the ludicrous visible on his face. He walked to the stand—mounted it in a kind of mockery—mirth & sadness all combined and said—"Gentlemen—this meeting is larger than I *knew* it would be. I knew that Herndon & my self would come, but I did not know that any one Else would be here, and yet an other has come—you John Pain. These are sad times & seem out of joint—all seems dead—dead, dead—but the age is not dead—it liveth as sure as our Maker liveth. Under all this seeming want of life & motion the world does move nevertheless. Be hopeful, & now let us adjourn and appeal to the people."

2. Owen Lovejoy was probably the most prominent Illinois abolitionist.

3. Known as his "Lost Speech," these much-admired remarks went unrecorded because they were said to have been so eloquent and commanding that no one present took notes. A more realistic explanation is that the speech was considered too radical for the constituency the burgeoning Republican Party was hoping to appeal to.

This speech is in substance just as he delivered it and substantially in the same sad, but determined spirit—and so we did adjourned and so we did go out & so we did witness the fact that the world was not dead.[4]

Before the foregoing facts took place I wish to relate an other event that went before. Sen Douglas and Mr Lincoln held their joint debate in the Hall of the House of Representatives in the Month of Octr 1854—during the State Fair. The debate took place in this city in the State house. Douglas spoke about 2 1/2 hours & Lincoln about 3 1/2 hours. This State Fair called thousands to the city. We abolitionists all assembled here taking advantage of the Fair to organize and disseminate our ideas &c. As soon as Lincoln had finished his speech Lovejoy, who had been in the Hall, rushed up to the stand & notified the crowd that there would be a meeting there in the Evening—subject Freedom. I had been with the abolitionists that day and knew their intentions—namely to force Lincoln into our organization and to take broader & deeper and more radical views & ideas than in his Speech which was simply *Historic Kansas*. See copy of Lincoln's speech in your records: he Lincoln, *then had not announced himself for Freedom*—only discussed the inexpediency of repealing the Missouri Compromise line. The abolitionists that day determined to make Lincoln take a stand. I determined he should not *at that time*, because I the time had not come when Lincoln should show his hand. I cared nothing for the ruin of myself but did not wish to see Lincoln sacrificed—hoped & believed that the time would come & it did come—as above first related. Lovejoy announced the abolition gathering in the evening. I rushed to Lincoln and said to him—"Lincoln—go home & take bob & buggy and leave this County—go quickly—go right off, and never mind the order of your going." Lincoln took a hint—got his horse & buggy and did leave quickly not noting the order of his going. He staid away till all Conventions & Fairs were over. When 1856 had come I thought *the time had come* when my pet should take a stand—an open stand on higher and more radical grounds. From 1854 to 1860 I kept putting in Lincoln's hands the Speeches & sermons of Theo Parker—the speeches of Phillips and Beecher—. I took the Anti-Slavery standard for years before 1856, as I now remember it—the Chicago Tribune—the New York Tribune &c I took at the same time—at least for most of the time—kept them in my office—kept them purposely on my [*illegible*] and would read to Lincoln good—sharp and solid things well put &c. Lincoln was a natural anti-Slavery man as I think and yet he needed watching—needed hope—fire—faith—Energy and I think I warmed him. Lincoln and I were just the opposites of the other. He was cautious—& practical. I was spontaneous—ideal & speculative. He arrived at truths by reflection. I by intuition—he by reason—I by my soul: he calculated—I went to toil asking no questions—never doubting. Lincoln had great *faith* in my intuitions and I had great faith in his reason.

---

4. WHH may exaggerate, or confuse this with another occasion. Springfield newspapers reported an enthusiastic local meeting to ratify the nominations made at Bloomington, at which AL also spoke. For articles in *Illinois State Journal*, June 11, 1856, and *Illinois State Register*, June 12, 1856, see *Collected Works*, 2:344–45.

Even before this event—even before these events I had my Eye on Lincoln & I was known to be an abolitionist and an avowed enemy of Know-nothingism. A number of gentlemen from Chicago—among them was the Editor of the Star of the West—an abolitionist paper published in Chicago and which sunk into the Chicago Tribune afterward. These gentlemen waited on me in my office and asked me my advice as to the policy of going into the Know nothing lodges and ruling it for freedom. I opposed it as being wrong in principle—as a fraud on the lodges &c—wished to fight it out in open day light—Lincoln was opposed to Know nothingism, but did not say much in 1854 or 5—did afterwards—told Lincoln—argued the question with him often & often, that as we were advocating *freedom for the slave*, in tendency under the Kansas Nebraska bill it was radically wrong to enslave the religious ideas and faiths of men, &c. The gentleman who waited on me as before stated asked me if I thought that Mr Lincoln could be trusted for Freedom &c. "I said to them—"Can you trust yourselves? If you can you can trust Lincoln forever" See a letter in your records from that man—the Editor of the Star of the West & who was appointed Consul to some place in England. I have his Exact image in my mind, but can't call his name just now. The man—the gentleman then went back to Chicago and from that day *trusted* Lincoln.[5] Mr Lincoln by this event—by the speech at Bloomington among other things was made the hero of Ills and came near being nominated for Vice Presdt of this Republic in 1856.

This letter should be read backwards as the last written event was first in order and the next above was the Second Event was in order & the first last.—have no time to be orderly or methodical and if you don't like it say stop and I'll thank you much—truly—honestly & indeed. I cannot help thinking what a difference it makes with men—whether a thing is popular, or unpopular. When abolition-ism *stuck* here all men avoided Lincoln, but when Freedom became popular and Lincoln elevated to the Presidency men & women rushed around him—kissed his feet—rolled in the dust, begging noticed, through a kick. Even—begged for a hair from the tail of his old horse: the very dogs & kittens pups & chicks running around Lincolns house assumed forms of beauty & power. Beggars for office—flatterers—mean men—sycophants surrounded Lincoln and he poor man beloved all. I never put my foot in his house but once and that on business which I could not avoid after he was elected President. I dread power—love to fight it &c. But God bless Abm Lincoln & his memory forever

Your Friend
W H Herndon

HL: Ward Hill Lamon Papers LN2325

---

5. This editor was Zebina Eastman. See §41.

94. To Ward Hill Lamon

Springfield Ills. Mch 3d 1870

Friend Lamon—

I have said in one or more of my lectures that there are two broad classes of men on this globe of ours. One class is the Spiritual—Ideal & Speculative; & the other class is the material—sensuous & practical, using scientific language. Mr Lincoln preeminently belonged to the second class: he was a material—sensuous & practical man

Lincolns Philosophy.[1]

Lincoln's Philosophy bears on his Religion—explains its tendency: it may be that they both have the same root. Mr Lincoln believed in a law or laws special or general, that at once created and rules every thing. At the beginning of his young life here he believed that every thing was *a preordained thing*—springing and coming out of God's for knowledge. Hence he was a fatalist—as much so as any Mahommedan. His notions of pre-ordination grew and developed into a blind irresistable fatalism. He subsequently climbed up to a contemplation & belief in a law of the universe. "For knowledge in God is fate in man"—"Every thing is governed by law." "God starts causes, & effects follow those causes; & those Effects are at once, in the ages, causes as well as Effects—Hence the universal chain of causation" "Man is a child & creature of these causes and effects—a waif beating its legitimate course under its law". Such were Lincolns ideas and substantial expressions. To accept fate is to deny free will. Lincoln followed his logic—or the logic of his thoughts. As there was no free will there was no sin; and hence no punishment & no hell. As man was simply a child of Effects—a creature of circumstances, which he neither made nor controled he was neither to be blamed nor Eulogized for what he did—he was neither a criminal nor a saint: man was what he was by God's ever driving circumstances. In the political world—"what was to be would be" was his belief: he never tried to guide men nor circumstances nor shape events because he verily believed that God through fate did it. Mr Lincoln waited patiently to discover the paths & currents things were taking: and when discovered he would aid the rush—never before. His Philosophy was—"Wait: its all a question of time". Mr Lincoln condemned no man and censured no man: he neither complimented nor eulogized man. I speak generally—for it is true that sometimes he did charily praise and did sometimes bitterly & hotly condemn. Mr Lincoln seemed Stolid—passive—deaf to suffering: it was fate & who could resits the decrees of the gods. If a man had to suffer *he suffered*. If a nation had to suffer *it had to suffer*, & there was no help for it. Suffering was medicinal &

---

1. What follows is WHH's first concerted attempt to explain AL's "fatalism." For a survey of this and later attempts, see Douglas L. Wilson, "William H. Herndon on Lincoln's Fatalism," *Journal of the Abraham Lincoln Association*, 35, no. 2 (Summer 2014): 1–17.

educational—not punitive. He had no imagination to create or call suffering to him nor to paint it, if evoked by the imagination. Mr Lincoln was not emotional nor Sympathetic unless his eye could see it, and his heart catch a throb, through his senses, of the aches of the sufferer. Then he was deeply emotional & keenly & quickly Sympathetic—not otherwise. As a general rule Mr Lincoln seemed cold—passive—indifferent or what not. Mr Lincoln was cold, *as opposed to heat*; and that is what I mean in my lectures &c, as to Lincoln's coldness. *Mr Lincoln was not a positively cold or hot man: he was negative & passive.*

Apply this Philosophy & this nature, and show how it applies to Religion—his ideas of Christianity. The result is that Mr Lincoln was an infidel—*denied Revelation—Inspiration* &c. &c *except under law.* His mind was mathematical—logical—cautious—skeptical—causative. *His mind looked back of diversity and sought unity.* I say put all these things together, and you will find that what I say is true Philosophically and in addition you have men's words—good mens words & their veracity as to what I say of Mr Lincoln's Christian views.

LINCOLN'S PRAISES & BLAMES.

I again repeat that Mr Lincoln was a peculiar man—sometimes he appeared to me to be great & sometimes small—sometimes inspired & sometimes dul—sometimes good and sometimes bad—, & sometimes foolish and sometimes wise & sometimes sane and sometimes otherwise: he was a medley. Mr Lincoln was a decidely peculiar man and what I now shall state will be hard to understand even by the best analysis or otherwise. Mr Lincoln so far as my knowledge goes—so far as I knew him, and so far as I have read him in his letters—speeches & public documents—messages &c., was hard to comprehend in all the phases of his character. I said he—as a general rule—never praised or blamed a man—never Eulogized a man nor condemned him—. I never heard him complement mortal man nor did I ever hear him much condemn mortal man. In his praise or blame he was Equally chary—equally passive—equally negative: it was neither good Lord nor good devil. Condemnation & censure made by others *seemed* to be sweet to him. Eulogies of the living *seemed* to burn him, but it was a passive sweetness and a passive fire. The feeling showed itself in his eye & features—which I have watched a thousand times & *tried* to analyze. Mr Lincoln hated Thomas Jefferson as a man—rather as a politician, and yet the highest compliment I ever heard or read of his was paid to the memory of Jefferson. In a letter addressed to the Republicans of Massachusetts April the 6th 1859 Mr Lincoln said— *"All honor to Jefferson"* [2] I heard Mr Lincoln deliver his Eulogy in the Hall of the House of Representatives here on the   day of   18   and in that Eulogy it appears that Mr Lincoln was a Eulogist by *adoption*—that is he quoted the language the fulsome language of some Newspaper: he was in his nature, I am satisfied, no Eulogist: he had not the imagination:

---

2. *Collected Works*, 3:376.

he had not the emotion: he had not the love nor spirit—nor feeling of a eulogist[3] The question which I wish to get at is this—Was all this envy in Mr Lincoln? Each man is Entitled to his own opinion. Mr. Lincoln was a terribly ambitious man, and hence a terribly jealous man. He who loves power is jealous of it in the hands of others. If this is Envy then Mr Lincoln was an envious man. A man that never loves is never jealous, and a man that never desires never envies. This is my Experience with man and woman. We envy the possessions of others—their conditions &c. We are jealous of what we have. We are jealous of others about things which either can get if successful. We are jealous of our rivals for power or fame &c.

This jealousy—this Envy or what not I think sprang from his nature and his philosophy somewhat: it sprang from the nature of his mind what ever dwelt on and hovered over principles & laws. He regarded no man living or dead: he loved principles that conserved mankind and their forces. He looked through the concrete man and saw a principle in the back ground. *That* he worshipped. Goodness & badness—greatness or littleness were qualities or attributes—or conditions of the man and he did not worship the man nor his qualities, but he did man's natural & God given rights. *He was a fatalist at bottom* and thought that qualities & conditions were accidents as it were of the individual and for which he was not to be eulogized nor blamed—Mr Lincoln did not care for the individual, and concrete man, but that attribute—that quality or rather the principles which underlie man in his creation—Liberty he did fervently worship. If what I say is true then by nature Mr Lincoln was no Eulogist—and no condemnor: he praised no man & blamed no man.

I went to Washington—as well as did others—many others—say in 1862—saw Mr Lincoln—had a short conversation with him: he enquired for no man and about no man: he enquired not for man—woman nor child.[4] I thought it strange for a moment and so did others when they observed the same thing as they visited Lincoln. This was natural, I told them, after reflection and analysis. Mr Lincoln was an unsocial man as I understand that word: he is quite reticent—cautious— confiding his deeper secrets to no man: he loved—dearly loved no man as I think: he loved justice—right & principle—not man. Hence he cared for no man and enquired for no man—at least he enquired for no man—no woman—or child of me. Many—Many others state this to me, while some others state that he was extremely Social—very communicative—very warm and Enthusiastic over their reception & the very sight of them. Some men have told me this whom I know Lincoln used to scorn. I know two or three of these men: they took it as a great honor if Mr Lincoln looked over towards where they stood. These men came home and Exagerated an intimacy that never existed.

But I wish to get back to the point. Mr Lincoln was no great Eulogist. This might have sprung 1st from the idea that his Eulogies were dangerous to his political policies—that is, his eulogies might have been quoted against him, shutting

---

3. Probably a reference to AL's Eulogy on Henry Clay, July 6, 1852, *Collected Works*, 2:121–32.
4. See §121, p. 151.

his mouth to contradictory views subsequently Entertained; or 2dly it may have been jealousy or envy—a fear of raising others to office & position for which he might struggle in the future. Lincoln kept his Eye on the main chance; or 3dly his mind—at least while in Washington was so absorbed in his duties that he could not find time to eulogize. He may have eulogized some men while at Washington, but I do not recollect it I incline to the idea that Mr Lincoln was not more jealous or envious than most men. I think Mr Lincoln worshiped principle and cared not for men. I think that Mr Lincoln's coldness or passiveness was not because of the want of a good kind & tender heart, but it sprang out of the fact that his great love of justice—Right—Liberty; & Principle swallowed up men & totally, in his mind, sank them out of view—. They were wholy gone to oblivion so far as he was concerned unless they should concretely appear and tap Lincoln on the shoulder & say—"Here we are again." It was then that Lincoln recognized them—not when they were absent.

One more word—If any person was treated better by an other man than Lincoln was treated by the same man then Lincoln was cut to the quick. If other men were more popular in the Community and eulogized & hurrahed more so than he was then Lincoln was sorely grieved and hated it badly. If he was mistreated in any way—if he was not appreciated by his fellow men it stung him to the quick. On one occasion he was indiscreet enough to put his feelings into print—see the commencement of his Speech here in 1839, against Van Buren and his administration.[5]

I have stated much of general human nature in this letter and especially much that bears on Mr Lincoln's nature. Take them and apply them in your Biography. Every thing, if you will be sharp, which I say will crop out in Washington by what Lincoln says & does. What I say may help you explain many things. I regret that I have no time to sit down and write out with care what I say. I send you some additional testimony of Jno. T. Stuart & Jas H. Matheny and can send you *"dads"*—your *"dad's"* if you want it: I mean Logan's evidence, if you wish it—Can send you a hundred others. Mathenys is really important and what is beautiful, *it is true*. I can affirm it all. except what is special to Matheny—. I cannot say that Lincoln ever told me he wrote a little Book on infidelity—nor can I say *he did not*. It seems that he did, but I will not assert it ~~as my own knowledge~~.

Your Friend
W H Herndon

HL: Ward Hill Lamon Papers LN2327

---

5. "Speech on the Sub-Treasury," December [26], 1839, *Collected Works*, 1:159.

95. To Ward Hill Lamon

Springfield Ills. March 6th 1870 [1][1]

Friend Lamon—

I have sent you several things—letters &c, which may be of more or less value to you. I hope they may assist you some in your Biography of Lincoln. As to Lincoln's legitimacy I do not wish you to understand that I assert that he was illegitimate. What I mean to say is this—It is my opinion that the weight of the Evidence tends—strongly tends to prove that he was an illegitimate. That preponderance of Evidence, as I think, has led my mind to the affirmative. It appears from your records that one—*Haycraft*—Clk of the Circuit Court of Hardin Co (in Elizabeth) Ky wrote to Mr Lincoln about his mother, evidently to find out some facts. Mr Lincoln, I say as appears from your records, answered the letter, saying in substance that—*"You are mistaken in my Mother."* Mr Lincoln does not state wherein the man was mistaken—gives no light. I regret that Lincoln did not state wherein the man was mistaken.[2] Prentice got up some evidence on this question in 1860, and the rumor thereof reached here, and I was told all the particulars as early as 1861 or 1862 as I now recollect.[3] Human memory is uncertain & it is possible that somewhat of my ideas & opinions is made up of rumor & rumor alone. I state this to you to put you on your guard as to what I say, and what all men say. Much of the matter is 10 years old, and watch all men—weigh well what is said—search for opportunities—casts of mind—Education & veracities. Follow no man simply because he says *So & So*. Follow your records, sharply criticizing as you go. When I was around taking Evidence soon after and long after Mr Lincoln's death *much—much* was told me which I did not reduce to writing, but which, *much of which*, floats about in my memory. Time may have modified—altered or changed what was told me. I rejected much which was told me, because what was told me was contrary to what I knew—contrary to my records, and contrary to nature—Still I now wish I had written it out to show the follies—prejudices— errors & falsehoods—the foundations of all human history.

I used to believe in the substantial history of the world—used to believe in the truthfulness of biography, but since I knew Lincoln and read & hear the multitudinous follies—prejudices—errors & falsehoods, I doubt all—nay reject all. I am sorry for this, but I can't help it. When I was a student of history, as well as of biography I only doubted—*slightly doubted*. I then made a resolve that I would, if ever opportunity offered write out a truthful history or biography of the man—mental—moral—religious &c analytically, as well as otherwise, so that the reader would have a full view of the whole subject—thus enabling the student and reader to judge more correctly than if he only saw a part of the subject. This idea grew on me as I got older and doubted more the older I grew. To fulfil this

---

1. First letter of this date.

2. AL to Samuel Haycraft, May 28, 1860, *Collected Works*, 4:56–57.

3. Presumably a reference to George Prentice, nationally known editor of the influential *Louisville* (Kentucky) *Journal*.

origional idea fully & completely—as I had now a good man—a good subject with
fair opportunities, *I determined* to get up a complete record of Lincoln, so far as it
was in my ~~memory~~ power to do so. I threw off, so far as I could, all preconceived
opinion & prejudices—all friendships or enmities—every thing that clouded my
vision. I was determined, at one time, to write out Mr Lincoln's history—biography rather, cost me what it would—loss of money—loss of friendship or loss
of every thing but honor. Pecuniary circumstances over which I had no control
compelled me to sell my records to you. When I was getting up the records people
tried to induce me *to state only what Mr Lincoln was* & not what *he was not*. I kept
on in pursuit of my original idea, determined to give the world light if I could. I
think that to state only what a man *was* only presents half the man, and to get the
whole it was necessary to state what *he was not*—the first part of this proposition
showing what he did & why he did it, & the second showing what he *did not* and
the reasons why. I thought that all the man, his positive side & his negative side
should be known. Hence the records which you have are as they are—both sides
fully represented, as I think. I am satisfied that I was correct, and yet correct—still
correct in other words.

Mr Lincoln was my good friend—well tried and true. I was & am his friend.
While this is true I was under an obligation to be true to the world of readers—
living & to live during all coming time—as long as Lincoln's memory lived in this
world. Lincoln rose over so many disadvantages that he seems to me a hero—having
lived a grand good life—. Such a life shoots faith & hope deep into the souls of
the young aspiring men of this land. Seeing Lincoln, as I see him, he is a grand
character. I see him in my mind from his cradle to his grave, and I say Lincoln's
life seems a grand march over the forces & resistances of nature & man. Do not
think me a hero worshiper. I know so much of Lincolns trials and troubles &
difficulties that I see & feel them all as my own—so closely do they touch me and
my good dead friend.

Now in writing your Biography I wish to say one word more, and it is this—you
state in one of your letters to me that you suppose that I am under obligations of
secrecy to many persons. To a certain extent I am, as I suppose. I wrote you and
gave you the names of such persons as I had pledged a secrecy. I do not remember
others just now. Possibly Leonard Sweat says something in his evidence about this
secrecy. Probably it was in his letter coming with his evidence.[4] Probably I am
under obligations to others. Do I understand you as saying that in your biography of Lincoln you intended to use the names of all persons giving this or that
particular or general information. For instance Mrs Lincoln—Mrs Edwards &
others gave me information. Do you intend to give up their names as authorities
of this or that assertion? If this is your plan I think it is wrong. Assert it somewhat
this way—From the Evidence before me this seems to be true, or it is true by
my records—Herndon's Records or in any way so as to avoid giving the names
of men, & women for every assertion. You are at perfect liberty to give up my

---

4. This probably refers to Leonard Swett's letter to WHH, January 17, 1866, *Herndon's Informants*, 162–68.

name and quote me as often as you see proper. I think I state nothing but what is true—at least, nothing that I do not ~~know~~ believe to be true. If I err it is in favor of Lincoln as I very believe, because I am prejudiced a little in his favor. In fact I was accused of being partial toward Mr Lincoln when I promised in my lectures or publically that I would strip myself of all prejudice. I was likewise said by Mr Lincoln's friends—mere blind hero worshipers—to be prejudiced against him. I felt then that I was correct—quite correct; and feel so yet. Would it not be better, friend Lamon,—not to refer to any name except such as you get the absolute consent of? Write, say to Stuart—Sweat—Speed—and all other men & women, and ask them if their names may not be used as authority.

Again—would it not do to say in your Preface or Introduction or what not to state that you have records &c; and if any men doubt—if any women doubt, let them come to you and convince themselves of the fact & truthfulness of what you say. I am afraid that the giving up names will blow this social American world wide open. What say You? What think you? Be cautious—be wisely discreet—be prudent & shrewd. Let us create no ill feeling or severe criticism from a morbid press eager to say something.

If you will send me the proof sheets of your Biography Early and long before you are ready to issue it, I will give you all the assistance I can in the world of *fact* & the world of *opinion* and in the world of *prudence*. As to other things you are better judges—you and friends than I am. You had better be in no very great hurry in finally issuing your book. Hard times will cut a material figure in its sale, as I see it. You are the better judge however of this than I am.

Please copy and send me as quickly as you can what I said in reference to Mr Lincoln's Philosophy and fatalism—one or two pages in my last letter sent to you per Express. I only want that part as to Fate & Philosophy. I wish to use it—had no time to copy nor correct. Please do this for me.

Your Friend
W H Herndon

HL: Ward Hill Lamon Papers LN348

96. To Ward Hill Lamon

Springfield Ills. Mch 6th 1870. [2]¹

Friend Lamon:

Once Lincoln got kicked at a mill and knocked Crazy. Mr Lincoln told me this—that he had to shell the corn with his hands & to take it to mill on horse back—corn in one end & rocks in the other: That he went to mill on his father's old mare—That he *"had to wait his turn "to grind"*—That it was getting late in the evening—he then being some *two* (2) miles from home—not *fifty* as stated by Holland—That he hitched in his old mare to the sweep-pole or lever that turned

---

1. Second letter of this date.

the wheel, and Lincoln being in a great hurry to get through with his grist urged up the old mare to her full speed round & round—round & round faster & faster— That he thought she ought to go faster & that he struck her with a stick—saying at the same time—or *intended rather to say*—"Get up—you lazy old divil", and just as he struck her and got to the words, which *were uttered*—"Get up—" the old mare protested with her heels on Lincoln's head against such treatment. Lincoln just as he had uttered—"Get up", was kicked—knockd crazy—was picked up—carried home—came *to* that night, say about 12 o'c; and that upon coming to consciousness—Lincoln finished the sentence—"you lazy old divil." He finished the sentence just as he intended to speak it, commencing where he left off. Lincoln told me this; and he and I used to speculate on it. The first question was—why was not the whole expression uttered; & the second one why finish at all? We came to the conclusion—I being somewhat of a psychologist as well as physiologist—he aiding me & I him—, that the mental energy—force had been flashd by the will on the nerves & thence on the muscles; and that that energy—force or power had *fixed* the muscles in the exact shape—or form or attitude or position to utter those words—That the kick *shocked* him—*checked* momentarily the action of the muscles; and that so soon as that check was removed or counteracted by a returning flow of life & energy—force & power in their proper channels, that the muscles fired off, as it were—functioned as per nervous energy flashed there by the will through the nerves—acted automatically under a power in repose—This seemed to us to be the legitimate conclusion of things.[2]

Let me say a word or two about Lincoln's mother and Lincoln's opinion of her. As I told you before Mr Lincoln openly & candidly and sincerely told me that his mother *was a bastard*. The exact *idea* that suggested the thought to tell what was told me by Lincoln was this—Lincoln & I had a case in the Menard Circuit Court *which required a discussion on hereditary qualities of mind—nature* &c. Lincolns mind was dwelling on his case—mine on Something Else. Lincoln all at once said—"Billy—I'll tell you something, but keep it a secret while I live. My mother was a bastard—was the daughter of a nobleman—so called of virginia. My mother's mother was poor and credulous &c. and she was shamefully taken advantage of by the man. My mother inherited his qualities and I hers. All that I am or hope ever to be I get from my mother—good bless her.—Did you never notice that bastards are generally smarter—shrewder & more intellectual than others? Is it because it is Stolen." This is a substantial statement made to me by Lincoln just on a hill overlooking Spring Creek on the road to Petersburg 2 1/2 miles west of this city about [1851?], and about which there is nor can be any material mistake and in these last expressions I have sometimes thought that Lincoln intended to include himself. I do not assert this to be so: it only *seems so*, by a loose intendment made by me—a loose inference made by me. The manner of Lincoln I never shall forget—nor what was said nor the place. Whatever may become of time.

---

2. For a more concise version of this story, see §88.

There is much in Holland's life of Lincoln which is true, as I gave him much; though he did not record what I said correctly. See Lincoln's Holland page 23–28 as [toled?]—correct[3]—I doubt the Parson Elkin story—that part which says that Lincoln wrote to the Parson—Lincoln was about 8 ys old—lived in a wilderness—had no paper always at hand—no ink—&c.—think the story came from Dennis Hanks—*Holland* 29. Mrs Lincoln died—as said by some with the milk sickness—some with a galloping quick consumption. Lincoln's readings are Exagerated in Holland—31–2. Lincoln didn't read the Bible much, if any—Didn't read Henry Clay's life by Prentice in 1830—nor 28–9; because it was not then printed, as I remember.[4] It came here about 1833, when Lincoln read it if ever. Look up the matter. Lincoln borrowed of Mr Crawford Weem's Washington and not Ramsey's Washington.[5] Is there such a life of Washington as Ramsey's life. I know that Ramsey wrote a History of the U.S., but did he write Washington's life? Look into this. It is said that Lincoln read Plutarch's lives. This is not so—. The boat story as told by Holland is untrue. Lincoln never tried to build a boat for himself nor his father to carry off the extra products of the Lincoln farm. Pshaw: the idea is ridiculous!! if the Lincoln family got enough to eat on a few acres of ground tilled by Thomas Lincoln and *"Abe"*, they should have thanked God and taken courage. I doubt the dollar story. Therefore See Holland 33. The dollars part may have happened or taken place at some other time & place & yet I doubt. Holland tells many things in the 1st 2d 3 & 4 chapters which is true. I was told them by Lincoln and I told Holland—will read Holland and pick out what I know to be true as I learned them from Lincoln and others. Be it remembered that I have walked over the Lincoln farm—saw every body, &c in Indiana, and know whereof I speak.

Mr Lincoln once made a mistake with a woman in counting money—correct see Holland 43—The Tea story is correct Holland 43. Mr Holland makes Mr Lincoln dream of his destiny about 1837—mistake—it was in 1840—Holland 46. Holland Exagerates Lincoln's popularity. Holland 53—I gave you the true reason in one of my letters to you. Holland tells a story about Lincolns honesty as post master—page 55—This is substantially so—think I was present at the time or heard it directly after it happened. Lincoln & I were going to Petersburg in 1850, I think. The political world was dead. The Compromises of 1850 seemed to settle the negroe's fate &c. Things seemed to be stagnant and all hope for progress in the line of Progress &c Freedom &c, seemed to be crushed out. Lincoln was speculating with me about the deadness & despair of things, and deeply regretting that his human strength & power were limited by his nature to rouse and stir up the

---

3. WHH seems to mean here that the information given on pages 23–28 in Holland's biography, presumably provided by WHH himself, is accurate.

4. First printed in 1831.

5. WHH got this from AL's cousin Dennis Hanks (*Herndon's Informants*, 41), repeating what he had read in "The Presidents Life," which probably refers to William M. Thayer, *The Pioneer Boy, and How He Became President* (Boston: Walker, Wise, 1864), 175+.

world he said gloomily—despairing—sadly—"How hard—oh how hard it is to die and leave one's country no better than if one had never lived for it. The world is dead to hope—deaf to its own death struggles—made know by a universal cry. What is to be done? Is any thing to be done. Who can do anything & how can it be done. Did you ever think of these things."

Holland has got a part of this 83. The fight of Lincoln—his offer to defend Col E. D. Baker and what he said on that occasion is true to the letter. page 97.

I think none of all these things are in your Record and yet I know them to be true, as stated herein substantially. Your record will complete what is incomplete. I did not record many things that I knew to be true, because they were familiar to me, and I knew I could draw on my memory if I should attempt to write the Biography of Lincoln. Much in Holland especially in the 1st—2—3d—4 & 5 chapters are true and yet I have said nothing about them & much that I think is false. Your record will show you what is true & what is false and what it does not & to which I do not refer, as a general rule, I know nothing of—either of good or bad—the truthfulness or falsehood. What I meant to say about the Lincoln geneological tree was that—: That so far as my investigation of witness in this matter, I failed to be satisfied, through such investigation. Lincoln's biographies make it plain, and yet I could find myself no human testimony—proving & clinching beyond doubt the truthfulness of the genealogy of Lincoln. So made by his biographers—&c. &c.

Some few days—probably on the day he received an invitation to deliver his Cooper Institute Speech he came into the office and looked much pleased—not to say [*illegible*] He said to me—"Billy—I am invited or solicited to deliver a lecture in New York. Should I go?" "By all means"; I replied "and it is a good opening too". "If you were in my fix what subject would you choose"—said Lincoln. "Why—a political one—that's your forte" I said to Lincoln. Mr Lincoln had some year & two before this, delivered a lecture here—at Jacksonville—and other places and it was so poor that it was a failure—utter failure. I heard it. Mr Lincoln had not the fire—taste—reading—eloquence &c which would make him a Lecturer—had no imagination—no fancy—no taste—no emotion and no readings in that peculiar line and hence I advised him as I did. He would, in the absence of a friends opinion, as soon take up the Beautiful as any other subject for a Lecture when he had no sense of it.[6] Lincoln had poor judgements of the fitness and appropriateness of things. He would wade into a ball room and speak aloud to some friends—"how clean these women look—". Mr Lincoln was a curious being: he had an idea that he was equal to—if not superior to all things—thought he was fit and skilled in all thing—master of all things, and graceful in all things—. Lincoln had not good judgements: he had no sense of the fitness—appropriateness—harmony of things. This nature forced itself on my observation and I could not avoid reflections and

---

6. On AL's sole attempt at an entertaining and enlightening public lecture, see Wayne C. Temple, "Lincoln the Lecturer, Part I," *Lincoln Herald* 101, no. 3 (Fall 1999): 94–110; "Part II," *Lincoln Herald*, 101, no. 4 (Winter 1999): 46–163.

conclusions and the most of these I think you have in my lectures &c. &c. Mr Lincoln was a strong man—a good man—an honest man—a tender man—full of the integrity of human purposes—had a tenacity of purpose—a persistency & continuity of thought, the Equal of which I never witnessed—and never expect to see—: But about the Cooper institute Lecture. I advised Mr Lincoln to go by all means and to lecture on politics. I told Mr Lincoln I thought it would help open the way to the Presidency—thought I could see the meaning of the move by the N. York men—*thought* it was a move against Seward—thought Greely had something to do with it—think so yet—*have no Evidence.* The result you know Mr Lincolns Cooper institute speech was a profound one—as I think.[7]

In one of my letters to you I said substantially—that it did Mr Lincoln's soul good to hear censure—condemnation &c.; and this is true when that censure—condemnation &c. were directed to his *Equal & rival*—the great who were struggling for the things—offices &c that Lincoln had his Eyes on—his hopes on & his Soul. As to little men—or great men who did not "run counter" to Lincoln's ambition he was passive—indifferent &c—saying by acts—"Go it husband—Go it bear." Let what I say here modify what I said in my former letter. I write by snatches—& *"ketches"* in Court, during Court hours—being disturbed by this man & that &c. for this purpose & that—&c. &c.

RELIGION AGAIN

Jas H. Matheny tells me that from about 1854 to 1860 that Lincoln played a sharp game here on the Religious world—that Lincoln knew that he was to be a great man—was a rising man—was looking to the Presidency &c. and well knowing that the old infidel, if not Atheistic charge would be made & proved against him and to avoid the disgrace—odium and unpopularity of it tramped on the Christians toes saying—"Come and convert me": the Elders—lower & higher members of the churches, including ministers &c flocked around him & and that he appeared openly to the world as a seeker—that it was noised about that Lincoln was a seeker after Salvation &c in the Lord—That letters were written more or less all over the land that Lincoln was soon to be a changed man &c and thus it was he used the Revd Jas Smith of Scotland—old man Bergen and others. I have often thought that there was something in this; but can't affirm it to be so. This is Matheny's honest opinion and no man is superior to Matheny's judgements &c of human nature—actions & motives &c: he knew Lincoln as well as I did I think. One thing is true that the said Revd Doct Smith of Scotland presented Lincoln with a book written by said doctr[8]—Lincoln brought it to the office laid it down—never took it up again to my knowledge—never condescended to write his name in it—never spoke of it to me—Never let me know much about his Religious

---

7. "Address at Cooper Institute, New York City," February 27, 1860, *Collected Works*, 3:522–50.
8. See James Smith to WHH, January 24, 1867, *Herndon's Informants*, 547n.

aspiration from 1854 to 1860 in the above line—always appeared different—that scorning all christian views—It is said by some one here that Lincoln told him that he was about converted—but that man I do not know & can't find out—is said to be a blab—&c. I do not think that Mr Lincoln was a hypocrit & yet I know he scarcely trusted any man with his more profound secrets—. I had to read them in his facts—acts—hints—face, *as well as what he did not do nor say*—however absurd this last Expression may appear to be. Mr Lincoln was a secretive man—had great ambition—profound policies—deep prudences &c—was retired—Contemplative—abstract—as well *as abstracted*. Lincoln was about as shrewd a man as this world ever had, & yet he was honest—fair & manly—incapable of falsehood—of base deception or of fraud as I think. But you shall have all opinions and all sides and all facts & acts that I can find and when you have all these you can judge for yourself.

I send you the Revd Doct Smiths letter from Scotland, giving me *"gass"*. I sent the Chicago Tribune's article on the Ann Rutledge lecture: it says that the Ann Rutledge Lecture is exploded—gone to the dogs—was imprudent—[saucy?]—&c.[9] When that Ann Rutledge lecture shall be exploded—the substantial facts of it— then Lincolns name & memory will explode with it. You have the facts of it—the most of them in your record. You can see for yourself & you must judge for yourself. Smiths letter is simply folly—bombast—&c. and what he says of Lincoln's Religion—the Bible &c. means nothing. It is too general in its Expression: he might say the same things of me speaking generally & yet it wouldn't express my ideas at all—nor my philosphy nor my religion. I believe that the Bible is the Revelation of God—& that Jesus was the son of God—& so do I believe that the Declaration of Independence is the Revelation of God & Gen Washington a son of God. I can talk a week to technical Christians and they will assume that I mean so & so when I don't mean *so & so*. Glittering generalities won't do. I believe in miracles—think a man is a miracle & God's grandest miracles—believe in Miraculous Conception—think your conception was a miraculous one. Glittering generalities won't do. Read my letter to Smith & notice the questions closely. Then read Smith's letter to me and watch the answer closely & you will see that he answered no question. About Miraculous Conception &c he said no word. In fact he made no specific answer to any thing. He knew I would prove him false if he should be precise—so he dealt in generalities. I could not answer Smith at the time of his letter 1st Because I was engaged in more important things; & 2d I would have to drag Mrs Lincoln into the field, because Smith took refuge under her—fought from behind her; & 3d because I should be compelled to say something of Smiths morals, temperance—integrity & character generally & 4th because I knew I had the facts & truths in my own hand—knew it would all come to light sometime &c. Hence I bided my time. If Smith is correct do him justice. Do Smith and all men exact and equal justice. Criticise all, thoroughly—and well. If I make any broad mistakes with pen or otherwise in my rush and great hurry give me an opportunity to correct

9. *Herndon's Informants*, 547–50; *Chicago Tribune*, March 7, 1867.

I send you Lincoln's letter to Wallace on Protection—don't know that it was ever Copied in the Records—think it was, but for fear it was not I send it to you.[10] Lincoln was a strong Protection man. He & Jno Calhoun of Kansas Notoriety, in this city in 1844, held a long discussion—say 3 or 4 nights on Protective Tariffs.[11] Both these men were strong men—strong on this question. Calhoun in 1844 was a strong—very strong & clear headed man—Lincoln's equal & the Superior of Douglas, but *whiskey—whiskey* ruined him long—long before he went to Kansas. Calhoun was a noble man in his origional nature—went to school to him—but *whiskey*—poverty—&c. &c did their work. He fell and yet in his fall he was a gentleman in every sense of the word—He loved Lincoln & as well as Lincoln could he returned it.[12] I heard this discussion—*"toted books"* & *"hunted up authorities"* for Lincoln, as I did in law.

Your Friend
W H Herndon

HL: Ward Hill Lamon Papers LN366

97. *To Ward Hill Lamon*

Springfield, Ill., Mch. 15 1870

Friend Lamon—

Your letter making certain enquiries is this moment handed to me. If I were you I should tell the truth as I saw it. I should suppress no truth & suggest no falsehood. If I thought Mr Lincoln an illegitimate I should so state it. I would draw a strong contrast between *what he was born and how he died*. He was born into the social world with a curse on him—a mill stone tied to his neck, and yet by his own inherent force of a sacred purpose he on the tide floated to glory. *Show his origin & end*—sharply contrasted. Contrast is a power: it makes things distinct—. Sympathy is a power. State the facts of his origin so as to arouse active sympathy and to bind it to him. Sympathy is a power. Give me the sympathy of the world and you may have its cold iron logic. Lincoln the unaided—uneducated—lone penniless bare foot boy, through holiness and persistency of an honest purpose carved upon the world's history—the character of *Honest Abe*. I should show his *low origin* and *high end* in bold contrast—running such parallels as history suggested &c. I should then applaud this Democracy—this Government, and show that such a character under such lowly conditions would be an impossibility in Europe &c—would show these things, holding them up to the young in this land for all coming time as stimulants—as living hopes urging them to a life of integrity—faith & hope. This all seems grand to me; and whether you know it or not Lincoln's life to me was a grand life, knowing what I do of him. This is my

---

10. AL to Edward Wallace, October 11, 1859, Lamon, 423; *Collected Works*, 3:486–87.

11. Debates with John Calhoun and Alfred W. Cavarly in Springfield, Illinois, March 20–25, 1844, *Collected Works*, 1:334–35.

12. In 1835, Calhoun had given AL employment as a deputy county surveyor, by which he supported himself.

idea and I think the best course for you. You must do so, if you want your Hero to shine. Without this whole truth business, I do not think it possible to make his life a grand struggle, making [*rest of letter missing*]

HL: Ward Hill Lamon Papers LN349

98. To Ward Hill Lamon

Springfield Ills Mch. 23d 1870

Friend Lamon—

I have been very busy in Court for a month or more and had no time to finish anything or polish anything—wrote on a gallop—with a whoop. I wrote you a hasty letter yesterday stating to you what you ought to do & what you ought not to do in relation to quoting authorities. I have an other view of the case which I wish to present to your view and it is this—: If you indiscriminately quote men & women on all questions they will turn on me in this way—"When I gave you the information I trusted *you*—gave *you* the information not expecting you would sell it to an other: it was a personal trust in you."

On general questions not affecting Lincolns *mother*—Lincoln's *birth* & parentage—Lincoln's *domestic* relations and his *religion* I can see no objections to quoting names. To that extent I will trust your discretion. In all cases affecting the above things including Lincoln's *courtship* you must get the consent of those who gave me the information. Your Records will show you where to write & to whom. I will see as many as I can and get their consent—will write to as many as I can and ask them for authority, but this must not release you from like Efforts to all persons—for I may not get time—have got to go out on the circuit and plead for bread. I am satisfied that I gave promises to more persons than I have spoken about—have no doubt that I gave my word to Haycraft & to the clerk at Hodgenville—as well as to Speed and Helm. I do not say this simply because I can say it, but because it is probably true. It has been a long time since I got the information and as I have passed through several Hells since 1866 & 7 I may have forgotten my promises. To break this honor is to ruin me and your book. We must walk discrett and have no attacks made on us that we cannot well & truthfully defend. Where we are discrett as well as true there we can stand and laugh, defying all charges of little base men and women. Your book must not go out with this this danger around it. Think well of these things.

Any question which will not raise a howl against us—me—yourself and your book quote freely from men and if you will & must women. If I can only stand on truth & honor I do not care for the howls of Christianity—of cringing timids—of policies—of fools & asses. I expect to be attacked as no man has been attacked lately, but I do not care for that *much*, when I know I have Truth—Honor & Propriety on my side. I have long since determined to tell the Truth & the whole

---

1. Ann Rutledge's suitor's real name was John McNamar, but he was known to her as John McNeil.

Truth in reference to Mr Lincoln's life, come weal or woe. *The world wants one true life of one man to swear by and they will get it I hope in your life of Lincoln*

I have just seen Jno. T. Stuart and he gives you this authority—"use my name on all things except where it would create unpleasant feelings and on this question I give Lamon a broad discretion" If you would only write to men and women you could get their consent without any trouble and how much better & safer for me—for you and your book

There is nothing in Indiana that you cannot use that I now remember of—. There is nothing in the County of Menard including Lincolns religion—insanity—courtship &c that you cannot use—Green—Cogdale—Irwin—Hill—Bail—Spear—*Mrs* Green—*Mrs* Armstrong. Probably I told Ann Rutledge's man—Lincoln's rival—forget his name just now—that I would not use his name—left it blank on the Ann Rutledge Lecture as I suppose for that reason—you can learn his name from your record. I think his name is McNeil or McNamara. Nult Green—L. M. Green Graham[2]—and others on that section will make no objection—: it is only in cases that would create unpleasant feelings—cruel criticisms &c. from which you forbidden the use—So you see you have a broad field; and if you wish to broaden it—widen it—deepen it—thunder cloud it in order to flash & blaze please write to the persons.

Suppose I know that I made no promise to any and all persons, do you not know enough of human nature to know that timids, cowards—policy men—squeamish women—grey hard youths—fools & asses—would turn on me if they could make a dollar out of it or dodge a consequence of [unsavory?] circumstances and how could I prove that I made no promise. You now have my ideas—would like to hear yours

Your Friend
W H Herndon

HL: Ward Hill Lamon Papers LN350

99. To Ward Hill Lamon

Springfield Ills. Septr 15th/70

Friend Lamon—

Enclosed please find Pho of Dennis Hanks: it is not a very good one, but will do, I hope. It is genuine, I know. I do not think that Dennis Hanks is the man who taught Lincoln how to read &c. Dennis is a good clever fellow but don't rely too much on what he says. Dennis loves to swell & rant &c.

I saw Judge Logan to-day and he says he will never tell what Lincoln's religion was. Lincoln was sometimes almost Atheistic. Judge Logan caught that view of him in Lincoln's gloomy moments. I do not think that Lincoln was an Atheist, though at moments he bordered on it. Logan once said to me this—"Lincolns religion

---

2. That is, L. M. (Nult) Greene and Mentor Graham.

was terribly low—sad to think about." Logan has always refused to communicate much—has been careful & cautious.

How are you and your secret—hidden—incog friend?[1] Both take my best respects and then *you* Lamon go to thunder

Your Friend

W H Herndon

HL: Ward Hill Lamon Papers LN359

100. To Caroline Healy Dall

Chinkapin Hill P.O Sangamon Co Ills Jany 24th 1873

My Good Friend

I this moment recd your last letter, dated the 4th inst. I am glad you are writing the life of Lincoln. There are Fame & the $ in it. The world ought to see what a woman thinks of L.

The terrible want of the $ forced me to sell my *records* to Lamon—ie the bound volumes—copies of the originals only. The originals—many of them are in my hands now & belong to me & no one Else. Many of the letters which Lincoln wrote to me I gave away, but they were copied. Lamon has those copies. I think they appear in Lamon's life of L. I loaned Lamon my lectures—& those little books you saw in my drawer: he has them now in Martinsburg West Va. With the exception of some letters—some speeches &c I yet have the originals of L's life—will dispose of them at a fair price—

You are a little mistaken in what you say in reference to Mr L's writing to any one wishing to know who his Father was. Mr Haycraft of Ky wrote to Mr L wanting to know who his—L's mother was, suggesting that her name was &c. &c. Mr Lincoln wrote to Haycraft this—"You are mistaken in my mother"—

I have opened my box of papers & have found the Paper given to me by Lamon and which you want.—Have found one of my lectures on Ann Rutledge—have found a letter of mine in answer to Hollands mistake about Lincoln & Douglas—I do not wish to risk them by mail. Shall I send by express.

I really wish you success in your life of L. *Privately—the life of L has yet to be written.*[1] Success to you. My materials would enable you to write a life of L that would crown you with fame

Your Friend

W H Herndon

MHS: Caroline Healey Dall Collection

---

1. A reference to Lamon's silent partner and ghostwriter, Chauncey F. Black.

---

1. WHH appears to be expressing reservations about the Lamon biography published the previous year and based largely on WHH's informant materials.

101. To Ward Hill Lamon

Fairview. Sangamon Co Ills. Mch. 9th 1873

Friend Lamon—

. . . I, as soon as I recd your life of Lincoln, instantly wrote to you thanking you a thousand times for it. As soon as I read it, though hurriedly I wrote to your publishers my opinion of it. The Biography is truthful—*solid facts*, and where you express an opinion I think it is generally correct. It will take its stand among the best biographies of this age. I may not agree to every thing you say or infer, but that shows your own independent judgements

You seem to feel pained—hurt by the critics & yet you ought not. No book ever rose to eminence uncriticised. Do critics notice d——d fools. Critics notice the great through envy. If I were author I would crave criticism if honest & independent. Unworthy books are never noticed Be not afraid of your book.

The *Christians* as a matter of course will hate your book—will hate me & all other free men and good books: they cannot, as you justly say—distinguish between Christianity—a Jewish form of Faith & Religion—that which is universal. But never mind. "Wag along," Holland is simply a tody—a coward—a fool—a timid ass. His review of your book is a Struggle of desperation—an Effort to save character. Let him rave

I do not agree with you when you say that a man is a fool for writing the truth. Your reward is in the future. You have made it possible for all young men who aspire to write good books to dare—brave criticism &c You should be content and in fact proud

Now friend Lamon go and take a good horn in my name and when you feel jolly & good give my best respects to your partner, though a stranger to me

Your old friend

W H Herndon

HL: Ward Hill Lamon Papers LN360

102. To Caroline Healy Dall

Chinkapin Hill Fairview Ills. Mch 10th/73

Mrs Dall—

I sent you on yesterday several important papers by express. The papers were 1st the News Paper which Lamon gave to me & which you wanted[1]—2dly A lecture of mine on Lincoln - Ann Rutledge &c.—3d a letter of mine on Lincoln & Douglas; & 4th a lecture of Mr Lincoln delivered before the Springfield Lyceum in *1838*.[2] Mr L was then 26 years of age. This Lecture will compare with any production of any man of the same age. Please read it & see how prophetic it is—see if you cannot feel that Mr L does not have an *instinct* of the times—an intuition of his

---

1. Not identified.
2. See *Collected Works*, 1:108–15.

heaven imposed duty—if not his fate. I tore this out of my bound volumes to aid you; it is the only copy in existence unless Lamon has got one copied from it. I kept it back for my own Biography of Mr L when I should write one, but I now give it to you. *Please have it copied* & the original put in some fire proof vault. I heard the lecture delivered in *1838*—not 1837 as Matheny has it. Will not some of the Printers of Boston issue a pamphlet Edit of the speech? For heaven's sake don't let it get destroyed.

You will perceive that the paper which Lamon gave me and which I send to you misnames Mrs Lincoln. Mrs Lincoln's name was Nancy. The writer calls her Hannah, I think.

All the assistance I can give you from corn fields—pig pens—Cattle yards &c I will—will cheerfully do it

Your Friend
W H Herndon

MHS: Caroline Healey Dall Collection

103. To the Editor of the Daily State Journal[1]

SPRINGFIELD, Ill., Jan. 12th, 1874

To the Editor of the Journal:

I delivered a lecture in this city on the 12th day of December last, and to which, or part of which, I understand that Mrs. Lincoln has taken some exception. I wish to state the exact truth in relation to this matter, so that the public may understand—know what to believe and who to believe.

About the year 1865 I finally determined to write the life of Mr. Lincoln, the tenderest, the kindest, best and noblest of men, ever doing and executing the good, the just and true to men in all paths and walks of life. In fact, he was the patriot of patriots; and now, as such, he looms up against the deep blue among the grandest figures of the age. The quick failure of Lamon's Life of Lincoln—its speedy repudiation by the public, caused in part by its being tampered with about the time it went to press, and by its wrong and injustice done to the great dead, has only intensified my original idea to write the life of Mr. Lincoln. Let me say here, once for all, that I am not one of the authors of Lamon's Life of Lincoln. I never wrote a sentence or a word for the biography. I am quoted by Lamon, and to that extent I am responsible, and no farther. It is probable that I never shall rest satisfied till I write the life. Having this determination to write the life of Mr. Lincoln, and having heard—say about one year after the death of the President— that Mrs. Lincoln had arrived in the city, and was stopping at the St. Nicholas Hotel, I called on her, and after the usual running remarks about her health, etc, I made known my purposes and plans. I stated to her that I intended to write

---

1. An editorial note at the head of this letter says it was published "at his request." The letter also appeared in the *Illinois State Register*, January 14, 1874 and the *Chicago Tribune*, January 16, 1874. It also appeared as a broadside entitled "Mrs. Lincoln's Denial." The testimony of Mrs. Lincoln offered here is very close to a WHH manuscript transcribed in *Herndon's Informants*, 359–61.

the life of her husband, and if she would consent, I should like to have some facts—a short history of herself to insert in the biography. She remarked to me in substance, that it was not usual to mention the facts—the history of the wife, in the biography of her husband, further than to say that the two were married at such time and place, and to which I replied: "That is true as a general rule, but then there are exceptions to this rule, and should be." At my special request, and after some argument, she at last consented to give me a brief history of her life. I got pen, pencil, ink and paper, drew up a small table, and became prepared to take down, as well as I could, the *substance* of what she said. She commenced as follows, which I took down with care:

"I was born on the 13th day of December 1823, in Lexington, Fayette county, Kentucky Am the daughter of Robert S. and Eliza Todd. Maiden name Eliza Parker. My mother died when I was very young. Was educated by Mme. Mentelle, a French lady, opposite Mr. Clay's. She was well educated; was French; spoke nothing else; scholars were not allowed to. Finished my education at Ward's Academy. People from the North visited Lexington. Went to school here. I came to Illinois in 1837. Was in Illinois three months. Went back to Kentucky. Went to school two years after I first came to Illinois. I returned to Illinois in 1839 or '40. This was after Mrs. Wallace came out to Illinois.

"My husband intended, when he was through with his Presidential terms, to take me and family to Europe. Didn't in late years dream of death—was cheery, funny, lived in high spirits. He intended to return and go to California over the Rocky Mountains, and see the prospects of the soldiers, etc, digging out gold to pay the national debt. He and Sumner were like boys during the last days of the rebellion. They were down on the river after Richmond was taken; they acted like boys; were so happy, so glad, the war was over. Mr. Lincoln, up to 1865, wanted to live in Springfield, his old home, and be buried there. Changed his opinion— notion where to live. Never settled on any place particularly. Intended moving and traveling some.

"Mr. Lincoln was the kindest man and most loving husband and father in the world. He gave us all unbounded liberty. Said to me always, when I asked for anything, 'You know what you want, go and get it.' He never asked me if it was necessary. He was very—exceedingly indulgent to his children. Chided or praised them for what they did—their acts, etc. He always said: 'It is my pleasure that my children are free, happy and unrestrained by parental tyranny. Love is the chain whereby to bind a child to its parents.'

"I have none of my literary scraps, poems, compositions, except I know the Shields poetry, which is as follows:

"'Ye Jews harps awake! The A___S² won,
Rebecca, the widow, has gained Erin's son;

---

2. The abbreviated word here is the contraction "auditor's," referring to James Shields. The poem is a satire at the expense of Shields, possibly written with her friend Julia Jayne. For the context, see *Collected Works*, 1:291–92n

The pride of the north, from Emerald Isle,
Has been wooed and won by a woman's smile.
The combat's relinquished—old loves all fought.
To the widow he's bound, oh bright be his lot!
In the smiles of the conquest so lately achieved,
Joyful be his bride, widowed modesty relieved.
The footsteps of time tread lightly on flowers,
May the cares of the world ne'er darken his hours.
But the pleasures of life are fickle and coy,
As the smiles of a maiden sent off to destroy.
Happy groom! In sadness, far distant from thee,
The fair girls dream only of past times of glee—
Enjoyed in thy presence—whilst the oft blarmied store
Will be fondly remembered as relics of yore;
And hands that in rapture you oft would have pressed,
In prayer will be clasped that your lot may be blessed.
    "'CATHLEEN.'"

The piece of poetry to which Mr. Lincoln referred, but did not quote, will be found in Lamon's Life of Lincoln, at page 255. It partly led to the Lincoln-Shields duel:

Mrs. Lincoln continued:

"Mr. Lincoln had a dream when down the river at City Point, after Richmond was taken. He dreamed that the White House had burned up. Sent me up the river to see. Went. Met Stanton on the way down. Mr. Lincoln told me to get a party and come down, which I did.

"Mr. Lincoln found out that _____[3] was stealing, as he thought, the public moneys. Intended to turn him out. My husband had placed great confidence in my knowledge of human nature. He had not much knowledge of men.

"Our expenses at the White House were about $10,900 per month. Breakfasted at 9 o'clock a. m., lunched at 2 o'clock p. m, dined at 6 p m. Mr. Lincoln got up irregularly; saw the people; attended the hospital, etc. etc. He said he would turn Seward out when peace was declared. Hated Andrew Johnson. Once only Johnson followed Mr. Lincoln, when he said: "Why is this man following me?"

"A letter of Mr. Lincoln's to me got out in the army.[4] Mr. Lincoln was tender, etc. Our dinners cost us $500 for friends, diplomatic corps, etc. Sometimes there were twenty-four of the Todd connections or family at once at our table._____[5] wife's conduct while in Washington was extremely bad.

"Mr. Lincoln had a kind of poetry in his nature. He was a terribly firm man when he set his foot down. None of us—no man nor woman—could rule him

3. The name omitted here is identified in WHH's manuscript notes as Mary Lincoln's brother-in-law, Ninian W. Edwards. See *Herndon's Informants*, 358, 359.

4. See AL to MTL, August 8, 1863, *Collected Works*, 6:371–72.

5. The name omitted here but given in WHH's manuscript notes is Edward Baker, the editor of the *Illinois State Journal* and husband of MTL's niece, Julia Edwards Baker, whose conduct is referred to here.

after he had made up his mind. I told him about Seward's intention to rule him. He said: "I shall rule myself; shall obey my own conscience, and follow God in it." Mr. Lincoln had no hope and no faith in the usual acceptance of these words. He was a religious man always as I think and believe. His first thought—to say think—about this subject was when Willie died—never before. He felt religious more than ever about the time he went to Gettysburg. He was not a technical Christian. He read the bible a good deal in 1864.

"Mr. Sumner and Mr. Lincoln were great chums after they became acquainted with one another. They watched each other closely. Down at City Point once Andy Johnson followed us. Was drunk. Mr. Lincoln said: 'For God's sake don't ask Johnson to dine with us.' 'No, don't,' said Sumner, 'and I did not ask him.'

"I often said that God would not let any harm come to my husband. We had passed through five long years—terrible, bloody years—unscathed, so that I thought so. So did Mr. Lincoln. He was happy in this idea—was cheerful, almost joyous, as he got gradually to see the end of the war.

"I used to read newspaper charges—newspaper attacks on him. He said: "*Don't do that,* for I have enough to bear; yet I care nothing for them. *If I'm right I'll live, if I'm wrong I'll die* anyhow. So let them pass unnoticed." I would playfully say, "That's the way to learn—read both sides."

"Mr. Lincoln's maxim and philosophy was, what is to be will be, and no cares (prayers) of ours can arrest the decree.

"I could tell when Mr Lincoln had decided anything. He was cheerful at first, then he pressed or compressed his lips tightly, firmly, one against the other. When these things showed themselves to me, I fashioned myself accordingly; so did all others around him have to do sooner or later, and they would find out. When we first went to Washington many persons thought that Mr. Lincoln was weak, but he rose gradually with the circumstances of the case, and men soon learned that he was above them all. I never saw a man's mind develop itself so finely—his manners got quite polished. He would say to me, when I talked to him about Chase and those others who did him evil, 'Do good to those who hate you and turn their ill will to friendship.' Sometimes in Washington, being worn down, he spoke crabbedly, to men, harshly so, and yet it seemed the people understood the conditions around him and forgave."

I am more than glad that Mrs. Lincoln has by the force of her letter of denial, hereinafter mentioned, drawn this record from the bad influence of time, mist and rats. In my lecture of Dec. 12th, 1873, I used the following substantial evidence or testimony of Mrs. Lincoln. It is as follows, and takes from the above evidence of Mrs. Lincoln:

"Mr. Lincoln had no hope and no faith in the usual acceptation of these words, and Lincoln's maxim and philosophy were, what is to be will be, and no cares (prayers) of ours can arrest the decree. Mr. Lincoln never joined any church. He was a religious man, always, as I think. His first thought, to say, think about this subject was when Willie died—never before. He read the Bible a good deal in 1864. He felt religious more than ever about the time he went to Gettysburg. Mr. Lincoln was not a technical Christian. I told him about Seward's Intention.

He said: "I shall rule myself—shall obey my own conscience and follow God in it," &c, &c.

Mrs. Lincoln, on reading or hearing of my lecture, as I suppose, wrote a letter to the Hon. John T. Stuart, of this city, in which she says that the language attributed to her is perverted, false, etc, etc. Mr. Stuart was directed to show this letter around, which I suppose was well done. I know it is telegraphed all over the country that no conversation ever took place at the St. Nicholas Hotel or other place between Mrs. Lincoln and myself touching Mr. Lincoln's religion, etc. She, in the Stuart letter, expressly admits a conversation, she says that Mr. Stuart came into the room while I was taking down the substance of the conversation, but that it was stopped—suspended during his stay. This I understood from Mr. Stuart, if I remember correctly. However, Mrs. Lincoln does expressly and explicitly say that the quotation in my lecture is perverted, false, etc. Her language is general and not specific.

Does Mrs. Lincoln mean to say that the quotation in my lecture and given above is a perversion—a false statement of her conversation just related, and as related? If so, it only needs a comparison of her evidence and the quotations which are placed here face to face, to be compared. If that is her meaning, she is mistaken, for, on comparison, they are one and the same. But if she means to cut deeper and say that the above conversation, as well as the quotation, is false, perverted, &c.—not that she did truly say, then that presents a question of care on my part in taking her testimony, and a question of memory, &c., on her part. I took all due care in getting the substance of what she said. I state that I was careful as usual in such cases when substance was sought, and I aver it was correctly done. I acted in all matters with her and others in perfect good faith. It is now nearly eight years since I took down her testimony.

To put the above quotation taken from my lecture in another form—*in questions*—will show the folly, the spasmodic madness of her denial. 1st. Does Mrs. Lincoln mean to say that Mr. Lincoln had hope and faith in the Spiritual Unseen, in the usual acceptation of these words? She knows better, and so does the world. 2d. Does she mean to say that Mr. Lincoln had no belief in nature's law, or in other words, substantially, "what is to be will be, &c?' 3d. Does she mean to say that Mr. Lincoln joined a church? 4th. Does she mean to say that Mr. Lincoln was not a religious man always, as she thought? 5th. Does she mean to say that Mr. Lincoln did not first think—to say think, about the subject of religion was when Willie died—never before? 6th. Does she mean to say that Mr. Lincoln did not read the Bible a good deal in 1864? 7th. Does she mean to say that Mr. Lincoln did not feel more religious than ever about the time he went to Gettysburg? 8th and lastly. Does she mean to say that Mr. Lincoln was a technical christian and joined a church? The denial of these propositions singly—the general denial of the quotations spoken of is an affirmation that the opposite or contrary is true. Will well known facts—well known history bear her out? For all this world her friends would not let her answer these questions. The manner and method of putting the thing at first blush shows the folly of such a denial.

Her objection may be to the application made by myself of the maxim, "what is to be will be," &c., to the idea of Christian prayer, or in other words to this sentence or the lecture, "and if this is—taking Mrs. Lincoln's words as true—what becomes of the Christian idea of prayer? What becomes of Noah Brooks' cant and twaddle about Lincoln's praying," &c, &c.

Until I know what Mrs. Lincoln means—till more certain and specific denials and charges are made by Mrs. Lincoln, I wish to say no more at present on this question—hope she will write a letter defining herself and make direct charges. By all means let us have such a letter. It will be important and interesting to the reading world.

Yours truly,
W. H. HERNDON

Illinois Daily State Journal *(Springfield, Ill.), January 15, 1874*

104. To Mr. Noyes[1]

Chinkapin Hill P.O., Sangamon County, Ill.,
Jan. 15, 1874

Mr. N.:

You say you desire to know all possible things of the good and great dead. I have just now a few moments to spare, and I do not know how better to spend them than to tell you what Mr. Lincoln really was and what he was not. Mr. Lincoln was a kind, tender and sympathetic man, feeling deeply in the presence of suffering, pain, wrong or oppression in any shape; he was the very essence and substance of truth; was of unbounded veracity, had unlimited integrity, always telling the exact truth, and always doing the honest thing at all times and under all circumstances. He was just to men; he loved the right, the good and true, with all his soul. I was with Mr. Lincoln for twenty-five years, and I can truthfully say I never knew him to do a wrong thing, never knew him to do a mean thing, never knew him to do any little dirty trick. He was always noble. In his nature he felt nobly and acted nobly. I never knew so true a man, so good a one, so just a one, so uncorrupted and so incorruptible a one. He was a patriot and loved his country well, and died for it. Mr. Lincoln expressed his great feeling in his thoughts, and his great thoughts in his feelings; he lived in his thoughts, and thought in his feelings. By these his soul was elevated and purified for his work. His work was the highest and grandest religion, noble duty nobly done.

Mr. Lincoln was cool and calm under the most trying circumstances; he had unbounded charity for all men. In religion he was a Theist, somewhat after the

---

1. The *Boston Evening Transcript* printed this letter and the one that follows it dated February 4, 1874, with an accompanying note: "The two following letters about Lincoln may be of interest to your readers. They were written to my great-uncle by W. H. Herndon. T. B." Neither Mr. Noyes, whose name appears in the salutation of the second letter, nor his great nephew, T. B., has been further identified.

order of Theodore Parker. Mr. Lincoln was not a speculative-minded man; was, like Washington, severely practical; he never ran in advance of his age, and yet was always directing the ideas and feelings of men to purely practical ends, to something that would end in good. Mr. Lincoln never shaped his veracity, integrity or virtue to circumstances; he fashioned and formed circumstances, so far as he could, to virtue, veracity and to integrity. He scorned meanness everywhere and at all times, and was bold and manly in his denunciation of wrong, however and by whomever done; he was not a foxy, tricky man; he was a statesman high above all tricks. How such a man as Lincoln could walk up to the highest point of human grandeur, from such a low origin, God only knows. But so it was ordained from the beginning and so it is. Mr. Lincoln was a man of great fidelity to what he believed was right—was true to friends, never deserting them till they deserted virtue, veracity and integrity. Mr. Lincoln could be, and was, trusted by the people with almost omnipotent power, and he never abused it nor shook the public faith in him. He was true to his trust, true to his country, and true to the rights of man. What a noble man, and what a noble life he lived! Washington was America's creator; Lincoln was its saviour. Mr. Lincoln now stands up against the deep blue sky the grandest figure of the age.

I have now stated to you Mr. Lincoln's leading characteristics, and if you like him better for them I am well satisfied with what I have told you. I have weighed every word and sentence, and can truly say they are true to Lincoln and Lincoln true to them. Mr. Lincoln was not a very social man. He was not spontaneous in his feelings; was, as some said, rather cold; he was rather reflective—not cold. However, take him all in all, he was as near a perfect man as God generally makes.

Yours Truly

W. H. HERNDON

Boston Evening Transcript, *February 13, 1932*

105. To Mr. Noyes[1]

Chinkapin Hill P.O Sangamon Co Illinois

Feby 4th 1874

Mr Noyes:

I received your kind note, dated the 31st ult, this moment. The letter I wrote you cost me no trouble and to know that it pleased you I am more than paid for the little time consumed in writing it. You will perceive in my Lecture on Mr Lincoln's religion, I state that Mr Lincoln's jokes were *vulgar—indecently so*. Without some explanation those words may mislead you. Mr Lincoln was raised among a peculiar people—an ignorant but good people—honest ones. Hence Mr Lincoln preferred jokes to fables or maxims as they, for his people, had the pith—point &

---

1. This letter has been transcribed from the original manuscript. As explained in §104, n. 1, it previously was printed, with another to the same recipient, in the *Boston Evening Transcript.*

force about them to make the point luminous—clear—plain. Mr. Lincoln was
not a dirty foul mouthed man by any means. He by nature was chaste enough in
his ideas & language, and when talking on business or to a gentleman he was as
refined & chaste in his language as any man. He simply chose his jokes for their
pith—force & power and in my opinion for no other reason. Mr. Lincoln was cut
out for a perfect gentleman and was such. I have known Mr. Lincoln to keep—on
the circuit as the Court & lawyers travelled around from County to County crowds
of people in full laugh till near day light. In villages the whole male population
would assemble about early candlelight of an evening at the tavern at which Mr
Lincoln put up to hear his jokes. I have seen men, sedate old men, hold their sides
"to keep them from splitting wide open", to use their expression, at his jokes. Mr
Lincoln could mock or mimic or imitate the thing or man so well, as he told his
stories, that no man, be he Preacher of the very gospel, could help laughing. Mr
Lincoln was sometimes very moody—gloomy, but let him get with his chums and
tell two or three stories and then it was that the sunshine of happiness burst full
in him aglow.

   With this explanation—with my letter to you and my Lecture I hope you now
understand Mr Lincoln better than Ever before.

   If such is the case I am content. Mr Lincoln was not a courtly polished man,
and yet he was a polished gentleman.

Yours Truly
W H Herndon

This letter is subject to your control just as the other was. WHH

ALPL: William H. Herndon Papers

106. *To Caroline Healy Dall*

Chinkapin Hill P.O Sangamon Co Ills
March 3d 1874

My Dear Friend—
   . . . I honestly think that the story of *Nancy* Hanks having negro blood in
her veins is all *"bosh"*—. My own opinion is that she was the child of a Virginia
aristocrat. It is *thought*, after some investigation made by myself, aided by others,
that the Hanks emigrated from the State of Conn about 1730 or 40. If this be
so she has good blood in her veins. Mr Lincoln told me himself that his mother
was an illegitemate, but was very, very intellectual. I guess this is so, judging
from what all the neighbors of her have often told me while I was in Indiana
collecting Evidence. 7th The mother of *Nancy* Hanks was named *Polly*.[1] I know
nothing of her except what is recorded in Lamon's life of Lincoln. All that you
have asked for—*nearly all*, can be found in Lamon's life of Lincoln published

---

1. AL's maternal grandmother was *Lucy* Hanks.

by Osgood Co. in 1872 which see. That Book is generally correct as to facts, but when it speculates—*beware!*

. . .

Your Friend
W H Herndon

MHS: Caroline Healey Dall Collection

107. To Mr. [_____ Flagg?][1]

SPRINGFIELD, ILL, Oct. 2, 1875

My Dear Sir: -

I enclose to you a letter written by Abraham Lincoln to his step-brother, J. D. Johnston.[2] Mr. Lincoln, at the time of writing the letter, was away from home attending court at Shelbyville. The letter is dated November 9, 1851, when Mr. Lincoln's hope and fame were at their lowest ebb. The compromise measures of 1850 had apparently sealed the fate of the slave forever, and there seemed to him no hope of doing good to his fellow-man. His course on the Mexican war was, in this section, unpopular—odious to some. This was in 1846–48. Lincoln was sad, gloomy, hopeless. He was very ambitious, and having lost hope, and failed in his ambitious desires, he was somewhat soured in consequence. But he did then what he always did—*the right*—and risked the consequences. His heart and soul and head always stood firm for the right.

Let me illustrate to you, by new and unpublished matter, which I know to be authentic, his love of truth. Thomas Lincoln, the father of Abraham, was twice married. His first wife was Nancy Hawks,[3] the mother of Abraham. His second marriage was to a lady by the name of Johnston—a widow with three children. This second marriage was in 1819, when Abraham was ten years old; he had a step-sister, Matilda Johnston, nearly his own age. About the year 1825 these children had grown nearly to manhood and womanhood. Heretofore they had roamed in the wild woods together. But now Mrs. Lincoln forbade Matilda going with Abraham, when he went to chop wood, or maul rails, or rive boards. One morning Abraham took his axe and maul and went into the forest to maul rails. 'Tilda saw him start and was determined to follow. So after Lincoln had been gone some time she darted down the path, stealthily overtook him, sprang upon him, putting her knee in the small of his back, and clasping her arms around his neck, thus bending him backwards, and threw him to the ground. In the scuffle 'Tilda

---

1. Manuscript not located. Though the newspaper that is the source of this letter does not print the name of the recipient, it is presumably the same as that of the following letter, where the hard-to-read name appears to be "Flagg." The only correspondent of WHH known to the editors is Willard C. Flagg, an early Illinois horticulturalist, but confirmation of this Flagg as the actual recipient is lacking.

2. AL to John D. Johnston, November 9, 1851, *Collected Works*, 2:112. This enclosure, also printed in the *Advertiser*, was apparently a copy. For the disposition of the original, see §116, p. 129.

3. Nancy *Hanks*.

fell on the sharp edge of the axe and cut her foot badly. After stanching the blood Abraham said to her, "What will you do now?" "Why," said 'Tilda, "I'll tell my mother that I fell on the axe, and that will be the truth, won't it, Abe?" "Yes, that will be the truth, *but it won't be the whole, truth.* 'Tilda, tell the *whole truth* about this and trust your good mother's forgiveness," said Abraham. This little story needs no comment. When I was collecting materials for a life of Mr. Lincoln in 1868–70 'Tilda herself told me this.[4]

Again, let me give you another incident illustrative of Mr. Lincoln's sense and love of justice. A gentleman named Chandler, now of Chandlerville, Cass county, Ill., moved from New York to this State in the year 1829; he entered, soon after his arrival, under the acts of Congress, eighty acres of land, and it was then the custom among the old settlers—a custom as strong as law—that each man had a right to enter as many as a hundred and twenty acres adjoining his first entry and in addition thereto. About the year 1832 a kinsman of Chandler came to Illinois and stopped with him six months or more, free of charge. He was told by Chandler and others what was the custom among the people, and woe be to him who violated it! I have seen the old settlers armed to the teeth with rifle and knife to defend and enforce this custom. Woe to the speculator who violated *the law!* By this custom Mr. Chandler *owned* eighty acres adjoining his first entry; it was so rich, so fertile, lay so fairly to the sun and was so justly and evenly divided between tree and prairie, that his kinsman fixed his eye upon it. So gathering up all that he could borrow, in addition to what he had honestly made, he started for the land office in Springfield one morning by daybreak. Mr. Chandler, when informed by his neighbors of this plot against him, said it was impossible. He was soon, however, convinced of the truth of their statement. So catching his fleetest horse he put spur for the land office about thirty-five miles distant. His neighbors gave him the money to enter his eighty acres. He ran his horse as rapidly as possible for about twenty-five miles, and when within ten miles of Springfield he overtook two young men—one a short, red-faced man and the other a long, tall, uncouth-looking lad—both utter strangers to him. Chandler's horse was quite exhausted, and so was he. He halted for a few moments, and was asked by one of them why this hurry? Chandler told them the story, when the tall young man, who was riding a fleet horse, said: "Stranger, you take my mare; she is fresh and yours is worn-out; put her under whip and spur and she will take you to Springfield in one hour,—won't she, Green?" "Yes, in short sixty minutes," said Green. "Beat the scoundrel to the land office by all means. We are strangers, but your face looks right and I'll risk the mare. We will all meet at Herndon's store in Springfield, in two or three hours. Come, be off quickly," said the tall young man. Mr. Chandler and the stranger exchanged horses. The kinsman, supposing that Chandler was ignorant of his purpose, rode leisurely along, conversing with those he met, so that Chandler got ahead of him, and, arriving in Springfield in the short sixty minutes, walked into the land-office, threw his hundred gold dollars ringing on

4. Matilda Johnston Moore, interview with WHH, *Herndon's Informants*, 109–10.

the table, and entered his eighty acres of land, much to his joy and subsequent profit. Well, who was this tall, uncouth young stranger? Who was he? It was one who loved justice and fair-play, honor and truth—it was Abram Lincoln.

Shortly after Mr. Chandler had entered the land his kinsman rode up, hitched his horse, went into the land office, counted his good hundred upon the [*unknown amount of text omitted*] climbed by his *character* from the lowest to the highest position known to man—the liberator of a race.

I shall write to you again, giving you other incidents of Mr. Lincoln's life, which I hope will help you to while away the time. If I shall succeed in this, the success will be my compensation.

Very truly yours,

W. H. HERNDON

Boston Daily Advertiser, *October 22, 1875*

---

108. To Mr. [_____ Flagg?][1]

Springfield Ills. Dec. 7th 1875

Mr [Flagg?]—

I recd your kind note, dated the _____ day of Novr; and for which please accept my thanks. What you say in reference to my published letter in the advertiser is perfectly satisfactory.[2] What the Ed says is equally so. I am not a very exacting man—am never so when men try to do right, but do wrong by accident. Let me say to you candidly "that all is right." I thank you for your trouble & interest in the matter—know your condition and don't wish you to move.

Today I send you a *leaf* of the Copy book of Mr. Lincoln.[3] I know it to be true—genuine—know that Mr Lincoln made it—wrote it &c. I got it from Mrs. Lincoln—the step mother of the Presdit in 1866. I know it by the hand writing—figures &c. [*In margin:* Date of the leaf 1825—when Mr Lincoln was 17 ys of age.] The way to manage this leaf is to have it pressed out smoothly—and then put between 2 10 X 12 window glass and framing the whole. I did a leaf this way, and it is now hanging up in my room &c. I hope you will like it and treasure it; it is the best I can do for you just now. I have a Cog of the mill (wheel) at which Mr Lincoln got kicked, which I can send to you if you will pay express chgs. There is a curious psychologic fact about this kicking. Did you ever

---

1. For the uncertainty about the identity of the recipient, see §107, n. 1. It should be noted that in each of these two letters, WHH sent this recipient one of his most prized Lincoln artifacts.

2. WHH's reference is presumably to the previous entry, a letter apparently published without his permission in the *Boston Daily Advertiser* for October 22, 1875.

3. This leaf from Lincoln's Cyphering Book (sometimes called his Sum Book), like this letter, is now in the Houghton Library at Harvard University (MS Am 1326). The fact that it was an enclosure to this letter has been overlooked until recently, when the document was identified by Profs. Nerida Ellerton and Mackenzie Clements of Illinois State University. See Nerida F. Ellerton, Valeria Aguirre, and M. A. (Ken) Clement, "He Would Be Good: Abraham Lincoln's Early Mathematics, 1819–1826," in *Abraham Lincoln's Cyphering Book and Ten Other Extraordinary Cyphering Books* (Cham: Springer, 2014), 123–86.

hear the story? I may send you other things—such as lawyer's briefs &c. &c if you would be interested in them.

I promised you, in some of my letters, that I had a few new stories—*incidents* in Mr Lincoln's life, and that I would write to you what they were &c, but I have had no time to "run them down", as Mr Lincoln would say, and find out their truth or falsehood. I may do so hereafter, if I can ever get time. I am running a farm *and* the law business, and hence am hurried almost to total exhaustion. One business is enough—two is to many for one man Beleive me

Your Friend
W H Herndon

Houghton

109. To Jesse W. Weik[1]

Springfield Ills. Decr. 7th 1875.

My Dear Sir:

Some few days since I recd your note, dated the 23d ult, requesting an autograph of Presdt. Lincoln. Let me say to you I am, at this moment, of the belief that I have given away all I had, and could have given away 10 thousand more or less of Mr Lincoln's autographs. Europe sends for them, and almost all the States of this Union send for them. However if in looking among my papers I should find one I will send it to you. I will keep your letter as a reminder of my promise. You say that it is harder to get one of Mr Lincoln's autographs than Washington's. Washington loved to write. *Lincoln hated to do so.*

Truly Yours
W H Herndon

Brown

110. To Jesse W. Weik

Springfield Ills. Octr 8th 1881.

My Dear Sir

I promised, a few days since, to send you an autograph of Mr. Lincoln, if I could find one among my boxed papers; and that if I could not that I would send you something more sacred, at least in my own eyes, than a mere autograph. I, as long ago as '75, promised to send you such writing or signature, if I could find one. When I rec'd your note of July '81 I had not forgotten my promise nor you. This week I unboxed my papers and the result is as follows: I found two of Mr Lincoln's autographs only two as yet one is in a letter written by Logan & *Lincoln*—but signed or written by Mr. Lincoln in *person*, which letter is addressed to Messrs.

---

1. WHH's first letter to JWW, who was then 18.

Rouland Smith & C—of Louisville Kentucky and dated april the 24th 1844. The other autograph is on a leaf of Mr *Lincoln's* Copy book and is sacred in two accounts—first it is Mr *Lincoln* signature and 2dly it is a leaf of his arithmetical note or copy book; which as I now remember bears date—1824–26–28.[1] Now for *the how* of finding the precious book. Soon after Mr Lincoln's assassination I determined to gather up all the facts of his life—truly—honestly *&* impartially whatever it might cost in money or infamy, and to give the facts to the world as I understood them. I did so, and probably you know the result. I find that this age is not ready to meet its own great truths: it will meet and grasp old truths—great and noble ones that have cost tears and blood way in the morning of the race of man. In collecting and gathering up facts of Mr. Lincoln's young life I went in person to various places—towns—cities—counties *&* states. In order to get at what I wished I went and saw old Mrs. Lincoln—step mother of the noble lad—a boy—a mere boy in 1824–6–8,—in Coles County Ills. This was say in 1865. I examined her—interviewed her in person and took notes of her conversation. She rose in mind high above her surroundings: she was a true woman. She told me then that Mr Lincoln used, when a boy, to keep an arithmetical copy book in which he put down his worked out sums. She likewise then told me that the boy Abraham was in the like habit of putting down in another copy book—his literary one—all things that struck him such as fine oratory—rhetoric—science—and &c. He likewise put things—wrote sentences on boards and other places and then read them—looked at them—over & over—analyzed them—thoroughly understanding them. He would translate them into his boyish language and *would* tell his school mates—friends and mother what they meant for he understood them and tell his thoughts he *would* and his school mates—friends and mother *must* hear or he would "bust wide open."

The information thus given me by the good old lady—the kind and loving step mother—God bless her, put me on nettles, as it were, and so we commenced the search. and found this—the arithmetical copy book—a leaf of which you now have. We could not find the other book: it is lost—and lost forever as our search was thorough. Mrs Lincoln gave me the book with her own hand or by the hand of her grand son. On this leaf you will find some writing of young Abraham and is as follows—the want of *Caps* included

> "Abraham Lincoln—
> his hand and pen
> he will be good, but
> god knows when"

---

1. This leaf from AL's Cyphering or Sum Book is in LC: HW: Exp 1:1:1–2.

On an other leaf of the same book is this

"Abraham Lincoln is my name
And with my pen I write the same
I will be a good boy but, God knows when"

By this paper you can tell the extent of Mr Lincoln's education in 1824–6–8. The letter is dated in 1844 at which time and *at this place* he was a great lawyer. In 1836 Mr. Lincoln was a tolerably good mathematician, as he was surveyor of Sangamon County. What he knew he knew plainly—clearly—thoroughly: he saw things down to the ultimate point, beyond which no man ever went. Study what you see in these papers, and you will see the general extent of Mr Lincoln's—personally dug out—education—Mr Lincoln had unbounded and unlimited confidence in his own mental power: he was himself and wholy self reliant, asking no man anything: he searched for what he wanted—dug it out by the tap root—held it out before him till he knew it inside and outside. Some one has said—"Give me the amount of soap that a people uses and I can tell the height of its civilization". Apply this rule—if rule it is to these papers and run out the rule. Many person's will say to schollars—young men struggling to climb high—"Imitate Mr. Lincoln in his methods—". All of which is right, but remember that *it is the mind back of its manifestations* which is inimitable—not to be imitated: it is itself and nothing can be like it. A rat cannot be an eagle. I once said that Mr Lincoln was a deeply and thoroughly Religious man at all times and places and under all conditions and I now repeat it: his Religion was of the noblest and grandest and broadest kind. Lincoln was a noble man.

On looking at this leaf and knowing Mr. Lincoln as I do—what Memories cluster arond my central being, while I'm writing this letter. Here is the name of *Lincoln* before me & in my mind; and the news papers overflowing with the sad intelligence of Garfields death—. The mind remembers Socrates and Jesus—*double* stars of the old World—Lincoln and Garfield *twin* stars of the New. Oh—how each suffered in his own way and for the Eternal Right. The sublime thoughts—the noble deeds.—the grand acts of these men will enter into all future time as moral forces and divine energies lifting up to a higher level and a grander plain the whole race of man for all coming time. The hand of him who wrote these sums—this simple poetry—this letter may moulder into dust, but his name will outlast these eternal hills: *he dreamed dreams of glory, and glory is justly his.*
                                           Your Friend
                                         W. H. Herndon

P.S. You well percieve that this letter is a hasty one. I have no time to tone it up nor to re-write it.
     Herndon

LC: Exp 4:9:1746–50

111. To John E. Remsburg

Nov. 4, 1881

Some people say that Mr. Lincoln was an ungrateful man. This is not true, and especially when applied to myself. He was always kind, tender, and grateful to me—clung to me with hooks of steel. I know that I was true to him. It is said that no man is great to his valet. If I was Mr. Lincoln's valet, the rule does not apply in this case, for my opinion of him is too well known. His was a grand, noble, true, and manly life. He dreamed dreams of glory, and glory was justly his. He was growing and expanding to the day of his death. He was slow in his development, but strong and big when he did come. The last letter which I ever received from him concluded thus: 'God bless you, says your friend.—*A. Lincoln.*' He felt what he expressed, and in return I say, *God bless you, Lincoln.*

Six Historic Americans, *130*

112. To Jessie W. Weik

Springfield, Ill. Jany. 2d 1882

My Dear Sir:

. . .

As to Mrs. Lincoln, she has plenty of her own funds to keep her for life—say 20 thousand dolls besides her pension. Her friends here are wealthy and will willingly take care of her if she will only let them. Mrs Lincoln is a curious woman—an unfortunate one—and to a certain extent a despised one. Mrs Lincoln is in part an unbalanced woman—her mind is—as it were unhinged, and has been for years—*Privately*—Mr. Lincoln held his wife partly insane for years, and this shows his toleration of her nature—his great forbearance of her outlandish acts, otherwise not understood by the great world. If I get time I may write you more on this point, but am so weak that I can say no more just now

Your Friend

W H Herndon

If I ever come to Greencastle I will call & see you

LC: 6Exp 4:9:1753–54

113. To Mr. Graff[1]

Springfield Ills Jany 13t 282 [1882]

My Dear Sir:

I have a favor to ask of you, and it is this—I see in two publications—books—a *supposed* speech of Mr. Lincoln. One of the books is Six Months in the White House, by Mr Carpenter—see pages 198–9, and the other is the Lincoln Memorial

---

1. Not identified. At top left: "Entirely Private."

Album—see page 340. by Oldroyd.[2] The story runs thus—a Committee of Colored people in 1864 presented—Mr. Lincoln with a superb Copy of the bible. The Colored people—the Committee were from Baltimore. On presentation of the bible the story goes that Lincoln made them a short speech. The speech as published in those two books makes Lincoln say things which he never uttered nor any sane man would utter. The speech is false as printed. No doubt that Mr Lincoln said a few kind words, but this speech as published makes Lincoln a fool—or a hypocrite or an ass or a Combination of the three. Now what I want you to do is to get one of these books and read the speech carefully over & over. After this is done find out who some of the Committee were, who presented the book, & heard the speech. When this is done ask the person if Mr Lincoln wrote out the speech, and handed it to the Committee. If he did not write it out find out 1st Who did write it, & 2dly *When* it was written out—where it was written out and how long after the time when the book was presented &c. &c &c, and any other questions—shrewdly calculated, & put. A lie will be your answer unless you are Careful. Probably you had better have one of the books with you when you interrogate the man or men. I say the speech is false and I want to nail it so. The two speeches differ—The one in the 6 mo in the White House is the longest & strongest. The Revd S. W Chase was one of the Committee. Part of the speech is true and that is the beginning of it. *Please* hunt up the *Exact truth* of this matter and write me.

[*In margin:* See some shrewd Liberal—talk to him & see what is the best course to pursue—show him this, if you think proper.]

If you see W H Burr[3] of Washington City give him leave to read this, & if proper take a copy of it, and hunt it up in Washington—& write me. It is the latter half of the speech which is a lie made of whole cloth—

Your Friend
W. H. Herndon

Keep your own secrets and don't let anyone know what you are doing or intend to do, Except a liberal

Illinois: Illinois History and Lincoln Collections

114. To Jessie W. Weik

Springfield, Ill. Feby 17 1882

Friend Weik

I came home this moment & find your letter dated the 13th inst. awaiting my arrival. I have been Lecturing on Lincoln for a short time and am just now hurried or would write you a good long letter, advising or informing you about

---

2. Carpenter, 198–99; Oldroyd, 340. AL's remarks as reported in the *Washington Daily Morning Chronicle*, September 8, 1864, are reprinted in *Collected Works* (7:542), which notes that reports in the *New York Tribune* and *Baltimore Sun* are "less complete."

3. Probably William Henry Burr (1819–1908), known for exposing historical hoaxes featuring fraudulent letters.

Mrs Lincoln & *Bob.* I will send you a *private* letter sometime The People don't understand things & no congressman dare say "No" to a question allowing Mrs. L a pension—or any sum of money. *Bob.* & his mother never were good friends— Such as their relation would suggest. You may see me sometime, I hope & trust and then I'll tell you much which I well can't put on paper. Good heavens!—if you knew half of what I do about Lincoln & his wife—their marriage—what lead to it & how it came out. &c You would say—good Lord deliver us from such a condition! Write—"Hell" over your ideas of Lincoln's married life.

You are correct about your idea of old age—poetry—youth &C. A man never loses his imagination—his emotion—feeling &c. The change of age is from the mere love song & simple rhyme to higher poetry—such as on Child Harold— Macbeth—&c &c. Man simply [slows?] down but keeps his harmony and the music of the soul to the great end.[1]

. . .

Your Friend
W. H. Herndon

LC: HW3176; Exp 4:9:1755–56

115. *Open letter to public*[1]

SPRINGFIELD, ILL., NOV. 9, 1882

A Card and a Correction.

I wish to say a few short words to the public and private ear. About the year 1870 I wrote a letter to F. E. Abbot, then of Ohio, touching Mr. Lincoln's religion. In that letter I stated that Mr. Lincoln was an infidel, sometimes bordering on atheism, and I now repeat the same. In the year 1873 the Right Rev. James A. Reed, pastor and liar of this city, gave a lecture on Mr. Lincoln's religion, in which he tried to answer some things which I never asserted, except as to Lincoln's infidelity, which I did assert and now and here affirm. Mr. Lincoln was an infidel of the radical type; he never mentioned the name of Jesus, except to scorn and detest the idea of miraculous conception. This lecture of the withered minister will be found in *Holland's Review.*[2] I answered this lecture in 1874, I think, in this city to a large

---

1. This passage may be about the changing taste in poetry of AL, who read Byron intensively in early life but later favored Shakespeare and wrote in 1863, "Nothing equals Macbeth. It is wonderful." *Collected Works*, 6:392.

1. Printed as a broadside for general distribution, this defense of his own character and career was published at WHH's request in *The Truth Seeker* on November 25, 1882
2. "The Later Life and Religious Sentiments of Abraham Lincoln," *Scribner's Monthly* 6, no. 3 (July 1873): 333–43. Josiah G. Holland, with whom WHH had crossed swords (see §66), was the editor of *Scribner's Monthly.*

and intelligent audience—had it printed and sent a copy to Holland, requesting, in polite language, that he insert it in his *Review*, as an answer to the Reed lecture.[3] The request was denied me, as a matter of course. He could help to libel a man with Christian courage, and with Christian cowardice refuse to *un*libel him.

Soon thereafter, say from 1874 to 1882, I saw floating around in the newspaper literature, such charges as "Herndon is in the lunatic asylum, well chained," "Herndon is a pauper," "Herndon is a drunkard," "Herndon is a vile infidel and a knave, a liar and a drunkard," and the like. I have contradicted all these things under my own hand often, except as to my so-called infidelity, liberalism, free religious opinions or what-not. In the month of October, 1882, I saw in and clipped out of the Cherryvale Globe-News of Sept., 1882, a paper published in the State of Kansas, the following rich and racy article; it is as follows:

"LINCOLN'S OLD LAW PARTNER A PAUPER.

"Bill Herndon is a pauper in Springfield, Ill. He was once worth considerable property. His mind was the most argumentative of any of the old lawyers in the State, and his memory was extraordinary.

"For several years before Lincoln was nominated for the Presidency, Herndon was in some respects the most active member of the firm, preparing the greatest number of cases for trial and making elaborate arguments in their behalf.

"It is said that he worked hard with Lincoln in preparing the memorable speeches delivered by the man who afterwards became President, during the debates between Lincoln and Douglas in 1858, and in constructing the Cooper Institute address delivered by Lincoln a short time before the war.

"Herndon, with all his attainments, was a man who now and then went on a spree, and it was no uncommon thing for him to leave an important lawsuit and spend several days in drinking and carousing. This habit became worse after Lincoln's death, and like poor Dick Yates, Herndon went down step by step till his old friends and associates point to him as a common drunkard."

There are three distinct charges in the above article. First, That I am a pauper. Second, that I am a common drunkard, and third, that I was a traitor, or false to my clients. Let me answer these charges in their order. First, I am not a pauper, have never been and expect never to be. I am working on my own farm, making my own living with my own muscle and brain, a place and a calling that even Christianity with its persecution and malignity can never reach me to do me much harm. I had, it is true, once a considerable property, but lost much of it in the crash and consequent crisis of 1873, caused in part by the contraction of the currency, in part by the decline in the demand for agricultural products, which I raised for sale, in part by the inability of the people to buy, &c., &c., and for no other reasons. Second, I never was a *common* drunkard, as I look at it, and

---

3. WHH's reply to Reed was delivered as a lecture in Springfield on December 12, 1873, and printed in the *Illinois State Register*, December 13, 1873.

am not now. I am and have been for years an ardent and enthusiastic temperance man, though opposed to prohibition by law, by any force or other choker. The time has not come for this. It is a fact that I once, years ago, went on a spree; and this I now deeply regret. It however is in the past, and let a good life in the future bury the past. I have not fallen, I have risen, and all good men and women will applaud the deed, always excepting a small, little, bitter Christian like the Right Rev. pastor and liar of this city, to whom I can trace some of the above charges. In my case this minister was an eager, itching libeller, and what he said of me is false—nay, a willful lie. Third, I never was a traitor or untrue to my clients or their interests. I never left them during the progress of a trial or at other times for the causes alleged, drunkenness. I may have crept—slid—out of a case during the trial because I had no faith in it, leaving Mr. Lincoln, who had faith in it, to run it through. My want of faith in the case would have been discovered by the jury and that discovery would have damaged my client, and to save my client I dodged. This is all there is in it, and let men make the most of it.

Now let me ask a question. Why is all this libelling of me? I am a mere private citizen, hold no office, do not beg the good people to give me one often. My religious ideas, views and philosophy are to day, here, unpopular. But wait, I will not deny my ideas, views or philosophy for office or station or the applause of the unthinking multitude. I can, however, answer the above question. It, the libelling, is done because I did assert and affirm by oral language and by print that Mr. Lincoln was an infidel, sometimes bordering on atheism, and yet he was among the best, greatest and noblest of mankind; he was a grand man. Why do not the Christians prove that Mr. Lincoln was an evangelical Christian, and thus prove me a liar. One of my friends for whom I have great respect, says, that "Mr. Lincoln was a *rational* Christian because he believed in morality." Why not say Mr. Lincoln was a *rational* Buddhist, as Buddhism teaches morality? Why not say Lincoln was a *rational* Mohamedan? By the way, let me say here, that I have a profound respect for an earnest, manly and sincere Christian or an atheist, a profound respect for an earnest, manly and sincere infidel or theist or any other religion, or the men who hold it, when that belief is woven into a great manly character to beautify and greaten the world.

These charges, and I do not know how many more, nor of what kind, have been scattered broadcast all over the land, and have gone into every house, have been read at every fireside, till the good people believe them, believe that I am nearly as mean as a little Christian, and *all because I told the truth and stand firm to my convictions.*

Respectfully,
W. H. Herndon

LC: Exp 4:9:1790 (printed broadside)

116. To _____ [1]

Springfield, Ill., November 24, 1882.

My Dear Sir:

A few days since I received your kind note, for which please accept my thanks. Inclosed you will find a letter from Abraham Lincoln to John D. Johnson—Lincoln's step-brother—which I promised to give you; it is the only letter which I have left of Mr. Lincoln's; it is a genuine one, written by the great man himself. I have kept the letter up to this day as an evidence that Mr. Lincoln was not an atheist; and had he been one, that fact would not lessen him in my estimation, though not one myself. I had this letter once published, but before so doing I showed it to several of Mr. Lincoln's old and dear friends, who laughed at me for my credulity in believing that Mr. Lincoln believed in Immortality and Heaven, as stated in the letter; it was said to be merely a message of consolation from a dutiful son to his dying father. However, I had the letter published, and kept the letter as an evidence that Mr. Lincoln was not an atheist. I could have given the letter away many times—could have sold it for money—but I would not part with it. I think the question of his atheism is settled, and now I present it to you. I may say to you that the letter has the ring, it seems to me, of true metal, and yet I give no opinion. You have the letter and the facts of Mr. Lincoln's life before you, and you can judge as well as I can. I will soon in this letter give you a phase of Mr. Lincoln's life not generally known, and possibly it will not be believed by the worshipping world—I mean hero-worshipping world. I have no reference to the worship of the religious soul.

Mr. Lincoln for years supported or helped to support his aged father and mother; it is to the honor of Lincoln that he dearly loved his step-mother, and it is equally true that she idolized her stepson. Johnson, to whom the letter is addressed; was Lincoln's step-brother—the son of Mrs. Lincoln by her first husband. Thomas Lincoln, the father of Abraham, courted his second wife in his youth; she refused to have him; he then courted Nancy Hanks and was married to her. A man by the name of Johnson courted Miss Sarah Bush—Thomas Lincoln's first flame—and married her. About the year 1819 both Mrs. Lincoln and Mr. Johnson died. Lincoln then in about one year again renewed his suit and it was accepted, and they were married Each had two children by the first marriage and none by the second. John Johnson was an indolent and shiftless man, a man that was "born tired," and yet he was an exceedingly clever man, generous, and very hospitable. Lincoln deserves great credit for the care shown his father and mother—hard cash and warm heart-care. In the very letter which I give you this care is shown; he says in the letter: "You (Johnson) already know I desire that neither father nor mother shall be in want of any comfort, either in health or in sickness, while they live;

---

1. The recipient has not been identified. This widely reprinted letter was first published in the *New York Tribune*, January 21, 1883, where a prefatory note reads in part: "The following letter was written by Abraham Lincoln's former law-partner to a well-known clergyman of this city, and has been furnished to THE TRIBUNE for publication." For WHH's comment on what he withheld from this letter, see §121.

and I feel sure that you have not failed to use my name, if necessary, to procure a doctor or anything else for father in his present sickness." Dutiful and affectionate son! Noble man! Mr. Lincoln was very poor at the time this letter was written, not worth, in property, more than three or four thousand dollars.

Mr. Lincoln purchased a piece of property in Coles County in this State as a home for his father and mother, and had it deeded in trust for their use and benefit. The aged couple lived in Coles County at the time. I do not now recollect all the particulars, and yet I once did. The records in Coles County will show the facts, if anyone in the future wishes to look the thing further up. Here is exhibited parental love and duty, backed up by warm affection, care, good credit, land, home and money. This was true and genuine comfort and material aid. It was not all gush, sympathy and tears on paper; it was real, solid, genuine comfort and support, such as we can live upon.

I now wish to give you a phase of Mr. Lincoln's life which is not generally known, nor will it be believed readily by the multitude; and yet it will be true to the letter and the spirit of his life. He was said to be a very simple-minded man, devoid of the silences and ambitions of life. In this city he was known only to the few. I would advise you before you read this letter to read Holland's "Life of Lincoln" at pages 241–2, where you will find many diverse ideas of Mr. Lincoln. Consider it inserted here. Mr. Lincoln was thought, as before stated, to be a very simple-minded man. He was simple in his dress and manners, simple in his approach and in his presence. Though this be true, he was a man of quite infinite silences. He was thoroughly and deeply secretive, uncommunicative and close-minded, as to his plans, wishes, hopes and fears. His ambition was never satisfied; in him it was a consuming fire which smothered his finer feelings. Here he ran for every legislative office, from the trusteeship of our then little village to the Presidency, and during all that time I venture to say that he never wholly opened himself to mortal creature. He was sceptical, cautious and terribly secretive, confiding his plans and purposes, ambitions and ends, to no man. I have known men in our office to listen to Mr. Lincoln's conversation for a short while and then exclaim: "Oh, what a simple minded man is Mr. Lincoln! So plain! so unambitious! so confiding!" and the like, when Mr. Lincoln's mind was not in our office but on a hot chase for the end so devoutly to be wished Of all Americans he was, most emphatically, a man of the profoundest, widest and deepest policies. He had his burning and his consuming ambition, but he kept his secrets and opened not.

An interviewer, with the best of intentions in the world, once went to Mr. Lincoln's room in the White House while he was President, and said: "Mr. President, what do you think of the war and its end?" To which Mr. Lincoln politely and laughingly replied: "That question of yours puts me in mind of a story about something which happened down in Egypt, in the southern part of Illinois." The point of it was that a man badly burned his fingers in being in too much haste. Mr. Lincoln told the story admirably well, walking up and down the room and most heartily laughing all the while. The interviewer saw the point coming at him like the sting end of a hornet. As a matter of course he was cut to the quick, and quickly down-stairs he rushed with an oath in his mouth, saying he would "never interview that man again." He was as good as his word, and never tried to interview the President again. And thus it always was with Mr. Lincoln. The man that tried to pump him always found a shut safe, well locked, and the key lost. If a man was ever created in this world who did not let his right hand know what his left hand did or was doing, it was Abraham Lincoln. He was a profound, marvelous and mysterious man to the great majority of men. I judged the man by his questionings, his manner, his nervousness, his unrest and the play of his features, with their colors, giving a significance to his thoughts and his wishes, a mind's revelation to mind.

While I say that Mr. Lincoln was ambitious, secretive and somewhat selfish, do not infer from these words that he was a dishonest man, nor an insincere man, nor a hypocrite, nor a mean man, nor a base man. He was, on the contrary, full of honesty, integrity, sincerity, open, fair and candid, when speaking or acting. He was for Lincoln always, but always with Lincoln's intense honesty. Mr. Lincoln was a wise man, a shrewd man, a long-headed man, full of his own policies. He was a marginal man, always leaving a wide blank on his paper, so that the future might write the future lessons thereon. Mr. Lincoln hated speculation, had no cranks, was not visionary and impracticable. He had relatively no imagination and no fancy, was material and purely practical. He had one of the very best balanced heads in America; and it was poised well on his shoulders. Henry Clay was his ideal statesman, a purely material and practical man. Mr. Lincoln's mind was purely logical, and he followed his conclusions to the ultimate end, though the world perished. I never heard Mr. Lincoln harshly condemn any man, nor did I ever hear him praise but two men; one, Thomas Jefferson, on paper; and the other Henry Clay, in his speech and letters and in his heart. Was this jealousy, or what? I think he cared for principles and not much for men, especially if he did not want to use them for his own ends, which were generally high and noble. Mr. Lincoln had no low cunning, was not a trickster, a mere wire-puller. He scorned and detested all such political arts. His mind required and lived in facts, figures, and principles. He was destitute of faith which comes and goes without evidence. His own reason and human experience were his authority, and these only with him were authority.

It is a fact that Mr. Lincoln was a peculiar man, a wonderful, marvelous and mysterious man to the world generally. I was with him for about twenty-five years; and I think I knew him well. Mr. Lincoln never took the advice of any man or set of men, generally speaking. He never asked the opinion or advice of any man. He was self-reliant, self-poised, self-helping and self-assertive, but not dogmatic by any means. He clung like gravity to his own opinions. He was the most continuous and severest thinker in America. He read but little, and that for an end. Politics were his Heaven, and his Hades metaphysics. His tendency in philosophy was materialistic; he was an evolutionist; and yet, as the letter now presented to you shows, he believed in God, a maker, Immortality and Heaven. I am not now advocating any particular opinion on any subject, nor denying one. I am simply stating facts, letting each man and woman draw his or her own conclusions. I give no decided opinion about the letter, except I know it is genuine, and now yours, which I hope you will keep to the end of your time, and then it may descend to the family as an heirloom, a great treasure indeed.

May I say again that Mr. Lincoln was a shrewd man, a long headed man, a wise man, full of policies? Mr. Lincoln knew that Senator Douglas was in his way in the North, and so he, at Freeport, determined to kill him [politically]. He put a question—and that, too, against his friends' advice and importunities—to Senator Douglas, which he knew the Senator must answer one way or the other, and he further knew that to answer the question either way was death to Douglas—death in the North if he answered one way, and death in the South if another. It was cold, well-calculated death anyway. Douglas answered, and of that answer he died. Again, after Douglas's death, in the North was only Seward to oppose him, and Lincoln determined to kill or outstrip him. Hence his "house divided against itself" speech here in 1858, and his speeches, his "irrepressible conflict" speeches in Ohio. Lincoln ridiculed when he could Seward's "higher law" idea, scared some of the Republicans with it, and got the confidence somewhat of the extreme Republicans; and in his great Cooper Institute speech in New-York in 1860 he drove the nail in Seward's political coffin. All this was planned and coldly calculated by Lincoln. I know this to be true.

What! this a simple-minded man? this a politically "innocent-dear" man? this a mere thing without ideas and policies? Away with all such opinions! Look how he treated his Cabinet in the issuance of his great Proclamation of Emancipation. He consulted them simply about little and unimportant matters, and so said to them before he read it. He decreed to issue it. He simply wanted his Cabinet to hear it read, and that is all. This proclamation was issued as by doom, and what he did was not for the love of the slave or liberty, but to save the Union. It was to preserve his "oath registered in heaven." He kept his oath, saved the Union, and with a quick dash of the military pen he freed four millions of people.

In philosophy Mr. Lincoln was a realist as opposed to an idealist, was a sensationalist as opposed to an intuitionalist, a Materialist as opposed to a Spiritualist, and yet remember what he says in his letter. I said to you in a private letter that Mr. Lincoln was at all times and places and under all circumstances a deeply and thoroughly religious man, sincerely, firmly, broadly and grandly so. I do not say he was a Christian. I do not say that he was not. I give no opinion the one way or the other. I simply state facts and let each person judge for himself.

I say, in short, in terms of contradiction if you please, that Mr. Lincoln was a perfect and an imperfect man, a strong man and a weak one; but take him all in all, he was one of the best, wisest, greatest and noblest of men in all the ages.

Most respectfully yours,
Wm H. HERNDON

New York Tribune, *January 21, 1883*

117. To the Editor of The Liberal Age

Springfield, Ill., December 4, 282 [1882]

One of the very best, greatest, and noblest of mankind, Abraham Lincoln, was assassinated on the night of April 14th, 1865, in a theater, intently listening to the play of the Country Cousins.[1] Eighteen years will soon hav rolled by since that sad event. Soon after the tragic death of Lincoln, I was written to by many persons to giv the facts and my opinion of his religious life. I refused for some years to write anything for *publication*, though I talked about it freely and by private letter. At last, at the request of many, and among them, I think, Mr. F. E. Abbot, I concluded to comply with their wishes. I, in the year 1870, wrote the Abbot letter touching Mr. Lincoln's religion and his religious ideas.[2] That letter will be found in Lamon's "Life of Lincoln" at pages 492–7. I was from 1865 to 1870 gathering up and collecting the facts of Lincoln's life. The Abbot letter contains the sum and substance of my efforts in this particular line. The letter is correct and substantially true in general and in every particular, and I refer to it here and make it a part of this letter. I hav nothing to retract from that letter, but in this I shall add something thereto. No man has refuted the Abbot letter, and no man can, I think, on evidence, contradict this. It is now nearly twelve years since I wrote the Abbot letter. Since these long years another and a new generation of people has come upon the scene of human action. It is a brave, reading, intelligent, and searching generation, demanding facts, figures, and principles as the sure foundations of its belief; it has no faith in the unseen and unknowable; it has no faith that comes and goes without evidence; it is a doubting age—an investigating age; it follows science and flatly denies supernaturalism. It is for this new generation that I write this letter touching Mr. Lincoln's religion. This is at once my excuse and justification. I affirm at the outset that Mr. Lincoln was an Infidel of the radical type, sometimes bordering on Atheism; and now the great question is: Was Lincoln an evangelical Christian? That question resolves itself into two others. 1st. Did Mr. Lincoln believe in the fall of man as related in the Bible? and 2d. Did he believe that Jesus was the *Christ* of God—the truly and only begotten son, as the Christian world contends? These are the questions to solve. The Christians assert, though they know or should know better, that Mr. Lincoln was a Christian in a theological sense. If this is not their meaning then it is admitted that Mr. Lincoln was not a Christian—only a rational Christian, and *that is no Christian at all.* It is not a question of kindness, goodness, generosity, tenderness, affection, and morality. These Mr. Lincoln had and more; he had honor, integrity, and general nobility. Mr. Lincoln was not a Christian in the general acceptation of that term; he did not believe in the fall of man, nor the miraculous conception, nor in the so-called divine revelation, nor miracle, nor in inspiration, as the Christian world contends.

Mr. Lincoln came into Sangamon county, down the North Fork of the Sangamon River in a frail canoe, in the spring of 1831. I can see from where I write

---

1. *Our American Cousin,* by Tom Taylor.
2. For the text of the Abbot letter, see §89.

the identical place where he cut the timbers for his flat boat, which he built at a little village called Sangamon Town, seven miles a little northwest of Springfield. Here he had it loaded with wheat, corn, bacon, and other provisions, destined for New Orleans, at which last place he landed in the month of May, 1831. He returned home about June of that year and finally settled in another little village called New Salem, on the high bluffs of the Sangamon River, then in Sangamon county and now in Monroe county,[3] and about twenty miles northwest of this city. Mr. Lincoln lived in New Salem six years, and in 1837 he moved to the little town (now city) of Springfield, where he resided continuously till 1861, when he left for Washington—the president elect of this great people. I hav known Mr. Lincoln well since 1834; and since 1844, when he and I became partners in the law business, I think I knew him thoroughly inside and outside, top side and bottom side. There was a peculiar people in New Salem. The men were mostly doubters, skeptics, Liberals, Infidels, if you please. They listened to experience, nature, and reason; they were great, broad-minded Liberal men, brave, generous, kind, and a hospitable people to a fault. I knew them well—one and all; they were hard to whip and not easily to be fooled or cheated. With these rough but courageous people Mr. Lincoln was thrown for seven long years; he was one of them, and identical in his religious belief. I should before this hav said something of Mr. Lincoln's religious belief while he lived in Indiana. A gentleman who has deeply and thoroughly investigated this question, and who now livs in high life in the great state, says of Mr. Lincoln, while he lived in Indiana, that "he went to church there to mimic and came away to mock." This is substantially correct. Mr. Lincoln left Indiana in his twenty-first year an Infidel, and held to it at New Salem, Springfield, and at Washington, and so died. This is beyond all reasonable controversy, if we can agree what it is that constitutes a Christian and an Infidel. A Christian is one who believes, among other things, that Jesus was the *Christ* of God. An Infidel is one who denies this, among other things. This test is fundamental and decisiv. No man can show that Mr. Lincoln believed in the miraculous conception of Jesus. Such a belief is blasphemous. While Mr. Lincoln lived in New Salem, he came across the works of Thomas Paine, Volney's "Ruins," and other such Liberal books. So strong was Mr. Lincoln's Infidelity in New Salem, and so burning were his convictions of the utter falsehoods of the Bible, that he felt it his duty to *write* and *publish* a little book on his Infidelity. In this book or pamphlet he attacked the Bible on two grounds: 1st. Its inherent contradictions; and 2d. On the grounds of its injustice—on the grounds of the highest human reason. He denied in that book the fall of man and the miraculous conception. This pamphlet was read by Mr. Lincoln to Maj. Samuel Hill, a good and true friend of his, who agreed substantially with him. Maj. Hill snatched the manuscript out of Mr. Lincoln's hands and threw it into the stove and burnt it up. Other living witnesses know this to be true. His reason for this was that Mr. Lincoln was then—1835–6—a rising young man, and Hill, as a discreet friend, knew that the book would forever damn Lincoln. This was the best deed ever done for Lincoln by any man.

---

3. Menard County.

Mr. Lincoln, in the year 1837, moved to the city of Springfield, a very little town, and then and there came across many people of his own belief, and I among them. I distinctly recollect their views, language, ideas, and philosophy. They called themselves at that time *Freethinkers*. Some of these men were highly educated and polished gentlemen. Mr. Lincoln read in this city Hume, Gibbon, and other Liberal books. He was in this city from 1837 to 1861, an Infidel, Freethinker, Liberal, Free Religionist of the radical type. As Mr. Lincoln grew older he saw the absolute necessity of silence on this question; he only opened to a few, and then more by sharp questioning than by a long solid argument. When a certain nameless divine of this city delivered a lecture here on Mr. Lincoln's religion, he was compelled to entitle it, in substance if not in words, "The later life and religious sentiments" of Mr. Lincoln. No man ever said that Mr. Lincoln's life was not religious, or that he had no religious sentiments. All men are religious and hav religious sentiments, but all are not Christians. If such loose language as this divine's can screw up the courage of the Christian brotherhood to believe that Mr. Lincoln was a Christian, all right. Mr. Lincoln, while in New Salem, was accused of being an Atheist, and this arose from the fact that the people took the words Infidel, Freethinking, and Atheism as meaning the same thing; and even now the world cannot precisely distinguish the broad difference. Mr. Lincoln, I understand, denied that he was an Atheist. In Springfield, after the death of Mr. Lincoln, he was accused of being an Atheist by some. I felt it my duty, as I had the evidence—written evidence in my hand—to publish a letter written to John Johnson in 1851 by Mr. Lincoln. In that letter Mr. Lincoln acknowledges the existence of God, immortality, and heaven. The letter will be found in Lamon's "Life of Lincoln," at page 336.[4] I showed this letter to several gentlemen who thoroughly knew Mr. Lincoln and his religious beliefs. They said substantially to me this: "The letter is only a word of consolation from a dutiful son to a dying father." I leave the question to the reader, and he must judge for himself. Had Mr. Lincoln been an absolute, positiv Atheist utterly denying the existence of God, *that fact* would not hav lessened him in my estimation. At times in the moment of his terrible gloom, thick as a fog-bank, there is no doubt that Mr. Lincoln bordered on Atheism—if not an out-and-out Agnostic. In Lincoln's better moments he was a *Theist*.

Mr. Lincoln left this city in 1861 an Infidel—Liberal—and so remained till he died on the morning of the 15th of April, 1865. I personally *know* many of the above facts to be true, of my own knowledge; and what I do not know personally, but assert to be true, I hav the overwhelming moral evidence to support and prove. I hav examined many persons on this point, as well as all others relating to Mr. Lincoln's life, and what those persons told me I wrote down at the time and place of the interview, generally many years ago. I do not think that there are any substantial mistakes in the notes. If Mr. Lincoln was a Christian it is very easy to prove it. The burthen of proof is on the Christian; first, because he is in the affirmativ; and second, it is a well settled principle in the laws of evidence that when a given state of facts, with accompanying conditions, is once prove, that

---

4. See pp. 49 and 129.

state of facts must be accepted until *the contrary is proven*. No one denies that Mr. Lincoln was once an Infidel. Now let the Christians bring on their evidence, or forever hold their peace. If *truth* will canonize Mr. Lincoln and make him a saint, I shall favor it with all my heart; it is truth which I want for the present and the future—for biography and general history. If Mr. Lincoln changed his views, when was it, where was it, to what extent, and who has the legal and sufficient evidence to establish it? By all means let us hav it now.

Some good men and women say that Mr. Lincoln was a Christian, *because he was a moral man*. They say that he was a *rational* Christian, because he loved morality. Do not other people, who are not Christians, love morality? Morality is not *the* test of Christianity, by any means. If it is a test, then all moral men—Atheists, Agnostics, Infidels, Mohammedans, Buddhists, Mormons, and the rest, are Christians. A *rational* Christian is an anomaly—an impossibility—because when reason is left free it demands proofs; it relies on experience, observation, logic, nature, laws, and constant modes of operation. Why not call Mr. Lincoln a *rational* Buddhist, a *rational* Mohammedan, a *rational* Confucian, a *rational* Mormon? for all these, if true to their faith, love morality. The true test of Christianity is this: Did man fall as related in the Bible, and was Jesus the only begotten son of God? Did Mr. Lincoln believe either of these propositions? He did not. I hav never seen the word "Jesus" in any of Mr. Lincoln's productions, and I do not think any other man or woman ever saw it there. *That is a poor Christian, who never mentions Christ, never calls on him for aid, nor invokes him for any purpose.* I hav never seen but once, and that in the Johnson letter, where Mr. Lincoln used the "immortality" in substance or in idea. Mr. Lincoln appeals to God, *but never to Christ, that I hav seen* or remember. It may be otherwise, and if so, the language can be produced. Mr. Lincoln's compositions, speeches, letters, messages, and inaugurals must be read with care. All men in writing use the Christian's terminology, conventional language, and ideas more or less.

I am aware of the fraud committed on Mr. Lincoln in reporting some insane remarks supposed to hav been made by him on the 4th of July, 1864, on the presentation of a Bible to him by the colored people of Baltimore.[5] No sane man ever uttered such folly, and no sane man will ever believe it. That very feeble-minded effort contains such expressions as this: "It (the Bible) is the best gift which God has ever given to man." Speech—human speech—is nothing; human reason is nothing; the human soul is nothing; nor liberty, justice, the printing-press, the continent of America, democratic institutions. These are nothing. Again, the same supposed speech says: "All the good from the savior of the world is communicated to us through this book. But for this book we could *not know right from wrong*." What! human experience, observation, and reason, they do not teach us right from wrong! Every dog, by his natural reason, knows right from wrong; so does the lowest and the highest animal life. Each, in its sphere, knows right from wrong, as to its own kind. So with man. Some thick-headed Bushman just from Africa,

---

5. See §61, n. 7 and §113.

where they kill and cook Christian missionaries for dinner, wrote this speech, most undoubtedly. No one else was sufficient for such a task.

Did Mr. Lincoln believe in prayer as a means of moving God? It is said to me by the Christians, touching Mr. Lincoln's religion: "Did not he, in his parting speech in Springfield in 1861, say: 'I hope *you*, my *friends* will pray that I may receive,'" etc., and to which I say yes. In his last inaugural he said: "Fondly do *we* hope, fervently do *we* pray." These expressions are merely conventional. They do not prove that Mr. Lincoln believed that prayer is a means of moving God. Mr. Lincoln was a shrewd and a long-headed man—a man of his own plans and purposes—a most secretiv man, never opening himself wholly to any one. He was a man of the deepest and profoundest policies; he knew that if he could get the Christians to pray for him he could chain them to himself and throw them against disunion; he used the Christians, *as it were*, as tools. And now let me ask the Christians a question in return: Did not Mr. Lincoln, in his last inaugural, say this: "The Almighty has his own purposes?" If the Almighty has his own purposes, then it is a question of wisdom, will, and power. If God is all-wise, then he knows what is best, and that best he moves by law, universal and eternal, everywhere, underlying and overfloating and ruling matter and mind. If he can know the best, can he will it to be and enforce it? If this is so, will he, through our prayer, change and alter his own plans and purposes to please us lunatics here below? Mr. Lincoln said, in his oft-referred-to inaugural, that God had his own purposes, and that neither the North nor the South had its own way, but that God had.[6] Mr. Lincoln believed, as I understood him, that human prayer did the prayer good; that human prayer was but a drum beat—the taps of the spirit on the living human soul, arousing it to acts of repentance for bad deeds done, or to inspire it to a loftier and a higher effort for a nobler and grander life.

Mr. Lincoln, I say, was a prudent, a wise and politic man, and now let me ask the Christians still another question: Did Mr. Lincoln, in his said inaugural, say, "Both read the same *word of God?*" No, because that would be admitting revelation. He *did* say, "both read the same Bible." Did Mr. Lincoln say, "Yet, if God wills that it (the war) continue till all the wealth piled by the bondman's two hundred and fifty years of unrequited toil shall be sunk, and until every drop of blood drawn by the lash shall be paid with another drawn with the sword," *as was said by God three thousand years ago?* He did not; he was cautious and said, "*as was said three thousand years ago.*" Jove never nods. A Christian would hav said, "*as God said* three thousand years ago." Had Mr. Lincoln uttered the expression "*as God said* three thousand years ago, that would hav been an acknowledgment of divine revelation, inspiration, miraculous conception, the fall, etc., etc This inaugural, in this particular line, is a protest, as it were, against prayer. Mr. Lincoln concludes the sentence alluded to thus, "So still it must be said the judgments of the Lord are true and righteous altogether." No one can show that Mr. Lincoln believed in inspiration or revelation, as the Christian world

---

6. "Second Inaugural Address," March 4, 1865, *Collected Works* 8:332–33.

contends; he did not deign—did not think fit—to say what it was or who it was that said, "*as said* three thousand years ago." I never heard Mr. Lincoln use the word *infinit* God. He uses the word *maker* in the Johnson letter, and means by the word God the same as *maker*, leaving the idea indefinit. Had Mr. Lincoln believed that God was infinit, he would hav said it. If he ever used the word infinit God, I hav failed to remember it. If I am mistaken in any point touching *any fact* of Mr. Lincoln's life, I shall gladly and with pride revoke it, and make that revocation public.

Mr. Lincoln delivered a lecture in this city in 1837, before the Young Men's Lyceum, which I heard.[7] It was published in the Sangamon *Journal* early in 1838, as I remember. The burthen of that lecture was to show the necessity, *in the state*, of *law* and *order*. In his messages and inaugurals while president, he struggled for *union* and *liberty*. To condense: the inspiration of Mr. Lincoln's *political* life was *law* and *order, liberty* and *union. Religiously*, Mr. Lincoln was an Infidel—a Liberal. In his *philosophy* he was a realist, as opposed to an Idealist; he was a sensationalist as opposed to an intuitionalist; and was a Materialist, as opposed to a Spiritualist. As a *logician*, he lived on facts, figures, and principles. In short, Mr. Lincoln was a material, practical man—a wise, long-headed, deep-policied man, and one of the very best, greatest, and noblest of mankind.

Your friend,
W. H. HERNDON.

The Truth Seeker, *March 10, 1883*[8]

118. *To Isaac N. Arnold*

Springfield Ills Decr. 27th 1882

Friend Arnold—

Your good natured note, dated the 18th inst, is at hand. I guess it is true that, if you and I were to sit down together we could nearly agree about Lincoln's religion. Once define what was a *rational* Christian—what are the great *fundamental* principles of Christianity, then we could agree or disagree and say—yes or no. We will leave this subject for a short while.

I am glad of an opportunity to explain what I wished to say. Soon after Mr Lincoln's death, and for some time before, I took notes of what Mr Lincoln said and did. About this time—say in the Spring of 1865: Holland came into my office and asked me many questions in relation to Mr Lincoln. I answered all willingly & truthfully. He then asked me—"What about Mr Lincoln's religion", and to which I replied— *"The less said the better"*. He then made this expression— *"O never mind, I'll fix that"* with a kind of a wink and a nod. As a matter of course he went and saw

---

7. "Address before the Young Men's Lyceum of Springfield, Illinois," January 27, 1838, *Collected Works* 1:108–15.

8. Reprinted by *The Truth Seeker* from the January 1883 issue of *The Liberal Age*, no copy of which could be located.

Mr Bateman, and received from him *some* account of Lincoln's religion.[1] Holland's life of Lincoln came out in 1866 I think. I read it—saw what Bateman said—went to see Bateman, and said to him—"Bateman, in order to make Lincoln a technical christian *you have made him a hypocrite*." (for much of this see Holland's preface pge 7: see Holland 241 Lamon 492–7) Bateman looked puzzled—or ashamed. We then kindly conversed together. I told Bateman that the story was false. Bateman told me that Lincoln and himself at the time of their interview were comparative strangers and that Lincoln said to him—"Come here Mr School Master." It was at this moment that Lincoln related the facts about his little political book—containing the names of Christian ministers &c. &c. (See Holland 236–9). I took down notes of Bateman's conversation, and showed them to him, after they were written out, and he confessed to their substantial correctness: they are dated the 3d—12—& 28 Dec. 1866 (See Lamons Ln 496. *Read* my whole letter in Lamon 492–97. I was determined to *rip this great lie up by the roots*, and so wrote the Abbott letter[2] (see Lamon's Lincoln 492–7. This letter has never been answered by man nor woman: it stands, and will forever stand. Here the matter rested till James A. Reed delivered a lecture here in 1873, I think; and which is published in Scribners for July 1873 or 4.[3] In this lecture I am attacked severely—called a liar &c. &c. It was not necessary to call me a liar. I replied to this lecture in 1874.[4] I still, in my lecture, kept cool and simply called Reed the truthful minister: he had relied on some things that were false & I proved them so.

Now comes the material point that I am most concerned about. In gathering up and collecting the facts of Mr Lincoln's life I examined hundreds of witnesses and among them were Matheny—Stuart, and others.[5] My notes all or pretty much all ran thus—Matheny says—"*I* knew Mr Lincoln from &c &c." I let them, in my notes, all use the word *I*. So with Stuarts testimony as well as others. Some of my evidences were by letters—*signed* notes, & my own loose notes not signed nor witnessed. Lamon's life came out in 1872. Upon this Reed, as it appears, went and saw Matheny—Stuart, and others; and asked them if they ever wrote those notes, as put down in Lamon's Life. Unfortunately the notes are quoted—fixed—or put in such a way as to *seem* that the notes were written by the men whose names they bear. This was Lamon's *fault*: he calls the Matheny note a *letter* which is not exactly true. Reed gets Matheny and Stuart to say substantially—"*I did not write that thing*—." In this they told the truth, *but not the whole truth*. The whole truth is just here—: They talked, and I wrote down what they said, as I understood them—did it at the time and place—honestly—fairly & squarely. I do not say that Matheny did or didn't sign & attest the note. I do not *now* say that the conversation was or wasn't private. I am ready to discuss those points when they arise. Stuart did not sign the notes. Mr. Matheny says substantially,

---

1. For background on the contention over Bateman and Holland, see §43, n. 3.
2. See §89.
3. See §115, n. 1.
4. 1873. See §115, n. 2.
5. A longtime friend of AL, James Matheny was groomsman at AL's wedding to Mary Todd. John T. Stuart was AL's first law partner.

in his letter to Reed, that he would not have let those notes go out to the world, as covering *the whole of Mr. Lincoln's life:* the notes don't pretend to do it: There stand the figures *1834 to 1860* in the notes: they expressly limit Mr Matheny's evidence to *1860*, and do not cover his Lincoln's whole life, nor pretend to. Mr Matheny again says the notes were *private* ones. In what sense were they private? They were taken when no person was present except ourselves—but they were to be used, if I needed them—if attacked. They would do me no good without that privilege. Again, Mr Matheny says substantially that these notes were his discon-nected sayings rather, a mere collection of sayings &c. This is a mistake: the note was written *all at once*, as it appears on its face (see Lamon 487–9 and *read* it). Mr Matheny again says in his letter to Reed, that Mr Lincoln—about the years—say 1859–65 *investigated* the subject of Christianity. Good God—Lincoln *investigated* Christianity in these years! *You* & every intelligent citizen know that Mr Lincon was a fire blazing hot and high with his ambition, and his duty. Matheny says to me that he knows nothing of Mr Lincolns investigations into Christianity. Now comes a *nib*—Mr Matheny *never wrote the Reed letter*—he knows nothing about Mr Lincolns investigation into the *"great fundamentals"* of Christianity as stated in that Letter to Reed. You may ask me the question—" Herndon—"How do you know that Matheny did not write the Reed letter" (See Scribner for July 1873, I think & Lamon & Holland for much of what is here said in this letter. Read the articles in full, for I refer to them for certainty *as to what Reed—Matheny—Stuart myself & others say*)—In answer to the above questions I say I know it—1st Because the language is not Mr Matheny's—: 2dly Because the thoughts—ideas—opinions are not Mr Matheny's; & 3dly Because Mr Matheny told me that he *did not write it*, & *who did*, though he signed it hastily & unthoughtedly. Mr. Matheny admits indirectly that he was interviewed—does not deny the substance of what is in his note in Lamon. I never said that Matheny wrote that note—never thought or dreamed of saying so—all I do say is—*for the present*—that *he talked*, & *I wrote.* Mr Matheny inferentially admits that he was reported correctly—except as stated herein. Can you tell me where we differ?

Now about Mr Stuart—Mr Stuart admits that he was interviewed. He admits inferentially that he is reported correctly, except in this—"I could not have said that Doct Smith *tried* to convert Mr. Lincoln *as late as 1858* and couldn't do it". It appears from Stuarts letter to Reed that Doct Smith & Lincoln became acquainted about the year 1848. Inferentially it is admitted by Mr Stuart that between 1848 & at the time that I interviewed him, and took his notes that "Doct Smith tried to convert Mr Lincoln from Infidelity and couldn't do it." The difference between us is in *dates*—not in substance, but I repeat that Mr Stuart said what I make him say in those notes. I took those notes in 1865—his letter to Reed is dated Decr 1872., seven years after the notes were taken. When Mr Stuart commenced his *hearsay* evidence in this interview I quit taking notes & when *he got back on facts* I took notes. This I did in all cases. For this reason I wrote to Doctr Smith of Scotland for his *knowledge—not hearsay*—you will find Smiths letter in "Scribner, and in Reed's lecture. Smith writes to me, and uses language that means nothing—any one can say the same thing or believe such language: the language won't do for this critical age *on such a question as this*. Does Smith take us for fools. I admit to you *again and again* that Stuart *did not* write the notes—nor is it his language—nor did he ever see the notes till published so far as I know or believe. I never said he wrote the notes—never thought nor dreamed of saying it—Reed assumes that I did say so, and then, on that assumption, called me a liar. Here is his only reason. Is this mode of argument gentlemanly? I answered the Reed lecture in 1874 and only called Reed a trusting minister—overwhelmed his lecture by evidence: he then *got angry* and wrote a letter or letters in 1880 to some one in Ohio which or part of his letter was published: he in that letter substantially said that I was "a vile infidel & a liar—a knave and a drunkard." In Octr 1881—about the 10th of Octr I denied this letter in the State Register. This thing these charges flew around the country for years. The Cherryvale Globe news caught up the story. I made it correct the lie, and in a *mad fit* I wrote my card with corrections, which I sent you: it was bitter I admit, but it is true nevertheless.[6] You have the whole story now. I refer to Scribner for July 1873, I think, for certainty as to what Reed—Matheny—Stuart and others say. I quote in this letter only *substantively* and sometimes reason *inferentially*. I refer to Holland—and I refer to Lamon on this special subject—Lamon at pgs in 487–97 In the Lamon *Abbott* letter for *one* (495) great &c, read *our* great & good & merciful &c: it was corected in 1870. Supposing that Reed—Matheny—Stuart—Smith & others are wholy in the right, and *I am wholy in the wrong* that does not make Lincoln a Christian as the world understands that word. The difference between Matheny—Stuart & myself *is a little thing*, and yet I sincerely wish to stand upright—fair and square before the world and I'll do that if I can.

Now *you*, my good friend, *seem to have forgotten what I have said in writing*, if you ever read it. You, in your letter to me of date 18th Dec. 1882, ask me "What about the Lincoln-Johnson letter to be found at page 336 in Lamon"?[7] My answer is—turn to Lamon at pge 495.—to my Abbott letter—and you will see what I think of it. I quote it and stick to it, and *it seems* to me to be an honest utterance. It was published in 1870 before Lamons book was written. Mr Lincoln *here* by *many* was thought & firmly believed to be an Atheist, and to clear up this ground I published the letter and quoted it. That is what I think of the Lincoln-Johnson letter. I have studied this question—slept by it, and *know* what I am talking about—am guarded in all directions.

Now about Bateman & Holland. I hear that both are dead, and it is my opinion, founded on what Holland said to me—"O I'll fix that"—On what I *know* and believe—On my experience, that *Holland* is the man to censure. Bateman hated, *in my opinion*, to expose Holland and injure Holland's enterprise. Bateman in his

---

6. For the "Card and Correction" letter, see §115.

7. AL to John D. Johnston, January 12, 1851, *Collected Works*, 2:96–97. In this letter, AL advises that his dying father "call upon, and confide in, our great, and good, and merciful Maker; who will not turn away from him in any extremity."

letter to you evaded the question, & I am sorry for it. You may now with all the lights before you, review the subject in your life of Lincoln just as you please.

Your Friend

W H Herndon

You may show this letter to any one. I do not care who it is. The letter is hastily written. I will send you a copy of my lecture in reply to Reed, if I can find one.

CHM: William H. Herndon Collection

119. To the Editor of *The Truth Seeker*[1]

[Post December 4, 1882]

Sir:

I wrote a letter on Dec. 4, 1882, for the *Liberal Age* touching Mr. Lincoln's religion. I could not in that letter—a long one—conclude the whole subject of it, but will finish it in this. These two letters will, I think, settle in the minds of the people their opinions of Mr. Lincoln's ideas of religion forever.* [*Footnote:* *When I laid down a proposition in my prior letter to you that had Lincoln said that God uttered the quotations which he uses that would hav been an admission an acknowledgement of divine revelation, etc. I meant it would be inferentially so to some minds but not so to all minds. Mr. Lincoln cut up by the roots in these sentences such an inference, by not uttering the words, "God said it." Lincoln was wise, shrewd, foreseeing.]

Let me say in the first place something in relation to Mr. Lincoln's mind—its qualities and characteristics. If there ever was a man who required precision and exactness of language to convey his clean-cut idea, it was Mr. Lincoln. There was in him a clearness and precision in language in all that he said; he was so clean and clear that he could not be misunderstood, nor long misrepresented. Mr Lincoln's ideas and language were clean-cut and deeply stamped, like golden eagles just dropped from the mint, ringing current upon the counters of the intellectual world; he required a certainty to a certain intent in every particular, as the foundation of his beliefs. Mr. Lincoln was a terribly secretiv man—a very cautious man—a man who kept his own thoughts; he was, generally speaking, as secretiv and reticent in his ideas, purposes, and intents as the eternal silences themselvs. If there ever was a man born of woman in this world who did not, as a general rule, let his right hand know what his left hand was doing, it was Lincoln. I would earnestly advise all men to read Holland's "Life of Lincoln," at pages 241–2, and to see for themselvs the estimate which the people of Springfield put on Mr. Lincoln; he lived in this city twenty-five years, and yet no two men, scarcely, agreed in their

---

1. This letter may have been prompted, in part, by an inquiry from the editor of *The Truth Seeker*, E. M. Macdonald, about what WHH had said in his *New York Tribune* letter of November 24, 1882 (see §116). For Macdonald's letter, see *The Truth Seeker*, March 10, 1883, 152. For WHH's reply, see §120.

opinion of the man whom the world thought it knew so well. Had it not been for a few wise, and brave ones too, Mr. Lincoln would hav been in a hundred years or less a mere myth.

No man has better understood the qualities and characteristics of Mr. Lincoln's mind, in a special line, than the good Bishop Simpson. He says in his funeral oration over the dead body of the great emancipator this: "If you would ask me on what mental characteristics his [Lincoln's] greatness rested, I answer: On a quick and ready reception of *facts*, . . . and on a *logical* turn of mind, which *followed sternly* and *unwaveringly* every link in the chain of thought on every subject which he was called to investigate, . . . and by a *determination to perceive the truth in all its relations and simplicity; and when found, utter it.*"[2] This is exact, true, and well said. These remarks—this oration—was made in Springfield, Ill., in 1865, when Mr. Lincoln was finally placed in the tomb. I now and here wish to pay the good bishop a deserved compliment. In the delivery of this oration at the tomb of Lincoln, the good bishop did not say a word about Mr. Lincoln's Christianity, as I now recollect it; he suppressed no truth and suggested no falsehood. Doctor Gurley, Mr. Lincoln's pastor at Washington, was in Springfield at the time, and Doctor Gurley and Bishop Simpson were seen, as I am informed, in a private conversation together, as supposed. These men knew—or had reason to know—Mr. Lincoln's religious views, and though they were under strong temptations to proclaim Mr. Lincoln's Christianity, if it was the case, to the world, yet their honor, their integrity, their manhood, and their love of truth, forbade it. All honor to such men who stand firm, when temptation—strong temptation—is trampled under foot, and truth thrown high in the sky. But no voice came from the silent tomb—from the nerveless and voiceless tongue of Lincoln—to the good men on that day to be telegraphed over the wires of the world that "I am a Christian." Here was the place and the time and the occasion, if ever, to proclaim Mr. Lincoln's Christianity to mankind if such was the case. But the silences, the eternal silences, ruled and reigned supreme.

Bishop Simpson said that Lincoln searched logically for the truth, and when found, he had *the courage to utter it.* I wish to make an application of this truth. Mr. Lincoln did, in 1835–36, search for the truth, and found it to his entire satisfaction; and *did declare his Infidelity* by writing a little book against Christianity. Again, if Mr. Lincoln changed his views as expressed in 1835–36 he did it in on logical investigation. If he did investigate that subject anew, who knows that fact? If he changed his original opinion he had *the courage to utter it.* Who knows that fact of change? If any one knows these facts, let him by all means tell it. Mr. Lincoln never investigated the subject but once, and that in 1835–36; he never changed his opinions from that year to the day of his death. I may here say that Bishop Simpson on that day—the day when he delivered his funeral oration at the tomb of Lincoln, in the presence of twenty or thirty thousand people—fell into a terrible

---

2. Matthew Simpson, *Funeral Address Delivered at the Burial of President Lincoln, at Springfield, Illinois, May 4, 1865,* (New York: Carlton and Porter, 1865), 10–11.

mistake. I heard Mr. Lincoln deliver a speech in this city in 1839 against Martin Van Buren and his administration. The speech was grandiloquent—a mere boyish effort, so to speak.[3] Bishop Simpson takes that speech of 1839 against Van Buren and quotes it as delivered in 1859 against slavery and the slave power.[4] Those who wish to investigate the subject will turn to Holland's "Life of Lincoln," at pages 534–5, and to Lamon's "Life of Lincoln," at pages 232–7. The most nicely critical and veracious biographer, Doctor Holland, then pays this high compliment to the speech of 1839, supposing it to hav been delivered in 1859—a speech against Van Buren in 1839—as a speech delivered in 1859 against slavery. Hear him: "No inspiration finer than this breathes in any of Mr. Lincoln's utterances. It almost seems as if an intimation of his life and death were given to him at the moment—as if a glimpse into his own and his country's future had been vouchsafed to his excited vision."[5] This sounds most ridiculous to me, who heard the speech in 1839. This error is carried on in a book recently published in New York, called "The Lincoln Memorial Album" (see page 78).[6] One more word about Bishop Simpson, and no more: he wrote the introduction to this memorial album, and in it he says no word about Lincoln's Christianity. Would to heaven that all Christians were such as this honest, truthful Christian man. All honor to him! The above errors were mere mistakes, accidentally and honestly made; but, were I to make such, hades would be my doom, because I am a Liberal in my religious views. I can do a Christian justice, but woe to me if I, though human, err.

I hav a good Christian neighbor who now, at least in spirit, is looking over my shoulder, saying: "Herndon, you are always invoking some person's word as proof of Mr. Lincoln's infidelity. Why do you not quote something that Lincoln himself says?" In reply to my good Christian neighbor and friend, let me say: Now you hav asked of me a favor, and will you in return do me a similar kindness? I then shall willingly comply with the wish of my friend. In 1842 I heard Mr. Lincoln deliver a speech before the Washingtonian Temperance Society of this city. The original Washingtonians were men who had just crawled out of the gutter, with the mud and dirt fresh on their faces. Many of the Christians of this city twisted up their noses at the men who had risen up from degradation, struggling to be men once more. These men, as contended by the quasi aristocracy, were low men—base-born men, unfit to lecture to the *elite* of the city. This was the feeling here among the Christians somewhat. Mr. Lincoln delivered a lecture before that society, taking the part of the poor unfortunates in the fight. He scored the Christians for the position they had taken. He said in that lecture this: "If they" (the Christians) "believe, *as they profess*—that Omnipotence condescended to take on himself the form of sinful man," etc.* [*Footnote:* *The meaning of the whole sentence—a long one—is this: "If the Christians believe, as they pretend, that God condescended to take upon himself the form of man for man's sake, surely the

---

3. "Speech on the Sub-Treasury," December [26], 1839, *Collected Works*, 1:159–79.
4. Though Simpson did indeed misidentify this attack on Van Buren as an attack on slavery, he correctly identified the date of the speech as 1839. Simpson, *Funeral Address*, 17–18.
5. Holland, 535.
6. Oldroyd.

Christians should stoop a little in this world to save the drunkards from utter and eternal ruin."]⁷ This was spoken with energy; he scornfully and contemptuously emphasized the words "*as they profess.*" The insult was as much possibly in the manner of utterance as in the substance of what was said. I heard the criticisms of some of the Christians that night. They said the speech was an insult and an outrage. Remember, Mr. Lincoln was fresh from Menard county, where he wrote his work on Infidelity in 1835–6, his temperance lecture being in 1842. In this same lecture he said, in reference to denunciation by the temperance lecturer of the rum-seller, that it begot denunciation in return. His words are as follows: "To hav expected them not to meet denunciation with denunciation, crimination with crimination, anathema and anathema, was to expect a reversal of human nature, *which is God's decree and can never be reversed.*"⁸ "But was not Mr. Lincoln a man of prayer?" asks my friend who is looking over my shoulder, and to whom I reply substantially in Mr. Lincoln's language just quoted: *God's decree, and can never be reversed by human prayer.* I quote from the original lecture, written out by Mr. Lincoln himself and published in the Sangamon *Journal* in 1842, and likewise from the Lincoln Memorial Album, pages 87–94.⁹ Mr. Lincoln, in his farewell address to the citizens of Springfield in 1861, says: "I hope *you,* my friends, will pray that I may receive,"¹⁰ etc. He means those who believe in the efficacy of prayer as a means of moving God from his decrees. He does not say *I* pray. In his last inaugural he says: "Fervently do *we* pray." He means fervently do we as a people pray; he does not say *I* pray. It is my opinion that no man ever heard Mr. Lincoln pray, in the true evangelical sense of that word. His philosophy is against all human prayer, as a means of reversing God's decrees. If any man ever heard Mr. Lincoln pray, as the word "prayer" is understood in the Christian world, by all means let us hav the truth. When did he pray? Where did he pray? What was his attitude and position? What did he say?—and all about it. Let me say here that to pray is no evidence, of itself, of a man's Christianity; and yet it is important to know the truth in this matter. Let the witness write out a letter under his own hand and seal, and giv his honor as to the truth of what is said. By all means let the truth come, though the heavens fall.

Mr. Lincoln used to say to me that the great, leading law of human nature was motivs, and that at the bottom was pure selfishness; that all human actions reflectivly speaking, were moved by motivs; "that negroes, like other people, act upon motivs."¹¹ He has told me often that there was no freedom in the human will,

---

7. AL's sentence reads in full: "If they believe, as they profess, that Omnipotence condescended to take on himself the form of sinful man, and, as such, to die an ignominious death for their sakes, surely they will not refuse submission to the infinitely lesser condescension, for the temporal, and perhaps eternal salvation, of a large, erring, and unfortunate class of their own fellow creatures." "Temperance Address," February 22, 1842, *Collected Works*, 1:277–78.

8. Ibid., 273.

9. Oldroyd.

10. WHH here quotes approximately from a version of AL's Farewell Address of February 11, 1861. See *Collected Works*, 4:190.

11. A reference to language used in AL's letter of August 26, 1863 to James C. Conkling. See *Collected Works*, 6:409.

and no punishment beyond this world. *He denied God's higher law*, and wrote on the margin of a newspaper to his friends in the Chicago Convention in 1860 this: "Lincoln agrees with Seward in his irrepressible conflict-idea; but he is opposed to Seward's *higher law*." This paper was handed to Judge Davis, Judge Logan, and other friends. I do not know the particular one this paper was handed to. Mr. Lincoln used to say, "What is to be, will be; and what is, is right—if men could only see all the facts and consequences at one good broad look." This was his fatalistic idea. In his last inaugural he said this: "Woe unto the world, for it must *needs* be that offenses come; but woe to the man by whom the offense cometh." What is the meaning of the words *must needs*? Needs means *necessity*. Then offenses of *necessity must* come, and there is no hope that they will not come, and no human prayers can arrest their inevitable coming. No Greek ever held firmer to fatalism, substantially, than Mr. Lincoln. Now what becomes of prayer?

I wish now to quote a somewhat lengthy extract from one of Mr. Lincoln's letters, written in 1864, to a lady, I think, in Philadelphia, by the name of Eliza P. Gurney. This extract proves his fatalism—his philosophy—and all that I hav ever said about it. The extract is as follows:

"The purposes of the Almighty are perfect and *must prevail*, though we erring mortals may fail to accurately see them in advance. We hoped for a happy termination of this terrible war long before this, *but God knows best and has ruled otherwise*. We yet shall acknowledge his wisdom and our errors therein; meanwhile we must work earnestly in the *best light he givs us*, trusting that so working still conduces *to the great end he ordains*. Surely he intends some great good to follow this mighty convulsion, *which no mortal could make* and no mortal could stay." (See the Lincoln Memorial Album, p. 338.)[12]

Here then is the declaration of the perfect idea of God—that his ideas must prevail—that God knew best when the war should end—that he has ruled otherwise than men's wishes—*reason*, not revelation, is the *best light he givs us—that no mortal could make this mighty convulsion*, and *no mortal could stay the great end he ordains*. I infer, only infer, that Mr. Lincoln means by the *best light he givs* us that of reason; he does not say revelation—he does not say *has* given us, but *givs* us. The italics are mine in this letter wherever used.

Again, I wish to quote an extract from Mr. Lincoln's inaugural, the last one; it is as follows: "Both read the same Bible and pray to the same God; and each invokes his aid against the other. It may seem strange that any man should dare to ask a just God's assistance in wringing their bread from the sweat of other men's faces, but let us judge not lest we be judged. *The prayer of both could not be answered. That of neither has been answered fully. The Almighty has his own purposes.* Woe unto the world because of offenses, for it *must needs be that offenses come*, but

---

12. Copying from Oldroyd, WHH makes a few minor copying errors. See AL to Eliza P. Gurney, September 4, 1864, *Collected Works*, 7:535.

woe to the man by whom the offense cometh." (See Arnold's Lincoln and Slavery, pages 625–7).[13]

Here Mr. Lincoln nails his religion and his philosophy on every man's door, and bids each read for himself under the severe penalties of ignorance and error. Take all these quotations from authentic documents, beginning in 1842 and running up to 1866, and you hav his religion and his philosophy. The tendency of Mr. Lincoln was to a scientific Materialism—evolution—though, if his Johnson letter be his convictions, without denying soul, heaven, God. His idea of God was a kind of "Sufficient Cause," a mere *maker*, and that is as far as human reason can reach, fully admitting the force of the argument of plans and adaptations in nature; it can logically climb no higher, struggle and toil as it may forever.

My good Christian friend, I hav now referred to Mr. Lincoln's religious ideas and opinions, and, to do this fairly, I hav quoted authentic documents, coming from Mr. Lincoln's own brain and pen; and now will *you* hav the kindness to show me by like documents when and where Mr. Lincoln believed in the fall of man, as related in the Bible; when and where did he believe that Jesus was the Christ of God, his truly and only begotten Son, as the Christian world contends; when and where did Mr. Lincoln believe in special revelation, special inspiration, special miracle, special providence, the efficacy of prayer as a means of moving God to alter his laws, ordinances, or decrees; and when and where did Mr. Lincoln change his religious belief, as uttered in 1835 down to 1866? Come, be fair and square. If you cannot produce such authentic documents which proofs no one questions or disputes, then cease teaching the good people to believe a falsehood. Cease cheating the mind out of its wish for truth.

I wish to giv an illustration of the uncertainty and unreliability of those loose things that float around in the newspapers of the day, and how liable things are to be inaccurate—so made even by the best of men. Mr. Lincoln, in the morning he started for Washington to take the oath of office, and to be inaugurated as president of this great republic, gave a short farewell address to his old friends. It was eloquent and touching. That speech is copied in Holland's "Life of Lincoln," in Arnold's "Lincoln and Slavery," and in Lamon's "Life of Lincoln," and no two are *exactly* alike.[14] Two of them substantially agree. If it is hard to get the exact truth on such an occasion as this, how impossible it is to get at Mr. Lincoln's sayings which hav been written out by men weeks and months after what he did say hav passed by! All these loose and foolish things that Mr. Lincoln is supposed to hav said are like the cords of driftwood, floating on the bosom of the great Mississippi, down to the great gulf of—Forgetfulness. Let them go.

It appears that in 1864, say in July, the colored people of Baltimore presented Lincoln with a superb copy of the Bible. One of the colored men who presented the Bible made some remarks at the time and on the occasion; and most undoubt-

13. "Second Inaugural Address," *Collected Works*, 8:333.

14. For the various versions of this speech that were reported and for the version AL wrote out afterwards, see "Farewell Address at Springfield, Illinois," February 11, 1861, *Collected Works*, 4:190–91.

edly Mr. Lincoln made a short reply. The supposed, the fraudulent, speech of Mr. Lincoln is copied in Carpenter's "Six Months in the White House," and in the Lincoln Memorial Album, and in McPherson's "History of the War," of which last I hav only a copy furnished me by a friend. No two of these exactly agree. Two of them substantially do. Now two things are certain: 1st. That Mr. Lincoln did not write it; and 2d. That some one did; and now the question comes, when was it written out? How long was it written out, as printed, after Mr. Lincoln did make his remarks in fact? My information is that Lincoln's remarks were made about July 4th, 1864; and that the speech—the supposed one—appeared in the papers about September the 5th, 1864—two months or more after the supposed speech was made.[15] In that speech Mr. Lincoln is made to say this: "But for that book we could not know right from wrong." Does any human being, in his sane moments, believe that Lincoln ever uttered this insane speech? What did the whole race of man do to know right from wrong for a half million years or more before this book, this so-called revelation, was given to the world, if such was the case? What do those millions of people now living, who never heard of this book, do to know how to distinguish right from wrong? How about the hundreds of millions who hav died, who never heard of this book? How did the struggling race of man build up its grand civilization in the world before this book was given to mankind? A civilization quite as high in some respects as this existed before Moses and Jesus. Was Lincoln a fool, an ass, or a hypocrit, or a combination of them; or is this speech—this supposed—this fraudulent speech, a lie—a bald, naked lie?

I wish to make one more quotation, and then I shall be done with this subject, probably forever. It appears, only appears, from what is said below that Mr. Lincoln and a minister, whose name is kept in the dark, had a conversation about religion. It appears that Mr. Lincoln said that when his son—bone of his bone, flesh of his flesh, and blood of his own heart pulse—died, though a severe affliction, it did not arouse him to think of Christ; but when he saw the *graves* of so many soldiers—strangers to him—not in his nativ or adopted state—men who were not of his blood, bone, and warm heart pulse, that sad sight aroused him to love Jesus. I shall now quote the words as I find them in the Lincoln Memorial Album published in New York in 1882, page 336. Says Lincoln: "When I left Springfield I asked the people to pray for me. I was not a Christian. When I buried my son, the severest trial of my life, I was not a Christian; but when I went to Gettysburg and saw the *graves* of thousands of our soldiers, *I then and there consecrated myself to Christ. I do* love Jesus."[16] It is a fine thing for the reputation of the "Illinois clergyman" that his name is to the world unknown. It is a most heartless thing, this supposed conversation of Lincoln with the Illinois clergyman. What! Lincoln feel more for the *graves* of strangers than for the death of his once living, loving, and lovable son, now dead, moldering to ashes in the silent tomb! This charge is

---

15. According to *Collected Works*, this presentation and AL's extemporaneous remarks took place on September 7. The confusion about the July 4 date may have arisen because the presentation inscription in the Bible is dated July 4, 1864. See *Collected Works*, 7:542–43. See also §61, n. 6.

16. See Oldroyd, 366.

barbarous, savage. To make Lincoln a lover of Jesus, whom he once ridiculed, this minister makes him a savage—just as he once was made a hypocrit to make him an Evangelical Christian, as was done by Dr. Holland in his "Life of Lincoln." I hav no word by which to utter my feelings that burst up as I read the above quotations; and did I express myself fully and freely, I probably should go too far. I, however, brand this "Illinois clergyman"—this person—as a liar, a wilful liar; a mean libeler of the great dead.

I wish, in conclusion, to make a correction, and it is this: In the Abbot letter, written by me in 1870, there was a typographical error in one word, and that one word I want changed. The word is *one*; it should be read *our*. So the correct reading will be, "*our* great and good and merciful *maker*." Mr. Abbot, in the next issue after my letter appeared in the columns of his paper, corrected the error, and I hav done so several times since.

W. H. HERNDON

The Truth Seeker, *February 24, 1883*

120. To E. M. MacDonald, Editor, The Truth Seeker[1]

Springfield, Ill., Feb. 8, 1883

My Friend:

In my letter to a minister of the gospel in New York I was afraid to say that Mr. Lincoln was *not* a Christian. I went in that line as far as I thought I could succeed. This is my reason for not saying that Lincoln was not a Christian. If I erred, you know the reason. On the whole, I think the letter is plain enough—think the good people will understand it.

The Truth Seeker, *March 10, 1883*

121. To the Editor of the Daily Illinois State Journal

Springfield, Sept. 22 [1883]

To the Editor of the State Journal.

In the columns of the daily JOURNAL, of the 1st day of September, 1883, I find a communication from "Gath," correspondent of the Cincinnati *Enquirer*, which purports to be a true account of an interview between the Hon. Milton Hay, of this city, and "Gath," alias G. A. Townsend, held at Saratoga, sometime in the month of August last. The letter or communication is taken by you, as I am informed, for the *Enquirer*, date unknown to me.

---

1. The March 10, 1883 issue of *The Truth Seeker* reprinted WHH's letter of November 24, 1882, to an unnamed New York clergyman. Editor Macdonald reported that on seeing this letter, he wrote to WHH asking him why, when he had written in *The Truth Seeker* that AL was "an unbeliever in the Christian religion," he wrote to the minister as he did. This letter is WHH's response.

The article is untruthful. It was so meanly treacherous to Mr. Hay, in "Gath," that Hay was forced, by his innate love of truth and justice, to deny the correctness, the truthfulness, and justice of the letter quoted by you, if so quoted. I refer to Mr. Hay's letter denying the truthfulness and correctness of "Gath's" letter, which will be found in THE STATE JOURNAL (Daily) Sept. 8, 1883. I kindly thank Mr. Hay for it. All blind, infatuated, and wild hero-worshipers, all over this broad land, fairly ache to get at something which they hope will injure me in order that, by my injury, they can lift up to a higher level what they so superstitiously worship—a myth. The letter of "Gath," so far as it speaks of myself, in the interview with Hay, is false—viciously false, indeed.

I wish now to answer the letter of "Gath" myself, and will do so because no one knows the facts of the case as well as I do. When I make the revelation—tell the truth of the business—I hope the chatty and gossipy world will feel easy, contented and calm about the story. The question which has so much bothered the world—*i.e.* Did Lincoln give me, or offer to give me, an office during his administration? I will finally and forever settle. The reason why I have not done so before is because the subject matter was a private affair between Lincoln and myself. Before making a revelation of the matter I wish to dispose of some few charges, or allegations, of Gath.

1.—"Gath" Asks Hay: "Has not Herndon disseminated a great many views of Mr. Lincoln, which are merely his own theories and vagaries?" and to which I reply for myself, that in 1838–40, Mr. Lincoln, at Bell's store, in this city, made me what I am in religion by his "theories and vagaries?" This is known in this city by a few of my friends. Again "You see," so says Gath—rather he makes Mr. Hay say, "Herndon was a man that Lincoln picked up; he was a poor, forlorn fellow, who got on the right side of Lincoln." It would be quite as true to say, "You see, Lincoln was a poor, forlorn fellow, who got on the right side of Herndon." Gath says further, "It was Herndon's poverty and hard luck that made Lincoln take to him." The truth about this matter is just this: I, according to the best of my recollection, was at that time, in 1844, the monied man of the firm. My ambition ran in that direction at that time and it is equally as true, at that time, that I was *possibly* as popular a man as Lincoln, and *possibly* as good a lawyer soon thereafter. I was not at that time, a poor, forlorn man, and am not deserted now.

By the way, if the letter of Mr. Lincoln to his step-brother, which will be found in Lamon's Life of Lincoln, at page 336, contains his religion or his religious views, "his theories and vagaries," then he and I totally disagree. In conclusion on this part of the case, Lincoln took me in partnership with him, and held to me till his death, because he could use me to his advantage, and in this he was not disappointed. Lincoln says: "Man acts from motives and he chooses the best." Lincoln is under this universal law, and subject to it.

"Gath" said to Hay: "Mr. Hay, did not Herndon have a grievance against Mr. Lincoln?"[1] "Yes," says Hay, if truthfully reported "There is just where you find so

---

1. This sentence is presumably the beginning of the second item in WHH's list of three.

many statements underrating Lincoln from that source. After Lincoln became President, Herndon went on to Washington City and asked for some office. I do not recollect what it was, if I ever did know. Lincoln wanted to do something for Herndon, but not to give him anything which would expose his weakness in the public service. When he settled on what he would give him—Herndon, whose expectations had been raised very high, became dissatisfied, and returned to Springfield, and was very sour on Lincoln." This was said by Hay to Gath, as reported by Gath, but which is emphatically and with emphasis denied by Hay in the letter referred to in THE JOURNAL of Sept. 8, 1883.

I now wish to state the substantial facts in answer to the above paragraphs. Just a few days before Mr. Lincoln started to Washington City to take the oath of office and become the President of the United States in fact and law, he came into our office and said substantially: "Herndon, do you want to hold any office under my administration?" and to which I thankfully replied—"No, Mr. Lincoln, I do not. I now hold the office of Bank Commissioner of Illinois and besides, I have a good practice in my profession; and if I take office under you, I will lose my practice and my present office." This I said substantially. He then asked me if I wished to hold the Bank Commissioner's office under Gov. Yates, and to which I replied: "I do." Mr. Lincoln then went and saw Gov. Yates and had me continued in office. I heard the conversation between President Lincoln and Gov. Yates—*but dare say no more*, unless pushed to extremes.[2] Further—about the year 1862, I did go on to Washington City for the only and express purpose of getting an office—saw Mr. Lincoln—asked him for an office, and instantly on the request he dropped pen and paper, and did go and speak to some department of the Government for an office—not for myself, but for a friend of mine, Chas. W. Chatterton. I quickly got the office, "freely, without purchase; fully, without denial; and speedily, without delay." Farther, say in 1863, I again, for myself this time, asked Lincoln for an office, as I now remember it. Soon Mr. Lincoln telegraphed me that he wished to give me an office, and mentioned what it was. I telegraphed back to him this: "I accept your proposition," but at the same instant of time I sat down and wrote Mr. Lincoln that I could not accept the office. Not wanting the office I wished to turn it over to a friend, now Judge———; but he could not accept. The reason why I telegraphed back to Lincoln just as I did, was because I did not wish anybody to know anything about our private affairs. The reason why I did not accept the office was because I had to go away from my home and business The dispatches between Lincoln and myself will be found in Springfield and Washington City, and I refer to them for the particulars. In my opinion, I can further say that it is my honest belief that Mr. Lincoln would have willingly given me any office that my ambition had struggled for. Why, then, should I have a greivance against my best friend? Why should I be very sour against Mr Lincoln? He gave me everything

---

2. WHH here hints at what was later revealed in a footnote to his biography of AL, that when AL urged the incoming governor, Richard Yates, to re-appoint WHH, Yates asked for a favor in return. See *Herndon's Lincoln*, 290n.

I wished and asked for. I never had, for one short moment, a grievance against Mr. Lincoln. I never had high expectations about office, was not ambitious nor selfish, and was not disappointed I did not return to Springfield from Washington "sour" against Mr. Lincoln. Mr. Lincoln has conferred on me many favors, and for which I am grateful, but I owe Mr. Lincoln nothing. I paid him for all he did for me one hundred per cent interest per annum with compound interest paid quarterly. I respected the man when living and honor him when dead. I have said that Lincoln was not God, and if this underrates him so be it. I have said and now say that Mr. Lincoln was one of the best, wisest, greatest and noblest of mankind; and if by this acknowledgement I underrate the man, so be it too. Now I hope this great *national* question is settled, and settled forever.

3.—"Gath" says again: "In short, about the only great thing that ever happened Herndon was being taken up by Lincoln", and in answer to which let me say: Gath, you have now entered debatable ground, and assumed that which is not universally conceived, by any means. I have heard other men, equally as wise as "Gath" say: "Herndon, the greatest injury that ever befel you was in going into partnership with Lincoln. He was the elder of the two and overtopped you. He got the credit of all wise acts and good things, and you, for your part, got the disgrace for all foolish ones done by the firm or either of you." I do not assert this. I only repeat what others have often said to me and in my presence to other people.

When Mr. Lincoln returned from Washington, in 1848–9, he came to this city, a broken down and bankrupt politician, caused by his course on the Mexican war, which I tried to prevent (see Lamon's life of Lincoln, page 291 to 294). His old friends in this then Congressional District, for his course in Congress, deserted him. I then stood firmly by Mr. Lincoln and helped him to fight his way upward. In 1854–6 Mr. Lincoln, for the time being, was very unpopular here, caused by his antislavery views and opposition to the enroachments of slavery. His acquaintances and friends would scarcely speak to him or deign to notice him—would not go to hear him justify himself before God and man. I then stood firmly by Mr. Lincoln, and helped him by pen and word, money and tongue, at the bar, in the press, and on the stump, to fight his way up again; and it is said by "Gath" that Lincoln never went to Lincoln & Henderson's office to pour out his soul to Henson.[3] I never said this or even intimated it; but I will give the people a universal law of human nature by which they can judge of the intimacy When men are driven together from a common fear coming from a common foe, as was the case with us in 1854–60, the relation is close and tightly riveted. Then the souls are one, and thoughts are known in the minds of each without utterance loud and long.

I know it is indiscreet to blow one's own horn, but if in this letter I have blown mine pretty loudly and well, I have done so in perfect self-defense. I plead guilty

---

3. This passage references a passage in Gath's interview where Milton Hay, having mentioned the Lincoln and Herndon law office, is quoted as saying, "He [Lincoln] was tolerant and kind to him, but he did not go there to pour out his soul and communicate his thoughts." See "Lincoln's Near Friend," *Daily Illinois State Journal*, September 1, 1883. "Henderson" and "Henson" both should read "Herndon" and were presumably introduced by an inattentive typesetter.

to this extent only. I have kept silent amid outrageous abuse on this question for more than twenty years, and now silence is no longer a virtue.

In conclusion, facts, *facts* are human forces and truth the divinest energy of man. Justice will be done to all men sooner or later, if we are worth weighing. If not worth weighing, all the charities of men will throw a dark veil between us and the critical public gaze. I have been actuated in gathering up the facts of Lincoln's life and publishing them now and then, to the world, by this, that the reading intelligent and reasonable people might have one true biography of a true and great man, who in his day and generation conferred a great boon upon mankind—a biography on which all men could rest in the certain and satisfying belief that the life of Lincoln was not an ideal production of the imagination, but one of solid fact. If I have erred, it is not because I did not love the truth, but because I did not see the facts as they really existed and in all their relations, That is true to any man's mind that sees it as truth. My motives have been good, though I may have erred. I do not claim infallibility, nor do I expect, or hope to please everybody. I was true to myself as I saw things, and had, and have, the courage of my convictions.

Most respectfully yours,
WM. H. HERNDON

Daily Illinois State Journal, *Sept. 24, 1883*

122. To Isaac N. Arnold

Springfield Ills. Octr 24th 83

Mr. Arnold—

I will now answer your 10 or 12 questions. I have got the facts from men, boys & women.—1st The amusements of Mr Lincoln were Chess—Fives—Jokes. Fives are knocking a ball up against a wall. Parties choose sides and play at 5's: it is a fine physical exercise. 2d He gave no dinner parties: he gave what we call *here* evening parties—i e the company collected at L's house say at 7 o'c P.M.—conversed—played—chatted, & went to supper—say at 9 oc. I have no recollection of ever hearing of L's *dinner* party—. 3dly Mr. Lincoln was exceedingly fond of apples, & fruits generally—: he ate apples peculiarly—he clasped his finger—fore finger, and his thumb around the equatorial part of the apple—the stem end being toward his mouth—he never peeled apples—peaches—pears &c 4th His chief guests were politicians mostly—(I have seen Judges—) Legislators &c. &c at his parties—among the men would be such as Hatch—Browning—Stuart—Dubois—Judd—Brown—Edwards[1]—The women would be the wives and daughters of such men—& the belles of the city—young ladies of wit—refinement—&c. *Mrs* Lincoln got up the parties herself & *selected* the aristocracy you may "bet". The suppers were very fine indeed Lincoln would however choose a few of his

---

1. WHH here refers to Ozias N. Hatch, Orville H. Browning, John T. Stuart, Jesse K. Dubois, Norman B. Judd, Christopher C. Brown, Ninian W. Edwards or Benjamin Edwards.

boon companions to make things lively—such men as Peck and other good story tellers—back 'em up in the corner and commence—"Lincoln cant you tell us a good story"—says Peck;[2] and to which Lincoln would say—"*Peck* your question puts me in mind of a story"; and then things would commence and run till the party had broken up, and the guests gone home. Mrs Lincoln would be as mad as a disturbed hornet—would curtain Lecture L all night, till he got up out of bed in despair and went whistling through the streets & alleys till day &c. &c. It would take a ream of paper to write it all out just as it did often happen. *Mrs* Lincoln was stingy & exclusive—avaricious and select—cold & repulsive to visitors that did not suit her cold aristocratic blood. Lincoln dare not ever ask a friend to go to dinner with him, unless he first got *Mrs* Lincoln's *warm*—eager consent, and this was not got often. The house was cold—exclusive and aristocratic, with no soul—fire—cheer or fun in it. Did you ever enter and ice cave in mid summer—eh? No wine—beer—or liquor was ever used at such parties—that I saw or heard of. Mr Lincoln once asked a few of his friends—if he should have wines and he was advised along the lines of his inclination—ie not to have any: he *never* played cards—never drank whiskey—never chewed tobacco—never smoked or snuffed: he drank beer *sometimes* for health purely: he often said to me—"I cant drink—all stimulants are nauseous to me. I claim no credit for being a temperance man". 5thly Mr Lincoln was gone on the circuit *about* 6 mo in the year—rather say from 4 to 6 mo in the year. Logan sometimes would go around—so would Jno T. Stuart—Edwards—Robbins—Baker—Conkling—Ferguson—myself et al. in parts—say N west—North & a short distance East, say to Christian—. In the North Leonard Swet—Scott et al—. In the East & SE Thornton—Vandever—Ficklin Linder et al.[3] The above men generally went to some few places with Lincoln—none went *all around* with him. Lincoln took a wide circuit— his home was *Hell* and he did not wish to burn long nor often—absence from home was his *Heaven*. Lincoln's mode of travel was in a buggy usually with one old horse—"Bob," which he got of James Short[4] about 1843—horse died about 1853–4—6thly. He wrote in our office his legal papers—letters &c on Sunday when not rolling his baby in a little child's wagon on the pavement *"whipt"* whilst his lady went to church. Mr Lincoln would come down to our office & bring Tad & Willie; they would make houses of our books—tear up papers—scatter things generally. Lincoln had no control over them—didn't seem to know that they were in the office—so abstracted was he Mr Lincoln sometimes would go to church as other men do. It was mournful to see Lincoln drug to church. 7thly The routine of Mr Lincoln's daily life, when not on the circuit, was reading the newspapers—telling yarns & cracking his jokes—playing Chess—Fives—. Lincoln was a good Sleeper scarcely ever getting out of bed before 7–8 unless *Mrs* Lincoln

2. Ebenezer Peck, a Democratic politician who converted to Republicanism.

3. Stephen T. Logan, John T. Stuart, Benjamin S. Edwards, Silas (?) Robbins, Edward D. Baker, James C. Conkling, W. J. Ferguson, Leonard Swett, John M. Scott, Anthony Thornton, Horatio (?) VandeVeer, Orlando B. Ficklin, and Usher F. Linder were all lawyers on the Eighth Circuit.

4. A friend from New Salem days.

chucked beat him out with a stick of stove wood in order to make him go to market for some beef for breakfast. He went to bed about 11 oc'l and rose about 7–8. AM. Good God!—Arnold you don't know anything about this house. Mr. Lincoln ate breakfast about 8—dinner about 12 when he dare go home—supper about 6 P.M. Mrs Lincoln kept—when she could keep—one girl. Lincoln kept none—no servant—sometimes sawed his own wood—would curry—feed and attend to his horse—. Mr Lincoln bought a very common carriage about '50 for his little family: it was a common democratic thing. Lincoln on horseback would be a sight—beat anything that Barnum ever had or could by any possibility get. In very early days in the absence of roads he did ride horseback. Old "Bob" wore out and Lincoln got an other horse about '52 called Tom. This was his carriage horse. I do not think that Mr Lincoln was *fond* of horses—dogs—cats—rats or other such animals, *unless* they could be of service to him. I do not think that he was very *fond* of men, unless he could utilize them somehow & for some purpose—. Remember that Mr Lincoln was *a cool practical man always & everywhere, and under all conditions.* If L's children wanted a dog—cat—rat or the Devil it was alright and well treated—housed—petted—fed—fondled &c &c. Could Lincoln Sing? Can a Jack ass whistle or sing? If he Lincoln did try to sing it was some vulgar song. These vulgar songs—jokes &c of Lincoln were not sung or told because they were vulgar: they were sung or told for 2 reasons—1st to sing away the blues & 2dly To shoot a sharp point sharply. Mr L was not a vulgar man naturally: he was by nature a chaste man of fine feeling. Mr. Lincoln's favorite authors are as follow—Burns from 1835 to 1840. Byron from 1839—to 47.—Shakespear from 1835—to 1866. I do not know that Lincoln had any prose authors that were his particular favorites. What Mr Lincoln wanted in literature he looked up just as in his law cases—: he was not a general reader. Mr. Lincoln was not a literary man—had not much ambition that way—he generally read *specially for an end*—was practical—lost no time in the field of speculation, or the impractical—*he read—and read—and read*—newspapers—joked—spilt himself all over our office—his head on the sofa—one foot on the stove—one foot in a chair and his hands and arms round about the chairs—&c.—would read aloud—saying that "I can better understand the case that way, as I have two senses aroused—1st my Eye; and 2d my Ear, and thus I am sure of catching the sense. 9th He wore commonly a black broad cloth suit—of medium fineness—wore a frock tail coat—seduction pants—no cravat or stock or necktie. What Lincoln dance? Could a sparrow imitate an Eagle? Barnum could make more money on Lincoln's dancing than he could on Jumbo. Mr Lincoln had no ear for music except of the old common kind—had no heels for dancing, even our old puncheon floor dances. You have never asked "Did Lincoln love *women*?" "Did he ever write poetry?" Friend—it wouldn't do to be too inquisitive on these points to one who *knows* Mr L.

As to what Mr Lincoln ate—it made no difference to him—he sat down and ate as it were involuntarily, saying nothing: he did not abuse the meal ie what he ate—did not praise it—did not compliment the cook nor abuse her: he sat down and ate and asked no questions, and made no complaints. I have seen him do this as above on the circuit for years: he was a peculiar man: he was as cool as a cucumber and as practical as common sense could be after full observation—experiment—& Reflection. I have said and I say it again that Mr Lincoln was the *most perfect gentleman* that I ever saw to his host—wife and servants—and to all around and about him *on the Circuit:* he never complained—was never captious as to how he was served or treated. Others would growl—complain—become distressed, and distress others—with the complaints and whine about what they had to eat—how they slept—and on what and how long—and how disturbed by fleas, bed bugs or what not. Remember to travel on the circuit from 1837 to 1856 was a soul's sore trial, down here away at least. No human being would now endure what we used to on the circuit. I have slept with 20 men in the same room—some on bed ropes—some on quilts—some on sheets—a straw or two under them; and oh such victuals—Good God! Excuse me from a detail of our meals. I would not undertake for a considerable sum of money to write out my experience at the bar *while on the circuit*. Mr. Lincoln practiced under Judges Lockwood—Treat—Davis & Rice[5] around & about here. As to the more Estern—Northern—& S Eastern Judges—& circuits I know nothing & will say nothings. From supper time when on the circuit till 12 or 1 O'c in the night Lincoln would make bar rooms—bed rooms—court rooms ring with laughter—yells and shouts made by the People who had gathered to attend court in part and to hear L in particular at and over his jokes—stories—wit and good humor. It was a jolly time for us all. We could not enjoy ourselves otherwise His jokes—jibes—stories—wit and humor were not in behalf of Christian morals and progress—as I think. You may think differently. I have seen all this—heard it all—enjoyed it all and suffered next day for all—. I, as well Judges—Jurors—Witnesses—Lawyers—merchants—&c. &c have laughed at these jokes &c in the night till every muscle—nerve and cell of the body in the morning was sore at the whooping & hurrahing exercise. Such was Lincoln's pasttime & glory on the circuit: it was his *Heaven* and his home his *Hell*. No human being can describe these nightly revels. Such amusements—such sports & tricks would not be tolerated now in any American society, & yet for *us* on the circuit at that time & in those places it drove away the Devil for awhile. At each Court house or County seat these things would be enacted twice a year—whiskey was abundant and freely used. Fights—foot & horse races—knock downs—wrestling—gambling &c were a part of our happy programe on the circuit during those days; and he, who did not enjoy them, was to the crowd a dog & shuned as such. What a change, Arnold! and thank God for it. When I go around the Circuit now and look around to see those who once listened to Lincoln's voice I can only see one now & then: they are all gone—gone—some west with the bear and the beaver—the Buffalo & the wild wolf and more to—Eternity. This is sad—sad and I live in an other world amid strangers of a seeming different race. This is all for the best—and the

---

5. Samuel D. Lockwood, Illinois State Supreme Court; Samuel H. Treat, Eighth Circuit and State Supreme Court; David Davis, Eighth Circuit; Edward Young Rice, Eighteenth Circuit.

change most glorious. The dawn of a real civilization has broken on us, and we must bend to its laws & forces or be broken. I propose to bend.

If these hastily written lines suggest anything to you write me and I'll answer you the best I can. If anything is not full enough write and I'll fill if I can—so goodby for the present.

Your Friend

W. H. Herndon

Note
I have no time to rewrite this

H

CHM: William H. Herndon Collection

123. To Jesse W. Weik

Springfield Ills. April 14th '85

Friend Weik:

. . .

I prefer what Lincoln told me about his mother to what Dennis Hanks tells. You must watch Dennis—criticise what he says. and how he says it—when & where—"tight" or sober. Dennis loves to blow—. Dennis came into the world at the back door out of a Miss Hanks—his father is Chas _____ Dennis has got things mixed up: he purposely conceals all things that degrades the Hanks. Dennis came out of one Hanks and Lincoln out of an other: the girls were cousins as I now recollect it. Thomas Lincoln—Abm's father and Abm Enloe had a severe fight over things. How goes this *fact* with Dennis's 16 yr old boy?

. . .

Your Friend

W H Herndon

LC: HW3195; Exp 4:9:1791–92

124. To Jesse W. Weik[1]

Springfield Ills. Octr 21st '85

Friend Weik.

Mr. Lincoln's habits—methods of reading law—politics—poetry—&c. &c. were to come into the office—pick up book—newspaper &c. and to spread himself out on the sofa—chairs &c, and read aloud much to my annoyance. I have asked him often why he did so and his invariable reply was—"I catch the idea by 2 senses,

---

1. Upper margin: "I have been requested to write something for N. A Review—*Private*" (see §183, n. 1).

for when I read aloud I *hear* what is read and I *see* it; and hence 2 senses get it
and I remember it better, if I do not understand it better." Sometimes in reading
he would have his body on the Sofa—one foot on one chair and one foot on the
table. He spilt himself out easily over 1/4 of the room. I have had to quit the office
frequently because of this reading aloud. In reading at his private house he would
turn his chair down—up side down—lean it down—turn it over and rest his head
on the back of the chair it forming an inclined plain—his back and body on the
carpet—read aloud—stop—think and repeat to himself what he read and repeat
it to you he would or [feint?]. He was in no sense—except in politics—a general
reader: he read specially for a special object and applied it. Mr. Lincoln was practical
and thought things useless unless they could of utility—use—practical &c. &c:
he would read awhile—read till he got tired and then he must tell a story—crack
a joke—make a jest to ease himself: he hated study except for the practical to be
applied right off as it were. In other words he had an End in view always. He was
a long headed strong man: he was reflective—not spontaneous: he was not a very
generous man—had no avarice of the *get* but had the avarice of the *Keep:* he was
liberal and charitable in his views of mankind in all their relations. Mr Lincoln
was a man of *thought*. I have met him in the streets of this city possibly a 1000
times and said to him good morning Mr. Lincoln and he would spraddle—walk
along as if I were not in existence—so abstracted was he. Can you read this—am
hurried—will write you again and again

Your Friend
W H Herndon

LC: HW3199; Exp 4:9:1799–1800

125. To Jesse W. Weik

Springfield Ills. Octr 22d 1885

Friend Weik—

. . . Mr. Lincoln & I entered into partnership in 1843 I think. L was a perfect
case lawyer—not well read in the Elementary books—studied special cases thoroughly and got to be a good lawyer through that means: he remembered his special
reading and applied it to other cases and so on till he got to be a no 1. Supm Court
Lawyer—was not a No 1. *Nisi Prius* lawyer: he didn't care for forms—nor rules of
Pleading—Evidence nor a Practice. he went for substance only.[1]

Hurriedly your Friend
W H Herndon

LC: HW3200; Exp 4:9:1801

---

1. *Nisi prius* lawyer: one who mainly practices in a court of original jurisdiction, as opposed to an appeals
court.

126. To Jesse W. Weik

Springfield Ills Octr 28th 85

Friend Weik

By Mr. Lincoln's Course in Congress in the Mexican War he politically killed himself here: he offered some resolutions in Congress Calling for the "Spot" where the first blood was shed by the Mexicans.[1] This was in 1847–8 I think. Mr. Lincoln knew that he was politically dead and so he went most heartily to knowledge: he took *Euclid* around with him on the Circuit and of nights and odd times he would learn Euclid's problems. Lincoln & I slept in the same bed: he read by tallow candle light. The bed steds in some cases were too short & so his feet hung over the foot board. He would study till 12 or 1 o'c in the night. At this time he despaired of ever rising again in the political world: he was very sad and terribly gloomy—was unsocial and abstracted. The Kansas Nebrask bill was introduced into Congress in 1854 by Sen Douglas Lincoln saw his opportunity and Douglas' downfall: he instanly on the introduction of that bill entered into the political field and by force of his character—mind—Eloquence he became our abolition leader: he was too conservative for some of us—and I among them and yet I stuck to Lincoln in the hopes of his sense of justice and the Eternal right. I was the abolitionist and kept on my table such speeches as Theo Parker's—Giddings', Phillips', Sumners—Sewards &c. Lincoln & I took from 1853 to 1861 such papers as the Chicago Tribune—N.Y. Tribune, The Anti-Slavery Standard—Charleston Mercury—Richmond Enquirer—National Era. Garrison's paper was sent me by friends. The list of papers &c is important to know. Lincoln was well posted on both sides. I had a Southern work called Sociology by Fitzhugh I think.[2] It defended slavery in every way. This aroused the ire of Lincoln more than most pro-slavery books I purchased all the Anti-slavery histories—biographies &c. and kept them on my table and when I found a good thing—a practical thing I would read it to Lincoln. I urged him along as fast as I could. I think I had May's history of the Anti-slavery movements[3]—had the decennial report of the Anti-slavery Convention &c—cant call them all over now. Lincoln now from 1854 to 1861 was in his glory—had hopes—bright hopes to fill his aspirations—Will write again & again

Your Friend
W H Herndon

You fix up in order of time &c. &c

LC: HW3201; Exp 4:9:1803–4

1. See "Spot" Resolutions, December 22, 1847, *Collected Works*, 1:420–22.
2. George Fitzhugh, *Sociology for the South; or, The Failure of Free Society* (Richmond: Morris, 1854).
3. Samuel J. May (1791–1871), a radical abolitionist, wrote a number of works on the anti-slavery movement.

127. To Jesse W. Weik

Spgfd Ills Octr 29th 85

Friend Weik

Mr. Lincoln was a good while preparing his house-divided-against-itself speech: he was at it off and on about one month. If a good idea struck him—if a feasible one, he penciled down on a small slip of paper and put it in his hat where he carried quite all his plunder—check book for the Bank account—letters answered & unanswered—handkercheif &c. After Mr Lincoln had finished—his speech by putting piece to piece & note to note he came into our office early one morning and said—"Billy I want now to read my speech and after I am done I want your opinion of it in all directions;" and to which I replied "Certainly, Mr Lincoln, I'll listen attentively to it and give you my opinion of it in every direction": He & I forgot to lock the office door. When Lincoln had read the speech about half through Uncle Jesse Dubois—Auditor of State came into our office and said—"Lincoln what are you doing" and to which Mr Lincoln said sharply—tartly—"It is none of your d——d business" Dubois left the office in a huff. When he had gone Lincoln commenced reading the remainder of his speech and when through he then ask me for my opinion of it. I said to Mr Lincoln in reply this—"The speech is a good one—written with great power and will bring you prominently before the American people. It is in advance of the age, but deliver it just as you have written it—." He subsequently consulted some friends about it—some had one view of it and some an other. Some wanted this sentence struck out and some that &c. and then in the presence of the crowd he asked my opinion again and I emphatically said to him—Lincoln deliver and publish your speech just as you have written it: it will make you President of the United States. Lincoln did deliver it just as he had written it and read it to me in our office. Soon after the Election was over and Lincoln was defeated hundreds of friends flocked into the office and said to Lincoln—"I told you that that speech would kill you." This mortified Lincoln: he would say to them, "You don't fully comprehend its importance, but I suppose you all have or will desert me for that speech. There is one man who will stick to me to the end: he understands it and its importance and that man is Billy Herndon my good old & long tried friend."

Lincoln had a million of curses from his foolish friends about this speech. He hated it and yet he was thoroughly convinced that it was the thing in the right time and he lived to see it—

Your Friend
WH Herndon

LC: HW3202; Exp 4:9:1805–6

128. To Jesse W. Weik

Springfield Ills Novr. 11th 85

Friend Weik:

Mr Lincoln once had, in an early day, down in Coles County in this state a heavy and a tight law suit. After the trial & before the jury had agreed a question arose in the jury room as to what was meant by the *preponderance* of evidence: the jury at last came into the court room and said—"We are hung on the question of what is meant by the preponderance of evidence." The lawyers laughed at the ignorance of the jury but said nothing. The court put on its dignity and in writing—verbose & long—wordy & intricate, instructed the jury as to what was meant by the *preponderance* of evidence. The jury retired to the jury room and on counting *noses* they found that "Confusion was worse Confounded". Soon they came into the Court room again and said, "May it please the Court, we are hung again on the same question of the preponderance of evidence". The lawyer for the plaintiff by the consent of the court tried his hand on an explanation of the word to the jury: he only added darkness to midnight with the stars & moon blown out of sight: Mr. Lincoln then asked the Court if he might try *his* hand on the question: The Court Consented and said to Lincoln—"Do try your hand in this question Lincoln." Lincoln arose and said—"Gentlemen of the jury—Did you ever see a pair of steel yards or a pair of store scales? If you did I can explain, I think, to your satisfaction the meaning of the word. If the plaintiff has introduced any evidence, put that in the scales and have it weighed—say it ways 16 ounces. If the defendant has introduced any evidence in the case put that in the scales; and if that evidence weighs 16 ounces the scales are balanced and there is no preponderance of evidence on either side. There are 4 witnesses on each side of this case If the plaintiff's evidence weighs one grain of wheat more than the defendant's then the plaintiff has the preponderance of evidence—his side of the scales go down—is the heaviest. If the defendants evidence weighs one grain of wheat more than the plaintiffs then the defendant's side of the scales goes down—is the heaviest; and that movement of the scales tell what is the preponderance of evidence. Now apply this illustration to the state of your mind on weighing the evidence for the plaintiff and defendant." "We see the point, Abe." said the jury This simple illustration of Lincoln gained his case. The defendant had the preponderance of evidence—rather the plaintiff did not have it

Your Friend
W. H. Herndon

This illustration shows most emphatically that Lincoln struggled to be plain to all minds—and especially to ignorant ones. This was one of his forts. H

LC: HW3203; Exp 4:9:1807–8

129. To Jesse W. Weik

Springfield Ills. Novr. 12th '85

Friend Weik:

Mr. Lincoln was a peculiar man: he was intensely thoughtful—persistent—fearless and tireless in thinking. When he got after a thought—fact—principle—question he ran it down to the fibers of the tap root—dug it out; and held it up before him for an analysis; and when he thus formed an opinion no man could overthrow it: he was in this particular without an Equal. I have met Mr. Lincoln of a morning—or evening and said to him, "good morning Mr. Lincoln". He would be so intensely—so deeply in thought, working out his problem—his question, that he would not notice me, though his best friend; he would walk along, his hands behind his back, not knowing where he was going nor doing: his system was acting automatically. There was no thought in his actions: he only had *conciousness*. Some hours after he had thus passed me he, on coming to the office, would say—"Billy what did you say to me on the other side of the square this morning as we passed?" I would say—I simply said "Good morning to you Mr. Lincoln". Sometimes this abstractedness would be the result of intense gloom or of thought on an important law or other question.

I once saw Mr Lincoln look more than a man: he was inspired by the occasion. There was a man living here by the name of Erastus Wright: he was—his business rather was to obtain pension for the soldiers of the Revolution—heirs—widows &c—the soldiers of 1812—widows—heirs &c. An old revolutionary soldier's widow applied to Wright, about 1849–50, to get her pension, which amounted to about $400. Wright made out the papers—got the pension and charged the poor widow $200—half of what he got. The poor old woman came into our office quite blind—deaf and on crutches and stated to Mr. Lincoln her case. Lincoln at once sympathised with the woman and said—"Wright shall pay you back $100. or more." Lincoln went and saw Wright in person. Wright refused to refund. The old woman commenced suit, Lincoln giving security for costs. The case finally got before the jury with all the facts of the case fully told. Lincoln loomed up—rose up to be about 9 ft high—grew warm—then eloquent withfeelings—then blasting as with a thunder bolt the miscreant who had robbed one that helped the world to liberty—to Wright's inalienable rights. Lincoln was inspired if man was ever inspired. The jury became indignant and would have torn Wright up—mobbed him in a minute—burst into tears at one moment and then into indignation the next. The Judge and spectators did the same according to the time that Lincoln gave his eloquence. The jury made Wright disgorge all except about $50.[1]

Herndon

I write you nothing but what I know is true. Pick out what you like and throw the balance to the dogs—am in Court and hurried—so excuse me. Herndon

LC: HW3204; Exp 4:9:1809–10

---

1. See *Herndon's Lincoln*, 212–13, 350. For a very different account of this episode, see Paul H. Verduin, "A New Lincoln Discovery: Rebecca Thomas, His 'Revolutionary War Widow,'" *Lincoln Herald* 98 (Spring 1996): 3–11.

130. To Jesse W. Weik

Springfield Ills. Novr 13th '85

Friend Weik:

There were three noted story tellers—jokers—jesters in the central part of this state especially from 1840 to 1853. Lincoln of Sangamon County—William Engle of Menard and James Murray of Logan: they were all men of mark, each in his own way: they were alike in the line of joking—story telling—jesting. I knew the men for years. From 1840 to 1853 this section was not known for a very high standard of taste—the love for the beautiful or the good. We had not many news papers— People in all of these Counties would attend court at the respective County seats. Lincoln—Engle, & Murray would travel around from County to County with the court and those who loved fun and sport—loved jokes—tales—stories—jests would go with the Court too from County to County. People had not much to do at the time and the class of people that then lived here are gone—perished. It was a curious state of affairs indeed. As compared with the now it was rough—semi barbarous. In the evening after the Court business of the day was over. & book & pen had been laid by the Lawyer—Judges—Jurymen—Witnesses & the people generally would meet at some bar room—"gentlemen's parlour"—and have a good time in story telling—joking—jesting &c. &c. The bar room—windows—halls & all passage ways would be filled to suffocation by the people, eager to see the "Big Ones" and to hear their stories told by them. Lincoln would tell his story in his very best style. The people—all present, including Lincoln would burst out in a loud laugh & a hurrah at the story. The listeners, so soon as the laugh. and the hurrah had passed and silence had come in for its turn would cry out—"Now Uncle Billy (Wm Engle) you must beat that or go home." Engle would clear his throat & say—"Boys the story just told by Lincoln puts me in mind of a story that I heard ~~down East~~ when a boy:" he would tell it and tell it well. The People would clap their hands—stomp their feet—hurrah—yell—shout get up—hold their aking sides. Things would soon calm down. There was politeness and etiquette in it. Each must have his turn, by Comity, in which to tell his story. The good people would, as soon as quiet returned, would cry out—Now is your time, come Murray do your level best or never come here again to tell your stories." Murray would prepare himself with his best. At first he would be a little nervous, but he would soon gather confidence—rise up—walk about, telling his tale as he moved in harmony with his story: he would tell it well—grandly—and the people would sometimes before the story was ended ~~would~~ catch the point and raise such a laugh. and a yell that the village rang with the yells—laughs—and hurrahs &c. Lincoln—and Engle now were nervous and anxious for their turns to come around. Lincoln would tell his story & then followed Engle. and then came Murry and then this story telling—joking—jesting would be kept up till 1 or 2 o'c in the night, and this night after night till the Court adjourned for that term. In the morning we would all be sore all through from excessive laughing, the Judge—the lawyers—Jurymen—witnesses and all. Our sides & back would ake. This was a gay time & I'll never see it again. This is or was the way we old westerners passed away our time. We loved fun and sport—anything for amusement. We had no learning but had good common sense with a liberal broad view of things—were generous and as brave as Caesar. When Court had adjourned in Sangamon County we went to Menard and then to Logan Co. This story telling was kept up faithfully from County to County and from term to term and from year to year. This custom or habit was our platform—show—negro minstrell—was our all in the way of fun. The old know it—the young can't concieve it. Each age has its own sport. and so with each people. This may seem folly now, but it was real life to us then. All that we had to do—all that we could do was to have joy and happiness in our own way. This old state of society was rude but it had its virtues: *it was sincere—and honest.* My old settlers speech which I sent you will help you to paint the scene. Draw on your imagination and fill up: it will please the people who read the story—people—state of society. &c. &c.

Pick out what you like and cast away the balance. I have no time to elaborate—amplify &c. &c nor correct.

I forot to say in my Wright story—the old revolutionary woman story that Lincoln volunteered his services—charged nothing—and paid her Hotel bill &c. Correct the error[1]

Your Friend
W H Herndon

LC: HW3205–6; Exp 4:9, 1811–14

131. To Jesse W. Weik

Springfield Ills. Novr. 14th '85

Friend Weik

As early as 1860 Mr. Lincoln had reason to believe that he would be assassinated or that an attempt would be made to do it. On the day of the presidential Election in—Novr. 1860 I went into Mr Lincoln's office in the state house—~~our office probably~~—and said to Lincoln—"Lincoln you ought to go & vote for the *state* ticket: he replied—"Do you really think I ought to vote" and to which I said—"Most certainly you ought. One vote may gain or lose the Govr.—Legislature &c:" He then remarked "I guess I'll go, but wait till I cut off the presidential Electors on the top of the ticket." He then cut of the head of the ticket. Col. Lamon & Col. Ellsworth and myself only were in the room.[1] I winked to these gentlemen to go along with Lincoln and see him safely through the mass of men at the voting place. They understood me. Lamon went on the right side of Lincoln—Ellsworth on the left; and I at Lincoln's back just behind him. As we approached the voting place the vast mass of men who had gathered to vote & to see Lincoln vote, as it was

---

1. See §129.

---

1. Ward Hill Lamon would be appointed Marshal of the District of Columbia during AL's presidency. Elmer Ellsworth briefly studied law in AL's office and was one of the first casualties of the Civil War.

whispered that Herndon had got Lincoln to vote or agreed to do so—opened a wide gap for him to pass on to the voting place. The Republicans yelled & shouted as Lincoln approached: he was allowed to vote unmolested and when he had voted & come out of the Court room—the voting place, they again yelled and shouted. I must say that the Democrats on that day and place paid about as much respect to Lincoln as the Republicans did: They acted politely—civilly & respectfully, raising their hats to him as he passed on through them to vote: they acted nobly on that day & at that place & time. Lincoln voted & was glad of it.

Directly after the Lincoln & Douglas Campaign in 1858—soon after it was over—he Lincoln commenced receiving through the Post office all manner of odd pictures cut out of news papers, expressive of pain—starvation—sorrow—grief &c &c. Frequently threatening letters were received by him through the P. O.; all of which he burned at the time. The receipt of these showed the *animus* of the times to Mr Lincoln. He said to me once—"I feel as if I should meet with some terrible End;" and so the great man felt through time & space instinctively his coming doom.

Your Friend
W. H. Herndon

LC: HW3207; Exp 4:9:1815–16

132. To Jesse W. Weik

Springfield Ills. Novr. 15th '85

Friend Weik:

. . .

Again you ask me—"When will your article appear in N. A. Review or some paper?" and in answer to *that* question I say—I cannot tell. I am picking up—gathering up, facts for you every day or so; & will send them as quickly as I can. Remember I am still in Court and am somewhat busy watching my cases and attending to my practice before Justices of the peace. I shall send you nothing that is not *good* & *true* & *new*. What I mean by the word *good* is this—something that helps to explain Lincoln's characteristics—nature—quality &c. You must *finish* up the facts which I send to you. I give them to you in the *raw*. You must polish—amplify—enlarge & make readable. I have no time to write out the stories, jokes—facts &c. &c as I see and know them to exist. When you get your article done I will listen well to it; and after the piece is accepted, published & *paid* for I will accept what you see proper to give me &c. &c.

The story of Lincoln—Engle & Murray[1] cannot be exaggerated by you. I have seen these contests between these men year after year—have seen hundreds & hundreds of men wild & furious with laughter at these battles of the story tellers. Each tried to excell the other, and each contestant had his friends just as at boxing

---

1. See §130.

or sparring matches &c. &c. These contests were conducted with Etiquette, decorum friendship. I will write you as I get up facts & have time to scribble them out. Can you read what I write?

Your Friend
W H Herndon

LC: HW3208; Exp 4:9:1817–18

133. To Jesse W. Weik

Springfield Ills Novr. 17th '85

Friend Weik:

In some particulars Mr. Lincoln was a peculiar man. For instance, he was very liberal and charitable to his fellow man and yet he was not a generous man in his gifts or with his money: he had none of the avarice of the *get* but had the avarice of the *keep*. Mr. Lincoln was fully aware of the imperfections and foibles of the race, and had great charity for man. I never heard him abuse anybody nor did I ever, except once or twice, hear him Eulogize any one: he attacked no one on the stump, because he was aware of his own lowly origen: His motto, in this particular, was "those who live in glass houses should not throw stones." Mr. Lincoln loved such books as "Jack Downing"—"Phoenixiana," & "Petrolium V. Naesby":[1] he was a terribly gloomy man, & Yet he loved mirth, because it gave vent to his gloom and his melancholy. I have heard him say—"If it were not for these stories—jokes—jests I should die: they give vent—are the vents of my moods & gloom." If you were in your office and wished to read anything of interest, just beware how you talked. If you said much *that much* would suggest to him a story that he heard on the circuit or down in—Egypt—the lower part of this state. The thing once suggested there would be an End of your reading. Close the book you must—you couldn't help it: he would tell one story and that would suggest an other; and so the day would roll by pleasant or unpleasant to you: he had no *hold up* in this particular. Tell his stories he would and read you could not—pleasant to you or not the mill would grind. Lincoln was not a social man—loved no man much—was more or less selfish—was wrapt up in his own children—was childish in this—a tool or a slave to them—blind to their faults. Mr. Lincoln was Lawyer—Politician—Lecturer & Inventor. He succeeded in the law and in politics—was an utter failure as Lecturer & Inventor.

Lincoln sometimes drank liquor—was a good chess player—loved "fives"—ie to play ball, knocking it up against a wall with the hand 2 or 3 men on each side. This letter is purposely miscellaneous as you may wish to pitch—throw such things

---

1. Major Jack Downing was a character created by Seba Smith. Charles Augustus Davis later created a sort of pseudo–Jack Downing who claimed to be intimate with AL during the latter's presidency. John Phoenix was the pen name of George Horatio Derby, a Western humorist. David Ross Locke wrote ironic pieces of pro-Union propaganda during the Civil War over the pseudonym of Petroleum V. Nasby.

in your piece. Probably I repeat some things, if so excuse me, as I do not keep notes of what I write.

Your Friend
W H Herndon

LC: HW3209; Exp 4:9:1819–20

134. To Jesse W. Weik[1]

Springfield Ills. Novr. 19th 1885

Friend Weik:

Mr. & Mrs. Lincoln never lived a harmonious life; and when she wanted to go to church or to some gathering she would go at all events and leave Lincoln to take care of the babies. Mrs. Lincoln couldn't keep a hired girl because she was tyranical to her and Lincoln per force was compelled to look after the children. Of a Sunday Lincoln might be seen, if in summer in his shirt sleeves, hauling his babies in a little wagon up and down the pavement north & south on 8th street. Sometimes Lincoln would become so abstracted that the young one would fall out and squall, Lincoln moving on the while. Some one would call Lincoln's attention to what was going on: he would turn back—pick up the child—soothe it—pacify it &c; and then proceed up & down the pavement as before. So abstracted was he that he did not know what or how he was doing and I suppose cared less. If the little one fell out and Lincoln was told of it he would say—"This puts me in mind of a story I heard down in New Salem;" and then Lincoln would tell his story and tell it well. The man and Lincoln would sit down on the curb stone of the pavement and finish the forenoon in stories; and when Mr. Lincoln saw Mrs Lincoln coming from church—she screaming because Lincoln had the child out of doors in the fresh air, he ran into his room and gently took what followed—you know, a hell of scolding. Poor Abe, I can see him now running and crouching.

It happened that sometimes Lincoln would come down to our office of a Sunday with one or two of his little children, hauling them in the same little wagon and in our office, then and there write declarations—pleas and other legal papers. The children—spoilt one to be sure would tear up the office—scatter the books—smash up pens—spill the ink and piss all over the floor. I have felt many & many a time that I wanted to wring their little necks and yet out of respect for Lincoln I kept my mouth shut. Lincoln did not notice what his children was doing or had done. When Lincoln finished his business he would haul his children back home and meet the same old scolding or a new and intensified one. He bore all quite philosophically. Jesus—what a home Lincoln's was! What a wife!

One word about Lincoln's honesty and fairness. Many—Many years ago one Chas Matheny sold a piece of land to a Mrs. (I forget her name) who was Lincoln's

---

1. Note in top margin of first page: "Correct & go on." Note on top of last page: "I sent your book on yesterdy."

client. The numbers of the acres in the piece was guessed at or a great mistake was made. The lines of the survey ran East, west, north and south, but from well known objects to well known objects—called monuments. The price of the land was so much per acre and the deed showed the terms of the sale. About the year 1858 Mr Lincoln was written to by the lady to have her land surveyed—laid off into lots &c. Lincoln got a compass—chains &c and surveyed the lands. In running off the land and calculating the number of the acres he found that Matheny had lost 4 or 5 acres of land in this city and that his client had gained it—say 4 or 5 a—more or less. Old man Matheny in the mean time had died and leaving 8 or 9 children, some of whom had died leaving heirs—children. Lincoln wrote to his client what he had done and what mistakes had been made and advised his client that she ought in morals and in law rectify the mistake—pay the Matheny heirs what was justly due them according to the acres at the original price agreed upon. The woman at first declined to rectify, but Lincoln wrote her a long letter again stating what he thought was right & just between the parties. Some of the Matheny heirs were very poor & needy. Lincoln's last kind & noble letter brought the woman to her own sense of right—sent to Mr Lincoln several hundred dollars. Lincoln was a friend to the Mathenys as well as to his client: he took the trouble of hunting up the scattered heirs and their descendants and paid them every cent that was due them and thus this man—noble man was ever for justice and the eternal right—. I hope you can make out what I wrote—correct &c. &c—am this minute going to Court—"Excuse haste and a bad pen"—as this poor devil will say.

Your Friend
W H Herndon

LC: HW3210–11; Exp 4:9:1821–24

135. To Jesse W. Weik

Springfield Ills. Novr. 20th '85[2][1]

Friend Weik

Your letter, dated the 18th inst, is at hand. The Van Buren—Lincoln story is correct. Mr. Lincoln met, as one of a committe to escort Mr. Van Buren into the city, Van Buren at a little place East of the city about 7 miles, called Rochester. The roads were terribly muddy—almost impassible; and the "old time" stage could not reach the city that night & so Van Buren put up for the night at the hotel of the place. The people of the village sent word to the city; and to our citizens, out of respect to the Presdt of the U.S, went out to Rochester to meet and to greet & to welcome Van Buren to our city. Lincoln was one of the citizens & one of a committee &c who went to greet & welcome Van Buren. This was I

---

1. This is the second of three letters to JWW on this date. The first is not included in this edition.
2. AL and Martin Van Buren met at Rochester, Illinois on June 16, 1842.

think in 1836–7.[2] Lincoln felt well—was introduced to Van Buren. The crowd held conversation for some time. Things began to drag and at last Lincoln told at special request one of his freshest and newest stories: he told the story so well and the point so sharp, that it amused Van Buren. Not only did it amuse him, but it struck him that Lincoln was a marked man—a man of mark—a peculiar man—a man of force. Lincoln told his stories till 2 or 3 o'cl P.M, much to the amusement of the crowd of people who had gathered from Rochester—Springfield and surrounding places, including the Country people. Van Buren—Lincoln & the People had a glorious time of it that night and til 8 o'cl am next day. The next day Van Buren was driven into the city with great pomp & parade. Van Buren has been heard to say to some of our people—"Your man Lincoln is an original genius—a marked man—a man of clear ideas and will yet be a man who will be a success in the field of politics and a power in the land." This is in substance what Van Buren said of Lincoln: it is all authentic. Van Buren was struck with Lincoln's store of fun—his wit—wisdom and with his individuality &c: he saw genius in the raw in Lincoln.

I know nothing of the story of Rives.[3] Lincoln had the advantage as he always had in all quarrels and difficulties

Hurriedly Your friend

W H Herndon

LC: HW3213–14; Exp 4:9:1827–28

136. To Jesse W. Weik

Springfield Ills. Novr. 20th '85[3][1]

Friend Weik:[2]

You say that you want one more law case. I can give it to you. About 1859 there lived in a village about 17 miles west of this place two young men of the first families. One of the young men was named Quinn Harrison—grandson of the Revd Peter Cartwright. The other was named Greek Crafton—a young lawyer who studied law with Lincoln & Herndon. Harrison's father was rich, & Crafton's father comparatively poor and yet highly respected. The village was in this County and called Pleasant Plains. There seemed to be a long existing feud between the families of Harrison & Crafton—at least between the boys—young men about 23 years of age: they were young men of promise at that time. The young men met in a store in Pleasant Plains one day by accident and some hot

---

3. George W. Rives was an office seeker who sought AL's support in spite of having abused him politically. See Daniel W. Stowell, "Lincoln's Reluctant Recommendation," *Lincoln Editor: The Quarterly Newsletter of The Papers of Abraham Lincoln*, 8, no. 1 (January–March 2008).

---

1. The third of three letters of this date.

2. Note on first page: "Do your best on this It is worthy of it—I have no time to correct nor embellish. / H"

words passed between the two. Crafton struck & gathered Quinn Harrison and threw him. Harrison in the scuffle got out his Knife Cut & stabbed Crafton Fatally: he lived a day or so and died of the wound. Harrison was arrested and a grand jury found an indictment against Harrison for murder. Lincoln—Logan—and others were employed by Harrison: Govr. Palmer[3] and the states attorney prosecuted. The lawyers on both sides were among the ablest in the state. The case was one of intense interest all over the County. The case was opened and ably conducted on both sides—every inch of ground was contested—hotly sough. All the points of the law—the evidence—practice & general procedure were raised and discussed with feeling—fervor and Eloquence. Lincoln felt an unusual interest in Young Harrison, as the old man, Peyton Harrison his father had often accommodated Lincoln when help was needed. During the trial which was a long one—a complex and a tedious one the Court—Judge Rice[4]—decided a question against Lincoln's views of the law. Lincoln argued the question of the law decided against him with ability—Eloquence and learning, as Lincoln had thoroughly had studied the case in the facts—procedure and the law. Lincoln submitted to the decision for a considerable time, but finding that the point decided against him and a material one was one of the principle turning points of the case. Palmer was pushing his victory in the debate to its legitimate conclusion—the utter defeat and rout of Lincoln and the conviction of Harrison of the Crime of manslaughter. Lincoln begged time of the Court—to reargue the point. The court granted time. Lincoln prepared himself well with Law—came into Court with an armful of books and read the authorities plainly sustaining his view of the Case. The Court was obdurate—clung to his decision—overruled Lincoln's objection—admitted the Evidence &c. Lincoln could not stand the absurd decision—for it was absurd & without precedent in the broad world; and in his anger L's he rose up and seemed inspired with indignation, mingled with a feeling of pity and Contempt for the Judges decision. He actually was fired with indignation and spoke fiercely—strongly—contemptuously of the decision of the Court. Lincoln kept, in his anger and Contempt, just inside the walls of the law—did not do anything—say anything that would be a contempt of Court: he was Careful and yet the searing that he gave the Court, through its foolish decision, was terrible—blasting—crushing—withering I shall never forget the scene. Lincoln had the Crowd—the Jury—the Bar in perfect sympathy and accord. The courts decision was ridiculed—scoffed and kicked out of Court. Lincoln was mad—vexed and indignant. When a great big man of mind and body gets mad he is mad all over—terrible—furious—Eloquent &c. &c. The Court at last was Convinced or driven to pretend to believe that its decision was wrong—overruled his former decision—sustained Lincoln's views & so now. Lincoln had the field his own way—cleared his man went to the jury—was able—Eloquent—powerful &c. &c. Harrison through Lincoln's Courage—knowledge of the law and the facts of his case was honorably acquitted—the verdict of the jury saying—Justified. It

---

3. John M. Palmer.
4. Judge Edward Young Rice presided over Illinois's Eighteenth Judicial Circuit in 1859.

was a proud day for Lincoln. Lincoln was a grand man—an imposing figure that day—I assure you.

The Court was actually badgered by Lincoln into its final decision of the Case. Govr Palmer couldn't stop Lincolns force—and Eloquence. This was a grand trial and so paint it.[5]

Your Friend
W H Herndon

LC: HW3214–15; Exp 4:9:1829–32

137. To Jesse W. Weik

Spfd Ills. Novr. 21st 1885

Friend Weik

It seems to me that in your article you *should* say something about Lincoln's nature—qualities and characteristics; and so here goes—the predominant—the chief qualities &c. of Lincoln are as follow. He was morally and physically corageous—Even tempered & conservative—secretive and sagacious—skeptical and Cautious—truthful & honest—firm in his own convictions & tolerant of those of others—reflective & cool—ambitious and somewhat selfish—kind to all and good natured—sympathetic in the presence of suffering or under an imaginative description of it—lived in his reason and reasoned in his life—Easy of approach and perfectly democratic in his nature—had a broad charity for his fellow man and had an Excuse for unreflective acts of ~~man~~ his kind—and in short he loved justice and lived out in thought and act the Eternal right. The above is Correct in Lincoln's *general* life. [*In margin:* I have weighed all my words—well before I penned them H.] I do not say that he never deviated from his own nature and his own rules. His nature—the tendency of it, is as I state. I studied Lincoln critically for thirty odd years and should know him well. Lincoln struggled to live the best life possible. This I know. Sometimes he fell short of his own ideal, as he has often told me: he has told me facts of his life that were not Lincoln's but poor human nature's *in* Lincoln. I shall never tell them to mortal man and of this be sure. Lincoln *as a whole* was really a most noble man.

You say that you intend to write two articles—one on Lincoln as a lawyer and one as a politician. The idea is a good one & I approve of it. The fields are broad and good as I see it.

Your Friend
W. H. Herndon

LC: HW3216; Exp 4:9:1833–34

---

5. The only known transcript of this case affords little evidence of AL's behavior as depicted here. See *People v. Peachy Quinn Harrison*, Sangamon County District Court, 1859, in *The Law Practice of Abraham Lincoln: Complete Documentary Edition*, edited by Martha Benner and Cullom Davis (Urbana: University of Illinois Press, 2000). See also Robert Bray, "The P. Quinn Harrison Murder Trial," *Lincoln Herald* 99 (Summer 1997): 59–79.

138. To Jesse W. Weik

Springfield Ills Decr. 1st '85

Friend Weik:

You wish to know if Mrs. Lincoln and the Todd aristocratic family did not scorn and detest the Hanks & the Lincoln family; and in answer to which I yell—Yes. Mrs. Lincoln held the Hanks tribe in Contempt and the Lincoln family generally— the old folks—Thomas Lincoln & his good old wife. Mrs. Lincoln was terribly aristocratic and as haughty & as imperous as she was aristocratic: she was as cold as a chunk of ice. Thomas Lincoln and his good old wife were never in this city and I do not suppose that they were ever invited to visit Lincoln's house. Had they appeared I doubt whether Mrs Lincoln would have admitted them. A young lady by the name of Hanks—I think Dennis Hanks daughter, came to this city about 1853 and went to school here: she boarded with Lincoln, but this created a fight a fuss between Lincoln and his wife.[1] This young lady married a doctor by the name of Chapman I think.[2] She and her husband now live or did live in Charleston in this State: they are good people. While the young lady was here Mrs Lincoln tried to make a servant—a slave of her, but being high spirited she refused to become Mrs. Lincoln's tool. Mrs Chapman is a lady: she and I used to Correspond about the facts of Lincoln's life &c. &c.[3] She by nature and in soul was a better woman than Mrs. Lincoln. I personally knew both. If you tell the story keep Mrs. Chapmans name private as she would not like it probably. I am glad to know that your *Eyes are open* about Dennis Hanks: he is a grand Exaggerator, if not a great liar. I believed nothing he told me unless he was—rather his story was verified by John Hanks—as good a man as ever lived—an honest man and a truthful one. I am now busy in Court and must dry up for a while. As facts come up in my mind I will send notes to you of what I *Know*. You wish to know something of my visit to the abolitionists in 1858—will write you about this when I get time.

Your Friend

W H Herndon

How do you like Lamon's Life of Lincoln generally? It is the truest life that was ever written of a man in my opinion. I do not agree to all it says. I did not like the 19th chap in all particulars. I think it is the 19th chap.

LC: HW3221; Exp 4:9:1843–44

---

1. Harriet Hanks Chapman, who told JWW that she lived with the Lincolns from 1842 to 1844. See *Herndon's Informants*, 646.
2. Augustus H. Chapman.
3. For Harriet Hanks Chapman's letters to WHH, see *Herndon's Informants*, 144–45, 407–8, 512–14.

139. To the Editor of the Religio-Philosophical Journal
Springfield, Ill., Dec. 4th, 1885.

I have carefully read Mr. Poole's address on Abraham Lincoln, published in the RELIGIO-PHILOSOPHICAL JOURNAL of Nov. 28th, 1885.[1] Mr. Poole is a stranger to me, but I must say that he struck a rich golden vein in Mr. Lincoln's qualities, characteristics and nature, and has worked it thoroughly and well, exhaustively in his special line.

I know nothing of Lincoln's belief or disbelief in Spiritualism. I had thought, and now think, that Mr. Lincoln's original nature was materialistic as opposed to the spiritualistic; was realistic as opposed to idealistic. I cannot say that he believed in Spiritualism, nor can I say that he did not believe in it. He made no revelations to me on this subject, but I have grounds outside, or besides, Mr. Poole's evidences, of the probability of the fact that he did sometimes attend here, in this city, séances. I am told this by Mr. Ordway, a Spiritualist.[2] I know nothing of this fact on my personal knowledge.

Mr. Lincoln was a kind of fatalist in some aspects of his philosophy, and skeptical in his religion. He was a sad man, a terribly gloomy one—a man of sorrow, if not of agony. This, his state, may have arisen from a defective physical organization, or it may have arisen from some fatalistic idea, that he was to die a sudden and terrible death. Some unknown power seemed to buzz about his consciousness, his being, his mind, that whispered in his ear, "Look out for danger ahead!" This peculiarity in Mr. Lincoln I had noticed for years, and it is no secret in this city. He has said to me more than once, "Billy, I feel as if I shall meet with some terrible end." He did not know what would strike him, nor when, nor where, nor how hard; he was a blind intellectual Sampson, struggling and fighting in the dark against the fates. I say on my own personal observation that he felt this for years. Often and often I have resolved to make or get him to reveal the causes of his misery, but I had not the courage nor the impertinence to do it.

When you are in some imminent danger or suppose you are, when you are suffering terribly, do you not call on some power to come to your assistance and give you relief? I do, and all men do. Mr. Lincoln was in great danger, or thought he was, and did as you and I have done: he sincerely invoked and fiercely interrogated all intelligences to give him a true solution of his states—the mysteries and his destiny. He had great—too great confidence in the common judgment of an uneducated people. He believed that the common people had truths that philosophers never dreamed of; and often appealed to that common judgment of the common people over the shoulders of scientists. I am not saying that he did right. I am only stating what I know to be facts, to be truths.

Mr. Lincoln was in some phases of his nature very, very superstitious; and it may be—it is quite probable that he in his gloom, sadness, fear and despair,

---

1. Cyrus O. Poole, "The Religious Convictions of Abraham Lincoln: A Study."

2. A Springfield, Illinois, resident, John Ordway, is identified as a "spiritualist" in "The Spirits Last Night," August 21, 1874, *Daily Illinois State Journal*.

invoked the spirits of the dead to reveal to him the cause of his states of gloom, sadness, fear and despair. He craved light from all intelligences to flash his way to the unknown future of his life.

May I say to you that I have many, many times, thoroughly sympathized with Mr. Lincoln in his intense sufferings; but I dared not obtrude into the sacred ground of his thoughts that are so sad, so gloomy, and so terrible.

Your Friend,
WM. H. HERNDON

Religio-Philosophical Journal, *Dec. 12, 1885*

140. To Jesse W. Weik
Private

Springfield Ills. Decr. 10th '85

Friend Weik:

Your letter, dated the 6th inst, is at hand. I am glad that you like Lamon's life of Lincoln: it is the truest life that was ever written of man. I gathered up the facts cautiously—carefully and critically. I know every person whose name is used in the book, I think. I knew who were truthful—who were Exagerators and who were liars &c. Lamon gathered up a few facts.

Miss Owens is a Kentucky lady—is well Educated—Came to Ills in 1836–7.—Saw Lincoln at Ables. The lady's name is Mrs Vincent of Mo.[1] It is no exageration to say that Mrs Vincent is an accomplished *lady*.

The dash of which you speak stands in the place of a woman. I cannot in honor answer further.

Lincoln Came to this city in 1837—and from that time to 1843–4 he and Speed were quite *familiar*—to go no further with the women. I Cannot tell you what I know, Especially in ink. Speed was a lady's man in a good & true sense. Lincoln only went to see a few women of the first class—women of sense. Fools ridiculed him: he was on this point tender footed—Jno. T. Stuart is dead. Between Lincoln & Stuart from 1843 to 1865 there was no good feeling of an honest friendship. Lincoln hated some of the ways of Stuart. Lincoln felt no jealousy toward Stuart. Stuart did toward Lincoln. Stuart in his heart hated Lincoln. Jno. T. Stuart was 77 years of age: he was a weak brother & a sly one—"tricky—dodgy": he and Lincoln did not agree in politics since 1853. Stuart was intensely pro-slavery—L for freedom. S & L were in partnership only about 2 or 3 ys.

Friend Weik—Why my good Sir—I have given away 20 years ago all my Lincoln letters: he had not been buried before I was bounced for Everything I posessed

---

1. Mary Owens, whom AL courted in New Salem after the death of Ann Rutledge, married Jesse Vineyard in Kentucky and later moved with him to Missouri.

that Lincoln's fingers ever touched. I am a weak brother, you know & I gave till I had nothing to give. You should have my letters of Lincoln if I had any you know.

Your Friend
W. H. Herndon

Come & see me & I'll tell you much about men—times—women. Ill write to you as I get time—will write about my visit to Washington &c &c

LC: HW3225; Exp 4:9:1851–52

141. To Jesse W. Weik

Springfield Ills Decr. 16th '85

Friend Weik:

I have just thought of a new fact which is as follows—Sometime about 1855 I went into a book store in this city and saw a book—a small one, entitled—called, I think, "The Annual of Science."[1] I looked over it casually and liked it and bought it. I took the book to Lincoln & H's office. Lincoln was in reading a newspaper. He saw that I had something which I thought of value: He said to me—"Well Billy—You have got a new book, which is good I suppose. What is it. Let me see it." He took the book in his hand—looked over the pages—read the little—introduction and probably the first Chapter and saw at a glance the purpose and object of the book—which were as follow—To record, teach and fully explain the *failures* and *successes* of experiments of all philosophies & Scientists everywhere, including Chemistry—mechanics, &c. &c. He instantly rose up and said that he must buy the whole set—started out and got them. On returning to the office he said—"I have wanted such a book for years, because I sometimes make experiments *&* have thoughts about the physical world that I do not know to be true nor false. I may, by this book, correct my Errors and save time & expense—I can see where scientists & philosophers have failed and avoid the rock on which they split or can see the means of their success and take advantage of their brains—toil & knowledge. Men are greedy to publish the successes of Efforts, but meanly sly as to publishing the failures of men. Many men are ruined by this one sided practice of Concealment of blunders & failures" This he said substantially to me with much feeling—vim & force. The last time that he spoke of the book to me he spoke in glowing terms

Enclosed I send you a letter of mine published in the "Religio-Philosophical Journal of the 12th of Decr 1885.[2]

Your Friend
W. H Herndon

LC: HW3227; Exp 4:9:1855–56

---

1. Probably *The Annals of Science: Being a Record of Inventions and Improvements*, a serial publication appearing 1852–54.
2. See §139.

142. To Jesse W. Weik

Springfield Ills. Decr [21] 1885[1]

Friend Weik:

I send you now a fact that runs along parallel with the last one. About the year 1854 I had purchased and read an Excellent life of Edmund Burk, the English statesman. It was an English work and an Excellent life of Burk. I read the book with pleasure and profit. It continued 2 vols &c. &c.[2] Mr. Lincoln Came into our office Early one morning just as I had finished reading the work. I say I admired the book very much, and I said to Lincoln, after passing the Compliments of the morning as was our custom,—Do you not wish to read a most excellent life of Burk, the English statesman? and to which he replied—"No, I do not wish to read his life, nor any mans life as now written. You and I have talked over life writing many and many times and you know that biographies are eulogistic—one sided—Colored and false. The dead man's glories are painted hugely—brightly & falsely: his *successes* as are held up to Eulogy, but his *failures*—his shortcomings—his negatives—his errors—slips & foibles and the like are kept in the dark. You dont get a peep at them—You don't get a true understanding of the man—only see one side and that Colored and hence false. I have no Confidence in biographies—Why do not book sellers have blank biographies ready printed and piled on their shelves and published for sale—so that when a man dies his heirs or admires or those who wish it can find a life of the dead ready made and at hand; and all that has to be done is to buy the eulogistic thing—fill up the blanks and call it the life & writings of the admired and loved dead. This would economize time and save strains on the brain. This is my opinion of biographies as now written. I want none of them and will not read them."[3] This was with much Emphasis said to me by Mr. Lincoln on the occasion herein related. I distinctly remember it. This very idea has spurred me more than all other things to make the world truly acquainted with the facts of Lincolns life: Now you have my purpose told you and the why honestly given to you

My friend I do wish you to understand that I state nothing about Mr. Lincoln but what is true and where I doubt I shut my mouth and keep silent. I do try to weigh Mr Lincoln accurately and justly. If I Err it is on the Side of Lincoln and not against him. I do not pretend to be infallible,—and all that I can say is this—I wish to be fair, just and truthful. I am willing to give to the world as one of the Cotemporaries of Lincoln all the facts of his life as I understand them to the world without pay or reward in the present or the future.

What I write you does not come up [to?] the dignity of letters—only memoranda

Your Friend
W. H. Herndon

LC: HW3227; Exp 4:9:1875–76

---

1. Day of the month is supplied in his next letter to Weik (see §143, p. 178).

2. James Prior, *Memoir of the Life and Character of the Right Hon. Edmund Burke*, 2 vols. (Boston: Ticknor, Reed, and Fields, 1854).

3. For other versions of this incident, see §187, and *Herndon's Lincoln*, 264–65n.

143. To Jesse W. Weik

Springfield Ills Decr. 23d '85

Friend Weik:

Say in the Early part of 1858 Mr. Lincoln came into our office in a dejected spirit. We passed the Compliments of the morning—did some necessary and quite important business &c. &c. Mr. Lincoln sat down on the Sofa—seemed dejected—melancholic—spoke about politics—his chances for senator—his hopes & his aspirations—spoke of the dodging and wriggling of Douglas in the Kansas Nebraska question—said Kindly—"I think Greely is not doing me, an old republican and a tried Anti-Slavery man, right: he is talking up Douglas—an untrue and an untried man—a dodger—a wriggler—a tool of the South once & now a snapper at it—hope he will bite 'Em good; but I don't feel that it is exactly right to push me down in order to elevate Douglas.[1] I like Greely—think he intends right, but I think he errs in this hoisting up of Douglas, while he gives me a downward Shove. I wish that some one could put a flea in Greely's Ear—see Trumbull—Sumner, Wilson—Seward—Parker—Garrison—Philips[2] & others, and try and turn the currents in the right directions. These men ought to trust the tried & true men" This Mr. Lincoln said to me in substance; & I *inferred* from it—only *inferred* it—that Mr Lincoln wished me to go and see these men, and see what I could do in the matter: he Knew that I was with, the most of these men in constant Correspondence, and had been for years—long before Lincoln took his advanced anti-slavery grounds *on the stump*—So I bundled up—had plenty of money then, never supposing that I should want thereafter and started East, on the *inferred* hint to see what could be done—landed in Washington saw Trumbull—Seward—Sumner—Wilson: stated what I wished of them—They were all right and doing all they could to stem the rising tide of Douglasism. I then went to New York—saw Greely told him politely and cautiously my story—said to him that Douglas was a new convert—was not to be trusted—was Conscienceless and without political principles or honor &c. &c. I said to Greely—"You do right in patting Douglas on the back, but wrong when you indirectly hit Lincoln, a true—real & long tried Anti Slavery man, in order directly or indirectly to overthrow or kill Lincoln. Can you not assist Douglas & our Cause by helping Douglas without stabbing Lincoln." We had a long conversation, but this is the shell and substance of it. Greely said to me, as I *inferred*—as I *understood* it "that he would most assuredly assist Douglas in all honorable ways—that he liked Lincoln—had confidence in him and would not injure him—that he would somewhat change tactics, and be careful in the future. Greely was kind to me—introduced me to many of the leading Republicans of N. Y City—had Conversations with them about the way things were moving—. Most of them said—"Greely is all right—has a string to pull, but will in the end show you his intents &c and will justify. Greely for some

---

1. By opposing the pro-slavery Lecompton Constitution in Kansas, Douglas had alienated Southern Democrats and the Buchanan Administration but had attracted Republicans.

2. Lyman Trumbull, Charles Sumner, Henry Wilson, William H. Seward, Theodore Parker, William Lloyd Garrison, and Wendell Phillips.

time acted up to the square thing—up to his promises as *I understood* them—wrote to Greely that I thought he had passed the line &c. He & I had some hard words, but at last we understood Each other. He said something in his paper about me that was not correct. I again wrote to Greely correcting him: he apologized to me through the Tribune—ie he explained and withdrew the charge &c.[3] From New York I went to Boston—saw Govr Banks—Theo Parker—Garrison—Phillips—and put them all right, if they were not right before; which is more than likely—I was gone about one month—returned home—paid my own expenses. I did not then think that the trip was necessary at all, but to assure Lincoln—to pacify him—to make him feel better I went, and did all that I could for friend Lincoln. When I got home I told Lincoln what I had seen and done—gave him my opinion that the trend—tendency and march of things were all in his favor, and that all would Come out right side uppermost: he seemed pleased, if not gratified—thanked me most heartily. From the time that I saw these mentioned men and hundreds more, including many news papers &c I think now that things began more and more to work for Lincoln's success. I say I *think* so, but do not *know* the Cause, unless it be my assurance that Lincoln, to the Anti-Slavery Cause, was as true as steel—as firmly set as Garrison &c. &c.

I saw many Anti-Slavery ladies, and their heads were stubbornly for "Honest Abe." This cheered me for I knew if the women were for Lincoln that Lincoln was the Coming man. Many said—"Lincoln is not radical enough, but he is a growing man—has a conscience that Can be educated; and the times will do that, if he has an Ear to hear." I had a good time of it—was treated well by all persons—saw the cities &c. &c.[4]

In my last letter to you I did not date it. Date it the 21st inst—intended to date but in my hurry and flurry forgot it. Again—I said to you "I wish you to understand &c." I *intended* to say. "Friend I wish &c" I meant nothing by the awkward and uncorrected expression—. Excuse me. I don't have much time to look over—read & correct my letters to you. I depend on you to Correct &c. &c.

I may be mistaken in the year in which I went on my trip: it may be I went in 1857 or in 1857–8. Correct me if I am wrong. It is now 30 years since I went on the Lincoln business; and I may have forgotten much of what was said—when—where &c. &c. Probably if you will refer to Lamons life of Lincoln that it can aid you in dates and the like. I may err in some things.

I am about pumped dry—dry as a sand desert.

> Your Friend
> Wm. H. Herndon

LC: HW3228–29; Exp 4:9:1857–60

---

3. Greeley and WHH had professed different versions of a supposed understanding that Greeley would support AL in the 1858 Illinois Senatorial race. *Chicago Press and Tribune*, February 2, February 16, and March 8, 1859. See also WHH to Trumbull, July 22, 1858, and February 26, 1859. LC, Trumbull Papers.

4. A brief account of WHH's 1858 trip is in *Herndon's Lincoln*, 239–42; for his biographer's account, see Donald, 112–16.

144. To Jesse W. Weik

Springfield Ills. Dec. 28th '85

Friend Weik:

You said in one of your letters to me that you intended to write an article on Lincoln as politician. This is a good subject and now let me assist you a little in addition to what I have already said. Mr. Lincoln was not simply a politician, but he was something more: he approached statesmanship. A statesman is one who among other things has great reason and a profound judgement with practical sagacity in government; and who is throughly acquainted with the people—their wants—their wealth and means of happiness—his Country & its relations to foreign governments. He must know all about Political Economy—the laws of wealth—Social Science—the science of the relations of men in society, and the forces that play on them there. Such a man—a Statesman must have an originating power—an organizing power and the power to Control the People through reason—justice and the Eternal right. He should possess great moral Courage with a genius to govern. *These are some* of the leading traits of a statesman. Lincoln had many of these qualities: he had great reason, backed up by profound judgements when he had time to mature his ideas and apply them: he was unequaled in his practical sagacities: he had great moral Courage—loved justice and the Eternal right: he knew his People—his Country and loved them. This man knew much of the law of Political Economy & the Social Science: he had an iron will in the right—on principle. The great Civil war absorbed all other questions—drove all measures—except those of war, from the field; and hence Mr. Lincoln had no opportunity to show his power of originating *&* organizing. I think that Mr Lincoln was deficient in originating power *&* the power to organize, but he had the power to Control the People *through their reason—their love of Country—justice* and *the right.* Mr. Lincoln governed the People by these invisible views: his war government was a glorious success—a good evidence that Lincoln approximated to a first Class statesman.

Your Friend
W. H. Herndon

LC: HW3231; Exp 4:9:1863–64

145. To Jesse W. Weik

Springfield Ills Decr. 29th '85

Friend Weik:

I once had an excellent library which I was compelled to sell because I was too poor to hold it. I owed money and sacrificed it to pay my debts. I imported books from London, through the house of C S Francis & Co. When I heard of a good work I ordered it, English—German or French, if the two latter were translated. I kept many of my books in my office—Especially the new ones and read them. Mr. Lincoln had access to all such books as I had and frequently read parts of the volumes—such as struck his fancy. I used to read to him passages in the books that struck me as Eloquent, grand, poetical, philisophic and the like. I would talk in my own peculiar vein to Lincoln about what I read and thought: he would like or dislike what I read and thought—would discuss the subject with me, sometimes animatedly. Sometimes we would get into a philisophic discussion—sometimes on religious questions and sometimes on this question & on that. It was in the world of politics that he lived. Politics were his life—newspapers his food, and his great ambition his motive power. I have given you a list of the newspapers that we—one or the other of us, took from 1850 to 1861. Now let me give you the kind of books which Lincoln had access to and sometimes peeped into. I had all the following books—ie the writers of the works—their names and the books &c they wrote. If I did not have all I had the most of them—quite all and hundreds, if not thousands of others: they are as follow:

Emmerson	Darwin
Carlyle	Draper
Parker	Leckey
Mclaughlin	Lewes
Strauss	Renan
Morrell	Kant
Bucher	Fitche
Feurbach	Cousan
Buckle	Hamilton
Froude	&
Spencer[1]	the like[2]—took the Westminster Review

All the above class of books I purchased as soon as out. If in German or French and *translated* I sent for and got through the house of C.S. Francis & Co of New York. I kept abreast of the spirit of the age till financial troubles overtook me in 1871–5. Since that time I have not read much. My poverty keeps my nose to the grind stone and it is now raw. I was of a progressive frame of mind and tried to get Lincoln in the Same Channel of thought. How I succeeded time and criticism can alone tell. If I had any influence with him at all it was along the line of the good, I hope & believe. Possibly I have helped the world a little in my way—hope so. I shall never state fully or otherwise what I did for Lincoln. I shall never do this in writing. I will talk to Confidential friends somewhat in a *chat*—but never

---

1. Ralph Waldo Emerson, Charles Darwin, Thomas Carlyle, John W. Draper, Theodore Parker, W. H. L. Lecky, _____ McLaughlin, George Henry Lewes, David Strauss, Ernest Renan, John D. Morell, Immanuel Kant, Lothar Bucher, Johann G. Fichte, Ludwig Feuerbach, Victor Cousin, Henry Thomas Buckle, William Hamilton, James A. Froude, Herbert Spencer.

2. Alongside columns of authors: "I included publications up to 1861 only."

for use nor publication. I Can now see Lincoln—his image before me: it is a sad beseeching look. I feel sad.

Your good friend

W. H Herndon

LC: HW3232–33; Exp 4:9:1865–67

146. To Jesse W. Weik

Springfield Ills. Jany 1st 1886

Friend Weik

In my last letter I gave you a list of books which Lincoln more or less peeped into. I forgot some important ones on political Economy: they are as follow Mills political Economy—Carey's political Economy—social science. McCulloughs political Economy—Wayland and some others.[1] Lincoln ate up—digested and assimilated Wayland's little work. Lincoln liked the book, Except the *free trade* doctrines: Lincoln I think liked political Economy—the study of it. I had American and English works besides those mentioned above in political Economy.

The following Conversation between Lincoln and myself about 1858 is too good to be lost. One day I somewhat Earnestly Complained to Lincoln that he was not quick and energetic enough in a particular Case to accomplish our ends and what I thought was needed in the Case. In a wry good natured way he replied—"Billy I am like a long strong jack knife doubled up in the handle. The extreme point of the blade has to move through a wider space before it is open than your little short woman's Knife, which you hold in your hand, but when the jack knife is open it Cuts wider and *deeper* than your little thing. I am 6 feet 2 inches high and it takes me a good while to open and to act—so be patient with me." "To change the figure" he said—"These long Convolutions of my poor brain take time—sometimes a long time, to open and gather force, but like a long well platted heavy and well twisted ox lash, when swung around and around high in the air on a good whip stalk, well seasoned, by an expert ox driver and popped and Cracked and snapped at a lazy ox shirking duty it Cuts to the raw—brings blood—opens a gash that makes the lazy ox sting with pain; and so when these long convolutions are opened and let off on something—are they not a power and a force in action as you say. You yourself have often Complimented me on my force of expression and now in part you have the desired *Why*." This Mr. Lincoln said to me and the substance is his and many of the words are his just as he used them.

---

1. John Stuart Mill, *Principles of Political Economy with Some of Their Applications to Social Philosophy* (London, 1848); Henry C. Carey, *The Principles of Political Economy* (Philadelphia, 1837–40); John Ramsey McCulloch, *Principles of Political Economy* (Edinburgh, 1825); Francis Wayland, *The Elements of Political Economy* (Boston, 1837).

LINCOLN'S 1ST INAUGURAL

Mr. Lincoln sometime in Jany or Feby 1861 asked me to loan him Henry Clay's great—his best speech in 1850, and likewise told me to get him Presdt Jacksons Proclamation against Nullification in 1832–3 I think, and I the Constitution.[2] I did loan him Clay's speech of '50—Gen Jackson's proclamation, & the Constitution of the U. States. Lincoln was perfectly familiar with Webster's reply to Calhoun & Haynes in 1833, I think. Lincoln read Webster's reply to Calhoun and Haynes in 1834–5—in New Salem while deputy Post master under Saml Hill. Lincoln was thoroughly read up in the history of politics of his Country. Lincoln as soon as I got him what he wanted went over to Smith's Store on the South side of the public[3]—went up stairs above Smiths—his brother in law and got his room and then and there wrote his first Inaugural. Lincoln thought that Websters great speech in reply to Haynes was the very best speech that was ever delivered. It is my opinion that these books and speeches were all the things that he used in the writing of the 1st Inaugural

Now about Mrs Vineyard—not Vincent as I wrote to you. I have not heard from her. However I'll tell you where she lives, *if you will say to her that I referred you to her & that you are the only man, Except Lamon* I have mentioned her name to. This is the exact truth. Mrs. Vineyard—Mary—lives or did live in Weston Mo: She must be 78–80 years of age: She is if living an intelligent woman, well Educated and refined.[4]

One word about Dennis Hanks. When you see him ask him, in a round about way, if Thomas Lincoln was not castrated because of the mumps when young. Dennis told me this often and repeated it. *Please* ask the question; won't you and note it down.

If you see Mrs. Chapman and the Doctr. give them my best respects. You had better go down to Farmington in Coles and see Mrs. Moore if living: she is Lincoln's step sister, as I remember it.[5] As you live in Indiana you had better go & see Mrs Jones of Gentryville.[6] Lincoln kept Store or worked for Jones. When you Come up here I have an idea to suggest to you.

Excuse this paper and my blunder on it[7]

Your Friend

W H Herndon

LC: HW3238r, 3239r/v, 3238v; Exp 4:9:1877, 1879–80, 1878

---

2. WHH seems here to have meant to say "and I think the Constitution."

3. The public square, occupied then as now by the state capitol.

4. Mary Owens Vineyard died in 1877.

5. Matilda Johnston Hall Moore was the daughter of AL's stepmother, Sarah Bush Johnston Lincoln.

6. The widow of William Jones, Lincoln's Indiana employer and mentor.

7. This note seems to refer to the letter's having been written on two folded sheets with the pages out of order.

147. To Cyrus O. Poole

Springfield Ills Jany 5th 1886

My Dear Sir:

In the first part of the 19th Century a great and noble man was born to America specially and to the world generally. His life was a grand success and his name stands high up among the mountain Men of the world. Mr. Lincoln thought too much and did too much for America and the world to be crammed into an Epigram or shot off with a single rocket: he was too close to the touch of the divine everywhere and too near to the suggestions and whisperings of nature for such quick work, done with a flash. It is said that he was a many sided man. It will take close, severe and Continuous thought through an analysis of his character to understand him or give a just idea of the man. Mr. Lincoln was a riddle and a puzzle to his friends and neighbors among whom he lived and moved. You wish to see this puzzle solved and this riddle unriddled. You and the world wish—crave to know the elements of Lincoln's great and honored success. You desire—you wish for a knowledge of the causes of his power and the secrets of his success. Having been acquainted with the man for more than thirty years—twenty years of which he was known by me closely & intimately I have formed a settled opinion ~~of the man~~, founded on my own observation—experience and reason of the mind and the courses of his power and the secrets of his success; and I propose to give to the world my opinion of them. This is done *first* because the man was hard—very difficult to understand, even by his bosom friends and his close and intimate neighbors among whom he associated; and *Secondly* because the reading and thinking world does not know him to-day. I really and dearly wish to aid the good people in forming a good a correct and just opinion of the man. If Mr. Lincoln could speak to me this day, in reference to my purpose in writing this letter, he would say—"Tell the truth and don't varnish me"; and I shall follow its Spirit.

First: Mr. Lincoln's success in life rested on his qualities—characteristics and nature, which are as follows—*First:* he had great reason—pure and strong: he lived in the mind and he thought in his life and lived in his thought. Lincoln was a persistent thinker, and a profound analyzer of the subject which engaged his attention. Politics were his life, newspapers his food and his ambition his motive power. What he read he read for a proximate—near end: he was not a general reader: he was embodied reflection itself: he was not only reflective but abstracted. These wrought evils on his intellectual and physical system: he was a close—persistent, continuous and terrible thinker: he was self reliant—self helpful—self truthful, never once doubting his own ability or power to do anything any one could do. Mr. Lincoln thought—at least he so acted, that there were no limitations to the endurance of his mental and vital forces. In his case from a long—severe—continuous and exhaustive study of the subject which he loved, generally taking no stimulative food nor drinks, there followed as a consequence physical and mental exhaustion—a nervous morbidity and spectral illusions—irratability—melancholy and despair. Hence, I think, comes a little of his superstition.

Secondly—Mr. Lincoln had an active, breathing and a living conscience that rooted itself deep down in his very being, every fibre of which twisted around his whole nervous system. This Conscience of his was a positive quality of him, and it sent its orders and decrees to the head to be executed there: it was the Court of Courts that gave final judgments from which there was no appeal, so far as he was concerned: he stood bolt upright and downright on his Conscience. What that decreed the head and tongue and hands obeyed unhesitatingly, never doubting its justice. Lincoln lived mostly in the Conscience and the head; and these two attributes of his were the two great ones of his nature—the ruling and predominant ones of his whole and entire life. It is thought by some men that Mr. Lincoln was a very warm hearted man—spontaneous and impulsive. This is not the exact truth. God has never yet made and it is probable that he never will make any man—any creature all head—all heart—and all Conscience. His types are of the mixed element compounded to suit himself. Mr. Lincoln was tender hearted when *in the presence* of suffering or when it was enthusiasticaly or poetically described to him: he had great charity for the weaknesses of his fellow man: his nature was merciful and it sprang into manifestation quickly on *the presentation* of a proper subject under proper conditions: he had no imagination to invoke, through the distances, suffering, nor fancy to paint it. The subject of mercy must be presented to him. The main question with Mr. Lincoln was—"Is the thing right—is it just," and if a man was the subject of his attention the question which he put to himself was—"What great truth—what principle do you represent in this world?" If the thing was just he approved of it, and if the man was a sham he said—"Begone." He was a man of great moral and physical courage and had the valor and bravery of his convictions and dared cautiously to do what he thought was right and just: he was cautious and conservative in his nature—was prudent and wise in his acts and I have often thought over Cautious, sometimes bordering on the timid. Sometimes he stood long hesitating between the thought and the deed.

Thirdly—Mr. Lincolns heart was sufficiently warm and he sufficiently impulsive and Spontaneous for the broad field and noble sphere of his action ~~and~~ his and the nation's destiny. A governor—a judge—a president in office has not legally much to do with the heart, but has all to do with Conscience and reason—right and justice as defined by law. Had Mr. Lincoln been a man of no will and all heart this great government would have gone to [wick?] in 1863 or before. Come, was not Mr. Lincoln built and organized for the occasion? Was he not the right man in the right time—in the right place? Would you have made him different? How would you have grouped the atoms or mixed and mingled the elements of his make up?

Mr. Lincoln was a sad—gloomy and melancholic man and wore the signs of these in every line of his face—on every organ and every feature of it: they were chisseled deep therein; and now the question is—What were the Causes of these? The Causes were—*first*—possibly heredity and *secondly* his physical *organization*. Mrs. Thomas Lincoln—Abraham's own mother was an uneducated—somewhat rough, but by nature an intellectual—sad and sensative woman. It is quite ~~probable~~ possible that Mr. Lincoln inherited this sadness and sensativeness from his mother:

he was in some particulars a very sensitive man. It is ~~probable possible~~ probable that his physical *organization*, which functioned slowly & feebly, gave rise to feelings of uneasiness—nervousness, and irritability—gloom—melancholy and despondancy, if not sometimes of despair. Both of these heredity and organization may have acted as causes. These states, however caused, made him a fatalist in philosophy and a sceptic in matters of religion. His philosophy was—"What is to be will be and no wish of ours nor prayers can change nor reverse the inevitable decree. Lincoln's sad hopeless declaration to his friends in Washington, who advised him to be more careful of his person in the future than he ~~was~~ had been in the past in substance was—"My dear Sirs, it is writ—it is writ." The very idea that he was in the hands of an invisible, irresitable and inevitable deaf power which moved as an omnipotent force evidently harassed and worried him. There are two other minor causes that may have intensified his states—his melancholy and the like: they were *first*, his intense love for—courtship of and untimely death of Ann Rutledge, the handsome, sweet and lovely girl of New Salem and *Secondly*, his courtship of and marriage to Miss Mary Todd. Lincoln's married life was a domestic hell on Earth. The whole sad story *shall* be told sometime. Twice, in this man's life he walked that sharp and narrow line that divided sanity from insanity.

~~Mr. Lincoln's success in life rested in his qualities, characteristics, and nature which are as follows—First—he had great reason—pure and strong, he lived in his mind and he thought in his life and lived in his thoughts; he was a positive and persistent thinker and a most profound analyzer of the subject which engaged his attention: he was embodied reflection itself. What he read he read for a proximate end a more particular end. Mr. Lincoln's life was politics—news papers his food; and his great ambition his motive power. His ambition was remorseless.~~[1]

Men at once—at first blush everywhere saw that Lincoln was a sad—gloomy man—a man of sorrow. I have often & often heard man say—"That man is a man of sorrow, and I really feel for him—I sympathize with him". This sadness on the part of Mr. Lincoln and sympathy on the part of the observer were a hearts' magnetic tie between the two. This result gave Lincoln power over men—rather it was self imposed. All men and women always and everywhere treated him under all conditions with great and profound respect; and a close observer of human nature could see—detect that much of that deep respect issued from the heart. Let me translate such acts of respect and deference of those who ever saw him into my own words. Those words are—"I beseech you let me respect and favor you." Men who do not know Mr. Lincoln and never did have paraded his hardships and struggles in his younger days in glowing words—or sad ones. Such an idea—such a description of the man is not exactly true: he never saw the minute—the hour nor the day that he did not have many financial friends to aid him—to assist him, and to help him in all ways. His friends vied with each other for the pleasure or the honor of assisting him. Lincoln deserved all this respect and confidence: he

---

1. This stricken passage seems to have been written from the same notes as a passage near the beginning of the letter, and was likely stricken for that reason.

was all honor and integrity—spoke the whole truth and acted it: he like all boys in the great west as well as elsewhere had to study in order to learn. Life in his case was a comparatively easy life, as compared with the struggles of the ambitious young men of the East. There the struggle for life is the fiercer. Lincoln was the favorite of every body—man, woman and child where he lived and was known and he richly deserved it. Lincoln generally rejected all help, his idea—matter being—"Those who receive favors owe a debt of gratitude to the giver and to that extent are obedient and abject slaves"

First—Now if the reader will but put these four qualities of Lincoln together— *First* namely—his great reasoning power with a profound judgment, if he had time to fully evolve and apply his ideas to the facts of life—*Secondly*—a deep and living Conscience, with a tender heart *in presence* of suffering or want—*Thirdly*—his spirit of prudence and his genius for practical sagacity; and *fourthly*—a sadness—a gloominess with somewhat of fatalistic ideas in his philosophy and skepticism about his religion or beleifs—authority—creeds, & forms of religion, *and run them out as causes* into his daily life, and he will have the causes of his power and the secrets of his success. These have influenced me and thousands, if not millions of others. I felt these influences when he and I were younger, and I feel them now. Because of Lincoln's great reason—his Conscience, his heart—his sadness—his prudence and practical sagacities, women, men, the people & and the nation voluntarily and trustfully threw themselves into his arms, clothed with an almost infinite power, and as calmly and as confidingly and as trustfully rested there as when an infant goes to sleep in its mother's loving—tender and watchful bosom. Lincoln deeply impressed this trustworthyness upon the people and they were never decieved: they were an impressible mass and he stamped it deep into the word—*Trust*.

Secondly—Mr. Lincoln continuously lived in three worlds—states or conditions of his existence. *First*, he lived in the purely reflective and thoughtful—*Secondly*, in the sad thoughtless and gloom & *thirdly*, he lived in the happy world of his own levities: he was sometimes in the one state and then in an other, and at times the transition was slow and gradual and at times quick—quick as a flash. Writers, respected ones and biographers have said that Lincoln was a many sided man. If they mean that he was sometimes reflective and thoughtful—sometimes thoughtless and sometimes cheerful and happy then I have no objections to the idea of his many sidedness. I would suggest a better and a more accurate idea and that is that Mr. Lincoln was a many *mooded* man. To form a perfectly true idea of the man take the first four qualities as last mentioned above and the three last mentioned and bunch them and the reader has a true analysis of Lincoln's nature & a good insight into the inner man. Every feeling that Lincoln felt—every thought of his—every willing & action of the man issued, burst out of and from the qualities—attributes and states above given. His thoughts were tinged and colored and his acts fashioned by his moods. These must all be considered and taken as a whole when Mr Lincoln is to be thoroughly understood by any one.

Wishing to help the people to understand Mr. Lincoln they must indulge me in a repetican of an other idea so as to keep the full train of thought in view.

He thought, at least he so acted, that there were no limitations to the force and endurance of his mental and vital powers. In his Case from a long—continuous—severe—persistent and exhaustive thought of the subjects which he loved, as a general rule taking no stimulative food nor drinks, there necessarily followed, as a consequence physical and mental exhaustion—a nervous morbidity—a sadness—a gloom—a melancholy—spectral illusion—irratability and despair. Hence it may be comes his superstition. I state this that men may see Mr. Lincoln as I saw him and knew him. This is the sole reason.

In what Mr. Lincoln said he suppress no fact and suggested no falsehood: he told the truth and the whole truth and this truthfulness and sincerity were written on every organ and feature of the face. The observer saw this and firmly and fixedly believed and trusted what he saw & felt. I do not wish to be misunderstood. I have said and now say that Mr. Lincoln was a secretive—silent and a very reticent minded man, trusting no man, nor woman, nor child with the inner secrets of his ambitious soul. This man was easy of approach and perfectly democratic in his nature. No man however humble ever felt uneasy in his presence. Lincoln was an odd man—a singular man—awkward—uncouth—graceless and somewhat unsocial. But these, to some, repulsive aspects of his nature, like the lesser star in the heavens, were driven into the dark infinite background by the greater—and brighter flaming ones of his good intents beaming over his face.

This great man, for great he was, has given to the world a great—a grand Character and let us all lovingly cherish it forever. Mr. Lincoln is a true and faithful expression of this, our age and a good representative of it. Our generation and our times will eloquently speak to the great infinite future generations and times, through our good and great men, who will teach them our arts—sciences civilization & philosophies. The good deeds of to-day will run through the race and knit us all together by silver threads, along the lines of which we of to-day and of this generation shall speak through all times and to all generations of men.

Your Friend
Wm H. Herndon[2]

[*Note on same page*]
Jany 22d 87
Friend Weik:
You must expect some repetition where I write so many different letters to different men all over the Union, East & West—north & South. I cannot help it entirely and no man could. What I cannot help I am not to be censured for.

Your Friend
W. H H

LC: HW3240–46; Exp 4:9:1881–93

---

2. This is a retained copy, most likely the composition draft, that was later sent on to JWW, as shown by the note on its final page and by direct reference in WHH to JWW, January 22, 1887. See §180, p. 224.

148. To Jesse W. Weik

Springfield Ills. Jany 7th '86

Friend Weik:

I wish to say a few words about Lincoln's Education or the probabilities in him of a College & Classical Education. Mr. Lincoln was by nature a man of peculiarities and of strong individualities. His Expressions were strong—gnarly—& original: he had an exact & keen perception—the precise seeing of the thing or idea; and had the power of Expression: he studied Expression—the keen clear power of Exact utterance to convey his idea. Had he gone to College and *half* graduated, or wholy so; and before his style was crystalised—or had been Educated after he had read our rounded, flat, dull artistic style of expression—writing—or speaking, he would have lost—and the world would have lost his strong individuality in his speech—his style—manner & method of utterance. He would have been a rounded man in an artistic way—would have sunk into the Classic beautiful. But it so happened was so decreed that his style—manner—method of utterance— Expression—its strength—its simplicity—and rugged grandeur were crystalised long before he became acquainted with the smoothed—weak & artistic style of today. Lincoln was Lincoln & no one Else; and he spoke & wrote in Lincolisms. Polish—art and literature grind down our peculiarities—personalities and individualities and make us alike in Expression. We sacrifice strength and grandeur to art & beauty. If you remember, I told you that the process—way of Lincoln's mental evolution was through thought to Esops fables—through these to general maxims from maxims to stories—jokes—jests; and from these to Clear, strong— Anglo Saxon words of power. In his mental Evolution he passed through all these phases. I have heard Lincoln substantiall state this, including the probablities of the weakening process—methods &c of a Classical or College Education—so I was told this by all his friends in Indiana & his early friends in Illinois.

The [fawning?]—smoothe—sickly—weak artistic literature of the day, ocean wide and as shallow too, would like the rising tide & reflow—the pulses & surges of the sea have ground the sharp—jagged—and rough Corners off the man like the ground pebbles into a round polished thing—like the pebbles on the beaches of the ocean, all quite alike.

Lincoln you know was a Complete success in Law—in politics and as a rule as Presdt of the United States: he was a flat failure as inventor—Eulogist and lecturer: he once tried to demonstrate the undemonstrable: he thought that he could completely demonstrate—square of the circle: he purchased tools &c with which to make the attempt, but failed. Lincoln was keenly sensative to his failures and it would not do to mention them in his presence. Mr. Lincoln, had he taken up the idea—had he thought it necessary, would have taught the graces of motion—civilities of life—Etiquettes of society & its fashions. Lincoln thought that he could do anything—that other men could or would try to do: he had unbounded Confidence in himself—in his Capacities & powers: he asked no man's advice and sought no man's opinions as a general—quite universal rule.

These peculiarities *and* failures show that Lincoln had narrow & shallow shoals in the river of his being o'er which the waters danced and rippled, but which broke in the flashing sunlight into millions of flashing mirrors, reflecting wondrous beauty to the human Eye and yet these narrow & shallow shoals only proved that above them and below them that there were deeper waters all up and down the great streem of his grand life that flowed onward and onward to the deep wide seas of the Eternal. Such was Lincoln.

It is now late and in the night—am tired from my daily toil. Will you have the kindness to write me out a copy of this and send it to me. I have no time to do it—want said Copy for a friend in New York—so good night, my friend.

Your good friend
W H Herndon

LC: HW3247–48; Exp 4:9:1898–1901

149. To Jesse W. Weik

Springfield Ills Jany 8th '86

Friend Weik:

It was the habit—custom of Mrs. Lincoln when any big man or woman visited her house to dress up and trot out Bob—Willie or Tad and get them to monkey around—talk—dance—speak—quote poetry &c. &c. Then she would become enthusiastic & eloquent over the children much to the annoyance of the visitor and to the mortification of Lincoln. However Lincoln was totally blind to his children's faults. After Mrs Lincoln had exhausted the English language and broken herself down in her rhapsodies on her children Lincoln would smooth things over by saying—"These children may be something sometimes, if they are not merely rareripes—rotten ripes—hot house plants." I have always noticed that a rare-ripe child quickly mature, but rots as quickly." Lincoln was proud of his children and blind to their faults—. He—Lincoln—used to come down to our office on a Sunday when Mrs. Lincoln had gone to church—*to show her new bonnet*, leaving Lincoln to care for and attend to the children. Lincoln would turn Willie and Tad loose on our office and they soon gutted the room—gutted the shelves of books—rifled the drawers and riddled boxes—battered the points of my gold pens against the stoves turned over the ink stands on the papers—scattered letters over the office and danced over them and the like. I have felt a many a time that I wanted to wring the necks of these brats and pitch them out of the windows, but out of respect for Lincoln and knowing that he was abstracted, I shut my mouth—bit my lips and left for parts unknown. Poor boys—they are dead now and gone! I should like to *Know* one thing and that is—What caused the death of these children? I have an opinion which I shall never state to any one. I know a good deal of the Lincoln family and too much of Mrs. Lincoln. I wish I did not know as much of her as I do: she was a tigress. I can see poor Lincoln woman whipt and woman Cowed and yet sometimes he would rise and cut up the very devil for a while—make things move lively and "get." This woman was once a brilliant one, but what a sad sight to see her in any year after 1862 and Especially a year or so before she died: she refused to see any and all ministers of the Gospel—any preachers—about her hopes of heaven or fear of hell—about God or her own salvation. I guess her religion was like her husband's—rather infidel—agnostic or atheistic &c. &c. ascending to moods or whims.

You state to me that I am the only one of Lincoln's friends—cotemporaries that is willing to tell anything or much about Lincoln or his family. There are two good reasons for this—1st he was not well and perfectly known by many and 2dly he tramped too often hard on the toes of those who did know him. Lincoln outstript his cotemporaries & companions and they feel a terrible jealously against the man who overheaded—outstript them. I have seen this meanness often. I have often said to you that Lincoln was terribly ambitious and to that extent he was egoistic—selfish—cold. The ruling people here—say from 1856 to 1861—do not, as I think, do right: they are mum about him except they are forced to say something good of him occasionally. The people—the middle Class worship Lincoln and the very bottom class blindly fall in the currents. I feel it my duty to state to all Peoples my ideas of Lincoln and my knowledge of the facts of his life so far as I know them This is my religion—has been for 20 years and will be probably for 10 more years. I want the world to know Lincoln

Your Friend

W H Herndon

LC: HW3249–50; Exp 4:9:1902–5

150. To Jesse W. Weik

Springfield Ills. Jany. 8th 1886

Friend Weik:

I have heard Lincoln tell the following *facts* on himself. In 1850 Mr. Lincoln was an applicant, under Fillmore's Administration, for Commissioner of the General Land office: he made arrangements to start for Washington and started from Ransdell's tavern in this city: he had a companion in the stage—for it was in old stage times, who was a gentleman from Kentucky—educated—cultured and a man of accomplishments, but like all warm and good hearted men he loved the good and cheerful. The two men—Lincoln & his friend started for Washington early in the morning, eating their breakfast before day. After they had got in the stage and had ridden some miles the Kentucky gentleman pulled out of his pocket a small plug of the very best tobacco from the "Sacred soil of Virginia," and handed it to Mr Lincoln, with a fine tortoise shell pen knife and said to Lincoln—: "Stranger, will you take a chew," and to which Mr Lincoln said—"Thank you, I never chew." The two rode on for some miles when they got near Taylorville, some 25 miles from this place and East of it the Kentucky gentleman pulled out a fine cigar case filled with the very best and choicest of Havana Cigars—opened it—got out his lighter and said to Lincoln—"Please have a fine Havana Cigar"; and to which Mr. Lincoln replied in his kindest manner—: "Thanks, stranger I never Smoke." The gentleman lit his cigar & very leisurely rode along, thumping and bumping over the rough road, smoking and puffing away, conversing all the while. Lincoln and his Kentucky Companion became very much attracted to each other. Lincoln had told some of his best jokes and the man had spun out his best ideas. They were really much pleased with Each other—seemed to fit one an other. The Kentucky gentleman was graceful and Lincoln graceless, but somehow or other they fit Each other like brother chums. They rode on merrily and pleasantly for a long—long while to them, for it was a tiresome journey. The stand where the two were to Eat their dinners was being approached—was seen in the distance. The Kentucky man threw out of the stage the stub of his cigar—opened his sachel or other thing, and took out a silver Case filled with the very best French brandy—took out the cork—got a silver cup—and handing them to Lincoln, saying "Stranger—Take a glass of the best of French brandies—, won't you?" and to which Mr Lincoln Said—"No—I thank you mister—I never drink." This peculiarity Seemed to amuse the Kentucky gentleman very much: he threw himself back against the front of the stage and good naturedly and laughing Said—"See here stranger—rather my jolly companion, I have gone through the world a good deal & have had much experience with men and women of all classes, and in all climes; and I have noticed *one* thing—" Mr. Lincoln here breaking in anxiously asked his companion.—"What is it—what is it?" "It is this—" Said the Kentucky man. "My observation—my experience is, among men—that those who have no vices have d——d few virtues." Lincoln was fond of a joke as you know—looked at his friend sharply to see if it was a joke or was intended for an insult; intending to pitch him out of the stage if it was an insult; and to laugh over it if a joke. Lincoln was quickly convinced that the man was good-natured kind—gentlemanly &c.; and then he burst out into a loud laugh saying—"It's good—it's too good to be lost & I shall tell it to my friends. Lincoln really laughed himself tired kicked out, in fact, the bottom of the stage—tore out the crown of his hat by running his hand through it &c &c The two friends became bosom ones and landed in Washington together. The Kentuckian got what he wanted & Lincoln got defeated &c

Your friend

W H Herndon

Polish this up—run it out. It is too good to be half told or lost H

LC: HW3251–52; Exp 4:9:1906–9

151. To Jesse W. Weik

Springfield Ills. Jany 9th 1886

Friend Weik:

I know a man now living or did live in Menard County: he, if living, must be 80 years of age. The name of the man is Minter Graham: he was an intelligent man—a good and a truthful man & yet in some things he was "sorter cranky". About the year 1817 he was travelling from _____ to Elizabethtown Ky. In passing from _____ to the latter place he saw at a little place a crowd of men—stopt—hitched his horse & went among the Crowd—soon found out that a man. had Killed his wife. Persons were expressing their horror at the act. Soon after Graham had stopt Thomas Lincoln and his boy Abraham came along and stopt—went among the crowd—found out what was the matter—had some conversation with the Crowd—and now comes the nib of this letter. After all the people had expressed their ideas one of the men said to Abram "My little boy what do you think of such a deed?" The boy studied a moment—and gave a terse and eloquent idea of the cruel deed. Graham says that the boy was very sad—that his language was Eloquent and feeling for one so young. The remarks which he made astonished all present—were pronounced good—plain—terse and strong and says Graham—"I have now known Mr. Lincoln for more than 60 years and I can see the same trait of character and the same style now in Lincoln that I did in 1817 in Ky: he studies to see the subject matter clearly and to express it tersely and strongly.[1] I have known him down here in Menard Study for hours the best way of any of these to express an idea: he was a strong man and an honest one. I knew Lincoln's relatives way back in 1802–4. Thomas Lincoln was a blank, but a clever man—a somewhat social creature. How he raised such a boy as Abe the Lord only Knows."

The above I know to be true so far as this—Lincoln always struggled to see the thing or the idea exactly and to express that idea in such language as to convey that idea precisely. When a young boy he read pretty much all the books in the neighborhood, and they were not more than a dozen. If he found anything worthy of his thoughts he would write it down—commit it to memory—then analyze it while he held it firmly in *conciousness*—in his mind. When this was done he would tell it o'er &o'er to his step mother and friends; and I can say the same thing with this addition—That he used to bore me terribly by his methods—processes— manner &c. &c. Mr. Lincoln would doubly explain things to me that needed no explanation. However I stood and took it out of respect for the man: he was terribly afraid that I did not understand him when I understood even his thoughts *at it*. Lincoln despised "glittering generalities" and even hated the man that used them. Mr. Lincoln was a very patient man generally but if you wished to be cut off at the knees just go at Lincoln with abstractions—glittering generalities—in-definite mistiness of idea or expression. Here he flew up and became vexed and

---

1. Graham's recollection may be a case of mistaken identity, as AL moved away from Kentucky in 1816 at age seven.

sometimes foolishly so: his mind was so organized that he could not help it and so we must excuse him. Lincoln's ambition in this line was this—he wanted to be distinctly understood by the Common people: he used to say to me—"Billy dont shoot too high—shoot low down, and the common people will understand you: they are *the ones* which you wish to reach—at least they are the ones whom you ought to reach. The educated ones will understand you anyhow. If you shoot too high your bullets will go over the heads of the mass, and only hit those who need no hitting." This Lincoln has said to me many times when I was on the stump or at the bar, or writing leaders for our newspapers which I did from 1854 to 1861, advocating Liberty and Lincoln.

Your Friend

W. H Herndon

LC: HW3258–59; Exp 4:9:1920–23

152. To Jesse W. Weik

Springfield Ills Jany 9th '86

Friend Weik:

Justice North of this city was once in St Louis hunting up an auctioneer. North kept in this city an auction room and wanted a number one auctioneer—a practical and a good one. Some gentleman in St Louis recommend one Chas Lewis—if I have not forgotten the name: he was somehow a nephew of Mrs Lincoln or probably other relative. North and Lewis made a contract. Lewis came up to this city as North's auctioneer: he had money and asked no favors—got $60 per month from North for his services. As soon as he landed here he as a relative of *Mrs* Lincoln thought it his duty to call on his *aunt*. So he went to see her—knocked at the door—was coldly admitted—told Mrs. Lincoln who he was &c. &c. Mrs. Lincoln's avarice at once arose and she told the young gentleman, in coarse—cruel and brutish language, that she did not wish her poor relatives to pile themselves on her and Eat her up. The young man tried to explain to her that out of respect he had called to see her—said he had plenty of money and had a good position and did not need her charaty and did not deserve her coarse—savage and brutal language: He quickly left the house deeply mortified, leaving *Mrs* Lincoln in one of her haughty—imperious and angry states. When Mr. Lincoln returned home in about two hours he at once saw that Mrs. Lincoln was standing square on her ears. Lincoln asked *Mrs* Lincoln what was the matter: she told him: he knew that she had acted the fool and the savage. Mr. Lincoln instantly went down to North's auction room, expecting to find rather a rough young, but unexpectedly he found a rather accomplished fellow, in order to apologise to the young man for the cruel treatment he had received at the hands of his wife. The young man made his statement to Lincoln—Lincoln once saw how it stood—apologised to the young man—talked to him tenderly and in a fatherly way—offered to assist him in all ways—loan him funds, if the young man needed it—invited him to his house &c.

&c. The young man thanked Mr Lincoln and told him that he did not need his assistance, but was much obliged to him &c &c he never went to see Mrs Lincoln again. The young man was heard to say—"Uncle is one of the noblest of men, but aunt (or cousin) is a savage" This story illustrates the difference between Lincoln & Mrs. Lincoln. This was about 1858—probably 1860. Lincoln as a general rule dare not invite any one to his house; because he did not know what moment she would kick Lincoln and his friend out of the house This woman was to me a ter- ror—haughty—poor when she married Lincoln—imperious, proud, aristocratic, insolent witty and bitter: she was a gross material woman as she appeared to me. Look at her picture and you can see what I have seen. In her domestic troubles I have always sympathized with her. The world does not know what she bore and the history of the bearing. I will write it out sometimes. This domestic *hell* of Lincoln's life is not all on one side. I do not & cannot blame Lincoln; and do not wish you to suppose that I could censure him, for I could not. Wait patiently for all the facts. Mrs. Lincoln acted out in her domestic relation the laws of human revenge: This is somewhat of my meaning. Sit still and "wait for the glory of the Lord."

You will please take my notes, called letters just as they are. I have no time to read them and correct them. When you Copy all or parts please correct. I have to write in a run and a rush as you know the facts of my business and the conditions of my life. I have to struggle to-day for my tomorrow's bread.

Your Friend
W. H. Herndon

Note.
By the way, did you save a copy of the long letter which I wrote to you about Lincoln and Garfield which you had published?[1]

LC: HW3260–61; Exp 4:9:1924–27

153. To Jesse W. Weik

Springfield Ills Jany 10th '86

Friend Weik:

Some days since I told you that Lincoln was a success as a lawyer—a politician & as ruler—Presdt of the U.S. I said that he was a total failure as inventor—eulogist and lecturer. When Lincoln passed the line of politics he was a weak brother of the race. Lincoln delivered 3 lectures here, I think. One was on the Iron age of the Bible or substantially that. I heard it—The second one was on the Young American or substantially that and the 3d one I cannot recall just now—will try to hunt it up. Lincoln in the first lecture traced the discovery & use of Iron as stated in the

---

1. Not found.

Bible from the beginning to end: it was a dull and miserable affair, and I would not put it among my records—wish I had now. The second was no better, if any.[1] People heard them—a few of 'em and were struck astonishment. Lincoln was a somewhat sensative man generally, and particularly so when his productions were criticised. If no attention was paid to them he was sad. To tell Lincoln that he was a failure in some walks of life was to make him miserable: he thought so much of his Lectures, they were written out & read, that supposing the persons to whom he gave them would print them—have them bound in gold or gilt and worship them, but the poor man was terribly mistaken: he gave one of these to a lady by the name of Brown as I recollect it now. What he did with the others I do not know or don't recollect.[2] It is said by Hon Isaac N. Arnold, Lincoln's late biographer, that Lincoln was a *first rate conversationalist*. This is simply nonsense. Mr. Lincoln was not a cultured man—not a general reader—had not much Education—didnt go much in society—was all head & conscience—all respect—somewhat unsocial—abstracted and a little cold—: he did not seek society—man nor woman for its—his or her sake: he sought each in order to shoot off his stories—very vulgar & dirty one too—the very vulgarist and nastiest that possibly could be told. Lincoln was not a vulgar nor nasty minded man by any means. On the contrary I think he was a pure minded man—not nasty nor obscene for the sake of such stories: he told his stories because they had a *point—a cut—and a sting* in them. Now let Mr. Lincoln get into politics among political groups of men who were his friends or among groups of men who loved the smutty—pointed and cutting stories, then Lincoln could *talk & chat* well. He was no *Conversationalist* as I understand that word. Mr. Lincoln was a poor listener. If the subject of the talk was politics he occupied the stand; and if stories—jokes &c then he was the Centre of the of the Circle—and voiced the wishes of the Crowd. Mr. Lincoln would use his chums, companions, if that word would apply to Lincoln, use them to make himself successful or happy and then throw them away as old tools. Lincoln—what—Strangers know him—pshaw! Lincoln—what—he go about telling his religious views to priests & preachers whom he in his inmost soul hated—thunder! good Lord!

Lincoln lived in the head, and conscience—not much in the heart: In the political field he was a man of profound judgements, if he had time to think—a man of sagacity—*the very genius of practical sagacities.* In this field he was without an Equal, standing like a great light house on some Continental Shore to light up the ocean—welcoming the good—bidding the Commerce of the world a most hearty coming. Here is a Singular man for your young study and worthy of it; he was a good man and a great one—an honest man & a man of integrity, loving justice &

---

1. The two elements WHH remembers belong to the same lecture. Wayne C. Temple has shown that AL had only one lecture, which he delivered at least six times. See Temple.

2. The manuscript of AL's only public lecture was in a portfolio of miscellaneous manuscripts left in the custody of Mary Lincoln's cousin, Elizabeth Grimsley, later Brown, who dispersed them to AL's friends after his death. See §213, n 1.

the Eternal right. As this man plowed through the sea of life he has left us streaks
of light—lines of light which tell us the whither of his going. God bless him!
Your Friend
W. H. Herndon

P.S If history is to be written it is worthy of being truly written. I may err—am
not infalleable—If wrong I hope to correct *Herndon*
You ought to tell me to take a different turn—a different cut if things don't suit
you. H

   LC: HW3262–63; Exp 4:9:1928–31

154. To Jesse W. Weik

Springfield Ills. Jany 12th '86

Friend Weik—
   While I have said that Mr Lincoln was skeptical—a doubting man—a man
that requires proofs before he believes a thing, *do not* understand that he was not
a credulous man. When you told him anything that was contrary to nature or his
experience he would think that you were mistaken or a liar. Tell him any thing
that he had no experience in—or story—tale—a given state of circumstances he
would a vast liar,[1] because he could test the fact by his experiences: he was not a
judge of human nature: he was honest and could not see how any man could sit
down and tell a lie, without some terribly strong motive: he was honest himself
to the bone and supposed that others were so constituted. *Mrs.* Lincoln used to
help Lincoln from being imposed upon: he frequently said to her—What is your
opinion of this man—that story. &c. &c
   Again *do not suppose* that because Lincoln had a powerful self esteem in his
own ability in the intellectual world to do anything that any body could do that
he was egotistic and so exhibited himself to the world and *do not* suppose that he
was dogmatic. Mr Lincoln was not egotistic, excepting in the mind—not open to
the world nor was he dogmatic: he was very careful in his statements and generally
so limited by facts & principles that what he said was truth and that he stated
firmly—bravely and corageously. This man is hard to understand. If you wish to
see what estimate his neighbors and old friends placed on him here in 1865 please
turn to Hollands life of Lincoln at pages 241–2. Please read those pages—and see
for yourself how he was estimated here in 1865.
   Lincoln was positive yet he was not arrogant nor dogmatic nor insolent nor
overbearing: he was credulous & yet incredulous—skeptical & yet a deeply religious
man. Lincoln had strong appetites—affections for _____ his children and strong
passions: he never looked to see what he ate but filled up and said nothing: he was
selfish in the love of his children—blind as a bat: like other men among women

---

1. Apparently WHH meant to write "he would believe a vast liar."

he occasionally boiled over. I have been around on the Circuit not to have noticed these things. When other lawyers were anxious to get home from the circuit and see wife and babies Lincoln did not nor would come home & meet the face of that terrible woman who by her cruel ways drove him home.[2] Is it any wonder that Lincoln sometimes *loved* woman & slopt over when he had no wife whom he loved. Poor man. The world is indebted to Mrs Lincoln indirectly: she drove her husband from home—made him study—kept him among men & in society and away from the domestic circle. Lincoln naturally love home sweet home and would have been quite a domestic man had he a chance, but it was decreed that he should keep thinking and moving along. Mrs Lincoln was a stimulant to Lincoln in a good sense: she was always urging him to look up—struggle—conquer and go up to fame by becoming a big man: she coveted place—position—power—wanted to lead society and to be worshipt by man and woman: she was ambitious and helped Lincoln along in her own providental way, while she crushed his spirit in an other way: she was like the tooth ake—kept one awake night and day

When you see errors read right along—When you see bad grammar or bad spelling—say—d——n it and go ahead—no time to read over what I have written

Your Friend

W. H. Herndon

I have spoken to several of my friends to give me material which they have promised to do and when they give me the facts I'll write to you H

LC: HW3264–65; Exp 4:9:1932–35

155. To Jesse W. Weik

Springfield Ills Jany 13th '86

Friend Weik

There was a curious streak in Lincoln and it was that of a *seeming* ingratitude. Lincoln came to this city in 1837; and Joshua F. Speed gratuitously took him into his room—gave him bed—house room &c. Wm Butler was a man of some wealth for the time—was successful in business—was making money &c: he took Lincoln to his house, gave him a bed—sleeping room and boarded him from 1837 to 1842 when Lincoln got married to Miss Todd—*The female wild cat of the age.*[1] Butler was a whig & so was Lincoln. Butler did not charge Lincoln one cent for the board for years—lodging &c. &c—. Butler saw in Lincoln a gloom—a sadness—melancholy &c and deeply Sympathized with him—wanted to help him.

---

2. WHH apparently meant to write "drove him *from* home."

---

1. AL seems to have lodged with Speed above his store until Speed left Springfield in 1841, but boarded with Butler. Thereafter, AL probably lodged with Butler until his marriage to Mary Todd in November 1842. On the question of whether Butler's hospitality was gratuitous, see §155, §159, and §234.

Lincoln is painted by men who do not know him as having a hard time of it in his struggle for existence—success—fame. This is all *bosh*—nonsense. No man ever had an Easier time of it in his early days—in his boyish—in his young struggles than Lincoln he had—always had influential and financial friends to help him: they almost fought each other for the privilege of assisting Lincoln: he was most certainly entitled to this respect. I have watched men & women closely in this matter. Lincoln was a pet—a faithful and an honest pet in this city: he deserved it. Lincoln was a poor man and must work his way up: he was ambitious—fired by it: it eclipsed his better nature, and when he used a man and sucked all the uses out of him he would throw away the *thing* as an old orange peeling. This was not always the case—*probably* not Lincoln's general rule. Lincoln was elected to Congress in 1847, I think: he had some patronage to bestow and his old friend Butler applied to him for the office of the Register or receiver of public monies in this city. There was an other applicant for the same office by the name of King—a kind of worthless man, in my opinion, and Lincoln gave the office to King over the head of Butler. Butler and Lincoln did not speak for years see note, over. [*note* Butler opposed Lincoln in all his aspirations for office from 1847 till about 1858. Butler frequently with others defeated Lincolns schemes. Lincoln thought it best for himself to bury the hatchet as I suppose / H] Lincoln was again—say in 1867–8 approached by Butler for an office, and Lincoln *did* give it to him, and out of which he made a fortune.[2] Such are the tricks and ways of politicians in this world. If politics make as noble a man as Lincoln was—as great a man too—God deliver me from the struggles, and ambitions of a political life. I saw Judge Matheny this morning, and asked him his remembrance of the facts and he remembers it substantially as I do—and as stated herein. History if it is worth writing is worthy of true writing and so I give you this note. I hope that you may never be a politician—pray so.

You may think that because I cut men—state the truth of them that I am a soured disappointed man, and in this thinking you are mistaken. I never was ambitious along the lines of politics, and on this line even I have been successful. My ambition was not for office—nor money, nor fame. My ambition in this life was to be an intelligent man, and a doer of good to my fellow man. To day I am a progressive and an advanced little thinker—a reformer—an optimist—an altruist, believing in an infinite Energy—Universal soul—God—in universal inspiration, revelation—sons of God. I am credulous to this extent—am broad and generous in my views. This infinite Energy has no *pets*—rules mind and matter by laws—absolute—universal and Eternal—. Now you have my philosophy and religion. I am today under my beliefs a contented and a happy man, and always have been and expect—hope to remain so.

It seems to me that I have written to you enough matter [to] make a respectable life of Lincoln. I feel that I am about pumped dry. However I shall continue to

---

2. Possibly a reference to what Butler described as "the cotton letter" given to him and others by AL in 1864, enabling them to engage in the highly profitable sale of Southern cotton. See *Oral History*, 23–24 and *Collected Works*, 7:213–14.

send you well authenticated facts & *only such*. Had you not better change your plans and issue a little life of Lincoln yourself? Answer this last idea. . . .

Your Friend
W. H. Herndon

LC: HW3266–67; Exp 4:9:1936–39

156. To Jesse W. Weik

Springfield Ills. Jany 15th '86

Friend Weik:

The great popularity of Mr. Lincoln in 1832 when he lived in Menard County— then in north West part of Sangamon County, arose almost wholly out of some measures he advocated, touching the personal and pecuniary interests of those in a locality. Mr. Lincoln advocated the cleaning out of the Sangamon river, so as to make it a navigable stream and likewise giving the Sangamon River a double mouth, so that the waters could run out quickly, thus helping the land owners in and along the Sangamon bottom & bluffs: he likewise advocated the digging a kind of canal from near the mouth of the Sangamon river to Beardstown below some 15 or 20 miles.[1] This would give a double outlet for the waters in the Sangamon and help to drain all the bottom land from the mouth of the Sangamon on to Beardstown. Every man woman & child in L's precinct now yelled for Lincoln—. he got all the votes of the precinct excepting three—in other words he received 277 votes out of 280. This was in 1832 and Lincoln was defeated in other parts of the county—not being popular out of his own precinct. Lincoln grew gradually in popularity in all parts of the county. Lincoln never carried a thing nor a people with a whiz, and a rush: he moved slowly through intellectual Conviction, and the people followed as they learned the man. Hon Jno J Hardin in 1844–5 beat Lincoln in Menard L's own old home and Baker defeated him in Sangamon L's new home in the same year—*in Conventions*, though not before the people. Had the Elections been before the people the result would have been the same. Lincoln had no furor, nor fuss, nor feathers in his nature and never carried anything by a storm: he grew like a giant oak annually a ring around a ring: he never grew downward but upward and outward, joint on joint and ring around ring; and then this giant man breasted the storm. The more people tested & knew Lincoln the better they loved him and the closer they stuck to him. Baker Col E D was popular with a kind of momentary furor but like all furors it had a short life. Lincoln—Col E. D. Baker—Col Jno J Hardin and S. T. Logan were all great men, each in his way. There were too many great men in this city for all to thrive, and so Baker went to Galena & then on to oregon to seek popularity and found it. These four men

---

1. See "To the People of Sangamo County," March 9, 1832, in *Collected Works*, 1:6–7; "Resolution Introduced in the Illinois Legislature Concerning the Incorporation of a Canal Company," December 11, 1835, *Collected Works*, 1:40; "Amendment to An Act to Incorporate the Beardstown and Sangamon Canal Company," [December 12, 1835], *Collected Works*, 1:40.

agreed among themselves that they should go to Congress by turns. There was a struggle for existence among them, and the fittest survived—Lincoln. Logan was little and unpopular—cold & parsimonious. Hardin was killed in the Mexican War—Baker in the great Rebellion and Lincoln rose and rose and died by the hands of the assassin in the same rebellion; and Logan died here about 3 years since and is now forgotten. Baker was Eloquent—Hardin chivalrous—Logan little—cold—selfish—and Lincoln honest, sincere, truthful, Eloquent in his strength of character. Lincoln triumphed over his enemies here—men who belonged to the same politics—and he was secretly *hated*. This is the reason why none of these people will talk to you about Lincoln. Jno T. Stuart and such men in their hearts hated, bitterly hated Lincoln, but he—L—was too big a Lion to attack. All of these men were men of great energy and ambition and more or less [bitterly?] selfish To see these fight & bite Each other like dogs in a ring settled my ideas about politics forever This is my opinion founded on observation. This city had some 10 or 12 great men in it from 1837 to 1862. I doubt if even Athens had in her bosom as many great men *at once* and for the same number of years as this city did have. These men though uncultured were naturally great. Some of these men were democrats and some whigs—subsequently Republicans—

Below you will find a kind of diagram showing what I mean in the first part of this note. The Illinois river runs about SW from NE and the Sangamon from East generally, running with the Illinois at right angles nearly.

The dotted lines show the canal & improvements Beardstown was then in Morgan Co if I recollect aright. Lincoln's precinct in Menard only.

                          Your Friend
                          W. H. Herndon

LC: *HW3268–69; Exp 4:9:1940–43*

157. *To Jesse W. Weik*

                                              Springfield Ills Jany 16th '86 [1]
Friend Weik:

Your kind letter, dated the 12th inst, is just handed to me, and in reply to part would say that I *never* told you that *Mrs* Lincoln wanted to marry Douglas. I *did* say to you that Douglas wanted to marry *Mrs*. Lincoln when a girl. *Mrs*

Lincoln, when a girl was courted by Douglas & Lincoln at the same time. Mrs. Lincoln was a keen observer of human nature—an excellent judge of it—none better: She was a terrible woman, but I must give her credit for a keen insight into men and things. Had *hell* not got into her neck she would have led society anywhere: she was a highly cultured woman—witty—dashing—pleasant and a lady, but hell got in her neck, which I will explain to the world sometime, if I live. This will be a curious history. When all is known the world will divide between Mr Lincoln & Mrs. Lincoln its censure as I believe. *Mrs.* Lincoln saw in Mr Lincoln honesty—sincerity—integrity—manliness and a great man in the future. *Mrs.* Lincoln saw in Douglas a rake and a roue by nature—a demagouge and a shallow man. This I *know*. Probably I know too much of all these things. *Mrs* Lincoln chose Lincoln and the choice showed her insight and her wisdom. I *know* the whole story from beginning to end. I know that *Mrs* Lincoln acted badly, but hold your opinion for a while. I have always sympathized with Mrs. Lincoln. Remember that every Effect must have its Cause. Mrs. Lincoln was not a she wolf—wild cat without a cause.

I am glad that you save and have saved all things written to you by me. I want them saved, because they will have much in them probably that the world will want. I am willing to be tested by them during all coming time, by the severest criticisms. If I misrepresent wilfully the world will know it, & if I am honestly mistaken the world will know that; & if I am true they will know that too. We cannot escape criticism if we are worthy of it.

Your Friend

W. H. Herndon

In a day or so I will write you more about Lincoln's domestic relations

LC: HW3270; Exp 4:9:1944–45

158. To Jesse W. Weik

Springfield Ills. Jany 16th '86 [2]

Friend Weik

You wish to know more about Lincoln's domestic life. The history of it is a sad—sad one, I assure you. Many and many a time I have known Lincoln to come down to our office—say at 7. oc am, sometimes bringing with him his then young son Bob. Our office was on the west side of the public square and up stairs. The door that enters our office was—the up half of glass, with a curtain on the inside made of calico. When we did not wish any one to see inside we let down the curtain on the inside. Well, I say, many and many a time have I known poor Lincoln to come down to our office, sometimes Bob with him, with a small lot of cheese—crackers & "bologna" sausages under his arm: he would not speak to me for he was full of sadness—melancholy and I suppose of the devil: he would draw out the sofa—sit down on it—open his breakfast and divide between Bob and himself. I would as a matter of course know that Lincoln was driven from home, by a club—knife or tongue and so I would let down the curtain on the inside—go out and lock the door behind me taking the key out and with me. I would stay away—say an hour; and then I would go into the office on one pretense or an other and if Lincoln did not then speak I did as before—go away &c. In the course of an other hour I would go back and if Lincoln spoke I knew it was all over. ie that is his fit of sadness &c. &c. Probably he would [say?] something or I would and then he would say—"Billy that puts me in mind of a story": he would tell it—walk up and down the room laughing the while: and now the dark clouds would pass off his withered and wrinkled face; and the God blessed sunshine of happiness would light up *those* organs o'er which the Emotions of that good soul played their gentle dance and chase. Friend I can see all this now acting before me and am sad.

Your good friend
W. H. Herndon

LC: HW3272; Exp 4:9:1948–49

159. To Jesse W. Weik

Jany 16th '86 [3][1]

Friend Weik—

Let me give you an exact idea of Miss *Todd*—Mrs Lincoln afterwards. I said to you and now say to you that when Mrs Lincoln was a young and unmarried woman that she was rather pleasant—polite—civil—rather graceful in her movements—intelligent, witty, and sometimes bitter too: she was a polished girl—well educated—a good linguist—a fine conversationalist—was educated thoroughly at Lexington Ky: she was poor when she came here about 1837—a little proud—sometimes haughty. I have met Miss Todd many times at socials—balls—dances—& the like—have danced with her. I think that Miss Todd was a very shrewd girl—somewhat attractive: she discreetly kept back the fundamentals—the ground work of her organizations: she was a shrewd girl and a sharp one—a fine judge of human nature and of the appropriateness of conditions. However after she got married she became Soured—got gross—became material—avaricious—insolent mean—insulting—imperious; and a she wolf of this section. The wolf I guess was in her when young and unmarried, but she unchained it—let it loose when she got married. Discretion when young kept the wolf back for a while, but when there was no more necessity for chaining it it was unchained to growl—snap & bite at all. But remember that in finite thing that every effect has its appropriate Cause. Keep your judgement open for subsequent facts.

I intended to say that—in the Butler note—Butler gratuitously—freely and without charge boarded Lincoln from 1837 to 1842 when Lincoln got married.[2] I think that in my hurry that I forgot to state this fact distinctly. I now say it. The

---

1. Pagination suggests this was written as a continuation of the previous letter and sent at the same time. *In margin:* "I write hurriedly of evenings and mornings—just after court and just before it—correct as you read & go on. / H."

2. See §155, §159, and §198.

reason why Lincoln appointed—had King appointed, was that King lived in a northern county in this state.[3] This county Lincoln wanted and King could carry it. Butler lived in this county and couldn't be of any use north to Lincoln. Hurrah for politics & politicians. Politics rob us of our better nature & politicians rob us of our money &c. Hurrah for politics & politicians

Your Friend

W. H. Herndon

LC: HW3271; Exp 4:9:1946–47

160. To Jesse W. Weik[1]

Springfield Ills Jany 19th '86 [1]

Friend Weik:

You once asked me for a history of Lincoln's paternity and as I remember it I promised to give it to you sometime, if I had the time to do it. The facts are about as follow. Lincoln once told me that his mother, Nancy Hanks, was the illegitimate child of a Virginia planter: he told me never to tell it while he lived and this I have religiously kept and observed. This is *one* fact in the chain of *inferences*. Thomas Lincoln the father of Abm in the spring of 1805 commenced going to see Sally Bush: he courted this finely developed and buxom girl: she refused him—did not at all reciprocate his love. This lady whom I knew was far above Thomas Lincoln—somewhat cultured and quite a lady. Mr. Lincoln—Thomas—then—say in the summer of 1806 commenced going to see Nancy Hanks—Abm's mother. Nancy Hanks accepted Thomas Lincoln's hand: they were actually married in Washington County Ky. The marriage took place the 23d day of Septr 1806 and the first child born to *Mrs. Lincoln* was on the 10th day of Feby 1807—a little less than five months from the day of the marriage.[2] This is a *second* fact which you must carry along in order to draw correct inferences. About 1815 one *Abraham* Enloe was caught by Thomas Lincoln in such relations and under such conditions with his wife that he was convinced that his wife was not like Caesar's wife above suspicion. Thomas Lincoln jumped on and into Enloe for what he had been doing, as Lincoln supposed. Lincoln bit off Enloes nose in the terrible fight. This is a fact number *three*. Lincoln—Thomas was so annoyed with Enloes visits and conduct that he was driven from Kentucky: he moved from there to Indiana about 1816–17. While *Mrs.* Lincoln bred like a rat in Kentucky, she had no more children in Indiana. This is fact number *four*. Mrs. Lincoln died about 1818–9 in Indiana. In about one year thereafter Thomas Lincoln went back to Ky to see Sally Bush, who had in the mean time—say in 1807–8, married one _____ Johnson.

---

3. See §155, p. 198.

---

1. *Two notes in top margin:* "Religiously private H"; "*Please send* me an exact copy of this, break up it into paragraphs if you can. H."

2. This date is mistaken. The correct date for the Lincoln marriage, June 12, 1806, was later discovered in the Washington County, Kentucky Marriage Register. See Warren, 9, 218n.

Johnson & *Mrs.* Johnson had two children or more. I knew them both. Johnson died about the time that Mrs. Lincoln did—One died in Indiana and the other in Ky. Miss Bush—now Mrs. Johnson was a finely developed woman and so was Mrs. Lincoln. The reputation of Mrs. Lincoln is that she was a bold—reckless—dare devil kind of a woman, stepping to the very verge of propriety: she was badly and roughly raised—was an excellent woman and by nature an intellectual and sensative woman. Lincoln, Abrm, told me that his mother was an intellectual woman—sensative and somewhat sad. I distinctly remember what Lincoln told me and the cause of the conversation. Lincoln said to me on that occasion this—; 'all that I am or hope ever to be I got from my mother, God bless her"; and I guess all this—what Lincoln told me, was the truth. Thomas Lincoln went back to see Mrs Johnson, as said before, and they were married in Elizabethtown Ky about the year 1819. Remember that Mrs. Johnson had children by Johnson. This is a *fifth* fact. Mrs. Johnson, now Mrs. Lincoln went to Indiana with Thomas and there had no children while in the prime and glory of her good life: she was a good woman a kind—clever and polite one. I knew her. Mrs. Thomas Lincoln, his 2d wife, now took possession of things in Indiana—dressed up—taught and Kindly cared for Thomas Lincoln 2 children by his first wife—Abm & Sarah. Mrs. Lincoln Thomas 2d wife had no more children while in Indiana, though she bred—had children in Ky by Johnson. Here is the *6th* fact. The two Lincoln by his first wife and the two by his last wife—Johnson the father—were raised up together and actually loved one an other. In other words Lincoln had 2 or 3 children by his first wife and none by his last. Mrs Johnson had 2 or 3 children by her first husband and none by Thomas Lincoln. The four children were raised up—vegetated together

   In addition to all the above facts—or supposed ones, for I give no opinion, Dennis Hanks told me that Thomas Lincoln when tolerably young—and before he left Ky was castrated. Abm Enloe said—often said that *Abm Lincoln was his child.* All these facts, if facts they are I received from different persons at different times and places. I reduced much to writing at the time—have letters on the subject from Ky and some of the facts I remember—ie that is I well remember what was told me, though I did write all down.

   Now let me give you something on the other side. The clerk of the court of Elizabethtown—Winterbottom, I think is his name, wrote to Mr. Lincoln in 1859–60 something about his mother and Lincoln said in reply—"*You are mistaken in my mother.*" I have seen Lincoln's letters to the Clerk, whatever may be his name.[3] The clerk and I corresponded some little, but I may miss his name. Here is the whole story as it has been told to me and I give you no opinion of fact nor inferrence. You must judge for yourself. It's a curious story and may all be true.

                                   Your Friend
                                   W H Herndon

   LC: HW3274–75; Exp 4:9:1952–55

---

3. Samuel Haycraft was the clerk's name. See AL to Samuel Haycraft, May 28, 1860, *Collected Works,* 4:56–57.

161. To Jesse W. Weik

Springfield Ills Jany 19th '86 [2]

Friend Weik:

Sometime in the early part of the winter of 1860 my friend, the Hon Joseph Medill of Chicago, wrote me a letter which protested against the appointment of _____ Cameron of Pa as one of the Cabinet and it was *intended* that this letter should reach the Ears of Lincoln.[1] I received the letter and handed it to Lincoln; and he read it over and over again and again. If I recollect the letter it was an Eloquent protest against the appointment of a Corrupt and a debased man. I do not think that at the time Lincoln had made any arrangement—no promise express or implied, as to who should be his Cabinet—do not think that Lincoln had thought much about it—the subject of his Cabinet. You know—now know that Lincoln had no organizing power—no drilling, & no driving power over men, excepting through their reason. The letter was a good one and an eloquent one. I think it had its influence with Lincoln and shall always so think. This far I spoke positively and without doubt. My memory is sharp and distinct on the above facts. I put in a word edgewise against Cameron. After Lincoln had read the letter o'er & o'er—he, it *seems* to me now—said that he would like to appoint men for his cabinet—half from the North and half from the South, to put it no stronger. It seems to me—*it is like a dream* that he mentioned the name of Botts of Va and Stephens of Georgia and the Senator _____ from Tennessee, whose name I have forgotten: it sounds like Manard.[2] The man was the brother Senator of Johnson vice president under Lincolns 2d admr. Johnson was senator at the time of Lincoln's conversation with me over Medill's letter as I now remember it. It may be that Lincoln was more open and positive than I put it, but I cannot now assert it. I knew that Lincoln respected Botts—Stephens—&c. I think that Lincoln at the time of our conversation did not positively appreciate the danger to the Union, though he had declared that "a house divided against itself cannot stand." Lincoln could not from his nature think that the Southern people could design the overthrow the government—the best government in the world. While Lincoln used the above expresson as an abstraction—a figure to convey an idea, I understood it as a fact—a law—as a necesity—inevitable—irresistable. You must remember that I was a radical abolitionist—a reformer—a progressive—a [distructive?] when speaking of slavery. I am yet the same in all things that obstruct justice—right—and the unlimited progress of men. I am an enemy to all cowardly conservatism in politics—religion—in the social and all other human worlds—. I am in hopes that something will turn up hereafter to prove what I say about Lincoln and our conversations over the Medill letter or to disprove it. If the whole facts ever come out they will be stronger than I put it here.

I think that your last letter, dated the 17th inst contains much for suggestion. The world is full of the lives of Lincoln and the people are tired of them, as I think.

---

1. Simon Cameron. Joseph Medill was managing editor of the *Chicago Tribune* in 1860.
2. John Minor Botts, Alexander H. Stephens, and Horace Maynard.

The thing which we should publish should be something like this—"Reminiscences of Lincoln at home" or something like that: it should not be a life of Lincoln, though facts—dates &c. &c of his life might be strung along unartistically—unthoughtfully as it were When the thing is finished or about to be then it will be time to write to publishers. We better agree first as to what shall be done, and then how to do it and last who shall set up the type—publish &c &c. Think of this? Have you made any arrangement with any syndicate to publish your letters? What syndicate &c. &c. Let us write to each other on this question so that we can understand things. I am glad that my ideas struck you about enlarging the piece—pamphlet—book or what not. We must publish things as they are. Robert or no Robert Lincoln. We can be gentlemanly in the record. If peoples feet are in the way—why let them take their toes away right off. More hereafter on this point.

I hope that you will come and see me sometime this winter. If you come—about to come rather notify me as to time: I do *not* think that it would pay to see Mrs Vineyard if living—. See Mrs Chapman and give her and her husband my best respects[3]

Your Friend
WH Herndon

LC: HW3276–77; Exp 4:9:1956–59

162. To Jesse W. Weik

Springfield Ills. Jany 27th '86

Friend Weik:

Your note dated the 8th inst is just at hand, and in reply to which let me that I have forgotten that Kentuckian's name. Lincoln told me the man's name, but I cannot recall it. If I ever do I will write to you. I do not think that the man was politician, but a merchant. I thank you for a copy of my letter to you

I have read the Allen letter and know all about it.[1] Allen was a great blow a [*illegible*]—a wild exaggerator & somewhat of a l——r. Lincoln knew the man and shot off his Caricature—burlesque of Allen. Lincoln, when he wrote the letter, was in one of his best joking moods. Did you take it as all done in good faith. Allen's idiotic son—weak minded son rather, after his fathers death and not knowing the facts as well as the people here—the old settler—published the letter—a most foolish thing. Had he consulted friends—his fathers old one it—the letter would never have seen the light.

I wish to state some facts about Lincolns domestic relations which I do not want to be forgotten. About the year 1857 a man by the name of Barrett was

3. For Mary Owens Vineyard, see §146, p. 182. For the Chapmans, see §138.

1. See AL to Allen, June 21, 1836, *Collected Works*, 1:48–49.

passing along 8th st. near Lincoln's house: he saw a long tall man running and saw a little low squatty woman with a butcher knife in her hand in hot pursuit: he looked and saw that Lincoln was the man and Mrs. Lincoln was the woman. Lincoln's house on 8th st fronts westward. He ran eastward down the walk in his own lot. Stephen Whitehurst lived in the same block. His house fronted east—the house being east of Lincolns. The consequence is that the back doors look into each other. Whitehurst was on that day—Sunday if I recollect the time—the day, standing in the back door of his own house and saw what happened. Lincoln ran down the walk in his own lot but seeing the people coming from church or going to it he stopt short and quick; and wheeled around—caught Mrs. Lincoln by the back of the neck and at the seat of her drawers—carried or pushed her squealing along the walk back to the house—Lincoln's home, got her to the door of the kitchen—opened it—pushed her in, at the same time—to use Whitehursts expression gave her a hell of a slap on her seat—saying to her—"There now, stay in the house and don't be a d——d fool before the people.

Again in the winter of 1857 the Supm Court was in session and Lincoln had an important suit to argue. He came in the clerks office—the law library room too: his nose was plastered up—fixed up with court plaster. Now for the facts. Lincoln had in the day before become somewhat abstracted—thoughtful and let the fire in Mr & Mrs. Lincoln's sitting room nearly die out. Mrs Lincoln came to the door of the sitting room from the kitchen and said—"Mr. Lincoln put some wood on the fire." Lincoln did not hear her and neglected the repair of the fire. Mrs Lincoln came to the sitting room again and said "Mr Lincoln—mend up the fire," it having got low down. Lincoln did not hear Mrs. Lincoln: she came in again and picked up a stick of wood and said—"Mr. Lincoln I have told you now there three times to mend the fire and you have pretended that you did not hear me. Ill make you hear me this time" and she blazed away at Lincoln with a stick of stove wood and hit him on the nose and thus banged it up. Some one in the Court room asked Lincoln what was the matter: he made an evasive reply in part to the question. Lincolns girl stated this, if others did not know it. From what I know of the facts it is more probable that it is true than untrue. I believe it: it went around among the members of the bar as true. Many such quarrels did take place between Lincoln and his wife. Lincolns domestic life was a home hell on this globe

Your Friend
W H Herndon

LC: HW3278–79; Exp 4:9:1960–63

163. To Jesse W. Weik

Springfield Ills. Feby 10th '86

Friend Weik:

I this moment received your P.C. dated the 9th inst and you guess rightly when you say that I am pumped literally dry of Lincoln facts—incidents &c. I have seen Judges Matheny—Broadwell and others;[1] and they have promised me to write out some facts—incidents &c. and give them to me; and when they do this I'll send them to you most assuredly. You know that the People in this city do *not* like to talk much about Lincoln: they have no disposition to tell good things about him & when cornered the people here *in private* will willingly tell you Lincoln's weak points—and damaging facts as they look at it. Lincoln outstript them and they *in secret* hate him This you know or believe from your own experiences. Prophets have honor in the world except in their own country. Hero worshippers here and everywhere hate me, because I dare tell the whole truth about Lincoln; and this is particularly the case with the Christians. To tell the truth—the exact truth as you see it is a hard road to travel in this world when that truth runs square up against our ideas of what we think it *ought* to be. I shall continue to send you more of the *facts* of L's life if I can think of any new ones that are true. Guesses I shall not send you—only well authenticated facts.

No—I am not frozen up—only pumped dry—. A new vein may burst in and fill up the vacuum again, and if it does I'll send to you the result.

. . .

Your Friend
W. H. Herndon

LC: HW3281; Exp 4:9:1966–67

164. To Joseph Fowler:

Springfield Ills. Feby 18th '86

Friend Fowler:

It may help you to understand Lincoln somewhat thoroughly by stating to you his philosophy. Mr. Lincoln believed that what was to be would be and *no* prayers of ours could arrest or reverse the decree: he was a thorough fatalist, and thought the fates ruled the world: he believed that the conditions made the man—does make the man: he believed that general—universal and Eternal laws governed both matter and mind, always and everywhere. This philosophy as a whole will account for much of the facts and laws of his splendid life. Things that were to be *would* be, and hence he patiently waited on events: his calmness under bloody war was the result of the same. His charity for men—their feelings—thoughts— willings and acts sprang out of his philosophy, that the conditions made them: his want of malice sprang out of the same. Lincoln neither hated nor did he love:

---

1. James H. Matheny was one of AL's oldest friends; Norman Broadwell read law with AL and WHH, later serving as a state legislator and circuit judge.

he never but once or twice Eulogised men, nor did he ever curse them. Men were mere tools in the hands of fate—were made as they are made by conditions; and to praise or blame men was pure folly. Men were not entitled to credit for what they were or did—what they thought or said—how they felt or acted. The thing was to be and no prayers of ours could arrest or reverse the decree: men are made by conditions that surround him—that have somewhat Exhisted for a hundred thousand years or more. Man is compelled to feel—think—will and act by virtue and force of these conditions: he is a mere child moved and groomed by this vast world machine, forever working in grooves—and moving in deep cut channels; and now what is man? he is simply a simple tool—a cog—a part, and parcel of this vast iron machine that strikes and cuts—grinds and mashes all things that resist it. The fates have decreed it and what they decreed is irresistable and inevitable. Mere human prayers are blank absurdities. What a man is, he *is* because of the great world's eternal conditions, and is entitled to no credit for virtue nor should he be blamed for vice. "With malice toward none and charity for all" I live for men was Lincoln's felings—thoughts—wills and acts. Man does but what is commanded by his Superiors. Lincoln used to quote Shakespear's philosophy.

"There is a divinity that shapes our ends
Rough hew them how we will".

If a man did him—L—an injury—a grievous wrong the man was a mere tool, and obeyed the powers; and if the man did him a great good—blessed him and made him happy, still he but obeyed orders, and he was not to be censured for the wrong nor praised for the right. Everything everywhere is doomed for all time. If a man was good or bad—small or great—and if virtue or vice prevailed, it was so doomed. If bloody war—deathly famine and cruel pestilence stalked over the land it was to be and *had come*, and to mourn for this—to regret it—to resist it, would only be flying in the face of the inevitable. Lincoln was patient, and calmly waited on events: he knew that they would come in their own good and appointed time: he was not surprised at their coming nor astonished at their extent, nor depth, nor fury. The fates and the conditions were *the* powers. Laws ruled everything everywhere, both matter and mind from the beginning to the end, if there was a beginning and an end. Such was Lincoln's philosophy: he was in religion [a Li] beral—, naturally and logically so. Do not misunderstand me—Probably Lincoln *did not* believe that Brutus was specially made and ordered to kill Caesar with a dagger in the Senate chamber; and yet he fully believed that Brutus & Caesar stood in the line of the most of the forces of nature let loose millions of years ago and let go at full play. I hope that these remarks will assist you in finding Lincoln—the real man as he lived among us.

You spoke in your eloquent letter of Emmerson and Lincoln: they differed widely.[1] Emmerson had the genius of the Spiritual and ideal. Lincoln had the genius of the real and the practical. Emmerson lived high among the stars—Lincoln lived

---

1. Ralph Waldo Emerson.

low among men. Emmerson dreamed, Lincoln acted, Emmerson was intuitional, Lincoln reflective. Both were Liberals in religion and were great men.

Your Friend
W. H. Herndon

LMU: photocopy

165. *To Jesse W. Weik:*

Springfield Ills. Mch 5th '86

Friend Weik:

I have just thought of a good thing—if I have not told it to you before.— About the year 1856–7 Mess. Stuart and Edwards[1] brought a large suit, involving much money and some principles—leading & important principles of Law against our client. At this time we had but 2 or 3 terms of court, and the docket was crowded—over crowded. Mess. Stuart & Edwards were pressing our client hotly for a trial and we L, myself &—our client were struggling against a trial at present. We—Lincoln & myself as well as our client wanted *time*—wanted a Continuance. We could not make any affidavit for a Continuance founded on *fact*—pertinent and material and good ones, because no such facts existed. However a Continuance we must have. I, in the absence of Mr Lincoln having heard a hint fall from Mr Edwards that he was afraid of some *facts* & some [*points* of?] law, drew up in a legal form a fictious and a sham plea, covering the exact grounds of the doubts and fears of Mr Edwards. The plea was scientifically and legally drawn, and if we had the facts to back & sustain it it would not only cause a continuance but it would defeat the case finally. It would cause a continuance, because Edwards as well as Stuart thought the facts were as pleaded and well pleaded. The plea could not be demurred to nor could S & E's foolishly take issue on the plea. The plea bothered S & E for some time: they did not know exactly what to do. However the issues were made upon the plea. The day of trial was just approaching and so Lincoln looked over the papers carefully in the case as was his custom and said to me this—"Is this seventh plea a good plea. "Yes" I answered—"But" said Lincoln—"Is it founded on *fact*" and to which I replied "No Sir." I then explained to Lincoln what the facts were—what S & E's doubts were &c. &c—that our client must have time or be ruined. He then scratched his head—thought a moment and said to me—"Erase—withdraw that sham plea—it's a lie, and shall not go on record." and so it was erased—withdrawn from the record. By some accidents

---

1. John Todd Stuart and Benjamin S. Edwards.

that took place the Cause was Continued and our man and his fortune accidently saved. This shows Ls honesty and hate of shams.

Your Friend

W. H. Herndon

I hope you can read this—I am nervous yet. Do the best you can. Rewrite it—correct it &c

LC: HW3282; Exp 4:9:1968–69

166. To John W. Keyes

Springfield Ills April 14th 1886

My Dear Sir:

You ask me for a short account of my acquaintance with Abraham Lincoln. I became acquainted with him in 1834, and from that time to the day of his death I knew the man well—I may say—intimately. He moved to the City of Springfield in 1837: it was then but a small town or village—now quite a city. I studied law with Logan & Lincoln—two great lawyers—in 1842-3. In 1843-4 Mr. Lincoln and I became partners in the law business in Springfield, but did business in all the surrounding Counties. Our partnership was never legally disolved till the night of his assassination—his death. The good man—the noble man would take none of my fees made in the law business after his election to the Presidency. Mr. Lincoln was a safe Counsellor—a good lawyer and an honest man in all the walks of Life. Mr. Lincoln was not appreciated in this City, nor was he at all times the most popular man among us. The cause of his unpopularity—rather the want of popularity here arose out of two grounds—1st He did his own thinking; and 2dly he had the Courage of his Convictions and boldly and fearlessly expressed them. I speak generally and Especially of his political life. Mr Lincoln was a Cool, Cautious, Conservative, and a long headed man. Mr. Lincoln could be trusted by the people: they did trust him, and they were never deceived: he was a pure man—a great man and a patriot.

In the practice of the law he was simple—honest—fair and broad minded: he was Courteous to the bar and to the Court: he was open—candid and square in his profession, never practicing on the sharp nor the low. Mr. Lincoln met all questions fairly—squarely and openly, making no Concealments of his ideas nor intentions in any Case: he took no snap judgements nor used any tricks in his business. Every man knew exactly where Mr Lincoln Stood and how he would act in a law case. Mr. Lincoln never deceived his brother lawyers in any Case. What he told you was the Exact truth.

Mr. Lincoln was a sad man—a gloomy man and an abstracted one; and hence he was not very social in his nature: he seemed to me to be an unhappy man at times: he dearly loved his children, but he was not the happiest man in the world domestically. As a friend Mr. Lincoln was true—true as steel: he thought in his life and lived in his thought. In many things Mr. Lincoln was peculiar: he did not trust any man with the secrets of his ambitious soul. I knew the man so well that I think I could read his secrets & his ambitions. He was a wonderful man and his fame will grow on the ages.

The desk made of walnut with four shelves in it with two leaves—doors belonged to Lincoln and myself in our early practice. The desk contained the most of our books for years. The table is made of walnut with two drawers: the desk & table were placed in our office on the same day—say as Early as 1850—probably before. You now own the same desk & table that Lincoln once owned: he gave me the desk & table; and what you have is genuine and true: they have never been out of my sight since they were delivered to Lincoln & myself. Please take good care of the Sacred things—mementoes of the noble man—Abraham Lincoln.

Most Respectfully
Wm. H. Herndon[1]

HSP

167. To Jesse W. Weik

Springfield Ills. July 10th 86

Friend Weik

. . .

In answer to your question let me say that Mr. Lincoln was *not* at Chicago nor nearer there than this city, during the week—time of his nomination for the presidency in 1860. Mr. Lincoln was in this city during the Convention—all the time of it, playing ball and drinking beer with the boys. He was nervous that day and played ball and drank beer to while away the time: he hoped and despaired that day in this city. I was in Chicago during the time of the Convention, but Lincoln was not there: he was *here* and had *not* been in Chicago for months, probably, before the Convention.

Your Friend
W. H. Herndon

LC: HW3286; Exp 4:9:1976

168. To John G. Nicolay

Springfield Ills. Aug. 26th 86

Friend Nicolay:

A few days since my wife found, after long search, the Pho of Sally Bush—Mrs Thomas Lincolns, 2d wife of "old Tommy". I sent the Pho to Mr. Drake of N.Y, I

---

1. For the Lincoln Memorial Collection, Keyes purchased a number of Lincoln-related items from WHH in this period. See Donald, 314–15. Notarized on final page: "Acknowledged before me this 13th day of April AD 1886 / Alfred A. North / Notary Public."

suppose your Artist and he is pleased with it. My wife is still on the search for the map—of New Salem, and if she finds it I'll send it to Drake.[1] Sally Bush—Mrs Thomas Lincoln was a lady by nature—accomplished for the times & crowds—for the places & the people. She is *the* mother of Abe: She raised him & flashed her good soul into him, God bless her. I love that old woman.

If you wish any fact about Lincoln—or an opinion of him, *draw* on me and if I have the fact or the opinion I'll freely give it to you.

I hope that you are having a glorious time among the mountains, seeing sights & catching fish &c

Your old Friend
W. H. Herndon

Brown

169. To Jesse W. Weik

Chicago Ills. Novr 4th '86

Friend Weik:

. . .

Let me suggest that you draw a canoe with 3 men in it paddling down the North fork of the Sangamon—one is Lincoln—one is Jno Johnson and one is Jno Hanks: they get out at a little place now called Riverton—walked to Springfield & took up quarters at the *Buck Horn Hotel*. The sign, hung on a post some 20 or 30 feet high with a Buck on it, well drawn. The sign swung in a square frame or nearly so—and moved with the wind. The Hotel was kept by Andrew Elliott The house was built of logs 2 stories high and a passage way running through the house—house ran east & west—was on I think Adams—between 1st & 2d street and on the south side of the street. Can't you draw it?—do it roughly and you have it just as I saw & played in it more than 50 years ago—say as early as 1826-7. The stories were low[.] Stairs went up from the passage way—through the house running north & south. Can't you do it? I shall call your attention—now to much—many things. Our court house was at this time or a little before made of unhewn logs—jail on 3 st was make of hewn logs, near the corner of 2 st & Adams I think—have seen it a thousand times.

. . .

There are in this Keys & Munson Collection some 200 relics.[1] You can get phos of any or all of said collections. Would it not pay you to come up about the

---

1. WHH is here assisting Nicolay and his partner John Hay in preparing their biography of Lincoln for serial publication in *Century* magazine, though he frequently criticized its contents as it appeared.

---

1. From November 1886 through mid-January 1887, WHH acted as curator of a collection of AL memorabilia that was exhibited in Chicago by John W. Keyes and S. B. Munson as the Lincoln Memorial Collection.

1st Jany '87. Did you get a copy of the catalogue &c of the collection which I sent you?[2] If you didn't Ill send again

I am well-content here—will be till I get homesick

Hurriedly Your Friend

W H Herndon

LC: HW3300; Exp 4:9:2002–4

170. To John J. Lindman

Chicago, Dec 3 1886

My dear Sir

From our short and hasty conversation about Mr Lincoln on the evening of the 26th ult, in the hall of the Lincoln memorial collection, Chicago, I judge that you wish to know something of president Lincoln's philosophy. This part of Mr Lincoln's life is less known than any other phase of it. A man's philosophy, when well known to the world, leads the world to a full knowledge of his life and explains many acts of it, otherwise inexplicable: it is something that can be appealed to in case of doubt as evidence of an act or a system of acts or a method of life. To know a man's philosophy is important. Mr Lincoln to use a Christian word believed in preordination—that is that all things are preordained—decreed beforehand. To use a somewhat classical word, he believed that fate ruled and doomed everything: he has been heard to say, often and often that what is to be will be; and no supplications nor prayers of ours can change or reverse the decree: it is inevitable. An other part of his philosophy was that conditions make & rule the man & not the man make and rule the conditions. In short Mr Lincoln to use a scientific word, believed in laws—laws general universal and eternal—that they ruled and governed both matter and mind from the beginning if any to the very end if any. Such was his idea or ideas of the operations of Nature under law. There were no miracles in his opinion outside of law.

Would it not follow, my good sir, if those ideas were Lincoln's—were his philosophy that he was a calm—cool and patient man and would it not follow that he had a broad—nay—an unbounded charity for the weakness—the foibles and vices of mankind? Mr. Lincoln could look out of his great nature—his noble being and see the sad stern realities of active life—the ludicrious—the grave and the gay—the foolish and the wise, and whisper to himself—"All this was decreed, was inevitable—was *to be* and *now is*". Would it not follow that Mr Lincoln would wait patiently on the logic of events with more than a woman's patience and would it not follow that he waited on the blossoming and ripening of events, their evo-

---

2. WHH probably refers to a publication of the Lincoln Memorial Collection of Chicago, *Abraham Lincoln* (Chicago: Clohesey, 1886), which appears to have been the forerunner of *Catalogue of Articles Owned and Used by Abraham Lincoln: Now Owned by the Lincoln Memorial Collection of Chicago* ([Chicago]: Lincoln Memorial Collection, [1887]).

lution and wisely seize his grand opportunities—gain his ends—catch the flow of events and tide himself to glory thereon. Would it not follow as a consequence that, come weal or woe—come victory or defeat—come life or death Lincoln was cool—calm, neither dispairing nor exulting in the event: it was to be—it was inevitable—it was decreed—it was doomed. To fret or despair—to exult and shout under such circumstances would be flying in the face of the inevitable or wooing her. So strong was this philosophy of Mr Lincoln that it was a part and portion of his being. He has been heard to say—"I fear some terrible end"

Now let me give you some of Mr Lincoln's leading characteristics: he was a man of fine feeling—a serene, continuous and persistant thinker and had a genius for the practical: he had a strong will on questions of importance involving some principle: and his feelings & his thoughts, when acting through his will, burst into noble deeds. Mr Lincoln was cautious—& conservative—honest & full of integrity—wise & far seeing, never going in advance of his people and his age in his policies or his measures. When the people were ready to advance he moved forward, never taking a back-step.

(Signed)
Respectfully yours
W. H Herndon[1]

LC: HW3308–11; Exp 4:9:2018–21 (copy)

171. To Jesse W. Weik

Chicago. Decr. 9th '86

Friend Weik

I am here and somewhat lonesome and I will have to talk to you—make a companion of you. You once quoted Judge Davis on me to the effect that Lincoln was a *great* lawyer. That I never denied, but I said that he was not a first rate *nisi prious* lawyer.[1] I further said that he was not a learned lawyer; and that he was a case lawyer &c. &c. Just hear what Judge Davis does say: he says of Lincoln: "he could hardly be called very learned in his profession, and yet he rarely tried a cause without fully understanding the law applicable to it."[2] This I agree to and now the question come, how was he a *great* lawyer? Says Judge Davis—"*he read law books but little*, except when the cause in hand made it necessary."[3] The next question comes—What books did he resort to to get his information? He went to

---

1. In margin: "Copy of letter to J J Lindman." Enclosed in WHH to JWW, December 18, 1886, this letter appears to be in WHH's hand, though written with more care than usual.

---

1. See §125, n. 1.
2. This is quoted from Lamon, 315, but is not the judgment of Davis; rather, it comes from Judge Thomas Drummond.
3. Judge David Davis eulogy of AL at Federal Court in Indianapolis, May 19, 1865, as quoted in Lamon, 313.

the *reports* and hunted up like cases: he was a case lawyer and that only: he never as a general rule went to the text books. [*In margin:* What—make a *great* lawyer of a man who never read law much!] Mr Lincoln was his own commentator: his conscience judgment and reason worked out the law. There is no use in calling Lincoln a *great* lawyer for he was not: he was a first rate lawyer *under conditions*: he must have his own time—a good *long time* to prepare his case in—study it—learn the facts & the law by heart and *then* he must feel that he was in the *right*. Without these things he was a weak brother in the law. Judge Park's says—and it is true "I have often said that for a man who was a quarter of a century both a lawyer and a politician the most honest man I ever saw: he was not only morally honest but intellectually so. xx *At the* bar when he thought he was wrong he was the *weakest* lawyer that I ever saw."[4] I know Judge Parks well and the above judgment of his is correct. Lincoln's soul was afire on politics and he did not care much about law: his soul was afire with its own ambition and that was not law. How are you going to make a *great* lawyer out of Lincoln? You can only say he was a *great* lawyer under conditions. Take Lincoln all in all it is my judgment that he was a 2d rate lawyer. A *great* lawyer is one who is the master of the whole law—and who is ever ready to attend in a *masterly* way all cases that come before him right or wrong—good or bad—ready or not ready, except *ever* ready through his legal love and his own sagacity. Now you have my opinion right or wrong—wise or foolish.

. . .

Your Friend
W H Herndon

LC: HW3316–17; Exp 4:9:2031–32

172. To Jesse W. Weik

Chicago, Decr. 22d 1886

Friend Weik:

. . .

I hope that you and Wartman will find new matter of interest in Indiana—and I do hope that you will get the "Chronicles."[1] The man who had them while I was in Spencer Co would not spare them under any Consideration. I had no money *with which to Coax him*. As to the anonymous letter I never paid much attention to it, because, as I recollect, the fact is that Sarah Lincoln was the oldest child of Mrs. Lincoln—Nancy Hanks and hence Abm may have been the child of Thomas, upon the condition that Thomas was not castrated & upon the further condition that Enloe never had connection with Nancy at any other time thereafter.[2] I do

---

4. See *Herndon's Informants*, 238.

---

1. James W. Wartmann was a WHH contact in Rockport, Indiana. For "The Chronicles of Reuben," see §176.

2. For Abraham Enloe (or Enlow or Inlow), see §92, n. 2.

not like anonymous letters anyhow. However push your investigation with vigor for something may come of it.

. . .

Your Friend
W. H Herndon

LC: HW3321; Exp 4:9, 2040–41

173. To Jesse W. Weik

Chicago, Decr. 30th 1886

Friend Weik:

1st Did you ever hear the story about Lincoln & Stanton, wherein Stanton, his Secy of War, in 1855 called Lincoln a Giraphe or ape? The case took place in Ohio in a big patent suit in which Lincoln & Stanton were engaged. Stanton called Lincoln a d—-d ape.[1]

2d Did you ever hear of the great Law case in Ills wherein Lincoln was employed by the Ills Central RR and McClellan's reply to Lincoln when he—L—presented his bill of $5,000 for his services &c?[2]

Lincoln in both cases was snubbed—outrageously treated—in one case by Stanton & in the other by McClellan. One of the cases was in 1853–5 and the other in 1855–6

Your Friend
W H Herndon

LC: HW3324; Exp 4:9:2046

174. To Jesse W. Weik

Chicago, Jany 2d 1887

Friend Weik—

Have you read the Jany no of the Century? If you have you will see that N & H have suppressed many facts—material facts of Lincoln's life; and among them are L's genealogy—paternity—the description of Nancy Hanks—old Thomas Lincoln—the Ann Rutledge story—L's religion—L's insanity—the facts of L's misery with Mary Todd—L's *back down* on the night that he & Mary Todd were to be married &c.&c.[1] I do not say that they did not mention some of these things in a round about way, but I do say that the kernal—"nib" & point of things have been purposely suppressed. N & H do *know* the facts fully as I am informed on

---

1. See §175, §245.
2. See §217, n. 4.

---

1. WHH refers to a chapter in the biography of AL by his former private secretaries, John G. Nicolay and John Hay, then being serialized in *Century* magazine.

good authority. Mr. Drake told them to Keys & Munson tolerably plainly.[2] Do you call this history—do you call it biography? No wonder that L had a contempt for all history and biography: he knew how it was written: he knew the motives & cowardice of the writers of history & biography.[3] Lincoln wanted to know the whole truth & nothing less. *This I know.* N & H write correctly as far as they go, or probably *dare* go. The reading world is not ready to hear the whole truth, if it is an unpleasant thing: they love to be put to sleep by pleasant stories or humbugged by falsehood. Barnum is the beaux ideal of the American. Nothing succeeds like success; this is what the general American worships—it and the ring-roll and glitter of the Almighty dollar. Probably the idea moves N & H to do what they are doing. N & H handle things with silken gloves & "a cammel hair pencil:" they do not write with an iron pen. If some sharp critic knew what you and I know he would shiver the future of N & H's biography in a minute. I say that the boys write well & tell the truth very correctly as far as they go. Who is to blame—the people or N & H? I am of the growing opinion that we must *state facts* while we give no opinion, leaving all men and women open to form their own opinions *on the facts.* This I have stated to you before and now I should like to have a hint of your ideas and feelings. What say you? Come out with them in full. I used to tell Lincoln in my wild way in 1858–9–60 this—"Lincoln, you must take an advanced step if you wish to be successful in your hopes and your ambition." I thought that he was too conservative at that time. *He moved and won.* If you wish to succeed in our life of L you must take *an advanced step.* You must strike the world with a grand surprise. This is just what the world demands and without such a stroke the people will go to sleep over your biography. This is my opinion. To tell the whole truth about L would be a grand surprise. Now you have my opinion in full, good or bad—wise or foolish. Give me your opinion of the literary merits of N & H's life of L. Come, out with it, won't you my good fellow.

Your friend in haste
W. H Herndon

LC: HW3326–27; Exp 4:10:2050–53

175. To Jesse W. Weik

Chicago, Jany 6th 1887

Friend Weik:

Mr. Lincoln was employed in 1855 by a man by the name of Many[1] to go to Cincinnati Ohio and defend for him a case before Justice McLean[2]—a case for

---

2. Mr. Drake was involved in production of the Nicolay and Hay biography; Keyes and Munson, proprietors of the Lincoln Memorial Collection, purchased Lincoln memorabilia from WHH (see §287).
3. See §142 and §187.

---

1. John H. Manny, a manufacturer of reaping machines in Rockford, Illinois.
2. Supreme Court Justice John H. McLean presided over the Manny trial.

an infringement of a patent and wherein McCormick was the plaintiff and Many was defendant. The case was an important one and big attorneys were employed on both sides—Seward—Stanton[3] & others. Mr Lincoln went on to Cincinnati to attend to the case—Probably Many came out to Illinois & accompanied Lincoln to Ohio. This is only my recollection. Mr. Lincoln landed in Cincinnati on time. Many accompanied Lincoln in the morning after Mr. Lincoln had arrived in Cinc to Stantons office—was ushered into the Ante room. Many left Lincoln for a moment in the Ante room—went and said a word or two to Stanton. Between the Ante room & Stanton's office there was a door with a large glass in it, so that Stanton could look through and see Lincoln. Stanton did look through the glass, and did see Lincoln who was rather illy clad according to Stantons notions of what great lawyers ought to wear. Many was in Stanton's room and Stanton contemptuously and grossly said to Many—"Why did you bring that d—d long armed ape here for: he does not know any thing and can do you no good."[4] Many was surprised. Lincoln distinctly heard what Stanton said: he was deeply insulted and felt indignant—left the room in and never appeared in the case any more—staid in Cincinnati a few days till the trial was over, as some say and as others say he left Cincinnati instantly in high dudgeon. My recollection is that he staid in Cincinnati till the trial is over; though he did not have any thing to say in his case. The lawyers with Lincoln treated him badly—discourteously and meanly from the beginning to the end. When Mr. Lincoln came back to Springfield he looked sad & sour and gloomy, and I never asked him how his case ended—thought probably that he had lost his case and felt badly over it.[5]

Your friend in haste

W. H Herndon

In this case too Lincoln sank his private griefs—wrongs &c out of view—appointed Stanton Sec of War for the public good.

LC: HW3328; Exp 4:10:2054–55

176. To Jesse W. Weik

Chicago, Jany 8th 1887

Friend Weik:

Inclosed you will please find a letter from Mr. Lamar of Indiana.[1] The story, as I related it to you once, is this—One of the Grigby boys married Lincoln's sister,

---

3. Edwin M. Stanton, the Pittsburgh lawyer who would be AL's secretary of war.
4. For WHH's reservations about whether or not this part of the story came directly from AL, see §245.
5. For an account of AL's mistreatment at the hands of Stanton on this occasion, see William Lee Miller, *Lincoln's Virtues* (New York: Knopf, 2002), 414–18.

---

1. See John W. Lamar to J. W. Wartmann, January 3, 1887, *Herndon's Informants*, 598–99. The story WHH attempts to recapitulate in this letter is that of AL's lost satire, "The Chronicles of Reuben." For a recollection of the text, see Elizabeth Crawford to WHH, January 4, 1866, *Herndon's Informants*, 150–52.

Lincoln thought that the Grigby's mistreated her, and the Lincolns & Grigbys fell out, one with an other &c. The two Grigby boys were subsequently married on the same night and *probably to two sisters.*[2] Old man Grigsby, for the 2 boys, had and held an *infair*, as was the custom at that time, at his house. The neighbors were invited except Abraham and all went along as merry as a Christmas bell. Abraham got the Ears of some of his chums who were in the house and *at the infair.* Abraham was not invited, and *so he felt huffy & insulted.* He therefore told the boys inside—This—"Let's have some fun—"Well" said the boys inside. It was arranged between the insiders & outsiders that the two married Couple should be put to bed, but A's husband was to be put in B's bed and B C was to be put in D's bed—all changed around & in the wrong places. Both husbands got in the wrong bed by direction, made between Abraham and the *invited insiders*—So it was arranged & so it was executed. The girls were aloft when they and their husbands were put to bed. Soon however a scream and a rattling of boards aloft were heard and all was "confusion worse confounded." A candle was lit and things found out and explained to the satisfaction of the women and the men. Probably the women knew the voices of their loved ones and by that means the terrible mistake was found out—but who caused it & what for were not found out for sometime—Here is Abraham—who was joyous & revenged that night—the good saint at one of his *jokes.* I have forgotten the names of the boys—their given names, and likewise the girls given and sir names. You will get the names when you go to Indiana. [*In margin*: Think the name of the boys was Charles & Reuben. Grigsby.] The story was told to me by one of the Grigbys—Root out the story. It's true—Can you read this?

Your Friend
W. H Herndon

LC: HW3330; Exp 4:10:2058–59

177. To Jesse W. Weik

Chicago, Jany 10th 1887

Friend Weik:

I wish, in a good natured way, to state to you my ideas of biographical writing; and in the first place what are the purposes of writing the life of *a man*—what are the objects to be gained by writing it and secondly what should be written? First The purposes—the objects of writing the biography of *a hero* is to make him *fully known* to the reading world in order that that reading world may profit somehow by his life—the example of it. The well written life of the great rouses men to struggle for a broader and deeper life—to climb up higher through the influence of the great's example. The lives of the great stimulate the young and help upward—push them onward. Every great man has his methods—methods peculiar to himself.

---

2. Reuben and Charles Grigsby married Betsy Ray and Matilda Hawkins, respectively.

The young seize the methods—imitate them and plow their way through life by *that seizure*, it may be. There is a glory in a great life of a great man and ambition in all classes seeks to walk to glory by the successful life of the good and great. Ambition is maddened by it and hence the human struggles to gratify it. So much for the influence of an example—Secondly—What should be written? Why—all, yes all the facts of the hero should be told—the whole of his life should be stated, including the smallest facts—and including feelings—thoughts, determinations and deeds. Every fact—all feeling—each thought—every determination—and all deeds are but manifestations of the man in this state or that, under this star or that. The *whole* of the man, objectively and subjectively, should be truthfully and fully, without suppression, suggestion—or evasion—or other form of falsehood, stated—generously written out. Suppose a great man does a small deed or mean thing or does a big thing or a grand thing—makes a failure or is a glorious success, there is a cause for it, and it is the religious duty of the biographer to state *all the facts* which were the cause of the man's acts. You may say that such acts are caused by this or that state—this or that judgement. You may be in error. Give all the facts to the reading world and let each person form his own opinions on those facts. To cheat the public judgement in any way is a high crime—treason truth—rebellion to the public welfare. The public good is founded on truths—facts—logical conclusions. Falsehood in these is the very highest crime as I think. It follows from what I have said that I am in favor of writing the life of Lincoln according to the above ideas—Again the mind demands that you or I give *a time—a place* and *a subject* for every thing written about. Hence we should give a full correct and broad description of the persons mentioned in our biography of L & especially of Thomas Lincoln—Nancy *Hanks* Lincoln, Abraham Lincoln—his wife—Mrs Thomas *Bush* Lincoln—Abraham's step mother. Let the subjects—the person stalk before the reader when reading. Now—friend—you have an outline—a rough one it is true, of my ideas of biographical writing. Read it carefully before you reject it.

Inclosed is a letter from Jesse K. Dubois to Mr Whitney of this place—rather a copy of it.[1] Please read the conclusion of it and you will see, as you have seen from Sweat's notes to me and Judge Davis's notes that there is much in it which I can explain to your satisfaction when I see you no time now.

Your Friend
W. H. Herndon

LC: HW3331–32; Exp 4:10:2060–63

---

1. See DuBois to Henry C. Whitney, April 6 1865, *Herndon's Informants*, 620. DuBois complains of AL's seeming ingratitude, as president, toward old Illinois friends.

178. To Jesse W. Weik

Chicago, Jany 11 1887

Friend Weik:

In my letter of the 9th inst I spoke to you of Dubois letter and Lincoln's *apparent* ingratitude. I sent you a copy of D's letter written to lawyer Whitney of this city. Lincoln like all men was moved by his motives and built up his character by his policies: he had a deep policy for every important move. You will see what Swett says and what Judge Davis said about Lincoln by looking at their testimony which you will find by looking at the notes now in your possession.[1] Let us look at this matter. First, if Lincoln had a friend he made that friend a friend by his, L's, character as a general rule and not by purchase. If that friend and a man who was only a *quasi*-cool half friend—not his warm particular friend wanted office, Lincoln would argue with himself about thus—"This man my warm particular friend always & was so made without purchase and will so remain without a bribe. This other man my *quasi* friend & not my particular friend can and will be made so by price—gifts—purchase. I shall run some risks of losing my old warm personal friend, it may be, if I do not give him some office, and yet it is not certain that I shall lose him. I can make this other man my friend by giving him office to a certainty. Things being equal or nearly so I shall make one friend without losing one with a certainty. This will aid *me* and give *me* strength in my struggles with other men who are my competitors & opponents." Here are Mr Lincoln's motives. I know the man and I know the facts in which I found my opinion—Secondly, Mr Lincoln was ambitious to build up a strong administration and a wise one—1st for his own name and fame & 2dly for the good of the people and the government and his country

LC: HW3333; Exp 4:10:2064–65

179. To Jesse W. Weik

Chicago, Jany 14 1887

Friend Weik:

. . .

From the critcisms of the press it would—it does appear that the reading world wants to know every and all events—facts—incidents—thoughts, feelings and adventures of Lincoln, including the books he read and the girls he "hugged," and the like, upon the fact of human experience that the man grows out of the boy and the boy out of the child. The foundations of manhood are laid in the boy—deep

---

1. For David Davis, see *Herndon's Informants*, 218, 346–51, 484, 529; for Leonard Swett, see *Herndon's Informants*, 159–60, 162–68, 213–14.

down in the boy. Mrs. Thomas Bush Lincoln did her job well in making Abe: she is the good angel who did it: she had too *choice material.* . . .

Your Friend
W H Herndon

LC: HW3335; Exp 4:10:2068–69

180. To Jesse W. Weik

Springfield Ills. Jany 22d 87

Friend Weik:

I am at home once more and I am glad of it; and I suppose that you are because I can have more time to write my notes. In a few days I shall send to you the books on Lincoln which I wrote to you about sometime since. By this time I guess that you have read my letters—evidences &c about Lincoln; and by the way let me ask you a question which is as follows—How did you like my Ann Rutledge lecture as a whole and especially that part which talks about the old settler. There was not much of "the *Malaria*" in them nor any of "*the Miasmatic*" sickly indolence in them, as H. & Nicolay write: they were a brave, generous—hospitable, jolly—rollicing set of boys, I assure you: these people were the very devil for fun and were warmly social: they were the most social of creature, these people in and about New Salem: they were rude and rough it is true, but full of truth and honesty: they were not a gloomy nor a sad people: they were full of life—oversouled, and that is all. These people were not touched by "the Malaria" nor dwarfed by "the Miasma."[1] The "boys" say this in order to show that the sadness of Lincoln was of the *forest*. This is all nonsense. Lincoln's sadness—gloominess &c. were the result of his *organism* and *facts* subsequent to his birth: he knew a great deal of his birth &c—more than one thinks. *Forest* life does not make a man sad—nor gloomy—nor melancholic: it makes a man sincere—earnest—thoughtful. Away with "the Malarial" and "Miasmatic" idea: it is nonsense or worse than that.

. . .

There was a story current here some years since that Lincoln courted a young lady here by the name of Rickard. My wife's step mother was a Rickard and the sister of the courted girl. My wife says that her step mother told her that Lincoln wanted "Su" that is Susan Rickard: she is still living here and I'll try and get the truth out of her.[2] Women, as a general rule do not love to blab about these things, especially to the general public. I once had Miss Rickards confidence and I think I hold it yet. I'll see about the matter when I have time and the fruit sought is ripe. I *do* want to get at the Exact truth of all the Lincoln facts. I have tried to do so

---

1. John G. Nicolay and John Hay, "Abraham Lincoln: A History: Lincoln in Springfield," *Century Magazine* 33, no. 3 (January 1887): 378–79.

2. WHH's wife later changed her testimony on the identity of this Rickard. See *Herndon's Informants*, 640.

for twenty years or more and will to the very End. The reading world is entitled to truth: it is their right to have it, and it is our religious duty to tell it.

I will see Mrs Francis and Mrs Edwards and get out of them some facts which I want and they know—at least I think they do know what I want. Mrs Francis once was quite a woman—a shrewd one—a friend of Miss Todd and Mr. Lincoln: it was she who patched up Miss Todd's & Lincoln's grievances. Mrs Francis belonged to the aristocracy of this city till she moved to Oregon—or to the great open wide wild west from which she has returned to her old west to die.

. . .

Hay & Nicolay say in the Jany number of the Century substantially this—That Speed was the *only intimate* friend that Lincoln ever had; and that Speed and Lincoln poured out their souls to each other. Possibly I do not understand what they mean by the word *intimate*. If they mean to say that Lincoln had no friends, after Speed, to whom he poured out his soul, then it *may* be true, but the question comes—Did he pour out his soul to Speed? Lincoln's nature was secretive: it was reticent: it was "Hush." Did Lincoln violate that whole nature? He may have opened to Speed *in one direction* under conditions. He was courting Miss Todd & Speed was—Well—you can guess. These facts brought the two close together, and on the love question *alone* Lincoln opened to Speed—possibly the whole. Did Lincoln tell Speed his love scrapes with Ann Rutledge as well as others? He did not. See Speed's letter to me in Lamon's life of Lincoln at page . Still an other question comes—Did Lincoln and Speed or either of them open the facts—their minds—to Hay & Nicolay about the *intimate* friendship? Who authorizes H. & N. to assert what they do assert? How do H & N know that Lincoln and Speed poured out their souls to one an other? If to tell a friend some facts in *one line* or direction constitutes *intimate* friendship then Lincoln always—before & after Speed left Illinois—had intimate friends, and if Lincoln's refusal to tell all the secrets of his soul to any man shows a want of intimate friendship then Lincoln never had an intimate friend Poetry is no fit place for severe history. I think the truth is just here—namely—That under peculiar conditions and under *lines* of *love* and in that direction alone they were *intimate* friends. No man pours out his *whole* soul to any man: he keeps millions of secrets in his own bosom—with himself and God alone: he would keep them secret from God, if he could. Such broad assertions as H & N's are lies and nothing less. Did H & N enter Lincoln & Speeds minds and read the story? Nonsense. Let us keep shy of poetry or poetical license in our book, if we can. Let us ever keep in mind facts—truths—and then write tersely and to the point—plainly to the understanding of the great mass of men—to the common people. Lincoln has often said to me—"Don't shoot too high—aim low."

Inclosed with this is a letter which I wrote to Mr Poole in '86 which you can read and file away.[3] In the letter I say, and now affirm, that Mr. Lincoln was a riddle and a puzzle to his neighbors generally. Some few knew the man inside and

---

3. See §147.

outside: he was at once a many *sided* and a many *mooded* man. At times he had his spells in which he seemed to be destitute of reason. In the Poole letter, in my hurry while writing it, I may have pressed the idea of *heredity* too far or give it too much force. I shall correct the letter and the idea sometime when I write to you. The letter was in fact hurriedly written and I had no time to correct nor rewrite it. Read it and tell me how you like it in general &c—. I do not in fact pride myself in the letter

Your Friend
W. H. Herndon

LC: HW3336–39; Exp 4:10:2070–77

181. To Jesse W. Weik[1]

Springfield Ills Jany 30th '87

Friend Weik:

I wish to, as it were, repeat some things in order to make my ideas clean and clear. I have tried to understand some of the philosophy of N & H. They say in the Jany No of "The Century" at page—378–9, I think, that Lincoln's sadness—gloom and melancholy were caused by his constitutional tendencies *slightly*—"taint"—to use their expression; and that that constitutional tendency was intensified by the *malarial* and *miasmatic* idea: they further say, to add to the force of the argument, that we of the great west in an early day lived a forest life, and that a forest life made us *sad*—*gloomy* and *melancholic*, and hence Lincoln's sadness—gloom and melancholy: they use the three words—sadness—gloom and melancholy, as I remember it. I have not the Jany No of the Century, having loaned it to my son. N & Hay further state that we of the great west of an early day were unsocial and never *smiled*—only laughed. Now all this is but to prove that Lincoln was sad gloomy & melancholic *slightly* through his organism, which *slightness* was intensified by the malarial & forest life idea. Let me see as to this argument. What is sadness—gloom and melancholy? They mean a state of *sorrow*—*dejection* & an *idea* that bodes *an evil*, which throw their shadow over the face of the man. That Mr. Lincoln was a sad—gloomy & melancholic man, I admit: his sadness &c were *principally* and *chiefly* caused by his organism—his make up and his constitution which certain tendency of it was intensified by a series of facts happening to him in his after life and a knowledge coming to him of the lowness of his origin—his mother's illegitimacy—his aunt's loosness—his father's loss of manhood possibly, & doubts of his own paternity &c. &c—these with the untimely death of Ann Rutledge, and his unfortunate marriage to Miss Mary Todd, and the hell that came of it, caused Lincoln's sadness &c ie—intensified his original nature. Lincoln's philosophy was a gloomy belief—terribly so—But let me continue. Does a forest life make men

---

1. In top margin: "No. 2 Read No 1 first." If this implies that two letters were sent under one cover, positive identification of the other letter is lacking, though the letter of January 22, 1887, is a good possibility.

& women sad—gloomy and melancholic? Remember what I said, as to the nature of sadness &c. That a forest life makes men and women sincere—thoughtful—earnest—sedate—reticent—contemplating—determined, which appear on the face, there is no doubt; & this state has been called *sadness—gloom* & *melancholy* by N. & H. Nonsense. A nation may probably be *sad* alone—not dejected—not feeling—not having the idea on the face of a coming evil—a boding desolation. A people may be sad—that is be serious—earnest &c, and this is the case with the American people. The Americans are comparatively a sad people. They have an unconscious destiny before them, and that makes them sad. Again N & H say that we of the great west in early times never *smiled*—only laughed. Had these gentlemen been raised in the wild—wide west where Lincoln was raised they would never have talked so wildly. Had they been here in an early day they would have seen men and women *smile* and *laugh* at every dance and at every corn shucking—at every social gathering—and at every hoe down—at every muster and at every election—at every camp meeting and shooting match—at every fire & on every highway: they would have seen had they been here a social—jovial—cheerful—generous and an honest people, smiling and laughing everywhere as occasion demanded. To *smile* is but a half tickling, but to laugh is the highest outburst of the human soul in the line of joyous feeling. The boys should not speculate: they should stick to facts. Lincoln's sadness in short &c. were constitutional and those states were intensified by facts & knowledge of his after life—by his conditions and his environments—socially—morally—mentally—the death of Ann Rutledge and his marriage to Miss Mary Todd and the Hell that grew out—come out of it. Lincoln's philosophy played its part in his gloomy states. I'll explain. Lincoln's marriage was a policy marriage & he paid the penalty of it, and the payment of that penalty wrote its receipt on his face.

Your Friend
W. H Herndon

LC: HW3340–41; Exp 4:10:2078–81

182. To Jesse W. Weik

Springfield Ills Jany 87

Friend Weik:

Judge Matheny tells me this story of Mr. & Mrs. Lincoln: the story was told him by one of the parties to it. About the year 1860 there lived in this city a man by the name of Tiger,[1] who was a personal friend of Lincoln: he was a kind but a powerful man physically. Tiger heard that Mrs. Lincoln was without help and knowing that Mrs. Lincoln was a tigress and could not for any length of time keep

---

1. In a memorandum book, JWW identified the man called "Tiger" in this letter as Jacob Taggart. See *Herndon's Informants*, 667.

a girl, thought that he had a niece, who was a fine girl, industrious, neat, saving, and rather handsome, who could satisfy any body on Earth. So he sent the girl down to see Mrs Lincoln: she, Mrs L, was anxious to get a girl and arrangements were made between the two that Sarah—the girls name, should stay and help Mrs L. Everything went on well for sometime, Mrs L bragging on her Sarah all the while to her neighbors & visitors. Sarah herself was no common hired girl, but a fine woman and rather intelligent, pleasant and social. Mrs. Lincoln at last got on one of her insane mad spells, insulted and actually slapt the girl, who could and would not stand it—: So she quit Mrs Lincoln—went home to her uncle Tiger's and told her story weeping and crying all the while. Tiger felt bad about the matter, but knowing that all quarrels generally have two sides to them, he was determined to find out the truth of the matter—so he went down to Lincoln's and when he got there he saw that Mrs. Lincoln had thrown the girls trunk and clothes out of the house and on the pavement in the street. On approaching the house he saw the things; and just in the yard stood Mrs Lincoln ready for a fight. Tiger advanced and spoke to Mrs. Lincoln in a kind and gentlemanly way—said he came to see her and find out who was in fault, and what was the matter—all about it. Mrs L at once blazed away with her sharp and sarcastic tongue, having her insane mad spell on her—abused Tiger shamefully, calling him a dirty villain—a vile creature & the like. Tiger stood still, waiting for an opportunity to pitch in a word of peace and reconciliation, but to no purpose. Mrs. Lincoln got madder & madder—boiled over with her insane rage and at last struck Tiger with the broom two or 3 times. Tiger now got mad, but said nothing to Mrs. Lincoln—not a word—stood the licking as best he could. Tiger at last gathered up the clothes of the girl and being a strong man threw the trunk on his shoulder and carried it and the girls clothes home to his niece. The older the thing—his licking by Mrs L, got the madder Tiger got and so he swore to himself that no man's wife should thus treat him and go free from a whipping or at least the husband should humiliatingly apologise for the wrong done him by his wife. The longer the thing stood in Tigers mind the more furious Tiger got, and so he went down into the city in search of Lincoln, in order to make him correct the thing or to whip him—to apologise or to stand a thumping—licking—a severe whipping: he after some considerable search found Lincoln in Edwards' store reclining on the Counter telling one of his best stories. Tiger caught part of the story that tickled him very much. However Tiger, being a man of *will*, called Lincoln out of the store and told him the facts of the fight between the women, and his licking by Mrs Lincoln; and said to Lincoln that he must *punish* Mrs. Lincoln and apoligise to him—Tiger or———and just here Lincoln caught what was coming—looked up to Tiger, having held his head down with shame as Tiger told the story of his wrongs, done him by Mrs L & said calmly—kindly—and in a very friendly way, mingled with shame and sadness—"*Friend* Tiger, can't you endure this one wrong done you by a mad woman without much complaint for old friendship's sake while I have had to bear it without complaint and without a murmur for lo these last fifteen years"—Lincoln said what he did so kindly—so peacefully—so friendly—so feelingly so apologetically in manner and tone and so sadly that it quickly and totally disarmed Tiger who said to Lincoln—"Friend give me your hand. I'll bear what has been done me by Mrs. Lincoln on *your* account and *your* account alone. I'll say no more about the matter and now; Lincoln let us be forever what we have been—friends." Lincoln instantly took and grasped, warmly grasped Tiger's hand and shook it in a real friendly western style—saying—"Agreed, friend Tiger and so let us be what we have always been, warm personal friends" and they ever were afterwards. Thus ended in the very best feeling and warmest friendship what at one time threatened to be a terrible [person?] fight. Both men were physically powerful and personally brave; and it is very doubtful which of the men was the most powerful. Lincoln was wise in not letting Tiger say what he intended to say which was—"I'll punish—whip you for your wife's wrong." That would have offended Lincoln and a fight would have certainly ensued. Lincoln tapped the cloud before the bolt came. I say that Lincoln was wise in the right—exact moment where wisdom was most needed and coolness. This little story brings out one of Lincoln's best characteristics—patience, love of peace, shrewdness & practical wisdom: it affects me as much any little story that I ever heard of Lincoln. God bless the man: He has blessed him as he has blessed no other man. Sometimes I can see Lincoln standing before me as I write about him, and so it is just at this moment. I see Lincoln—the sad—the noble man.

I hope that you can read this fine little story, ending in peace and lasting friendship between two old personal friends: it is a good story and one that can be relied on: it comes from the right quarters and through men who know what they are talking about—men of truthfulness—honor—integrity.

Your Friend

W. H. Herndon

Mrs. Lincoln had the insanity of madness and not the madness of insanity before she left for Washington / H

LC: HW3342–44; Exp 4:10:2082–87

183. To Jesse W. Weik

Springfield Ills Feby 5th '87

Friend Weik:

It is said by some of the biographers of Lincoln that "he never drank a drop of liquor in his life" and that he never chewed nor smoked a cigar or pipe. It is not true that Lincoln "never drank a drop of liquor in his life": it is true that he never smoked or chewed tobacco. Mr. Lincoln did sometimes take a horn: he played ball on the day of his nomination at Chicago in 1860 with the boys, or the day before that, and did drink beer two or three times that day and during the game or play: he was nervous then—excited at that particular time, and drank to steady his nerves. Lincoln has been often heard to say that "I never drank much and am entitled to no credit therefor, because I hate the stuff." A friend once ask Lincoln this question—: "Don't you like liquor, Lincoln" and to which L replied—"No, it is unpleasant to me and always makes me feel flabby and undone." Lincoln had a low or slow circulation of the blood and hence he had not much wear and tear of the tissues of the body; and hence no very strong thirst or appetite for stimulative drinks—nor other tonics: he had a good but moderate appetite for food and was satisfied with almost anything that would satisfy hunger—anything with which "to fill up." Lincoln in thought and in act moved slowly mentally and physically. He reasoned from the simple to the complex—from the concrete to the abstract—from facts to principle—from there to Laws, through analogy: he was a worshipper of principles & Laws. To him everything was Law. Those persons generally who have a rapid circulation and somewhat nervous who think quickly and act quickly, have much of the wear and tear of the tissues of the body, and consequently desire stimulants—tonics and sometimes unfortunately much of them to restore the loss of tissues, or to arrest further loss or destruction of them Such men generally love strong food—heat giving food—and demand it—are somewhat dyspeptic, because of the strong food—and the excess of it, and their bad digestion. Lincoln had a good appetite and good digestion—ate mechanically, never asking why such a thing was not on the table nor why it was on it, if so: he filled up and that is all: he never complained of bad food nor praised the good. I, on the Circuit, have sat down with Lincoln a thousand times, it may be, at the table and he never made any fuss about the food on the table: he ate and went about his business, though the food was "cussed bad" as 8 out of ten at the table would say—. Some would swear at it and others would laugh at their misfortunes in not getting "goodies." Lincoln did drink when he thought that it would do him good: he was never seen under the influence of liquor more than once or twice in his younger days when it liquor was quite in universal use. Lincoln was rather silent at the table holding but little conversation there with any one.

Lincoln was a riddle and a puzzle sometimes: he loved best the vegatable world generally, though his food was of a mixed kind: he loved a good hot cup of coffee; and Especially did he love apples: he would wrap his forefinger of his right hand and his thumb around the equatorial part of the apple and commence eating at the blossom end, never using a knife to cut or peel the apple. I have seen him read—study his case and the law of it intently while eating his apple. His table at home generally was economised to the smallest amount: he never dared as a general thing to invite his friends to his house. Mrs Lincoln was a very stingy woman and yet she would occasionally have parties. Lincoln himself had none of the avarice of *the get* and yet he had a tinge of it in *the keep*: he was not generous in his money matters, unless he had some view in end. *Mrs* Lincoln was the cause of his poor tables: she economised here to swell otherwise Poor unfortunate woman!—wish that she had done better. The world will better understand the woman and the cause of much of her and Lincoln's troubles when Thorndike of the NA Review publishes my article on Lincoln—his marriage—&c until which time form no crystalized unchangeable opinion.[1] Rest easy & be content.

Your hurried friend
W H Herndon

Judge Davis told me that Lincoln never invited him to his house and have heard many others of Lincoln's best friends say the same thing.

LC: HW3345–46; Exp. 4:10:2088–89, 91, 90

184. To Jesse W. Weik[1]

Springfield Ills Feby 6th '87

LINCOLN'S PHILOSOPHY.

Friend Weik:

————That Lincoln had his peculiar *states* above described no one doubts, and that they sprang out of his organism admits of as little doubt. There is a physical organism and an intellectual one in every human being. Minds are of a different kinds. Some minds require much evidence before believing and some less. Every mind must believe or fail to believe on certain evidence and some minds are credulous and some incredulous. This difference comes out of the intellectual organism, as we call it for the sake of an idea. Mr. Lincoln's mind required much evidence to produce conviction: it was an incredulous mind and naturally disposed to doubt—deny—was skeptical. Now the question comes—"Did Lincoln's gloom &c come out of his intellectual organism, or his physical?" Or put in different words—"Did his mind with his philosophy make him sad—gloomy &c or did his physical organism alone make him so?" It was his physical side that did it. Lincoln's philosophy grew out of his mind which was bottomed on the physical as a boy grows out of a man—an oak out of an acorn: it *had* to be just as it was and could not be otherwise by any means; and now an other question comes—"Did his philosophy make him more sad &c than he otherwise would have been?" His philosophy *may* have tinged—have colored or intensified his sadness somewhat—a little but it did not cause his sadness &c. What was Lincoln's philosophy? He was

---

1. This and other references indicate that WHH was invited by the editor of the prestigious *North American Review*, Allen Thorndyke Rice, to contribute to a series of recollections of AL that were eventually collected and published as *Reminiscences of Abraham Lincoln by Distinguished Men of His Time* (1886). WHH's article, as he indicates here, was to be on AL's domestic relations, but it never appeared and is presumed lost.

---

1. The note in the top margin—"No. 2 Read this after No 1"—indicates that another letter, possibly that of February 5, was sent with this one.

honestly a fatalist and has been often heard to say—"I always was a fatalist," and quoted Shakespeare as follows—

"There is a divinity that shapes our ends
Rough hew them as we may."

he believed in predestination—foreordination—That all things were fixed—domed one way or the other, from which there was no appeal. He has often said to me—"What is to be will be and no efforts nor prayers of ours can change—alter—modify or reverse the decree." Lincoln was somewhat superstitious—had a kind of foreboding of his fate: he said to me more than a dozen times this—"I feel as if I shall meet with some terrible end;" and then would become more sad—. Lincoln always, to me in our private conversation, said that there was no freedom of the will—rather the mind as a whole: he maintained that there was no conscious act of any man that was not moved by a motive first—last and always. Finally Mr. Lincoln believed in constant modes of operation in nature—continuous and unchangeable ones eternally—Law in short that ruled both matter and mind. This philosophy of Lincoln I have heard him state many many times in our philosophical discussions—private office conversations. Mr. Lincoln was a natural—necessary and inevitable—doomed Infidel—*logically* and *absolutely* so: he was under his law; and it is all folly for any man to say that Mr Lincoln was a christian and believed in the Efficacy of prayer. You might put the following words in Lincoln's mouth and they would be substantially true—"What can I do—what can any man do—what can the whole race moulded into one man do, to arrest the workings of this terrible—this iron—this all powerful machine that by decree and doom moves in its inevitable and omnipotent way to its own ends, working *out* new life and grinding *in* death forever? What change this power and arrest its operation, which are certain—absolute—and eternal! This vast iron machine moves in no mysterious way—moves with an omnipotent force. I cannot act against it. No I cannot even *think* against it."————. Here you have Lincolns philosophy—his religion—and his thoughts—Lincoln in his younger days tended toward scientific materialism—that is, he believed that behind all these phenomenal manifestations of the universe there was a *Power* that worked for righteousness as seemed to us: he would not call that *Power* God: he called it *Maker*. In after life he used the familiar language of the day, and called it *God*: he did not use the word God in any religious sense—christian sense rather. He was most emphatically an Infidel—was so logically naturally—inevitably so, as his philosophy reveals—and demonstrates.

Your Friend
W. H Herndon

LC: HW3347–48; Exp 4:10:2092–95

185. To Jesse W. Weik

Springfield Ills Feby 9th '87

Friend Weik:

I have read the Feby No of the Century—the article by H & N, and find it a rather poor thing: it is wordy and windy and takes no note of time for the benefit of order in this short life of ours. I, and so can any one, write the substance of the article, so far as a knowledge of Lincoln is concerned, in ten lines. The writers say— tell a good truth when they state that "Lincoln recieved everybody's confidence and rarely gave his ~~in~~ own in return." This is most emphatically Lincoln. Again the "boys" state an other fact—namely that Mr. Lincoln had great individuality which he never sank in the mob nor mixed it with any class of men: his individualism stood out from the mass of men like a lone cliff over the plain below. Again the "boys" say that Mr. L had great dignity and that is the truth. I do not use the word "boys" in any contemptuous sense. I respect them very much: they are doing a good thing. Mr. Lincoln was a very plain man and of—to a certain point—easy approach—quite democratic—somewhat social, but beyond a certain ring of self respect which surrounded and guarded his person no man ever dared go without a silent but powerful rebuff. Lincoln kept aloof from men generally—few knew him: he would be cheerful and chatty—somewhat social and communicative—tell his stories—his jokes—laugh and smile and yet you could see, if you had a keen sense—perception—of human character, that Lincoln's soul was not present—that it was in an other sphere: he was an abstracted and an absent minded man: he was with you and he was not with you: he was familiar with you and yet he kept you at a distance, substantially saying to himself—"This nature of mine *is mine alone*, and it is sacred ground on which no man shall tread" It is well to note this pecu- liarity of Lincoln. This peculiar nature of Lincoln will explain to you why it was that Holland never found out anything while here gathering up facts of Lincoln's life; and it further explains why there was such a disagreement among the citizens of Springfield generally as to the nature—qualities and characteristics of L. Turn to my long article which I sent you—the one prepared for the Tribune, and you will see what Holland says as to the opinions of the good people of this city about L. Few knew the man and the many were ignorant; and hence the disagreement among ourselves as to the man. Lincoln was reticent—secretive—incommunicable in some—many lines of his character. The "boys" do not say all that I repeat here to you; and it is well to note what I say, if you wish to know the man which you are soon to write about. I have seen and felt all this in Lincoln a thousand times. I have stated all this many—many times to the reading world. See 6 mo in the White House—see Truth Seeker &c. &c and other letters scattered through the papers—from 1865—to 1887 and including my letters to you. What I say here is but a repetition, but it is well enough *to say it again and again.* Lincoln's individ- ualism was great—so was his dignity—so was his reticence—abstractedness and absent mindedness—a peculiar man, this Abraham was. . . .

Your Friend

W. H Herndon

LC: HW3349–51; Exp 4:10:2096–101

186. To Jesse W. Weik

Springfield Ills Feby 11th '87

Friend Weik:

Mr. Lincoln was not at all times *the* popular man in Sangamon County—the Capitol county of this state—L's home; and there is a good reason—many reasons for it. In the first place he was not understood by the mass of men: in the second place he was not a social man, not being "hail fellow well met;" and in the third place he was a man of his own ideas—had the courage of his convictions and the rules of their expression. Lincoln was social in *spots*—at courts on the circuit as we travelled around with the Judge: he was corageous in his ideas everywhere and at all times. Mr Lincoln was not a warm hearted man, positively so: he was abstracted and absent minded. When in one of his moods he was abstracted & absent minded and would not notice a friend on the street, though spoken to pleasantly: he would straddle along—stride along, not noticing his friend nor reply to any good morning salutation. All this was taken for *coldness—dignity—pride* &c &c by some and hence to *that some* and his friends Lincoln was misjudged and disliked. These moods of Lincoln, when I have met him on the street, caused him to pass me unnoticed, though spoken to warmly and kindly; and yet I knew the man so well that I paid no attention to it, rather I have felt for him—sympathized with the suffering—sorrowful—sad man. *Hell* was to pay in his family frequently and this intensified his *states*. Lincoln was a many *sided* man and a many *mooded* one; and how do you expect the mass to understand greatness in misery. I was the firm—devoted friend of Lincoln from 1833 to 1866 and nothing could move me from my convictions of Lincoln's goodness—honesty and greatness. I [voted?] for him all the time against the world. I helped for years to write him up in our Ills Journal and other papers in this & other states—Lincoln and I frequently disagreed in measures & men, never on principle as I now recollect it. Before Lincoln was assassinated I doubted the policy & the principle of a tariff except for revenue alone and to-day I am a *radical free trade* man. In 1847–49 I saw that Lincoln would ruin himself about the Mexican war and his opposition to it, and so, being his friend and not seeing the question as he did, I tried to prevent Lincoln's destruction. I wrote to him on the subject again and again and tried to induce him to silence, if to nothing else; but his sense of justice and his courage made him speak—utter his thoughts, as to the War with Mexico. Lincoln and I had many hot disputes in our office and yet those disputes were friendly ones. He was never insulting nor dictatorial to me. No politician in America can vote and live if he opposes war in which the spread Eagle is concerned—America. When Lincoln returned home from congress in 1849 he was a politically dead and a ruined man: he wanted to run for congress again but it was no use to try. Judge Logan tried his hand as successor of Lincoln but Logan was a failure—and a fizzle. Here was a cold—avaricious and little mean man for you as the people saw him. Lincoln from 1849 to 1855 became a hard student and read much—studied Euclid and some mathmatical books—read much in the political world—The repeal of the Missouri Compromise acts roused Lincoln—waked him up to his new opportunities and he seized them and you know the results—. Lincoln was born out of the war and grew to the manhood of glory—such is life with an opportunity—Verily

> "There is a divinity that shapes our ends
>   Rough hew them how we may"[1]

Now as to Lincoln's ideas—the courage of his Convictions and the valor of their expression—*First*. Mr. Lincoln as early as 1836 issued a political hand bill in which he declared himself for woman's rights—.[2] His keen sense of justice could not refuse woman the rights which he demanded for himself—said to me often that that question was one of time only. *Secondly* he in 1835–6 wrote a little book against Christianity which was burned by Saml Hill his friend: he often in Conversation as late as 1850 avowed his ideas in this city. I have heard him—so has Judge Matheny—Stuart and many others—*Thirdly*. In 1844, I *think*, he advocated temperance in 1844 before the Washingtonian society, both temperance, and the society being somewhat unpopular at that time.[3] The Washingtonian Society was formed by a dozen or more of drunkards; and the elite and Christians of this city more or less turned up their noses at the men and what they advocated. Nearly all men drank during those days and hence to run up against custom and habit quite universal was unpopular. *Fourthly*—Lincoln bitterly opposed the Mexican war as you know: he did so while political death stared him in the face: it buried him and yet "he arose on the third day" and became our national savior. *Fifthly*: he opposed slavery everywhere and at all times when to oppose it was political death. From 1820 to 1860 it was a time of *"dough faces"*[4] in the north. Lincoln turned his face to flint on this question and he stood firm on his conscience. *Sixthly*: he opposed the repeal of the Missouri Compromise of 1819–20 with all his soul—first on the grounds of policy and secondly on principle. The repeal was for a time democratic—pro slavery and popular, but Lincoln with others made the repeal unpopular and justly odious. This repeal was his grand opportunity and he seized it and rode to glory on the popular waves—. *Seventhly*—He advocated the policy of free immigration of foreigners and their right to vote, when Americanism here was popular and rampant. The question arose in the city as to the right of foreigners who had not been naturallized, though they had lived in this state as residents for six months or a year as the case might be to vote at our city Election. I was city attorney at that time as I now remember it, and it was my duty as such officer to see that no one illegally voted and to have them punished for such violation of the charter and ordinances of the city. The question was a doubtful one—one in which different but honest opinions could be expressed. I spoke, as atty of the city I think, to Lincoln about the question—showed him the laws of the state—the

---

1. *Hamlet* 5.2.
2. AL to the Editor of the *Sangamo Journal*, June 13, 1836, *Collected Works*, 1:48. Here AL professed to be in favor of extending the right of suffrage to tax-paying women.
3. AL, "Temperance Address," February 22, 1842, *Collected Works*, 1:271–279.
4. "Dough Faces": Northern politicians with Southern principles regarding slavery.

charter of the city, and its ordinances, with changes *in the state law* and asked him his opinion of the Law. After looking over the matter and taking his time he said to me—"The question is a doubtful one—and the foreigner is taxed by the city and it is but justice that they should vote on all questions of city policy or interest." The precise question was—Does a *general* law passed by the Legislature repeal a city charter without including it—naming it directly or by just inference I said "no" & this cut off many votes: it was compromised at last however. The whigs—Lincoln being one—were opposed to the foreigners right to vote in City matters. Lincoln dared be just and stand bolt upright—*Eighthly*—Mr. Lincoln opposed Know Nothingism in all its phazes, everywhere and at all times when it was sweeping over the land like wild fire: he and I stood shoulder to shoulder on this as well as all the question mentioned herein except as stated.[5] *Ninthly*—Mr. Lincoln had the courage to issue his proclamation of emancipation when one side of the Republican party said that he was too cowardly to do it, and the other side said that the issue of the proclamation at this time would lose the fall Elections for the Republican party: he had decided to issue it and he decided the time. The proclamation come as by doom. He had the courage in his Greely letter to say that what he did or failed to do about Emancipation &c &c was not done for the negro—was done to save the Union[6] Nor could the Senate of the United States drive Lincoln to dismiss Secy Seward[7] and *Tenthly* & lastly when Mason and Slidell had been arrested by Capt Wilks of the San Jacinto and the Press and the People all over the land were wild with enthusiasm over the glorious event, demanding the punishment of these traitors—When the Secry of War—the Sec of State and his cabinet were wild and furious for the punishment of these men, one cool head and one brave heart rose up and said substantially—"This must not be—these men must be released—one war at a time. To punish these men now would cause a war between England and America; and that is just what the South wants. Take off the Shackles from these men—open the doors of their prison and apologise to England;"[8] and so it was done, though a bitter pill to take under the circumstance. England will some day rue her course. Here stands Lincoln a brave and a great soul who has the courage of his convictions—his ideas, and the swift valor of their Expression. How do you like the man friend Weik?

Your Friend
W. H. Herndon

Lincoln's ideas with his courage made him at times unpopular. Had not Mr Lincoln been assassinated just when he was he would have *governed* the Republican party

---

5. For Know-Nothingism, see §93, p. 92.

6. AL to Horace Greeley, August 22, 1862, *Collected Works*, 5:388–89.

7. In a confrontation with a hostile Senatorial delegation in December 1862, AL was able to forestall their demands for Seward's resignation.

8. James Mason and John Slidell were Confederate diplomats en route to Europe when on November 8, 1861, they were removed from the British mail steamer *Trent* by American Naval Captain Charles Wilkes, in violation of international law. Despite public enthusiasm in favor of the act in the United States, AL and the cabinet decided to release Mason and Slidell rather than risk war with Great Britain.

during his second term or it would have crushed him if it could. There would have been a struggle over policies & measures H

LC: HW3352–55; Exp 4:10:2102–9

187. To Jesse W. Weik

Springfield Ills. Feby [16][1] '87

Friend Weik:

Probably I have told you this story before; and if so excuse me. From the time that Lincoln & I entered into partnership in the fall of 1843 I was quite a reader "in biographical literature. Seeing a notice of a fine life of Burke the English orator and statesman, I ordered it from C. S. Francis & Co of New York.[2] I read it carefully—2 vols. and liked it very much. One morning I had it on our ~~office~~ table and was looking over some few pages, which I was desirous of reading again, when Lincoln came into our office: he looked rather cheerful and pleasant. We spoke kindly to each other—passed the compliments of the morning &c. I said, still thinking of the book—"Lincoln do you not wish to read an excellent and eloquent life of Burke, the English orator and statesman;" and at the same time handing him the book: he took it in his hands and hastily ran over some of the pages of it, reading a little here and there. And then handing me back the book, said—"No, I don't want to read it. Biographies as written are false and misleading. The author of the life of his hero paints him as a perfect man—magnifies his perfections and suppresses his imperfections—describes the success of his hero in glowing terms, never once hinting at his failures and his blunders." "Why do not" said Lincoln "book merchants and sellers have blank biographies on their shelves always ready for sale—so that when a man dies, if his heirs—children—and friends wish to perpetuate the memory of the dead, they can purchase one already written, *but with blanks*, which they can fill up eloquently and grandly at pleasure, thus commemorating a lie,—an injury to the living and to the name of the dead"?

This, Mr. Lincoln said to me in substance just as I have it. I felt the force of what he said, because I had *thought* the same. I may sometimes repeat stories to you, not keeping any record of what I do write. In writing so much to you how can I help it? Could you, if you kept no record?

LC: HW3356; Exp 4:10:2120–2

---

1. WHH supplied the date for this letter in a letter written two days later. .

2. For an earlier telling of this story, see §142. In the margins: "A good Story" and "This ought, by rights, to follow Mrs Moore's good story about Lincoln's love of truth" (see §107).

188. To Jesse W. Weik

Springfield Ills Feby 18th '87

Friend Weik:

I sent you an undated letter to-day: it should be dated the 16th inst. Please date.

On Saturday evening I was called out to write the will of Benj Bancroft and at the house of Bancroft I found an old friend of Lincoln, whose name is Fisk: he told me the following story which is correct. A man by the name of Pollard Simmons was a good friend of Lincoln in 1834–6. Jno Calhoun was the surveyor of Sangamon County—was "The Candlebox Calhoun"[1]—and a democrat in 1834. Simmons loved Lincoln, who was very poor at that time, and he tried to get Lincoln in some business: he applied to Calhoun as the friend of Lincoln to give him a deputyship in the surveying business. Calhoun as Simmons remembers it gave Lincoln a deputyship. Simmons got on his horse and went on the hunt of Lincoln whom he found in the woods mauling rails. Simmon's said "Lincoln I've got you a job" and to which Lincoln replied—"Pollard, I thank you for your trouble: but now let me ask you a question—Do I have to give up any of my principles for this job. If I have to surrender any thought or principle to get it I wouldn't touch it with a ten foot pole?" "No, you do not Lincoln," said Pollard Simmons, and to which Lincoln replied—"I'll accept the office and now I thank you and my superior for it"

You wish me to state some of Lincoln's customs & habits about the office in Springfield. Well, when he got to the office about 9 o'c in the morning the very first thing that he did was to pick up some news paper, if I had not hidden them, and read them aloud, much to my discomfort: he would spread himself out on the sofa—one leg on a chair—and an other on the table or stove. I have often said to Lincoln—"Why Lincoln do you always read aloud" and to which he said—"When I read aloud my two senses catch the idea—1st I see what I am reading and 2dly I hear it read; and I can thus remember what I read the better." Sometimes Lincoln would read something in the papers and that would suggest to him an idea and he would say—that puts me in mind of a story that I heard down in Egypt in Ills; and then he would tell the story and that story would suggest an other and so on. Nothing was done that morning. Declarations—pleas—briefs & demurrers were flung to the winds. It was useless to attempt to read anymore that morning. Sometimes Lincoln would—when his wife had gone to church or when she had kicked him out of the house, bring to the office Willie & Tad, *them* little devils to me—so bad were they, but now little angels, I hope. Those children would take down the books—Empty ash buckets—coal ashes—inkstands—papers—gold pens—letters &c. &c in a pile and then dance on the pile. Lincoln would say nothing, so abstracted was he and so blinded to his children's faults Had they s——t in Lincoln's hat and rubbed it on his boots, he would have laughed and thought it smart. Lincoln was a fool in this line. Lincoln was a selfish man generally and especially in the political world but was blindly generous to his *own* He worshipped

---

1. "Candlebox" referenced Calhoun's notorious role in an 1858 voting fraud in Kansas.

his children and *what* they worshipped he loved what they loved and hated what they hated rather *disliked* what the hated, which was every thing that did not bend to their freaks—whims—follies and the like. But poor Lincoln and Willie and Tadd. I am now sorry that I used to hate the children. I regret it, but human flesh could not have borne it better than I did. I *did* it out of pure and perfect respect for Lincoln.

In our disputes on law points—on principles in any line Lincoln was never *to me* insulting nor domineering: he was cool and patient—kind and tender. We used to discuss philosophy which I have written to you so much about. Lincoln never read much law—and never did I see him read a law book through and no one Else Ever did. Politics were Lincoln's life and news papers his food. I'll keep on this line a little while.

Your Friend

W. H Herndon

A law office is a dry place for incidents of a pleasing kind. If you love the stories of murder—rapes—fraud &c. a law office is a good place—but good Lord let me forget all about a law office—H

LC: HW3357–58; Exp 4:10:2110–13

189. To Joseph Fowler

Springfield Ills. Feby 18th '87

My Dear Sir:

Your excellent letter, dated the 7th inst was, a few days since, duly received and for which I am obliged to you. I agree with you about your historic references, and especially so when you mention Emmerson, whose spirit was a living part of the universe, and one of its highest manifestations in his peculiar line. He was a part of the thing which he saw and so truthfully—so exactly described. If you have ever read my poor lectures in 6 months in the White House you will perceive that Lincoln was "*brim full*" of the good spirit of the universe. Its spirit was forever *suggesting* something to him: he was just as great in his line as Emmerson was in his. Nature whispered her secrets to both of these men. They were both interpreters of Nature—one in one line and the other in an other. Lincoln read the logic of events—the result of causes in the human world: he had his own peculiar philosophy and patiently waited on the flow of events: he was calm—patient—enduring—sympathetic in the movement of the mass of men. This sprang from his philosophy which is as follows—1st Mr Lincoln has said probably a hundred times—"that what is to be will be and no prayers of ours can arrest or reverse the decree." 2dly That conditions make the man and not man the conditions; and 3dly that the Universe of matter and of mind was ruled by universal—absolute and eternal laws. Now then Mr Lincoln in his suggestiveness—rather the suggestiveness of nature *felt* coming events generally way in advance of others, though he was, as we call it, conservative. Lincoln was a part of the conditions which were ruled by law and he humbly submitted to the fates. Lincoln was a *fatalist* and has said to me—"I feel as if I shall meet with some terrible end. The spirit logic of events was in Lincoln. Something told Lincoln of his coming fate. I have sat in our office for hours watching this great man's face & the different plays of it—sometimes it was terribly sad and sometimes cheerful—sometimes it was deeply reflective and often abstracted, living as it were in another world. I had so much respect for the man that I did not dare to obtrude myself just then in his presence by any remark or question. Lincoln had great dignity—a strong and a distinct individuality and he never mixed it up in the mass of men. Hence I had to stop in my approach to the boundaries of that dignity and that individuality. Mr. Lincoln and myself used to discuss freely all manner—kinds of questions—social—political—philosophical—religious &c; and in all of our discussions each of us kept his own mind, and his own self respect. Mr. Lincoln was never insulting—nor insolent nor dictatorial to me: he understood me, as I did him: he was patient with me and sympathetic in my [means?], and may I say to your private ear he had great respect for my *intuitional* nature and often and often consulted it. I say this private to you. You wish to understand Mr Lincoln and it *may* be that I can help you a little in a short letter. Lincoln was a peculiar man and a great one: he never shrivelled up in my Estimation, it made no difference how close we got to each other, for the closer we got, the larger Lincoln grew. Lincoln loved the beautiful in the *moral* world—not much in the physical world. He was close to the spirit of Nature—rather it was close to him: it buzzed about his ear and revealed in one line—in one part Lincoln's thoughts and his duty: he was a man of fine feelings—keen and accurate thoughts—with a strong will on principles—in the right and doing noble deeds. If God were to touch me I should be a god. God somehow touched Lincoln and he was a god. You understand me: he was one of the very greatest, best and wisest of men; and yet he had his faults—mostly negative ones. I studied Lincoln for twenty five years closely: his nature in its different manifestations forced me to do so. If Lincoln's philosophy is true that conditions make the man it was conditions that made him president for an almost a divine purpose and those conditions were not thwarted.

Yet friend I was brave or fool enough years and years since to tell the truth about Lincoln—his philosophy and his religion and got abused for it roundly. We grow upward truly, do we not?

Your Friend
W. H. Herndon

Lincoln's assassination was the result of conditions—causes far back lying and no one will ever know the secret. Conditions may educate us to think we know. I cannot now discuss the question with you—would if I had time

H.

ALPL: W. H. Herndon Papers

190. To Jesse W. Weik

Springfield Ills Feby 24th '87

Friend Weik:

As I said to you a law office is a dry place. There is nothing in it but work & toil. Mr. Lincoln's habit was to get down to his office about 9 o'cl am, unless he was out on the circuit, which was about 6 or 8 mo in the year. Our office never was a head quarter for politics. Mr. Lincoln never stopt on the street to have a social chat with any one he was not a social man—too reflective—too abstracted: he never attended political gatherings till the thing was organized; and then he was ready to make a speech—willing and ready to reap any advantage that grew out of it—ready & anxious for the office it afforded, if any in the political world. If a man came into our office on business he stated his case, Lincoln listening generally atentively while the man told over the facts of his case. Generally Lincoln would take a little time to consider. When he had sufficiently considered he gave his opinion of the case plainly—directly and sharply: he said to the man "Your case is a good one" or "a bad one," as the case might be. Mr. Lincoln was not a good conversationalist, except it was in the political world, nor was he a good listener: his great anxiety to tell a story made him burst *in* and consume the day in telling stories. Lincoln was not a general reader, except in politics. On Sundays he would come down to his office—sometimes bringing Tad & Willie and sometimes not—would write his letters—write declarations and other law papers—write out the heads of his speeches—take notes of what he intended to say—How do you expect to get much of interest out of this dry bone—a law office, when you know that Lincoln was a sad, gloomy—melancholic & an abstracted man? Lincoln would sometimes lay down in the office to rest on the sofa, his feet on 2 or 3 chairs or up against the wall. In this position he would reflect—decide on what he was going to do and how to do it; and then he would jump up—pick up his hat and run, the good Lord, knows, where. Judge Davis was judge over, I think, ten counties and it generally took him from 6 to 8 mo to go around this circuit twice a year. Lincoln would never come home while the court was grinding out justice on the circuit to see his wife or family, while all other lawyers, Every Saturday night after court hours, would start for home to see wife & babies. Lincoln would see us start home and know that we were bound to see ~~home~~ good wife and the ~~babies~~ children. Lincoln, poor soul would grow terribly sad at the sight—as much as to say—"I have no wife and no home." None of us on starting home would say to Lincoln—"Come, Lincoln, let's go home," for we knew the terrors of home to him. I can see poor Lincoln now as we turn our backs on Each other—one bound for home and one back to the Court house. It's too sad to think about. I wish I did not know it all. Lincoln, you know, was not a social man, and hence those little *incidents* in his office and around his hearth which you want so much are hard to gather and to get, for they are few and far between. You know this relation between Mr & Mrs Lincoln and you ought to know by this time that the *rich incidents* at that house were—were—were—those of an unpleasant nature. You had better see Mrs Chapman of Coles Co on the subject—the question of rich incidents.[1] I know that she can tell you much about the customs—habits—methods of life &c about Lincolns home.

You wish me to state what year Lincoln & I entered into partnership: it was in the fall of 1843, and that partnership was never dissolved till the evening of his assassination (see Arnold's life of Lincoln pge 53). You further wish me to state what the motives were that actuated Lincoln in taking me into partnership. I answer—I don't know and no one else does. The Revd J. A. Reed of this city, *knows* all about *God*; and why does he not *know* all about *Lincoln*.[2] Reed is simply foolish in his attacks on me, because I said & published that Lincoln was an Infidel. Reed is a little bitter christian and that's all there is of it. How do you like the inclosed slip cut from the "*World*" Feby 8th '87?

Your Friend

W.H Herndon.

Mr Weik, I do not like to talk about my self—have never followed that practice and never will. I may say to you that Lincoln never regretted our partnership and that's enough. H

The Hon Jno T Stuart got mad at Lincoln & my self because Lincoln did not take him into partnership in 1843; and he pursued us all his life with more or less bitterness on the sly—H.

LC: HW3359–60; Exp 4:10:2114–17

191. To Jesse W. Weik

Springfield Ills. Feby 25th '87 [1]

Friend Weik:

You will find in this a piece on Lincoln's philosophy &c.[1] Do not get huffy about it: it is a good condensation of the subjects; & after studying it, I think that you will approve of it—Don't see how you can disapprove it. Please send me a copy of it *commencing* with the words—"Mr. Lincolns philosophy was as follows," and ending with "made in one short moment a criminal of Brutus and a murderer." I want to send it to friend Remsburg of Kansas: the piece knocks the efficacy of prayer into fits. It is said by fools or those who do not know better that Lincoln believed in the efficacy of prayer—Pshaw!— . . .

Your Friend

W. H Herndon

1. For Harriet Chapman, see §138.
2. For Rev. James A. Reed, see §115.

1. For the "piece on Lincoln's philosophy," see §192.

Note

You wish me to state the amount of the Confidence which Mr. Lincoln reposed in me. It is not a sufficient statement to say—*Look at his acts*—We were in partnership for near a quarter of a century in the most trying times of his life. Would he have kept me so long without great confidence. I simply suggest this to you—Lincoln's acts are better proof of his confidence than any pompous words *of any man*. I attended to the money matters of L & H mostly and I never heard of a charge that I wronged Lincoln. I have Lincoln's last letter to me while Presdt: it is now in the Memorial Collection at Chicago and ends with these words—"God bless you says your friend." Ill send you a copy when needed.

H

LC: HW3361–62; Exp 4:10:2118–19

192. To Jesse W. Weik

Springfield Ills Feby 25th '87 [2]

Friend Weik:

I want this to go in our book—at least in substance. Mr. Lincoln's philosophy was as follows—first, he believed that what was to be would be and that no prayers of ours Could arrest or reverse the decree—2dly, he was a fatalist and believed that fatalism ruled the world—3dly, he believed that Conditions made and do make—will forever continue to make the man and not man the Condition—4thly he believed that there was no freedom of the human mind; and 5thly he believed that universal—absolute and Eternal laws ruled the universe of matter and of mind, Everywhere and always. Mr. Lincoln also contended that motives moved the man to every voluntary act of his life. If the above was Lincoln's philosophy or a part of it then many acts of his life may be justly interpreted, and the man better understood by it. X[1] Lincoln's patience sprang from his philosophy—his calm quiet waiting on the Events of the times—his coolness—calmness under the times of terrible bloody war—his charity for men and his want of malice for them everywhere, all grew out of his peculiar philosophy. Lincoln neither loved nor hated—never admired and never censured—never—Eulogized and never condemned man. I speak of Lincoln's *general* nature. Is this true; and if so why is it true? Men had no free choice—things were to be, and they came—irresistibly came—doomed to Come—men were made or they are made by superior Conditions over which they had no control—the fates settled things as by the doom of the Powers—and laws, universal—absolute and eternal ruled the universe of matter and of mind. X[2] Men were but simple tools of fate—of Conditions, and of laws; and to promise

1. Marks the beginning of a passage characterized in a marginal note: "This is a good Condensation of all that I have said to you on these special subjects herein; and will probably supercede all other letters—lectures—&c. &c. This does not excuse Lincoln's sadness &c and the philosophy of it. Ill explain when I see you."

2. Marks the end of the passage referred to in the previous note.

men on the one hand or Censure them on the other was in the abstract wrong in principle at all times. The thing—the Event was to be just as it had Come, and no right and no wrong and no virtue and no vice should in truth be attached to it. The man—the people but obeyed their superiors. The man—the people and the whole races are made by forces conditions—Environments around them, set in motion a million years or more ago, sweeping swiftly around the Universe every instant of time, never flagging—ever onward. Lincoln used frequently to quote the following lines of Shakspear

"There's a divinity that Shapes our Ends
Rough hew them how we will"

Man is Compelled to feel—think—will and to act subject to these influences of these Conditions: he—man—is a mere child moved and made by this vast world machine, working in grooves and moving in deep cut channels forever and forever; and now what is man? he is simply a *simple* tool—a mere *Cog* in one wheel—a part—a small part of this vast iron machine that strikes and Cuts—grinds and mashes all things, including man, that resist it. Events—the fates decreed them and what they answer is irresistible and inevitable and *no prayers* of ours can arrest or reverse the decree. What a man is, he is because of the Conditions of the universe and is Entitled to no credit and should have no blame attached to him for the deed. If a man did Lincoln a grievous wrong the man was a mere tool, and did but obey his superiors. If the man did him a good, he but obeyed the powers and should not suffer for the wrong nor praised nor paid for the right. The man was compelled—driven to do what he did do. It was to be and had Come. If a man was good or bad—small or great—successful or unsuccessful—filled with virtue or overflowing with vice; and if war, pestilence or famine stalked abroad over the land it all was doomed from the beginning. Lincoln was patient and calmly waited on Events: he knew they would come, because cause and Effect—antecedents and Consequents are ever in action following laws. Every event in the universe was preceded by some prior Cause and gives guarantee of some subsequent event flowing therefrom. It is possible that Lincoln did not fully believe that Brutus was specially made to kill Caesar in the senate chamber of Rome with a dagger—and that Caesar was specially made to be killed by Brutus; and yet he would believe because it is true that both Brutus and Caesar were forced by conditions over which they had no control into the inevitable pathes and Center of forces that destroyed Caesar and made in one short moment a criminal of Brutus—a murderer

Now one word as to Mr Lincoln's religion. From Mr Lincoln's Tender heart and large head—from his philosophy; and from his feelings—his thoughts, his determinations—his willings; and his acts throughout life, one is Compelled to say that Lincoln's religion was of a broad and noble Kind—a liberal—an infidel—one who did *not* believe that the Bible is God's special and divine revelation.

This is all that I propose to say, where I have the say—about Lincoln's philosophy or his religion: it is a good condensation of all that I have said to you on those subjects; and all that is necessary to say. What is said is true and will offend no one as I see it. The truth ought not to offend, where that truth is stated in a kindly and gentlemanly way—said to explain the nature—qualities and Characteristics of one of God's great men, who once was with us & for us.

Your Friend

W. H. Herndon

LC: HW3363–64; Exp 4:9:1894–97

193. To Jesse W. Weik

Springfield Ills Mch. 16th '87

Friend Weik

Inclosed you will find a good notice of Nicolay & Hay's work which I cut from Puck of Mch. 9th '87: it is an excellent thing and shows plainly that N & H have introduced too much collateral & unimportant matter that does not touch any part of Lincolns life—fact philosophy—religion—qualities, characteristics &c. N & H have entered too deeply in trash—nonsense—collateral facts—unimportant events, and persons. they have wearied the people—tired them out. In writing our book let us avoid this step—this fatal step. Let us see the mark and shoot for that directly as with a rifle for the centre. In other words let us write directly of Lincoln and Lincoln alone, leaving off facts & principles that do not touch Lincoln. Strip Lincoln naked and write of him and him alone. All facts that explain Lincolns life—his religion—philosophy—his politics—his domestic life &c. &c should be directly stated, honestly—fairly and impartially. Throw light on this great man and not cloud him by verbiage—nor bury him under a mass of unimportant facts & persons—this is our duty. This is my idea. The people in this city are getting tired of N & H's life of Lincoln: they laugh at it in Menard where I have been. I will soon send you some information that I got while in Menard—was sick during court and couldn't do much. I saw Mrs Bell and she is to make us out a copy of the quilt in which Lincoln stuck a stitch or two, with a 1/2 eye on the needle, and 1 1/2 eyes on Ann Rutledge. It is the universal opinion of the old folk of Menard that Lincoln & Ann were engaged to be married absolutely. I have examined the right ones on this question—people that *Know* and who are truthful.

Your Friend

W. H Herndon

LC: HW3368; Exp 4:10:2136–37

194. To Henry C. Whitney

Springfield Ills. April 16th '87

Friend Whitney—

Your very kind letter, dated the 3d inst, was duly received. . . . I have carefully read your note and I see nothing in it that is not true. You hit Lincoln very well: he was a curious man and was moved by his moods. Lincoln had *no home* just as you say: he had a domestic hell that he did not like and went there only to eat & sleep. Lincoln aught never to have married anyone: he had no quality for a husband: he was abstracted—cool—never loved and could not from his very nature. What you say about Lincoln is substantially Correct

I cannot now tell you where you can get any of my 4 or 5 lectures on Lincoln. I never thought enough of them to preserve them, though others stenographed them and were thus sent over the Country. Nicolay & Hay are failing and as you well say—are getting "worse and worse." As to Lincoln's stories I do not remember any that would do to State to *a* mixed audience in *a* lecture; they would cut some one on some point—— Yes I am going to write the life of Lincoln as I saw him honestly—truthfully—corageously—fearlessly cut whom it may. What you say about Lincoln's gloom—sadness—high exaltation is substantially Correct. Lincoln felt the *Honor* and the *Burden*, ~~and to that extent~~ but he was Lincoln still. The Exaltation made him more thoughtful and more abstracted and more gloomy and to that extent more miserable. Lincoln once said to me this—"I fear that I shall meet with some terrible End" and this cloud always hung over him. I will answer your note—the parts unanswered, as soon as I can.

Your Friend
W. H. Herndon

Illinois: Illinois History and Lincoln Collections (copy)

195. To Jesse Weik:

Springfield Ills. June. 19th 87

Friend Weik—

Your very considerate and kind note, dated the 10th inst, was duly recd, and for which I am much indebted to you indeed. When I wrote you my note stating to you my wants—and necessities &c I did not intend it as a hint to you—did not refer to you, but to some friends here in or about this city. I expected the loan here, but as you have generously offered me the loan I shall accept because it will save me time—expense and trouble. For and in consideration of the loan of the $100 I give you a lien on the Lincoln materials now in your possession—~~from~~ my labor on our book and the book when completed and the proceeds of it till you are paid. You have the possession &c of all things and this letter gives you a lien so that you are safe and run no risks. If the law of Indiana requires other rentings than this—which is not probable I will execute them when I come to Greencastle.

For all expenses which you advance for the firm in writing this book—paying my board—travelling expenses &c &c you shall have a lien on the foregoing things—fully as for the $100 to be advanced. Please send me the hundred dollars as soon as you receive this—want to buy necessary clothes—pay some family grocery bills before I start for Indiana &c. &c. Send this money by bill draft or some other safe mode. The hundred dollars to bear interest from the day of the advance—say at the rate of 8 or 10 per ct. per annum.

. . .

By the way, had you not better go to Charleston in our state and see Dennis Hanks—Mrs Chapman & others as to the description of the person of Thomas Lincoln & Nancy Hanks Lincoln. You can get a description from them and from no one else. Mrs Chapman has heard Mrs Thomas Lincoln's—2d wife of old Thomas Lincoln speak of and describe Nancy Hanks Lincoln. Dennis Hanks knew her well and will—in his old age—still describe her. In this case his memory will be good and in it he has no motive to lie. Lincoln himself—Abraham Lincoln told me that his mother was an illegitimate child of a Virginia planter or farmer. Dennis Hanks told me that Nancy Hanks Lincoln was illegitimate and that her father was a Sparrow. Nancy Hanks kept her mother's name and not her father's.

I have to attend the July court in Menard Co—have recd a fee in advance in one case—must attend to it—court the 2d or 3d Mondy in July—I have to deliver a 4th of July oration in Menard. I will be in your city in due time and of this rest assured.—

Your Friend
W. H Herndon

It is as hot as fire & an old cock like myself can't stand much heat. H

LC: HW3374–75; Exp 4:10:2147–49

196. To Truman Bartlett:

Springfield Ills June 24th '87

My Dear Sir:

. . . (I knew Lincoln well for more than a quarter of a century and I studied the man inside and outside as well as I could. You spoke of Mr Lincoln's fine physical nature, but to see and study the man you would say that Mr Lincolns physical nature was comparatively low—course and not fine and high. He seemed to have no blood in his frame: his flesh was dark—wrinkled & folded: it looked dry & leathery—tough & everlasting: his eyes were small and grey—head small and forehead receding, but when this great man was moved by some great & good feeling—by some idea of Liberty or Justice or Right than he seemed an inspired man. It was just then that Lincoln's nature was beautiful and in complete harmony with the laws of the great Eternal. I have seen him in this inspired condition and thought that he was molded in the Spirits best mold. Lincoln was a great man—a good man, and a pure one, and beneath his rough exterior Nature wove her fine net work of nerve. In "Six Months in the White House" I tried to describe Lincoln. This book *may* assist you: it will not do you any harm. Lincoln was a gloomy man at one moment and a joyous man the next: he was conscious that a terrible fate awaited him: he said to me this—"I cannot help but believe that I shall meet with some terrible End". This idea seized him and it made him gloomy. At times his better nature would get the mastery and he would be happy till the shadow of his fate flitted before him. In phylosophy Lincoln was a fatalist and in religion a liberal—an infidel: he was a sensationalist as opposed to an intuitionalist—a realist as opposed to an idealist.)

. . .

May I say to your private ear that I am engaged in writing the life of Lincoln, the special purpose of it being to fill a blank, as I see it. I could tell you much about Lincoln if I could sit down and talk with you for a day or so, but we are too far apart to sit down in chairs and chat. I forgot to say above that in my poor opinion Lincoln had not arrived, when he was assassinated, at the meridian of his intellectual power.

Your Friend
W H Herndon

MHS: Truman Bartlett Papers

197. To Truman Bartlett

Springfield Ills July 8th '87

My Friend:

. . . .

(In your letter of the 28th ult you state these words—"When I spoke of Lincoln's fine physical nature I meant it from a physical point of view, that is, I would say he had a fine physical nature—was tall—healthy—strong—mobile in movement and of good proportion." I understand you and now you will pardon me if I state that he was not of good proportion—was six feet four inches high in his sock feet—was thin—wiry—sinewy—*not muscular*—weighed from 160 to 180 pounds and if you mean by the word *mobile* nimbleness of motion—ease of movement—grace of movement you are mistaken. If you mean to say and I do not so understand you that by the word *mobile* you mean that Lincoln—had mutability of temper then you are correct. There were *great contrasts* in Lincoln's life—mysterious ones—Sometimes Lincoln was great—very great, and sometime small. He was strong and he was weak—he was sad and cheerful by turns—he was good natured generally, but it was terrible to see him mad: he was all honor—full of manly integrity—sympathetic—practically wise—politically sagacious—never moved nor acted from mere feeling, but from thought—reason—he was cool—

conservative and courageous—was truly a noble man. When you read 6 mo in the White House by Carpenter *please tell me what impression it had on you as to Lincoln.* You are correct when you say that Lincoln's brain was one of *quality* & not size.) Will you pardon me for being so plain—outspoken? You ask me if I ever saw in this great wild west many men of Lincoln's type and to which I answer, *yes.* The first settlers of *Central* & Southern Ills were men of that type. They come from the limestone regions of Virginia—Kentucky—Tennessee &c and were men of giant strength—physical force and by nature were mentally strong. They were ~~agressive~~ original—were individualists. They had no education and no culture but good nature helped them. The strong *alone* from 1818 to 1830 could get here and the strong *alone* could survive here. Some of these men were politicians—some lawyers—some farmers &c. No one was like Lincoln, and yet many men were of his type. I cannot now further explain than to say that conditions made this class of men—may explain to you sometime. Limestone water—so scientists say gave us big frames and the struggle for life in the wilderness—& the South gave us if you please mental force. A forest life makes us sad—and thoughtful. I think that by nature we were a great people. We were rude and rough—had no polish nor culture. Each man and woman was himself or herself. Individuality—distinct individuality was the rule. Each followed his inclinations and despised imitatio[n]. Lincoln was Lincoln—Grant was Grant—Douglas was Douglas. Had Lincoln been a man of hig[h] culture—polish—of literary taste—habits &c &c he may have been a good Country lawyer—that's all. I hope that you understand me—can't by letter fully explain.

(You are entirely correct about the study of Lincoln: he was a man of "Extraordinary Contrasts"—he was Lincoln & Lincoln alone, and none Exactly like him. You must study him by himself and of himself. The reason why I stated so much about Lincoln in my former letter was this—give a sculptor one fact—a leading physical fact and that suggests to him an other in complete harmon[y] with the other; Lincoln had large hands & feet—foot flat. Hence a large frame &c. &c. Lincoln's religion was practical and hence materialistic, and hence to a certain extent was his organization &c. I speak generally. You would not look for a well rounded man in such a description. I have studied Lincoln inside & outside. Pardon me. I describe him to you as I saw him and knew him. I loved the man and worship, as it were his memory. I owe to truth a fidelity and mean to pursue that cause to the End.)

. . .

You state one fine truth ~~on~~ as the world thinks & moves; and it is this—"It is a sorry fact of human nature that the great truth about a man is not preferred to an artificial estimate of him, even by those who are supposed to love him best." Hero worship—the worship of the ideals in a man is the spirit of the age. Fact gives place to the ideal and truth—*solid fact* gives place to the imagination, and fancy revels in the unreal[.] I have been much abused for telling the truth about Lincoln; and this I shall continue to do[.] Lincoln will rise in the estimation of mankind the higher the more thoroughly he is known because that estimate will be formed from facts truthfully and courageously told. When public opinion is thus formed it never changes: it rests on fact—on eternal verities.

Your Friend
W H Herndon

MHS: Truman Bartlett Papers

198. To Truman Bartlett:

Springfield Ills. July 11th '87

My Dear Sir:

. . .

The article which you sent me about Lincoln & Douglas is untrue in part—in the main part. Mr Lincoln only corrected his speeches—made them talk as he had talked on the stump. This he did and no more. His corrections were only verbal & not otherwise. Mr Lincoln told me how it was. I will refresh my memory & correct the note sometime. You ask me to state to you Mr. Lincoln's attitude—pose—look—acts—gestures &c. &c while in the act of speaking—addressing bodies of people. I will do so just as soon as I can see some old friends who were close observers of Mr Lincoln. We will have a talk and then I will write to you in full. I have seen Mr Lincoln in every possible human attitude—have heard him speak for many years.

. . .

Your Friend
W. H. Herndon

MHS: Truman Bartlett Papers

199. To Henry C. Whitney

Springfield Ills. July 17th '87

Friend Whitney—

. . .

I will willingly, as I have time, give you any opinion which I have of Lincoln. The truth and the whole truth about Lincoln will *never* injure him: he will grow larger under the blaze of truth and the sharpest criticisms of the iron pen: he was too great—too good and too noble to be injured by the truth: he had his faults—more negative ones and who has not some of these spots. The blazing sun has them and so did Jesus have them. What would you give for a true life of Washington—the *inside* life of him? The great reading growing world shall have one of Lincoln, if I live, but I will catch the Devil for so doing. The world demands truth and truth it shall have. Lincoln was a curious—wonderful—mysterious man, incomprehensible by the mass of men. I studied Mr Lincoln for 25 years, inside and outside: he was a man of opposites—of terrible contrasts. One man to-day would see Lincoln in one state and the man would say this was Lincoln. To-morrow this same man would see Lincoln in a totally different State and say this was *not* Lincoln, and yet it was, for Lincoln *was under his law*, and that ruled him with the iron of logic. Mr. Lincoln was a many mooded man. One man would see *this* mood and one man *that*, and from seeing Lincoln in one mood each man would form his opinion on one phase of L, and hence the errors of judgement among the people as to L. This caused these contrasts in Lincoln Caused the differences of opinions among men in relation to Lincoln.

Your Friend

W. H. Herndon

Illinois: Illinois History and Lincoln Collections

200. To Truman Bartlett

Springfield Ills. July 19th 87

My Dear Sir:

I will now answer your questions put to me in your letter of the 4th inst. In this state and specially about the center of it we have no tables—boxes—stands behind which we address and speak either to jurors or to crowds. It is open before us and we speak from the level floor when we address the jury and about on a level with them. Sometimes the jurors are raised a little, the back seat being higher than the front, so that those behind can see and hear. We speak from stumps in the woods; if no better can be had—from boxes—from rude and temporary platforms erected in groves—woods or public squares in cities & villages. Every thing is open—visible and clear. We have no tables—boxes—boards—plank to hit, beat and to bang. The speakers stand out fully to public view, & the crowd is seen plainly by the speaker—so much for circumlocution to catch and idea.

Mr. Lincoln was six feet and four inches high in his sock feet: he was consumptive by build and hence more or less stoop shouldered: he was very tall—thin and gaunt. When he rose to speak to the jury or to crowds of people he stood inclined forward—was awkward—angular—ungainly—odd and being a very sensative man, I think that it added to his awkwardness: he was a diffident man, somewhat, and a sensative one, and both of these added to his oddity—awkwardness &c as it seemed to me. Lincoln had confidence, full and complete confidence in himself, self thoughtful—self helping and self supporting, relying on no man. Lincoln's voice was, when he first began speaking, shrill—squeaking—piping—unpleasant: his general look—his form—his pose—the color of his flesh wrinkled and dry, his sensativeness & his momentary diffidence, everything seemed to be against him, but he soon recovered. I can see him now—in my mind distinctly. On rising to address the jury or the crowd he quite generally placed his hands behind him, the back part of his left hand resting in the palm of his right hand. As he proceeded and grew warmed he moved his hand to the front of his person, generally interlocking his fingers and running one thumb around the other. Sometimes his hands, for a short while, would hang by his side. In still growing warmer as he proceeded in his address he used his hands—especially and generally his right hand in his gestures: he used his head a great deal in speaking, throwing or jerking or moving it now here and now there—now in this position and now in that, in order to be more emphatic—to drive the idea home. Mr Lincoln never beat the air—never sawed space with his hands—never acted for stage effect—was cool—calm, earnest—sincere—truthful—fair—self possessed—not insulting—not dictatorial—was pleasing—good natured, had great strong naturalness of look, pose—and act—was clear in his ideas—simple in his words—strong, terse and demonstrative: he spoke and acted to convince individuals and masses: he used in his gestures his right hand, some times shooting out that long bony forefinger of his to dot an idea or to express a thought, resting his thumb on his middle finger. Bear in mind that he did not jesticulate much and *yet it is true* that every organ of his body was in motion and acted with ease—elegance and grace—so it all looked *to me*. [*In margin*: I distinctly remember what is said herein though I conversed with others *to be sure*]

As Mr Lincoln proceeded further along with his oration, if time—place—subject and occasion admitted of it, he gently and gradually warmed up—his shrill—squeaking—piping voice became harmonious melodious—musical, if you please with face somewhat aglow: his form dilated—swelled out and he rose up a splendid form, erect straight and dignified: he stood square on his feet with both legs up and down, toe even with toe—that is he did not put one foot before an other: he kept his feet parallel and close to and not far from each other. When Mr. Lincoln rose up to speak, he rose slowly—steadily—firmly: he never moved much about on the stand or platform when speaking, trusting no desk—table—railing: he ran his eyes slowly over the crowd, giving them time to be at ease and to completely recover himself, *as I suppose*. He frequently took hold with his left hand, his left thumb erect, of the left lapel of his coat, keeping his right hand free to gesture in order to drive home and clinch an idea[.] In his greatest inspiration he held both of his hand out above his head at an angle of about fifty degrees—hands open or clinched according to his feelings an[d] his ideas. If he was moved in some indignant and half mad moment against slavery or wrong in any direction and seemed to want to tear it down—tramp it beneath his feet and to eternally crush it, than he would extend his arms out, at about the above degree—angle with Clinched big, bony, strong hands on them—.

   If he was defending the right—if he was defending liberty—eulogizing the Declaration of Independence, then he extended out his arms—palms of his hands upward somewhat at about the above degree—angle, as if appealing to some superior power for an assistance and support; or that he might Embrace the Spirit of that which he so dearly loved. It was at such moments that he seemed inspired, fresh from the hands of his Creator. Lincoln's gray eyes would flash fire when speaking against slavery or spoke volumes of hope and love when speaking of Liberty—justice and the progress of mankind—such was this great man to *me* and I think—*I know* such he was to thousands, if not to millions of others. I speak from long knowledge—observation—experience, but with my poor reason impartially. You know my criticisms of Lincoln as published in Carpenter, and *now take this letter and that criticism* and you have my exact ideas of Lincoln in the fields touched upon.

What is here written is written after thought and after investigation among close observing friends, my own knowledge—observation and experience included and if these hasty words will give you any idea of Lincoln's methods—ways—manners—&c &c of speaking—&c &c. I shall be amply paid.

I have this morning just returned from our Menard Circuit Court, where I was attending to my professional duties: it is hot and I am tired

Your Friend

W H Herndon

PS: In Carpenter's book and in my lectures I said that Lincoln had no dignity *"so called."* I used that word. I did so, meaning that Lincoln had no pride—haughtiness—self conceit—[pomp?] of carriage. Lincoln was a man of great dignity and yet democratic—easy of approach. He would up to a certain point allow any approach, but go beyond *that,* and his dignity soon protected itself, and wilted the man who dared go beyond the proprieties of the occasion. H

MHS: Truman Bartlett Papers

201. *To Truman Bartlett*

Springfield Ills. July 27th '87

My Dear Sir:

I promised to answer your letter of the 15th inst and will try & do so now. It is a hard and difficult matter for two men living a distance from each other, by running letters, to understand one an other, specially so if they follow different pursuits and use local words—words of art—law—science. When I said that Lincoln was not of a good proportion I compared him with others—the *general* man. When you said that he was a man of good proportions you looked at him alone and compared his parts—organs, one with an other—Lincoln's legs with Lincoln's arms &c. Now you see where we differed. We are both correct. Lincoln was a man of good proportions when we look at him alone and not by comparison with the *general* man—the great mass of man. Lincoln was out of proportion when compared with the mass of men. The world is full of fuss and fight simply because men do not understand one an other. You are correct when you say that Lincoln was *mobile* when looked at alone, one of his parts compare with an other of his parts. This I confess—You will find the plains, mountains & outlines of Lincoln's head & face hard to catch: they are so subtle. In this you are clearly correct. You will have to use many phos—side views, half side views—and front views to catch the man and the spirit of him. I said that your statue in clay is good; and I say so now. I have it in my hands while writing this: Lincoln had the grace of pose and motion. In my poor lectures in Carpenter—a mere sketch of two or three lectures, I said that he walked so that he seemed to *pocket tire*—walked easily and to that extent walked gracefully. This is what I meant and so you will perceive that we do not much disagree. I try to understand mens positions—natures—surroundings &c. &c. and I think I understand you. Again you are correct when you say that the photographers, ignorant—unscientific men—men of no taste—no judgement—wishing to make a show of art ruin the phos which they do take by pencil, paint—coloring &c. I would give a good many dollars for a no one pho of Lincoln, but there is none, as it appears to me. . . .

In one of my letters to you I said of us western people—especially of the old settlers—say from 1818 to 1845, that they had no culture and in reply to which you state that that expression in your section means a College Education &c. and not the culture that comes of observation—experience—and reason. The old settlers from 1818 to 45 were men of culture—so were the women—God bless 'em if culture includes sharp observation, quick & broad experiences, and a manly reason of or about men—commerce—laws—institutions—human nature and the world & its affairs generally, excluding College Education. I have never seen such a people. I have been in your state and know many of your men personally and all the great ones by reputation, but for good horse sense our people—the old settlers, were your equals, if not your superiors, as a mass. You ask me if I know Walt Whitman I do by reputation—have read his leaves of grass &c: he is a poet truly and indeed. I know Whittier & other of your poets by reputation—I like the heart and sympathy of Whittier and the bold originality of Whitman. I know Phillips—Parker—Garrison & others of your great men personally. One more word—you speak of Lamon's Life of Lincoln. May I say to you that take it as a whole it is one of the truest lifes ever written of a man. I do not agree to all it says.

Your Friend
W. H. Herndon

MHS: Truman Bartlett Papers

202. To Truman Bartlett

Greencastle Indiana Aug 7, 1887

My Dear Friend:

Your letter dated the 30th ult is just received and I thank you for it. I am glad that you and I *now* agree about Lincoln's physical form, and now for the relationship between his physical & mental make up. Keep in view Mr. L's form, including shape &c: (he was a great big—angular—strong man—limbs large and bony: he was tall and of a peculiar type. I said to you once that Mr. Lincoln had not arrived at maturity in 1865, and I *say so now*. Mr. Lincoln was of a low or slow mechanical power—inside of him; his blood ran slowly—had low or slow circulation and consequently a slow build up. As he had a slow build up he had a slow development; he grew up like the forest oak, tough—solid—knotty—gnarly, standing out with power against the storm, nearly defying the lightening. Hence I concluded that he had not arrived at his highest point in 1865. You see the value of getting some leading fact—great fact of the physical man. No other man on the continent could have stood what Lincoln did in Washington: he had a frame of *iron*. Now for the mind. As Mr Lincoln had a slow circulation and a slow build up—so his mind acted slowly and his mind was tough—solid—knotty—gnarly, more or less like his body: he was angular in body and angular in thought—in deed and speach: he was a tall and big boned man and his speech was tall—strong & big boned & enduring. The convolutions of his brain were long: they did not snap off quickly like a short thick man's brain: they had to have their time, but when those convolution opened and threw off an idea it *was* an *idea*, tough—solid—gnarly—big—angular. Tallness—height generally indicates power in the man. Mr. Lincoln was not what is called muscular, but was sinewy—wiry—. The enduring power of Mr Lincoln's brain—thought was wonderful: he could sit and think without rest or food longer than any man I ever saw. Please see Lincoln's strong—terse—knotty—gnarly and compact words—driven together as by a sledge hammer: his sentences—his thoughts, as uttered—are they not grand types of original expression? What say you? It is the force of the inner build up power, mechanical or spiritual, just as you please, which makes the physical and intellectual man. I have given you the correspendencies in my own rude rough way. The key of the [know?] I have given you, that's certain; and by running things out, with the assistance of that key you can see Lincoln as I saw and knew him.)

I am very busy here writing my memoirs of Lincoln and have no time to run things out for you. You are enough for that—my superior, I know. I will help my friends always, if I can. I am glad that you wish to know Lincoln and I'll assist you to know the man, if I can, but I must have a little time. I'll more fully hereafter answer your letter of the 30th July. Write to me as often as you please and Ill answer as well and as quickly as I can. Possibly I can help you some. I am a weak brother but will assist others with that weakness to the best of my heart and head

Your Friend
W.H Herndon

MHS: *Truman Bartlett Papers*

203. To Truman Bartlett

Greencastle Indiana Aug 16, 1887

My Friend—

Your letter of the 10th inst was duly recd and I shall proceed at once to answer it. (I did not intend to say that Lincoln's organization was a *low* animal organization. What I meant to say was that is was a slow working machine—blood ran slowly—& the like. Let me tell you some facts—in addition to the above. Lincoln's

flesh was coarse—pimply—dry—hard—harsh—color of his flesh saffron brown.—
no blood seemingly in it—flesh wrinkled. Mr Lincoln had an evacuation—a
passage about once a weak—ate blue mass—. Were you to read his early speeches
thoroughly and well you could see his; *then,* coarse nature—his materialism &c.
He grandly rose up more spiritualistic and this is one of the reason why I say that
Lincoln was not fully developed—in *mind,* at least: he may have just entered the
field of his power—intellectual power, but he had not got to the centre of it. If
I were you I would consult some of the best of Bostons physicians on the very
question of *low* organization. I have a kind of imperfect idea on this point. If your
physicians give you an opinion please write to me. Lincoln was superstitious—believed more or less in dreams—consulted Negro oracles—had apparitions and tried
to solve them: he said to me once this—"Billy I fear that I shall meet with some
terrible end". You may show my letters—on this point to your best physicians—
physiologists—histolegists—anatomists &c, but they—my letters, are otherwise
private Please get your learned men to assist us. The ideas is worthy of a search
and an opinion *from science.* I have a shadow of an opinion. The precise enquiry
would be this—"*Was Lincoln's physical organization as compared with other men, of
a low order and was it of a low order when only Lincoln was looked at by himself and
not compared to other men.*"? This is a question of much interest to me and will be
to the world of science. Lincoln is a kind of an enigma—When your Boston man
said—"Lincoln died at the right time &c" he did not know what he was talking
about, was sputtering in the dark. Lincoln would have lead us gloriously—peacefully to the end: his martyrdom may have increased his fame, through the horror
of his taking off, but you and I are not talking about the sympathy of the world,
but are looking deeper or higher, just as you please to express it The observations
of that man "were cruel"—your Massachusetts man I mean. Lincoln rose equal to
the emergencies & would have risen to them under all circumstances: he would
have seen the reconstruction measures clearly—clearly—. I have a decided opinion
on this point, but have no time to express it.

In a late letter to you—the one enclosed with the Ann Rutledge lecture, I made
a fool of myself and it was on this—I said to you "How do you like my description
&c. the old settlers &c.?" I did not intend *that.* I meant to draw out of you only
an idea of the people and their classes in and about New Salem &c. I corrected
the language on the outside of the letter. By the way—just *now*—Sunday morning
Mr Weik has handed me yours of the 4th of Aug. directed to me at Springfield
Ills & forwarded to me here—cannot answer it now—too late. The fact that I am
writing the life of Lincoln is now known to quite all persons. Inclosed I send you
a slip &c which please keep till you hear from me.

Your Friend
W. H Herndon

I use the words organization & organism about synonymous, though there is a little
scientific difference. Ask the physicians the exact difference and write to me. H.

MHS: Truman Bartlett Papers

204. To Truman Bartlett

Greencastle Indiana Aug. 22d, 1887

My Dear Friend

Your three letters of the 14th 17th & 18th of Aug are before me and I shall answer them in the order of their dates. Now as to the first one. I do not think that New Salem scenery and & her people had much to do with Lincoln: he had no sense of the beautiful in the *physical* world but had in the *moral* world. The people of New Salem had a good deal to do in forming L's life—probably not as much as one would suppose. Lincoln in head was above them. The Ann Rutledge story—the facts of it did effect Lincoln's life, *I know*, up to '42 and it is quite likely longer—possibly to his death. I fear that the world will damn me for opening things—unknown things, but I am determined to open. Great men have great mothers and if this nation wants great men it must build up great women; and in order to do that the nation must open all the avenues of life to her—make her equal to man before the law. She must be thrown on her own resources and thus in the struggle of life develop herself. You speak kindly of my lecture, but I shall have no time to write the life of Lincoln in such a style. I am exceedingly poor—poor indeed, and would starve if I tried to write a full life of Lincoln in such a style, as is in the Ann Rutledge lecture. My life of Lincoln will be a limited one—kind of subjective—inner life, with a mere thread of history running along. This life, if it ever sees the light will cause a squirm.

As to the 2d letter, I still adhere to my idea that Lincoln had *not* arrived *intellectually*, at least, to the height of his power; and you may answer that by the tables of facts made by insurance and other companies & ways that it is set down—the course of life of men—say at 45–50, but I reply did not Lincoln grow up to 1866— *over the average age*; and now will you fix the limit of L's development my friend? What authorizes you to do it? Come be fair. Compare his Gettysburg Speech with his speeches say from 1840 to 1850. I am firm in my convictions because founded on facts—If Lincoln grew up from youth to '66—over the average life of man, will you say "here is the limit of L's greatness," but how do you know it? You have no fact to prove it and so I have the logic of things on my side. As to his physical development I am not quite certain of my idea in that particular—am not *decided* on it—am thinking on it.

In your third letter you give me a story about Lincoln's ambition, the Scott story—the Chamberlain story; and to which I say—in part the story is evidently— *to me*, correct. Lincoln was ambitious and in that he was selfish. Mr. Lincoln's idea was that he ought to be retained the 2d term because he knew all the facts of the great rebellion, and that no man could learn and understand them in 2 years; and that it was best under all the circumstances to keep him there. Lincoln doubtless did consider his success in his 2d term of vastly more importance than the advancement of Grant, or all men on the Earth, No Earthy doubt of it—No doubt of it—none. No man had better take up this story unless he master Lincoln. I would say to all—be slow. Lincoln however did not intend to be understood that the Rebellion had better succeed than his—L's—defeat for the 2d term. Lincoln would have offered himself up as a sacrifice to squelch the Rebellion and free the slaves, for with him it was—the whole matter. The rebellion was a question of human liberty—white as well as black—see his Philadelphia speech. This is my opinion, good or bad. Lincoln remains unknown and what a big mysterious man. In one of your letters you ask me this question in substance—"Do you think that Lincoln wished to be known—*thoroughly known* and to which I answer emphatically—No—he was a hidden man and wished to keep his own secrets. As I trail the man step by step, like a dog trails a fox I find many new *spots*—many new *holes*—much to admire and much to regret. It nearly kills me in my old age to persist in my search. Please pardon allusion to myself.

Your Friend
W. H. Herndon

There is hard thinking to be done in writing L's life,

MHS: Truman Bartlett Papers

205. To J. E. Remsburg

Springfield Ill. Septr 10, 1887.

Friend Remsburg:

Today I send you Speed's Lecture on Lincoln which you can keep till I send for it and this will probably be never: it is a very poor lecture, if the lecture Contains his knowledge of Lincoln, and I guess it does:[1] it shows no insight into Lincoln at all, though it is well enough written. It is said that Speed had a world of influence over Lincoln" This may be so, and yet I never saw it. Mr. Speed was my boss for 3 or 4 years & Lincoln—Speed Hurst & I slept in the same room for a year or so.[2] I was clerk for Speed. Speed could make Lincoln do much about simple measures, policies, not involving any principle. Beyond this power Speed had not much influence over Lincoln nor did anyone have. It is said by Nicolay and Hay that Lincoln poured out his soul to Speed—Bah. Nonsense. *probably*, except his love scrapes, Lincoln never poured out his soul to any mortal creature at any time and on no subject. He was the most secretive—reticent—shut-mouthed man that Ever Existed. You had to *guess* at the man after years of acquaintance and then you must look long and keenly before you *guessed* or you would make an ass of yourself. You had to take some leading—great leading and a well Established fact of Lincoln's nature and then follow it by accurate & close analysis wherever it went. This process would lead you correctly, if you knew human nature and its laws. Lincoln was a mystery to the world: he loved principle, but moved men just to

---

1. Joshua F. Speed, *Reminiscences of Abraham Lincoln and Notes of a Trip to California* (Louisville: Morton, 1884.)

2. Charles R. Hurst bought out Joshua Speed's interest in the Springfield mercantile business that WHH refers to on January 1, 1841.

suit his own Ends: he was a trimmer among men, though firm on laws and great principles; he did not care for men: they were his tools and instruments: he was a cool man—an unsocial one—an abstracted one, having the very quintessence of the profoundest policies. Lincoln's heart was tender, full of mercy, if in his presence or some imaginative man presented the subject to him. "Out of sight, out of mind" may truthfully be said of Lincoln. If I am correct, what do you think of the stories afloat about what Lincoln said ~~about~~ in relation his religion, Especially said to strangers? I send you two "Truth Seekers," which you will please read where I speak of Lincoln in 3 letters—pages marked at the top. You will learn something of Lincoln's nature in those three letters of mine—2 of them on Lincoln's religion, and one to a minister.[3] Please read them. There are some quotations in these letters which I have never had time to send you as I recollect it. They are good things—one on Laws of human nature and one on the pride—haughtiness of Christianity. Lincoln delivered a lecture in which these quotations are to be found.[4] I heard him deliver it.

W H Herndon

LC: *Alfred Whital Stern Collection*

206. To Jesse W. Weik

Springfield Ills. Septr. 10th, 1887.

Friend Weik—

Inclosed with this you have the condensed conversation of several people.[1] You will perceive that no two exactly agree. Orendorff seemed honestly to wish that the whole story should be told.[2] Matheny wished it, if it—the story touched no others, but that the story should be told, if you touch the subject. Palmer would give no opinion just now. Govr. Oglesby said that—for our *books' sake*, that we had better say nothing at all.[3] Senator Cullom & Jayne said that "if you say anything tell it all."[4] Now here are the opinions of six of our leading people; and no two agree. One is to open out seemingly so and honestly so—one gives no opinion—two are for letting out the whole story, if we touch it—one says tell it out, "if y don't touch others, and touch upon the subject at all;" and one says "you had better say nothing about it," though we may say what we want to about *Nancy Hanks* illegitimacy, saying that the people had got things mixed up. I am inclined as a policy only

3. *The Truth-Seeker*, February 24, 1883, and March 10, 1883; the letters referred to are §116, §117, §119.
4. "Temperance Address," February 22, 1842, *Collected Works*, 1: 271–79. In that address, AL asserted the irreversibility of human nature and criticized Christians for their lack of charity for reformed drinkers.

1. John Palmer, Alfred Orendorff, Shelby Cullom, William Jayne, James H. Matheny, Richard Oglesby. For these interviews, dated September 6, 1887, see *Herndon's Informants*, 637–39.
2. Alfred Orendorff had been a law partner of WHH.
3. Richard Oglesby was Governor of Illinois, a Civil War hero, and formerly U. S. Senator.
4. Shelby Cullom was then Illinois's senior U. S. senator. William Jayne was a Springfield physician and politician.

under all the circumstances to follow Govr. Oglesby because that will be the truth, I or we affirming after a thorough and searching investigation that Lincoln was the lawful child of Thomas & Nancy Lincoln and this in my opinion will be the exact truth as I understand the facts. In this event we need not touch on Thomas Lincoln's castration at all—so the "cussed" castration business need not bother us. What do you think? Write to me and then you can write out the first chapter, as you promised, and send it to me. You may say this in that 1st chap—"Lincoln is, upon the weight of the evidence after a thorough & searching investigation before me, the lawful child of Thos & Nancy Lincoln," first tell the whole story and the reasons therefor about Nancy Lincoln's illegitimacy—&c &c. Let that come out. We have said in print & in writing and by word of mouth that the world *wants the truth and will put up with nothing else.* I see now my way clearly. How does it strike you?

Give my best wishes and highest regard to *each* one and all of your father's family. Do not fail in this Weik

Your Friend

W. H Herndon

LC: HW3414; Exp 4:10:2213–14

207. To Jesse W. Weik

Springfield Ills Septr 15th, 1887

Friend Weik:

· · ·

Some year or more ago I was called upon to say something about Mr. Lincoln's *spiritualistic* life. I investigated the question and found that it was *probable* that Lincoln did attend one or two of the Seances of the spiritualists and saw much that he could not account for. If *he did not* attend the seances he *listened* attentively to what they said and did—gave them a respectful hearing and a good one, as he did to all persons, and to all ideas. Mr. Lincoln in my opinion *did not* become a spiritualist in the true sense of that Word. You know that Lincoln was a kind of superstitious man and having a belief that he would meet with some terrible End it is not impossible that he sought the advice of the *spirits.* This much I wish you would say somewhere in our book. The spiritualist claim Lincoln as a believer. Therefore say in substance what I say to you. Probably you have my letter addressed to the Religio Philisophical Journal.[1] If so see it too.

· · ·

Your Friend

W. H Herndon

LC: HW3418–19; Exp 4:1: 2217–20

---

1. See §139.

208. To Jesse W. Weik

Spfgd. Ills. Septr 22d, 1887.

Friend Weik—

Inclosed with these letters you will find one from Swett, promising to give us some reminescences &c; and one from Whitney—a long letter as usal. I have written to S. H Melvin of San Frisco for a copy of Lincoln's lectures. Melvin was one of the Commrs of the monument association. I have written to *Sarah* asking her to tell me the whole story of Lincoln's courtship &c with her. This must have been after Lincoln broke off his engagement with Miss Todd ~~after~~ in '41. However it may have been in '38–9. I'll find out the facts and write to you. I saw Jno [Decamp?] who came to this place in 1827: he says that Hancock wrote the poetry about the Talisman. I saw Louis or Lew Rosette. I went to see Mather—he was—was "tite." Whitehurst's paper was simply a Filmore paper and was called the Conservative and was published here in 1856: it was edited by Whitehurst,—and overlooked by such men as Jno E. Rosette—Stuart—Matheny. The other paper published here in 59 & 60 was called the Republican and was edited by Bros. Jamesons first and then sold to Jno. E. Rosette, who "busted." See the letter—the copy of it which you got at Oldroyd's. This will give the date when in the hands of Rosette.[1] I am busy as a bee gathering up facts which I have sent and will send to you. Why did you not answer my letter containing Cullom's—Jayne's &c. &c opinion? What do your people say about the matter? What is your idea of things in general and in particular. I will get all the phos that I can—have no money with which to get 'em—hope Matheny will have his taken, costing us nothing. Whitney will send his. If you will look at the Septr No of the Century at pges. 679–80 you will find a letter from Yancy which I would use in Lincoln's life when speaking of him in 1858–9. I would bring it in when speaking of the Lincoln and Douglas debates—to show Treason—Disunion on the part of the South in 1858.

[*Signature cut off*]

LC: HW3420; Exp 4:10:2221–22

209. To Truman Bartlett

Springfield Ills. Sept 22d, 1887.

Mr Bartlett—

I have been under the weather for some two weeks or I would have written to you in answer to your last. Nothing new has happened and no new views formed about Lincoln physically or intellectually. I stick to my opinions expressed to you. I will tell you a *secret* about Lincoln which must be kept *private*. I tell you the secret, because it lets light into Lincoln. Mr. Lincoln's mother - *Nancy Hanks*, was the illegitimate child of a *Virginia planter*, and right here it was that Lincoln got his mind; it never came out of a Hanks in this world. The Hanks' are the lowest people

---

1. For more on the Conservative, see §243, §245, §246, and §282.

in the world, if we may judge of them by their history of 1790–1814. It is held by some that Abm. Lincoln is the illegitimate child of one Enlow, but I do not think that they are borne out by good and sufficient evidence. I simply state the facts or supposed facts to you in order that you may understand the origin of things and by knowing this origin you may infer much, if you will carry it out. Lincoln knew all these facts or supposed facts and hence *in part* his sadness; his domestic life was a hell—a burning—scorching hell in the domestic world and hence an increased sadness & gloom. There flitted before this great man an apparition—an idea that he was to meet with some terrible end. And when you look at these things and know the peculiarities of his physical organization you will not be surprised at Lincoln's sadness—gloom and melancholy. This terribly reticent—secretive—shut mouth man never talked much about his history—plans—designs—purposes—intents; and when a man tells you this or that about what Lincoln said, believe what you *must* and no more. Lincoln had profound policies and never revealed himself to any man or woman and this his nature caused the devil domestically. Lincoln is unknown and possibly always will be. Sometime next month, nothing happening I will send you your *phos*. I will be glad to see you in Ills at anytime.

Your Friend
W. H. Herndon

MHS: Truman Bartlett Papers

210. To Truman Bartlett

Springfield Ills. Septr 25th, 1887

Friend Bartlett—

On the 22d inst I wrote to you a *private* & confidential letter in which I stated to you that Abm Lincoln's mother—*Nancy Hanks*, was an illegitimate child of a Virginia planter. I repeat what I said to you in that letter; and there is no doubt of the facts. Mr Lincoln told me the facts and the record of the woman bears out her son's statement that she was an illegitimate child of a Virginia planter. Here Mrs Lincoln got her *mind* and her *blood*; she was an intellectual woman beyond a doubt; her son told me so and all other persons who knew the woman prove that she was rather a great woman. She cared nothing for forms—etiquette—customs &c. &c but burst through them without a care for consequences: she was a social creature—very much so—loved the company of men more than woman and by her peculiar nature she got up a bad reputation; and because she had a bad reputation it was—it is still charged that Abm Lincoln is the child of one Enlow. My own opinion after a searching examination is that Mrs. Lincoln, Nancy Hanks, was not a bad woman—was by nature a noble woman—free, easy and unsuspecting. My own opinion after a sweeping and searching examination—investigation is that Abm Lincoln was the child and *heir* of *Thomas Lincoln & Nancy Hanks* Lincoln. I admit that all things are not perfectly clear to me; and yet I think that the weight of the testimony is in my favor on both of these grounds. Old Thomas

Lincoln—Abm's father was *castrated—fixed—cut*, but no one can fix the exact time of the loss of manhood. That *event* being *uncertain* lets in the presumptions of *chastity—Virtue* and *heirship* & on them hangs the weight of testimony alone. This is pretty close rubbing—is it not? I will write to you again and close up this subject forever, I hope. Now I want to ask you a question and it is this—shall I tell the whole story & argue things out as I see it?

Your Friend

W. H. Herndon

It will take an exhausting argument

MHS: Truman Bartlett Papers

211. To Truman Bartlett[1]

Springfield Ills. Septr. 30th, 1887

Friend Bartlett—

I wrote to you 2 letters dated about the 22d & 26th inst and in the first of which I tried to explain Mrs. Nancy Hanks Lincoln's parentage &c. In the one of the 26th I tried to explain the paternity of Abm Lincoln. Now I wish to explain the facts somewhat of Lincoln's origin—the doubt of it &c. It is said to me that Thomas Lincoln—Abm's father, was castrated and there is not much doubt of it, but the material question is— *When was he castrated?* Nancy Hanks—Abm's mother, married *Thomas Lincoln* when she was about 22 years of age: she had 3 children by Thomas Lincoln—at least the 3 children were born when or after Thos & Nancy were married. If she had been a bad woman why did she not have children before marriage? The first child, *Sarah*, was born in 8 mo less 2 days after the marriage and lived and married. *Abm* was born in 2 ys thereafter—after Sarah and *Thomas* 2 ys thereafter—after Thomas—making 6 ys from the marriage: she Nancy ceased to have children in—say 1812: she Nancy was in the vigor & prime of her life when she ceased to breed and why did she cease thus to bear children? Because Thomas was castrated. Mrs Nancy Hanks Lincoln—Abm's, mother died in 1816: she had no children from 1812 to 1816 and why, because her husband lost his manhood and because she was a virtuous woman. Had she bred right along—Thomas being castrated, then she would have let a stray bull in the pasture. Thomas Lincoln married a Mrs. Johnson: she had 3 children by her first husband Johnson: her first husband died about 1817 and she too, in the vigor & the prime of life, had no more children by Thomas Lincoln, because he was cut—fixed—castrated. If the time of Lincoln's castration was before marriage then Abm is the illegitimate child of some one, but if after Thomas, her youngest son, then Abm was got in

---

1. In top margin: "Please keep these 3 letters till you go hence & then hand them over as proof of legitimacy & virtue—H"

lawful wedlock. Under this state of facts, do you not see the importance of pre-sumptions. The law *conclusively* presumes that all persons born in lawful wedlock *shall* be presumed to be the lawful child & heir of the husband and his wife unless it should be conclusively proved that the man was incapable of procreation by nature or accident. No one now living can fix the time when Thomas Lincoln was castrated. The presumptions of law saves Abm's paternity. This is close shaving on so important a subject.

In addition to the above there appears to have been 2 *Nancy Hanks*—one the mother of *Abm* & the other the mother of *Dennis Hanks*—a bastard—an illegit-imate. Now at this late date when men say that they had connection with Abm's mother, can there not be a mistake in identity of persons. It appears in evidence before me that a Mr. Haycraft wrote in, 1860 or 1861, to Mr. Lincoln asking him some questions about himself—Abm. It appears, it is a fact, because I have copies of Mr. Lincoln's letter to Haycraft, that Abm Lincoln replied, in answer to a question about his own mother, & himself—"In the main you are right about my history. My father was Thos. Lincoln & Mrs Sally Johnson was his 2d wife. You are mistaken about my mother: her maiden name was *Nancy Hanks*."[2] This is all that Lincoln said in Haycrafts letter. Intelligent men do say that they did know the difference between the two Nancy's & so the matter stands. It however gets back to the question of *castration*. If Thomas Lincoln was castrated *before* he married *Nancy* then the fact is or was that Nancy Hanks—Abm's mother was a bad woman, but no one fixes the exact date of the sad fact. Now *you must presume* that every grown man has the power of procreation and *you shall* presume that all children born in lawful wedlock are legitimate, unless you can prove that the pair had no earthly opportunity of access—or that the man was by nature or by accident deprived of his manhood.

I promised you near the beginning of our correspondence that I would reveal to you some things. I have done as I promised and so you will have to judge for yourself. I am satisfied On thorough investigation that Abm. Lincoln was the lawful child of *Thomas Lincoln* & Nancy Hanks and that she was a virtuous woman. I hope that you can read my letter—hastily written *as you must know*.

Your Friend
W. H. Herndon

My life of L is nearly ready for the press. H

MHS: Truman Bartlett Papers

---

2. AL to Samuel Haycraft, May 28, 1860, *Collected Works*, 4:56–57.

212. To Truman Bartlett

Springfield Ills. Octr, 1887

Friend Bartlett—

. . .

My book will be ready for the press—say in Decr. or Jany next. I am bothered a great deal how to act in the matter. I thank you for your suggestions. You are correct in saying that the whole truth should be told of most men and yet it would not do for Lincoln. Lincoln is still going up—the growing great ideal man. I know a good deal about Lincoln—more than I dare state in a book. I watched the man closely for 30 years—20 of which were just across the table 10 X 3 ft. I was his friend—a fast one—an unswerving one and he knew it. I was from '34 to 1865 for Lincoln against the world—saw in him a great man—a man of destiny—took notes &c &c. Lincoln to the world is a profound mystery—an enigma—a sphinx—a riddle and yet I think that I knew the man: he was uncommunicative—silent—reticent—secretive—having [profound?] policies—and well laid—deeply studied plans. He moved men at pleasure and for his own ends: he was a remorseless trimmer with men: they were his tools and when they were used up he threw them aside as old iron and took up new tools. On principles he was as true as steel and while I say all this his ends were his Country's and man's.

You are correct again when you say that the noblest of women can lose their character quickly in a little village or in a new & sparsely settled country. Every body knows every body and any man's business is the business of the whole community. Such people love to tattle and to lie about one an other: they have nothing to do but to tattle and to lie in small things. In cities no man's business is his neighbors and to each man and woman attends to his or her business and goes on unnoticed and uncriticised, but wo to the woman in a little village if she makes a false step.

One more word about Thomas Lincoln—Nancy Hanks & *Abm* Inlow. Thomas Lincoln caught Inlow at his house under suspicious circumstances &c. Lincoln & Inlow had a fight about it and Lincoln bit off Inlow's nose. *Possibly* Thos. Lincoln left Kentucky to get rid of the devil. Nancy Hanks was as far above Thomas Lincoln as an angel is above mud. It is said that she didn't care anything for Thomas and now let me conclude this rambling letter by saying to you that Nancy Hanks was a great noble woman—a woman of a very fine cast of mind—was a broad minded—liberal—generous hearted—quickly sympathetic woman—a woman far above her surroundings—meditative—introspective—sad—daring—fearless & in some cases indiscreet. Lincoln himself told me much of this description of his mother. I know it by what her neighbors say of her & with which neighbors I have talked.

Your Friend
W. H. Herndon

Enlow was a kind of genius—a roue—a rake—a libertine—a man of force—& of mind—a broken down genius.

Since writing the above I recd your kind letter dated the 22d inst and for which I sincerely thank you. I wish greatly to be understood by all men. I have often said that Mr. Lincoln was an *Infidel* and *I say it now*. In 1835–6 Mr. Lincoln in the village of New Salem wrote a little book on Infidelity. In this little work, burnt up by a friend—Mr. Neill,[1] Lincoln denied the miraculous conception of Christ—ridiculed the Trinity; and denied that the Bible was the Divine Special revelation of God. *Here are facts - well settled facts.* Now what is an Infidel? As the Infidels use the word it means *those who deny that the Bible is the divine Special revelation of God.* If you will turn to Webster's dictionary you will find that that is the meaning of the word Whether this is so or not the Infidel has the right to define himself and the terms which he uses. Lincoln was a *Deist* if that word suits—fits the case better. *I well know that all this is no evidence of a want of religion in Mr. Lincoln:* it is rather an evidence that he had *his own* religion. I have said for more than *twenty* years that Mr. Lincoln was *a thoroughly religious man*—a man of exalted notions of right—justice—duty—&c. &c. Lincoln's religion was of the grandest & noblest type—kind. But when Mr. Bowditch[2] says that Mr. Lincoln was not an Infidel I am at a loss to know what an Infidel is. Lincoln was a strong believer in an overruling Providence—no man more so: he had a grand belief here. Am I understood friend? Rest assured, Mr Bartlett, that no theories go in my book—*facts*—*science*, if I can catch it only will be mentioned in the life. *Facts—facts—facts* shall be my guide. The Eastern people—bless 'em too, must give us poor devils of the great west some little credit for common sense and the practical. We pride ourselves on the useful & the practical. We are a people who have not a great pride in mental speculation nor in Theories. Write us down as "Practical."

Your Friend
W. H. Herndon

I judge that Mr B uses the word Infidel as synonymous with *atheism* which he is not warranted in doing—excuse me H

MHS: Truman Bartlett Papers

213. To Jesse W. Weik

Spfgd Ills. Octr 22d, 1887.

Friend Weik—

On last Saturday I recd your good long letter, dated the 10th inst, giving me much information—"much ideas." I guess that we had better bow to the semi omnipotence of public opinion and bend to the inevitable with grace and as much

---

1. WHH here confuses John McNeil with his partner, Samuel Hill, who is the one who reportedly burned AL's "little work." See *Herndon's Informants*, 61–62.
2. Not identified. Presumably someone quoted by Bartlett.

dignity as we can reserve. I do not see the use of fighting the unavoidable and losing what we have a chance of getting. We can tell all necessary truths—all those truths which are necessary to show Lincoln's nature &c. characteristics &c. We need not, *nor must we lie.* Let us be true as far as we do go, but by all means let us with grace bow to the inevitable. If the people will not take the truth—"God's naked truth" let the crime rest on them and not on our heads. Talk to me of the progress of this age! Sugar coat a lie and it goes down sweetly. The mass of men vomit at the truth unless it is sweetened with the lie. Falsehood is worshipped and the truth crucified: it always has been so and always will be so. *I say bow down to the inevitable.*

I am glad to know that you were in Chicago feeling your way—glad that Whitney was kind to you and did all he could for us. I agree with him that New York or Boston is the place for our contemplated book. I think Swett can do us good with Griggs &c. When the Mss are done I'll go to Chicago if I can. You and I will have to meet here say for a month and fix up things—understand one an other as to what things shall be said & how & when said. When & where shall we meet? I have written nothing as yet except a little on Lincoln's civil policy and will not till you and I see each other and well understand things. To write anything now would be folly. Bow to the inevitable with grace.

I recd the Preface & 1st chap.—have read them—are very good, but the 1st chap will have to be changed—re-written—modified—gutted. "Make things straight & rosy." Success is what we want We want no failures. Do what is necessary to gain that end, short of lying—or fraud. Please Lincoln's friends—the Publishers—and all mankind, past, present & the future. Go to any necessary expense in getting a type writer. Now you have my views in full

. . .

I saw Susan Talbott—Lincolns sweet heart as said: she says that Lincoln never courted her to the end of a proposal—have written 2 letters to Sarah, but I fear that she will not blab. Mrs. Talbott intimated to me that Sarah would not blab, if L courted her. It is enough that Lincoln & the girls were warm friends, if nothing more. I saw Brown: he says that Melvin has Lincolns Lectures—saw Mr Grimsby—the son of Mrs. Brown who says that his mother never had a lecture of Lincolns.[1] I have written to Melvin twice, but he has not answered. I am doing all I can to further things along & will to the end—am trying to please the world & all mankind & womankind too, bless 'em. By all means bow to the inevitable and do the best that you can under all circumstances.

Your Friend

W. H Herndon

I send you two letters to read.—Opinions like Swetts &c File 'em away. H

LC:HW3424–25; Exp 4:10:2229–32

---

1. On leaving for Washington in 1861, AL deposited his "literary portfolio" of miscellaneous speeches and papers with his wife's cousin, Elizabeth Grimsley (later Brown). See Carl Sandburg, *Lincoln Collector: The Story of Oliver R Barrett's Great Private Library* (New York: Harcourt, Brace, 1949), 75–85. For Melvin's story, see Jesse W. Weik, *The Real Lincoln* (Boston: Houghton Mifflin, 1922), 245–46. The editors are grateful to Michael Burlingame for assistance with this issue.

214. To Jesse W. Weik

Spfgd Ills Octr 29th, 1887.

Friend Weik—

I recd the ten dollars ($10.) which you sent me on last Saturday; and for which I am obliged to you. I wish to ask of you an other favor till our book is out. I raised nothing this year—everything burned up in the drouth; and am indebted to my grocery man to the amount of fifty five dollars. I wish to borrow this amount of you and for which I will allow you ten per ct per annum till the debt is paid. The loan shall be a lien on all things book, record—papers &c. &c as fully and completely as the note of mine now in your possession. The book, papers, & record are worth fifty times what I owe you. Please send me the fifty five dollars as soon as you get this & I'll sign any note which you will enclose. If you can please favor me or get it from some one in your city and I'll make him 2d mortgagee fully as you now are. I will consider the loan a great favor to me

I am at work getting up materials—

Your Friend
W. H Herndon

LC:HW3426; Exp 4:10:2233–34

215. To Jesse W. Weik

Spfgd Ills Novr 17th, 1887.

Friend Weik—

I recd the twenty five dollars which you were so kind as to send me. I thank you for it. Inclosed is my note for two hundred dollars, exactly like the one for $175—if I have made no mistakes. The note reads 10 per ct, but $25 only draws that sum. The $175 draws only 8 per ct as I understand it. I'll make any correction we note & I know you will. So much for the money matter. Weik, I thought when I wrote for the $55 that you were rich and could spare it. I am sorry that I did it though just now in a pinch. The $25 helps me out with what is due me. I know that H & W have largely drawn on W, but it will all come out right as sure as you live. Be not discouraged. I think that you are a little. The book will go now or in a few years. It is a good investment for your trouble, expenses—loans to me &c

Yes, I do know how difficult it is to get a publisher just now, but the *now* will not last always. A better time is coming for us as I think

. . . [*Unsigned and possibly incomplete*]

LC:HW3427; Exp 4:10:2235–36

216. To Jesse W. Weik

Spfgd Ills Novr 30th, 1887.

Friend Weik—

Inclosed is Swett's oration on the unveiling of the Lincoln statue at Chicago Octr 22d: it is very good & yet there are historical mistakes in it.[1] Swett says that Lincoln first moved to Coles Co. Lincoln first moved to *Macon* Co. The Lincolns moved to Ills in 1830 & not in *19*. Abm was 7 years old when he moved to Indiana. The Lincolns arrived here in the fall of 1830 & not in August. Abm, as I remember it, did not help to raise a crop in '31: he came to Spfgd Ills in the last of Feby or 1st Mch *1831* and went down the Sangamon River &c. Abm went to school about 6 or 8 mo in all: he went to the Legislature 8 ys & not 4. Abm never worked for a farmer on the Sangamon River: he never fired an engine on a steam boat at any time nor place—. Offit[2] had the boat built & not Lincoln. Lincoln was not struck as I think by the Negro. Lincoln, during the sessions of Legislature from 1834 to 40 did not walk to Vandallia nor from it to New Salem: he rode on horse back Squire Smoot loaning him some—say $200 to dress up in &c.[3] Probably there are other mistakes which you will detect & correct. However when Swett *speculates on* L's character qualities &c *he is very correct:* he has caught Lincoln nearly exact. The oration is a good one & preserve it. Follow it in his speculations—however not blindly Lincoln was *a poor listener in common social running conversations among friends, but when he wanted to get an opinion* gather up ideas *that interested him—on a subject on which he was about to act—one that would advance L's interest and through it his country's, then he was a most profound listener.* Lincoln in his serious and trying times in Washington heard patiently all men and weighed well all that was said. I have seen this in Washington myself on more days than one and on more occasions than one—often I may say——— I have drawn an ink mark around a truthful sentence. Swett & I see nearly alike.

Swett states Lincoln's religion Correctly: he says nothing about L's philosophy however Except incidentally. You have that in one of my pieces. I have drawn a mark around Swett's statement of Ls philosophy—fatalism &c

. . .

One more word about Swetts oration He says that Lincoln never loaned his money. This is a mistake. I have seen him loan people his funds & take a mortgage on real estate. L always loaned at legal interest when he could have got more. There is no mistake in what I say. You might quote in our book the most of what Swett speculatively says about character—characteristics—qualities &c. What he says is good—is true to the letter and the spirit, as I see things—as I knew Lincoln. What Swett says about L's self helpfulness—self reliance—self trustfulness and

---

1. *Oration upon the Unveiling of the Statue of Abraham Lincoln in Lincoln Park [Chicago] October 22, 1887.*
2. For Denton Offutt, see §92, n. 14.
3. Some of WHH's corrections are in error: the Lincoln family moved to Illinois in March 1830; AL reportedly worked for farmers along the Sangamon in 1830 breaking prairie and splitting rails; AL helped build Offutt's boat; he wrote that he and his partner, Allen Gentry, were "hurt some" when attacked by negroes on the Mississippi River in 1828. See *Collected Works,* 4:62.

self assertion in a good sense is very correct. Lincoln sat on his throne like a god and watched and noted the flow of events and the trend of things and made the most of them: he kept his own secrets & never was elated nor depressed. Things were as they were ordained and doomed and no man—no set of men could hasten—enlarge lessen—nor retard their flow or development. The movements of the world were inevitable powers—Such was Lincoln's philosophy

Your Friend

W. H Herndon

Swett says that Lincoln was of unknown parentage. Did he mean this as a hint? H

LC: HW3428–29; Exp 4:10:2237–40

217. To Jesse W. Weik

Chicago, Decr. 5th 1887.

Friend Weik:

In the month of August 1853 the Ills Central Rail Road employed Lincoln to defend a case in which the County of McLean was plaintiff and the Rail R Co was defendant: it was a case of taxation and involved a constitutional question, which I will explain when I see you. The Road advanced to Lincoln a retaining fee of $250. The case was decided in Bloomington and in favor of the Road. The case was appealed by the County of McLain to the Supreme Court of the State of Illinois and there it was argued twice and finally decided in favor of the R. Road: it was a big case and involved the question of the right of taxation by all the counties of the state through which the R. Road ran and this to all eternity—i e as long as the Rail Road existed. Mr. Lincoln was known alone in the case, though I was in it and recd my $2,500. When the case was finally through in 1855 Mr Lincoln presented his bill $5,000 to *Gen* McClellan—Yes *Gen* McClellan, who was engineer—probably treasurer &c. &c of the Road. When the bill was presented by Lincoln to the General, he, the Gen, rose up in his dignity & said haughtily and insultingly to Lincoln—"*Sir*, Daniel Webster ~~and~~ nor any other good attorney would not charge more—nor as much as *you* charge, *Mr. Lincoln*."[1] Lincoln was stung and maddened by the remark—walked away from the *Gen*—went down to Bloomington in McLain Co and, as I recolect it; sued the R. R company—recovered judgement for $5,000 and it was paid, I receiving my $2,500. I know that I got my money. This story is substantially correct in all particulars. Lincoln really hated McClellan for years, though for the supposed good of the country Lincoln

---

1. George B. McClellan was employed by the Illinois Central Railroad as its chief engineer in 1857 and is not known to have been involved in AL's dispute over his fee.

sank his individual hate for the public good—~~as he supposed~~ when he appointed
the Gen the Gen of the army &c

Your Friend

W. [H. Hern]don

Will write out the Stanton story soon: it will be a true story. When you are reading
my letters—Records &c take notes: it will help you—make Index &c

LC:HW3428–29; Exp 4:10:2237–40

218. *To Ward Hill Lamon*

Spfgd. Ills Decr. 16, 1887

Friend Lamon—

I recd your kind & friendly letter, dated the 4th inst. I likewise got your syndicate articles and for all of which I am much obliged to you. I have carefully read
the pieces and like them very much indeed: they portray Lincoln on one side of
his life admirably. Lincoln is the great unknown—the Silent—the reticent—the
incommunicable, having deep under currents, moving here and there as occasion
demanded: he used men as tools & when worn out he threw them away as old
lumber & got new ones: Lincoln cared nothing for particular men: he loved nobody excepting his children and hated nobody: he thought that the universe was
a vast machine grinding out facts as by fate which no one could rest. What was to
be would be and no prayers of ours could resist the Decree". Such was this man's
philosophy.

Now as to Lincoln's farewell speech to which you refer. I have read the speech
as you have it—as Arnold has it—as Holland has it—as others have it, including
Nic & H; and scarcely any two agree.[1] It does not seem to me that N & H's is
correct & yet they say the speech is, and I cannot dispute it. Nicolay & Hay make
Lincoln speak *too positively* when they make him say substantially that he is going
to undertake a business—more difficult than ever devolved in the Shoulders of
Washington. The speech that others use make Lincoln say—substantially that he
is going to undertake a business more difficult *perhaps* than has devolved upon
any other man since the days of Washington. I quote from memory and I refer

---

1. For different versions of this address, see AL, "Farewell Address at Springfield, Illinois," February 11,
1861, *Collected Works*, 4:190–91. See also Douglas L. Wilson, *Lincoln's Sword: The Presidency and the Power
of Words* (New York: Knopf, 2006), 10–18.

Lincoln & Douglas spoke in the State House—*not at* the fair grounds—in '54.[3] When Lincoln was done speaking Lovejoy rose up in the H H Rep and said that a meeting would be held in the Hall that night. I followed Lincoln out of the Hall and told him to run—take his horse & buggy & Bob & run, explaining to him the state & intention of things as I saw them. See Lamon pgs 353–359. Lincoln in my opinion left the city because I told him to run—go. &c. &c. I do not think that he intended to go to court—at all if there had been court which I doubt. Lincoln had thousands of distant friends in the city who were anxious to see him and arrange for the future. But Lincoln was off and I think that I could swear to the reason of the off—Your Friend

W. H. Herndon

LC: HW3441; Exp 4:10:2262–63

224. To Jesse W. Weik

Spfgd Ills May 6th 88

Friend Weik—

I recd the ten dollars which you were so kind as to send me. The ten dolls helps me over a shoal—a bad shoal indeed. I think that I can get along now without pestering you so much. I was needy and the ten under the circumstances makes me rich, at least I feel so. I am hard at work in the field, but my great hurry is over I think. I thank you for the money and am indebted to you more than you can well think. I'll write you as soon as I can answering all your questions if possible. Love to all.

Your Friend
W. H. Herndon

LC: HW3450; Exp 4:10:2275

225. To Jesse W. Weik

Spfgd Ills. June. 23d 88

Friend Weik

I not long since wrote you a kind and suggestive letter and you want more of them and so here goes—1st I wrote you a letter once in which I stated that Lincoln quietly broke social and dancing parties by his jokes—. Lincoln would corner a few men at the party and commence his yarns and jokes and thus attract the attention of the whole crowd. The women would say, "Mr. Lincoln please stop your stories as you are breaking up the dance." Sometimes Lincoln would quit and yet if old nick was in him he would go on worse and worse. I have seen this repeatedly[1]

---

3. In margin: "Simply called the state fair grounds speeches."

---

1. See §122.

2dly The letters which Wm F Herndon wrote us at Greencastle containing the substance of the laws during Lincolns legislative days shows better than anything can the state of our civilization from 1834 to 1841. I would repeat the substance of those letters sharing what Lincoln was called upon to legislate—vote and act about.[2] 3dly Lincoln's religion again. Lincoln in a letter to Mrs. Gurny virtually denies the efficacy of prayer—see Lincoln memorial album page 338—beginning at the 9th line and ending on the 20th—see as to his conversion at Spfgd same book pge 366.[3] He never was converted anywhere however.

. . .

Your Friend
W. H Herndon

LC: HW3456–57; Exp 4:10:2285–88

226. To Jesse W. Weik

Spfgd Ills. July 10th '88

Friend Weik

1st Mr. Lincoln would come down to the office about 8 oc am, sometimes in a good natured cheerful mood—speak pleasantly—tell a good story and thus he would continue til 12 oc. About 2 o'c p.m he would return to the office—in the same day in a sad terribly gloomy state—pick up a pen—sit down by the table and write a moment or two and then become abstracted & wholy absorbed on some question: he would often put his left elbow on the table in his abstracted moods, resting his chin in the palm of his left hand. I have often watched Mr. Lincoln in this state while he was lost in the world of his thoughts, gazing in the distance. In this condition of things neither he nor I would speak. Occasionally I did ask him a question in his moods but he would not answer, probably for 30 minutes. In the mean time I would quite forget that I had asked a question. To my surprise say in 30 minutes he would answer my question fully and accurately. He had pushed my question aside for the time being. Mr Lincoln in his abstractions or in his misery *seemed* to me to be a little off, so odd was he and yet I know that for the time being that he was in the lone land of his greatest thoughts. It has been said of Mr. Lincoln that he was a many sided man and if he was he certainly was a many mooded man. I can see Lincoln now in my mind looking sad & grim, sitting at our table, pen in hand while his chin rested in the palm of his left hand his elbow resting on the table, he gazing in the distance all the while. There is a sad picture for you truly and you can write it out to suit yourself. It is a correct and a true picture

2. Not found.

3. Oldroyd. Also see AL to Eliza P. Gurney, September 4 1864, *Collected Works*, 7:535–36.

2dly—I was deputy clerk of the supreme court of the state of Ills. and had some peculiar advantages to hear and to see.[1] Mr. Lincoln would come down from his home to the Supreme Court room about 7 or 8 ock in the evening. The lawyers—Browning—Logan—Bushnell[2] & other lawyers were studying their cases and making abstracts and briefs &c &c. Lincoln would come into the room in a good humor—in one of his best moods—speak kindly & pleasantly to all and say—"You men sitting here so mum puts me in mind of a story." The lawyers would say—"What is the story Lincoln, come tell it" and tell it he would, and that story would suggest an other and so he would break up all reading—abstract and brief business: he would keep on till 12 or 1 ocl in the night—

3dly—I have seen him break up, as it were, social parties—gatherings &c at dances &c as I have often told you: he would annoy the women dancers, because the men dancers would stop in the dance to hear the story.[3] Bear all these little incidents in your mind: it is these things that please the reader. Just think of a merry dance going on with music—women & wine and "old Abe" in the corner of the dancing hall with his 8 or 10 chums around him telling one of his best, *just loud* enough for the ladies to hear and you have a picture of the reality which I have seen more than once. "Old Abe" would enjoy to the ends of his toe nail his social crutch. You could see that it did him good all over. Lincoln would have his fun cost what it might.

4thly—Sometimes Lincoln would buy apples and bring them to the office, offering me some: he, in eating his apple, would clasp his fore finger & thumb around the equatorial part of the apple and commence eating it at the blossom end: he never peeled his apples but ate them just as he bought them—Curious man—an enigma.

Your Friend
W. H. Herndon

These little things are the charm of the life of the great.

. . .

LC: HW3458–60; Exp 4:10:2289–94

---

1. Margin note: "I have told you some of these things before this, but I want you to be sure and remember 'em".

2. Orville H. Browning and Stephen T. Logan were political and legal associates of AL. Nehemiah Bushnell was Browning's law partner.

3. See §122.

227. To Jesse W. Weik

Springfield Ills. Aug 8th '88

Friend Weik—

. . .

To-day I send you a letter by mail from "*Sarah*."[1] I have registered the letter for fear of loss. Mrs Barret says that Lincoln did propose to her and the letter bears internal evidence of its truth. The bible story is just like Lincoln.[2] Mrs. Barret is of good blood—truthful—a lady in every sense of the word—when young a pretty woman. I have known her since '31 and I can honestly say that her family is of the very[3] in this County. If you remember Speed's letter to me he tells me to erase a word if he has not done so. That word is "*Sarah*."[4] Speed evidently knew that L was courting "Sarah"—Miss Sarah Rickard—now Mrs. Barret. My wife has always strenuously Contended that L did court Sarah and did propose to her.[5] My wifes step mother was a Rickard & sister of Sarahs. She my wife has heard the mother of Sarah say that Lincoln courted Sarah and did propose to her—*Sarah*. You know that I saw Mrs. Talbot—a sister of Sarah about this matter and that she told me Lincoln did not court nor propose to Sarah so far as she knew. &c. Mrs. Talbott was insane a year or so since and was in the Lunatic assylum at Jacksonville Ills. It is a fact that Mrs. Talbott has lost her recollection of the past to a great extent. This I know through conversation with her. In short, whatever doubt has hung over the matter heretofore it is now all cleared up. I shall write to Sarah for her pho and for such facts about L's courtship, proposal &c as she will reveal. I had to write to her, I think, four times before I could get her to answer. My wife feels elated over her victory in the matter: she was in a good position to *know* and she did *know*. Mrs Barret wrote to her brother to tell me the story but he did not reveal, but I have not seen him:[6] he lives 20 miles or more away and is rather a shy man—rather a retired sensative—secretive—non communicative man.[7] When he sees me he will tell me I have no doubt. However we have it direct under Sarah's own hand and that is enough. Mrs. Butler was the sister of Sarah. Lincoln boarded for years with Butler and it was here that L first saw Sarah. By the way, I am convinced that the story about Butler's boarding Lincoln for nothing—keeping him on charity &c. &c is wholy false.[8] No doubt that Butler did assist Lincoln very much—when L was poor, just starting on the race for life—a noble & a grand race in the end

. . .

Your Friend
W. H Herndon

LC: HW3467–68; Exp 4:10:2306–09

1. Sarah Rickard Barret to WHH, August 3, 1888, *Herndon's Informants*, 663–64.
2. According to Barret's letter, when AL proposed, he suggested that according to the Bible, "Sarah will become Abraham's wife." Genesis 11:29
3. Presumably, WHH intended to write "the very best."
4. See Joshua F. Speed to WHH, November 30, 1866, *Herndon's Informants*, 431.
5. See *Herndon's Informants*, 640.
6. In margin: "The Rickard girls, like all girls did not tell their brothers anything about their love scrapes. Girls talk to girls—not to boys about such things—" H.
7. Sarah Rickard Barret's brother was John Rickard.
8. For WHH's earlier view, see §159.

228. To Jesse W. Weik

Spfgd Ills. Septr 24th '88

Friend Weik—

You remember that Lincoln in 1841—Jany—went crazy and did not marry Mary Todd according to promise.[1] I have a theory about it. Sarah Rickard—now Mrs. Barret says that Lincoln courted her and proposed in 1840–41. If these dates are right it appears that Lincoln had two strings to his bow and that at the time of his crazy spell he expected to marry Miss Rickard and did not want to marry Miss Todd. It further seems to me that on Miss Rickard's refusal he became desperate in Novr. '42 and married Miss Todd. Speed I think in one of his letters to Lincoln said—"*Have you seen Sarah?*" Is that date—the date of 1840–1.? If so, then my theory is probably correct. Give me the dates of these facts. You can find them in Lamon—in Speed's letter, I think in Lamon—in Miss Barret's letter and in Nicholays & Hays life of Lincoln—say in 1841. See Century of an early date. I have no books—papers, dates here. Will you please give me the dates wanted. It is true that had not Mrs. Francis formed her conspiracy with Miss Todd at Mrs. Francis' house between the 1st of Jany 1841 & 22d Novr. 1842 that Lincoln never would have married Miss Todd.

Jesse, 1st I shall ever contend *good naturedly* that my piece on the Pioneers of Ills should have gone in our book *in full*. I mean the piece in the Ann Rutledge lecture: 2dly The views of Lincoln & Jeff Davis should have gone in our book, so as to explain the issues &c: 3dly The causes why Lincoln held the People to him and his administration &c. &c or Lincoln's power over the People; as written to you in two or more of my late letters should have found a place in our book. The first of the above shows the state of civilization from 1831 to 1838 in Menard and about New Salem. Lincoln grew out of this civilization. The second of the above shows the views of the great men who formed the constitution &c that the Government was *National*, & that secession, developed from the idea of Nullification, had no foot hold—no resting place in the Constitution as made by our fathers & that it was a folly and a wicked delusion. Lincoln was a part of the war for the Union & the Constitution and to skip—pass over unnoticed the issues between Lincoln & Davis—the North and the South—the ideas & doctrines of the North & the South, seems wrong—and leaves a blank in our book as I humbly think.

. . .

Your Friend
W. H Herndon

LC: HW3479–80; Exp 4:10:2334–36

---

1. For the subsequently discredited story of AL backing out of a wedding to Mary Todd, WHH is here relying on the testimony of her sister, Elizabeth Todd Edwards, with whom she was living at the time. See *Herndon's Informants*, 443–44, 592.

229. To Jesse W. Weik

Spfgd Ills Octr. 10th '88

Friend Weik—

. . . [*In margin*: Lincoln said that his mother was by nature a great woman—great hearted & great headed—will write you about her—&c. &c soon according to my impressions—give it now on 3 & 4th pge.]

In Arnold's life of Lincoln he makes Abm's mother a *tanner* of cow skins &c. This is all nonsense. Write to Chapman and get Dennis Hank's recollection of the facts asserted. Women in this section never did any cow skin tanning—nor tanning of any kind. Arnold makes Lincoln's table groan with wild game such as venison—turkey—quail—duck—fish—squirrel &c. &c. This is all nonsense. Mrs. Lincoln was too avaricious for such things: she kept, as a general thing, a stingy table. Sometimes she would give parties and then it was that she flamed out in some splendor—. Mrs Lincoln kept or set a poor table. Lincoln never invited his friends to his general tables. Mrs. Lincoln would give him hell if he did and pay it down "right off," with tongue & broom stick.

Jesse—In one of my letters to you I stated that we wanted friends defenders &c. and to that end let us speak illy of no one. I said some hard things of Logan—wipe 'em out—So I said that Stuart pursued us, L & myself—wipe that out too—This is the prudent course, is it not?

While I am about it let me state to you the impressions which Mr. Lincoln's conversations made on me about his mother. I took no note at the time of what he said could not. I include the impressions left on me by conversations with David Turnham—old man Woods—Dennis Hanks the Grigsby's and some Kentuckians.[1] Turnham & Mr Wood were well acquainted with Mrs. Lincoln. In the first place Mr. Lincoln told me that his mother was a kind of genius—a great hearted & a big headed woman. He further stated to me that she was oversouled with goodness—tenderness & sympathy. Mr Wood verifies part of this—so does Turnham. Dennis Hanks and others say that she was a careless woman—careless of dress—show or glitter—Dennis Hanks says that Abm & Sarah did not know what cleanliness—civilization &c. were till Thomas Lincoln married Mrs. Johnson. Abm's mother despised forms—ceremonies etiquette—loved the company of men more than women's, because more like herself *in mind*. Mrs. Lincoln was a rather sad woman, especially at times in Indiana where she was high above her surroundings including all the Hanks' & I may say the same thing in Ky and when she broke out it was like the sunshine in a cloudy and stormy day, giving warmth & cheer to the world. I told you in one of our private conversations that one cause of Mrs. Lincoln's bad reputation among women, was because of her bold steps with men. Mrs. Lincoln was a good thinker rather than a good house & child cleaner: she was a rather gloomy woman in Indiana so says Mr Woods. Mr Wood takes for his idea of gloom from the fact of meditative mind—a mind

---

1. David Turnham, William Wood, and Nathaniel Grigsby were AL's Indiana neighbors that WHH interviewed and with whom he corresponded. For their testimony, see *Herndon's Informants*.

with an idea. Mrs Lincoln pushed aside all forms, ceremonies & what fashion builds—was sensative & secretive: she acted from within & not from the without. You know that Mrs Lincoln is charged with unchastity and the like. Do not these charges come from the fact, among the women—her neighbors, that she was a bold—reckless—courageous, daring self reflecting and self reliant woman—one with an idea of her own. I read a description of Mrs. Lincoln in some Ky paper some years since which in part comfirms my impression long since made. One or two words the author in the Ky paper changed after the first issue. Mrs. Lincoln was Mrs. Lincoln & no one else. In many things Mr Lincoln and his mother were alike, especially in self reliance—hate of forms—love of substance—in sadness—carelessness of dress looks &c &c sensativeness and secretiveness You now have my ideas of Mrs. Lincoln

Your Friend
W. H. Herndon

LC: HW3483–84; Exp 4:10:2353–56

230. To Jesse W. Weik

Spgfd Ills Octr 20th '88

Friend Weik—

. . . The reason why I did not take notes of Lincoln's conversation with me on the road to Petersburg was because it would have been done in his presence and he would have forbidden it, & because I had no paper and pen and ink.[1] The truth about it is, that in many particulars I did not take notes, because I was not prepared to do it—had no paper, pen and ink and sometimes I found men & women on the road—in fields at work—in wagons—on foot—on *Steam* boats—Rail Roads &c. In fact I did not, many times, see the importance of the information imparted to me till long after it was told me. Never saw the importance of much—many things till they rounded up as a whole. How is it with you? Think of 20 or 30 years in my struggles to get *facts* and you will understand my difficulties when you consider that I had to talk, as it were, to thousands of people.

. . .

As to Lincoln's courtship with Ann Rutledge let me say that L is not to be censured. The facts are that Hill—McNamar & Lincoln courted the girl at one and the same time; she preferred McNamar and L ceased to pay much attention to her, if any. McNamar after his engagement with Ann went to New York and was gone about two years. The relatives of the girl convinced her that McN had deserted her and at last, through the Rutledge's—Green's et al the girl consented to receive the visits of Lincoln.

Evidently somehow she let L know of her determination to cease expecting McNamar. Lincoln *then* & *not before* plunged in the second time, and won. The

---

1. See *Herndon's Lincoln*, 16.

poor girl unfortunately died a short time before L & her were to be married. I see nothing wrong in all this. Lincoln acted the man in this matter as he always did in all matters. Publishers of books know too much and would gut things of all pith and point if they could. You & I ought to know something after studying Lincoln for 30 years or more.

Your Friend
W. H. Herndon

P.S Please file all my letters good, bad & indifferent. They will be useful sometime H

LC: HW3487–90; Exp 4:10:2361–64, 2414–47

231. To Jesse W. Weik

Spfgd Ills. Octr 22d '88

Friend Weik—

. . .

So the wise critic does not believe in the Ann Rutledge story.[1] If he will only look over our evidence it is quite possible that he would have a dream of its truth. Lincoln will be in the great, no distant, future the Ideal man of America, if not one of the great Ideals of all the English speaking people and every incident of his life will be sought for—however apparently trifling—read with pleasure and treasured up in the memory of men. These little incidents will round up Lincoln's life and [globe?] the facts into a sphere of Ever rolling glory. This is my idea of a life of Lincoln, and especially so when these little incidents are *facts* truthfully told. Can critics destroy a truth? Their judgements are not infallible—oftener wrong than right. The judgements of the universal man are always correct & to them I appeal. You Know that we have been careful in all this matter to get the truth and nothing but the truth.

. . .

Your Friend
W. H. Herndon

LC: HW3491; Exp 4:10:2365–66

232. To Joseph Fowler

Springfield Ills. Octr 30th '88

My Friend:

With this letter you will find some short and rough notes on Nancy Hanks' & Abraham Lincoln's paternity which I promised you and which I hope will sometime

---

1. The "wise critic" was probably John Clark Ridpath, JWW's former professor at Indiana Asbury (now DePauw) University, who was acting as his advisor.

throw some light on Lincoln.[1] Some new fact may come bursting out to public view and when taken in connection with these notes will settle many things in the future. The reason why I scratched off these notes was a fear on my part that no one in the future would have the courage to wade through the ocean of my Lincoln evidences—records—papers. &c. &c and if such person did wade through I feared that the drift of things might not be noticed or distinctly seen. Hence you have my reasons—. My motive in writing the notes was that the people might know the truth about Lincoln in the future, if not a revelation to a few in the present. Right or wrong you have my reasons and my motives. The reason why I send them to you is because I know that you wish to understand Mr. Lincoln thoroughly inside and outside; and because I hope that you will sacredly keep these notes during your life and then hand them down till the proper time of publication. Now you have my reasons and my motives on this point. The facts in the notes have enabled me to understand much of Lincoln. When Mr. Lincoln told me that his mother, as related to you in a former letter of mine, was the illegitimate daughter of Lucy Hanks by a planter of Virginia, a flood of light burst on me and in that conversa-tion with Lincoln as I wrote you, I thought *only though* that Lincoln meant more than he said out & out. From that time—say in 1850, I have closely watched that man in certain directions. Lincoln was a terribly sad man and now the question comes, was that sadness inherited—or was it pre-natal, though not hereditary; or was it organic? Lucy Hanks might grieve over her seduction and thus stamp her grief on Nancy Hanks, making her sad: Nancy Hanks might have grieved over her seduction and stamped that grief on her son, making him sad, gloomy, mel-ancholic. From this point of view it probably—Lincoln's sadness &c, was partly inherited & partly prenatal. Lincoln's organism probably intensified that sadness; but what shaped the organism and made it function sadness? Mr. Lincoln, as a matter of course knew all about his ancestry and that might have helped to shade his sadness. Mr. Lincoln was terribly secretive—reticent—shut mouthed about himself and his relatives: he made but few revelations about his ancestry to me when it is considered the long years he & I were in partnership and the closeness of our relations; and when Nicolay & Hay say that this secretive—reticent minded man *by nature* poured out his whole soul to Speed—why nonsense! Lincoln may have told Speed much in one line and that line was his courtship with Mary Todd. Lincoln—Speed & I all slept in the same room for years. I was a clerk of Speed and I know what their Exact relation was. Nicolay & Hay it seems to me know nothing of Lincoln's nature—if they know any thing of human nature. If they do know any thing about it they either do not know how to tell it or analyze it. Please excuse this departure from the main thing in hand. Lincoln was a profound

---

1. Neither of these two sets of notes is known in WHH's hand, but versions of them do survive. Fowler, the recipient of the present letter, preserved what prove to be his own paraphrases of the notes on both Nancy Hanks and AL. Truman Bartlett, who had been promised access to these notes by WHH, retrieved them after WHH's death from his widow and made copies of each set of notes, which are located in the Bartlett Papers, MHS. The editors intend to publish these texts in a forthcoming edition of Herndon's lectures and memoranda on Lincoln.

mystery—a Sphinx sitting at the road side making no revelations of himself—his origin—his feelings—thoughts or purposes to any one. Lincoln would come into his office about 8 or 9 Oc AM and if in a good *state* he would speak pleasantly— tell a story—discuss philosophy—sit down at the table—pick up a pen—draw up the ink stand—catch up a scrap of paper—*stop* and then muse—become sad and then was my opportunity to catch an idea. I have looked into—his brain— the very back part of his little gray sad eye and thought a thousand, it may be, foolish things. I have asked myself on such occassions—"Why do you never Mr. Lincoln, on the stump, speak illy of any one? Is it because you open withering retorts, letting in an open light of the stagnant pool of your ancestry—or is it because you care nothing for men, only the idea which they represent; and why is it that you never eulogise men—speak strongly & favorably of this great man or that, is it because you are envious of their glory; or is it that no man is to be credited with his make up; conditions ruling & forming things absolutely without human consent & against that will. Is no man to be censured for what he does & is no man to be praised for what he is and what he does—Is it all fated &c. &c." Such questions as these and a thousand others come bubbling up on such occasions. I do not mean to be understood as saying that Lincoln never praised men—eulogised them—censured them nor condemned them, but such was his general life. I never heard Mr. Lincoln praise but two men—Jefferson & Clay, & never heard him censure but one—Douglas. Lincoln was a profound mystery and when you hear men say that they understand Lincoln set such down as mistaken men. Lincoln did write fewer social letters—& even political ones than any man that ever lived in such a high station: he was secretive—cautious—somewhat unsocial—abstracted—*loved* no man deeply—strongly & never *hated* any man more than a minute. A man who never loves never hates and a man who never hates never loves & such is nature. When all of Lincoln's letters shall have been gathered up & printed, the whole will only be a primer. Look at Washington's 10 or 12 vol of letters & then look at Lincoln's primer. I speak more particularly of Lincolns social friendly correspondence. In this letter I speak generally, bordering on the special closely. I have been asked a thousand time, it may be, this—"By what means was it that Mr. Lincoln so controlled men—why was he King ruler by a kind of divine right". If I ever get time I will give you my opinion—have no time now—am hurried—am poor—have to struggle today for my tomorrow's bread—regret having written such poor & uncorrected letters to you on such a subject as Lincoln & his attributes—characteristics & the like, but you have them and there is no use to whine about them. What I have said to you I have tried to tell the truth as I understand it. Try and reconcile the letters and understand me. My motives are good, because I want the world to understand this marvellously big man, great man—noble man & darkly mysterious man. Probably he stands a mystery to me because I tried to penetrate the soul of the man an essence—a thing not to be penetrated by mortal man. I give you ideas that may help you to see all sides—my weakness—my cranks as well as Lincoln's greatness—nature—attributes &c. &c. I withold nothing from you—tell it all, so that you may see clearly.

As to my book all that I claim for it is that it is truthful as far as I understand it. It is narrative in its style—no strain for effect. I would, as you believe, tell all the truth—"God's naked truth," if the publishers would let me. Publishers are parsimonious and their agent critics are good judges of *mechanical* literature, but good heavens what do such men, who never walked with men—the great mass of men, one minute, know of the great warm impulsive heart of the mass of men! They may feel the cold pulse of the closet and the ring & roll & glitter of the almighty dollar, but what else? My literary associate and myself have clung closely by Lincoln's side as he walked the earth & have not gone off to the war in search of him. You are correct in your estimate of Nicolay & Hays life of Lincoln, as I think. I have felt what you have felt in this direction and I suppose that is the general feeling of all. Nicolay & Hays book will fill a want in the future I think. In my book I have entered into no weighty estimate of Lincoln, because now is not the time to do that even were I capable of doing so. We are, all of us, too close to Lincoln & his times to judge fairly and profoundly. Your estimate of Seward—Chase & Co is I think very correct. You love the truth and my notes & my letters may possibly help you along in your studies of Lincoln.

You may give copies of the notes & my letters, all of them if you wish, to your friends, but with this understanding that none of them nor any part of them nor the facts of them are to be made public for years. Robert Lincoln hates me religiously for telling the truth about his father & mother and I do not wish that hate to be intensified, nor do I crave his love, but discretion is a good thing now & then—here & there. Excuse this long letter won't you?

Your Friend
W. H Herndon

Question—Could Abm Lincoln come from such a man as Thomas Lincoln without assistance H

[*In margin:*] Please read Nancy Hanks' piece before you read the Lincoln note—i e before you read the one on Lincoln

LC: Ethan Allen Hitchcock Papers, Box 1

233. To Joseph Fowler

Springfield Ills. Novr. 3d '88

Friend:

A few days ago I sent you some notes—short rough things, made for my own use alone when written. I likewise sent you a long, somewhat windy, letter, the best that I could do under all the Circumstances. I fear that the notes and the letter will prove disappointing, if not terribly vexatious to you and friends. I am aware of this. I know the point of vexation in your mind, and it is or will be this—I scarcely give and opinion, and fail to unriddle uprising questions in your mind. I am not a theorist run mad. I state facts and wish all persons to form their own opinions, free and untrammeled from any speculations of mine. Science may be said to be the revelations of nature to reason. This is what we want about heredity—transmission—pre-natalism and the like, when we talk about Lincoln's sadness—gloom—melancholy—morbid[1] irritability in the man. This man had his "black fits"—his illusions—his fears—his terrible despairs—his domestic crucifixions—his terrible sufferings. He walked much of his time on that narrow line that divides sanity from insanity, caused by nervous and mental exhaustion. He seemed to have an infinite power of study: he did not know his limitations however. I have not the science with which to deal with Lincoln's case. I state facts, hoping in the future to have a science of physiology and psychology in the world There is nothing lawless—neither matter nor mind. I will do my part for the future, by giving facts to the future. Science may unriddle in the future all of Lincoln. This man in a private conversation about his feeling said to me—"I fear I'll meet with some terrible end". Did he then see that terrible end in the dim future? I have had peculiar feelings when in the presence of Lincoln. Friend, do not think that I am exaggerating. No human pen, I think, could exaggerate in this field. Now if you will again pick up and read my poor analysis of Lincoln to be found in 6 Mo in the White House[2] and read it in connection with this and my last letter & my notes inclosed in my letter, you will begin to see Lincoln as I saw the man, I think.

Now as to Lincoln's physical system: He was, as I remember it, a healthy man—had a slow circulation—a hearty eater—had good digestion—tolerably good respiration, though inclined by build to consumption—flesh coarse—somewhat dry—hands sometimes a little cold and clammy—always very costive—was long—tall—weighed about 160–180.—very amarous—full of passion for woman—was wrinkled & shrivelled—big boned—slow to act, with slow thinking; and this peculiarity of Lincoln made Seward act the fool when he wanted Lincoln to let him run the government. Under Lincoln's coarse exterior he must have had an extra fine net work of nerve. O—how little did he know of Lincoln, who was only waiting the rich development of the *last fact* in the great coming drama where it was a crime to wait longer. He was gathering up all the facts—slowly, I admit, of the rebellion and watching their relations in every line and direction—one to the other, then and not till then could or would Lincoln act. Lincoln by his mental organization required, to use a law term or phrase, [certainty?] to a certain intent in every particular, before he could believe a thing and act on it. Pardon me for saying this—I think that I pretty well understood Lincoln: he was the great big man of our firm and I was the little one. The little one looked *naturally* up to the big one—watched closely—searchingly every act of the big one, saying or thinking to himself "what means this—to what end and from what motive". Here you have a confessed truth and remember it. You shall have it all, so that you can *see*. The thing, for you to know is, what was the person's opportunity to know his powers of perception or his capacity to see the things correctly which he relates to you including his veracity. My mouth is locked just here.

---

1. This word appears to have been stricken later at WHH's behest. See §235.
2. Carpenter.

Lincoln should never have married Mary Todd, ambitious to lead and control Society: she was a woman of fine intellect—quick witted—sarcastic—aristocratic—refined. In fact she once was a lady, but unfortunately she fell from that high position, as I think, from the Exessive use of morphine. To me she was always kind and respectful; and in return I respect her: she had much to bear. Lincoln was her opposite in many things—he was abstracted—unsocial, uncommunicative—sad—gloomy, having none of these little touches that please woman. The marriage between Lincoln & Mary Todd was a policy match and keenly did both suffer from it. Mrs Lincoln was a better woman than the world gives her credit for. She was a whip and a sting to Lincoln's ambition—she urged him to go upward. I admit that *at times*, in her *after life*, that she was a she devil, filled it may be with morphine. Let us be charitable for we are all weak creatures at best, no one knowing himself till conditions push him on to ruin. Bless this woman. She was Lincoln's best and wisest adviser when at herself and in her younger days. She had good judgement as to policies and a fine judge of human nature. She directed Lincoln rightly and kept him on that path. I speak of this woman in her younger and better days. This woman must have cut Nicolay & Hay, because they do not say any thing about her, nor did they insert, as I recollect it, her likeness in their life of Lincoln. This is a mean little revenge on a poor dead woman. I may be mistaken in my recollection about her engraving.

Lincoln should have married some village girl—some country lass, who had no political ambition—no ambition to lead and control society: she should have seen to it that Lincoln was kept clean—seen that he had plenty to eat—was kept warm—not vexing him about wood—fuel or food—rocked the cradle and teezed him with no questions and should have seen that he was comfortable every way in every particular, then Lincoln's domestic life would have been happy, while she looked up and worshipped, next to God, her husband; and in that duty well performed—the whole of it, her domestic life would have been an earthly heaven, but as it was Lincoln's domestic life was a domestic hell. People who marry for policy and not from sacred love violate a law of their nature and must inevitably suffer the dread consequences. Such are my observations and experience derived from policy marriages generally, if not particularly. As a lawyer I have seen much of this. Domestic misery follows close on the heel of policy marriages, but enough of this—

I have forgotten all along to state to you that Lincoln was an extremely sensative man and was *deeply stung by any kind of neglect*—stung, I say, to the quick and to the raw; and now comes the question—Had this any thing to do with a conciousness of his origen—his paternity—his lowly emergence into this world? I think that it is probable. I have known men to commit suicide because of it. Remember I give no opinion of L's legitimacy as *a fact* & yet I do as a legal proposition say most emphatically that he was the son—legitimate child—heir of Thomas Lincoln & Nancy Hanks there being no sufficient evidence of Thomas' incompetence at the proper time and here I rest. No court except for incompetence would hear any evidence against L's (legal) legitimacy, because he was born to Thomas & Nancy during lawful wedlock, they having been lawfully married and before he was born. This law question is a policy question & a wise one as you know without any words of mine.

I think that by this time you believe I am trying to tell the whole truth of Lincoln. I hope you do. I have lost friends & caste in society from that very fact. I send you a slip of paper[3] for *one purpose* and one purpose alone and that is to show you that I have lost friends & caste in society, because I loved and dared tell the truth. Lincoln is a large man and can well stand all the truth. I think that a biographer or one who writes of an other has a double duty to execute—1st to tell the truth about the dead respectfully and if you please reverently for his honor & his good name among men; and 2dly to write the truth—the whole truth—necessary ones—for the good of the living, in order that the living people now and coming people during all future time, may worship that truth in a real person and not a suppressed or suggested one. This has been my aim and my end and if I shall have succeed in learning the living and coming generations who Lincoln was and what in full—the full well rounded man I shall not have lived in vain.

Some of these days when you have nothing much to do please sit down and read carefully & thoughfully my analysis of Lincoln to be found in 6 Mo in the White House by Carpenter—then the notes—rude and rough just sent you, including the letter sent with the notes and lastly this poor scrall of a letter and then ask yourself this question—"What have I learned from all these things?" It may be that the response will be—"Not much, Sir"

When I get time, if ever and feel like it, I will write you and give you my reasons why Lincoln was King of men by divine right. I am a simple farmer—have been for about twenty years and have not much time to spare—am very poor and hard run—have to work hard to keep the wolf from the door and in spite of all these thing I am a contented and a happy man, trying still, in my old age to do good to my fellow man—it seems the main object of my life. Excuse in me whatever *appears* to you as egotism. You have got a good deal of me in my letters at any rate and be content and calmly wait on the future.

Your Friend
W. H. Herndon

P.S. I have stolen this time from my work in order that you may know what you so much want

LC: Ethan Allen Hitchcock Papers, Box 1

---

3. Not identified.

234. To Jesse W. Weik

Spfgd Ills Novr. 10th '88

Friend Weik—

. . .

We boys only went to the mouth of Spring Creek where we first saw the boat and thence we went up the River to Bogues mill—5 or 6 m—We did not go down as far as New Salem[1]

. . .

Be sure that Lincoln come all the way up to Bogue's mill. It *seems* to me that he did and that, I at that time, saw Lincoln, but be sure that I am right. The records will fix it—it has now been 56 years since I saw what now *seems* to be the truth to me. Try and get me right—. If L came up to Bogues mill I saw Lincoln & if he did not then I did not see him at Bogues mill.[2]

. . .

It has been thrown up to me recently that Butler did board Lincoln free from 1836—to 1843. I have written to [Mist?] Butler, asking him to see his sister too and get his & his sisters opinion on the facts. I think the charge is a lie. Butler was poor from '36 to 1843 and couldn't affort it, nor would L accept of such long continued gratuity.[3] Will send you Butlers letter in answer to mine, if he writes me.

. . .

Your Friend
W. H Herndon

LC: HW3499–3500; Exp 4:10:2381–84

235. To Joseph Fowler

Springfield Ills. Novr. 13th '88

My Friend:

I have received two registry return receipts from you—I am glad that you received the notes & my letter sent you. I hope that you will be interested in the notes. I regret that I had no time to rewrite and copy my letters, they would have looked better. The main object of writing this note is to ask you to *erase* one word in one of my letters. The word is this—*morbid.*[1] That word is too strong. The meaning of the term or word irritability I will now explain. Mr. Lincoln had

---

1. WHH is referring to an event in 1832 when the steamboat *Talisman* attempted to prove the Sangamon River was navigable, a venture in which AL was known to have acted as a guide and helped clear the river of debris.

2. WHH here expresses concern about whether what "seems to be the truth" about his first sight of AL could be confirmed by the testimony he himself had collected—his "Lincoln records," then in JWW's possession.

3. See §155, §159, §234.

---

1. See §233.

a slow but *healthy* irritability—that is his organism slowly responded to all stimuli. His irritability was *not* a *diseased* one, but *generally* a *healthy* one. The word irritability alone sometimes means a sickly or diseased irritablity Hence the above correction and explanation. If you think that the two words—*morbid irritability*, had better be stricken out do so. Probably the whole thing seems to be unnecessary and foolish, but yet it shows *to me* much of Lincoln & explains his tardiness—his sadness—&c. Science even by these words, as explained may seize a great fact—a law of Lincolns life. I hope that I am not getting too scientific. Was this irritability of Lincoln an organic result—and if so what made his organism so? Was it a kind of heredity thing? Or was it impressed on him by his mothers grief while yet in the womb? Was Lincoln's sadness the effect—the result of his peculiar organism? When Lincoln acted too slowly here is the cause: he couldn't help it. If Lincoln was sad and gloomy here is the cause and he couldn't it. If Lincoln read foolish stories, passed vulgar or other jokes in the midst of grave times and to grave men he *did so* to arouse this slow irritability and assume the life of Lincoln *awake* and not be in a sad, gloomy—dreamy state. Take all my letters in connection with this and form your conclusions from all. I am not a scientific man and don't pretend to be, and yet I do believe that through science Lincoln will be better known. Pardon my foolishness. I may see too much of Lincoln for practical human use just now—probably too little.

If you have given copies of my notes before this reaches you *please*, with your own eye, for a friend, see that the word morbid is *erased*.

Your Friend in haste
W. H Herndon

LC: Ethan Allen Hitchcock Paper, Box 1

236. To Truman Bartlett

Springfield Ills. Nov 16th '88

My Dear Sir:

. . . My poor book will I guess suit no one, but that I cannot help. The life is mostly an analysis of Lincoln—an attempt to let people peep into the inner man, a thread of his history running through the book at the same time. The time is not yet to correctly and accurately estimate & weigh Lincoln. We are too close to him and the times in which he lived and out of which, with conditions, he wrought his great glory; he is the ideal man of America and probably will be an ideal man of all English speaking people. Every thing about Lincoln should be preserved correctly and you will help to preserve important facts in relation to him. You will get in the book truths—facts—opinions, where I give one, with no admixture of falsehood, if I can avoid it. I have been working on facts—to get them twenty five years or more. The book treats of Mr. Lincolns as an individual—domestically—socially—as a friend, lawyer—statesman- politician—his religion

& philosophy—his philosophy &c. &c. don't go much into war matters—only a kind of a one eye glimpse of it. How does this ring—how does it suit, my friend?

. . .

Your Friend
W. H. Herndon

MHS: Truman Bartlett Papers

237. To Jesse W. Weik

Spfgd Ills Decr. 13th '88

Friend Jesse—

Some proofs recd. You ask me to locate in the book the story of Miss Sarah Rickard—now Mrs Barrett. Soon after Miss Todd come to Ills the 2d time—say in '39 Mr. Lincoln soon went to see her and courted her and they were engaged to be married on the 1st Jany 1841. Lincoln did not come to "taw"—to time. They separated forever as Lincoln intended it should be. After the smash up Lincoln went to see *Sarah*: She refused him. Lincoln through Mrs Francis & his own desperation went to see Mary Todd again and married her in '42. The location of Miss Rickard's story comes in between the 1st Jany '41 & Novr. 1842. as I and my wife make it. My wife has heard all the Rickard girls state the facts as I have heretofore said to you. If you will see a letter in Lamon from Speed, I think, to Lincoln in which is used this substantial expression—"Have you seen Sarah" that will help to settle this question as to when & what is correct. Miss Rickard may mistake the time that L went to see her, if there is any discrepancy—errors &c &c. You have my recollection & my idea. By the way you have left out the best thing in Sarah's letter: it is this—Lincoln said to Sarah—"And Sarah shall be the wife of Abraham."[1] . . .

The whole proofs read admirably well and as I said to you once before a thousand recollections—facts & incidents came bubbling up in my mind about Lincoln. Sometimes I wish that I had a stenographer present & take all down. I did not take down in writing 100th part of what I heard men and women say: they talked too fast for me, not being a stenographer—some I conversed with on the roads and other places and had no chance. Things which I did not deem of importance I paid not much attention to, but now I regret it, as I have often wanted the very things that I rejected

Your Friend
W. H. Herndon

LC: HW3521–22; Exp 4:10:2422–25

---

1. See §227.

238. *To Jesse W. Weik*[1]

Spfgd Ills. Decr. 22d '88

Friend Jesse—

    I guess that you will dislike this letter about as heartily as you *dislike* anything. Nevertheless I shall send it and ask it to be filed away. I suppose that you will agree with me that Lincoln had a low & feeble circulation. It follows physiologically does it not that he had a slow, but a somewhat healthful irritability—that is his whole organism moved slowly to the influences of all kinds of stimuli: he thought slowly and acted slowly, and as I said in one of my lectures on Mr. Lincoln in '66 his body and mind seemed as if they needed oiling. A man thus conditioned has his spells of sadness—gloom and melancholy, if not his spells of despair. This state of Mr. Lincoln made him, as it were at periods, unconscious of his surroundings and to arouse that somewhat dormant Consciousness he needed a stimulant and that was found in a story and tell it he would. The human mind is active and cheerful or sad & gloomy according to the quantity and quality of the blood sent from the heart through the brain. This story telling—this stimulant, sending more blood to the brain, aroused the whole man to an active consciousness—sense of his surroundings. Grave men in grave times, sometimes his ministers, would approach him in order to state the urgency of some matter that needed his immediate attention. Mr. Lincoln would look up to his minister half sleepily—dreamily, saying—"Mr Secretary take a chair": he would, in a moment or two, after the secretary had stated his errand, tell some story much to the disgust of his minister, who would censuringly say "Mr President, this is no time for story telling—the times are grave and full of war, and the country is fast drifting to ruin". Mr. Lincoln would good naturedly reply—"Come Mr Secretary, sit down—sit down—I have a perfect and a profound respect for you and were it not for these stories I should die: they are vents through which my sadness—gloom and melancholy escape". Mr. Lincoln would thus arouse his half dormant Consciousness into activity—into full play and power; and after he had been thus aroused he would listen to what the secretary or minister eagerly told him, like a philosopher and in a short moment he would make his answer, his reply, so wisely and so earnestly as to convince the man that that point or that subject had been thoroughly and maturely considered before, long, long before this moment of meeting. This state of Mr. Lincoln, particularly so if it was accompanied by mental & nervous exhaustion, produced by long and intense study, caused him to have delusions—saw apparitions—specters & the like. This man was, as a general rule a sad—a gloomy & melancholy man, but at exceptional times a momentarily happy one and it was a curious thing to see him sink quickly back into his usual state of sadness and gloom and become, as it were, oblivious of his surroundings, man and the world. Let no man blame Mr Lincoln for being sad or seeing apparitions: his sadness and his gloom came naturally out of his organism and his apparitions from the same source somewhat and from nervous & mental exhaustion. Let no man ~~blame~~ rudely censure Mr.

---

1. In margin: "*Lincolns 'nature'—one side*"

Lincoln for his story telling, because the telling of them aroused him and made him happy for a time.—Had this great man been of an ardent temperament with swift and strong volumes of rich blood pouring through his brain—had he been impulsive—quick to think and quick to act—rashly running before the complete development of the individual ideas with National ideas and of facts—marching with banners hastily before his people—blindly guessing at the trend and drift of things—hungry and longing for a quick end of the national quarrel—groping his way before ideas and facts, this great nation would have been two governments this day. This feeble and low circulation—this slow irritability which slowly responded to stimuli—this organism with herculian strength not having much wear & tear about it by nature conserving its forces—this great man with a great heart and greater head, with a sublime patience and an endless endurance saved the Nation from division and Consequent ruin. Was not Mr. Lincoln the right man, in the right time and in the right place? Surely—surely there is a Providence in the affairs of men, has been, now is, and forever will be, as we poor mortals see it.

Your Friend
W. H Herndon

P.S I know that this does not suit you—you dislike such stuff terribly, and yet some persons may like it. You dislike all speculation, including my piece on L's power over men and the piece on L's love of law & order. H

LC: HW3425–26; Exp 4:10:2436–39

239. To Jesse W. Weik

Spfgd Ills Decr. 22d '88

Friend Weik—

. . .

Let me say one more word about Lincoln's want of will in cases not involving a right or a principle. Once he did something that his political friends did not like and they told him that he acted the d__n fool: he came into the office a few minutes after this and told me what he had done that caused his friends to censure him. At the conclusion he said—"Well, I suppose, it's a d___d good thing that I was not born a woman".

Your Friend
W. H Herndon

LC: HW3425–26; Exp 4:10:2436–39

240. To Jesse W. Weik

Spfgd Ills Jany 4th '89

Friend Jesse

. . . my idea of Mr Lincoln's conversational power is this. On general subjects talked about (in society) in the social line Lincoln was a poor conversationalist: he was a very poor listener in the social line too. However when he wished—asked advice which was not often & on which he was about to act he was a good listener—an admirable one. . . .

Your Friend
W. H Herndon

LC: HW3528; Exp 4:10:2442–43

241. To Jesse W. Weik

Spfgd Ills. Jany 4th '89

Friend Weik—

Mr. Lincoln and I had various and diverse conversations in relation to the spirit of the times and about slavery from '53 to '61. I was an out and out abolitionist, radically so. Mr. Lincoln was a very conservative man & a cautious one: he thought slowly and moved slowly in the matter of his opposition to slavery. I declared often & often in his presence & *to him* that the fugitive slave law was a *thing* engendered in hell. I said to Mr Lincoln repeatedly from '53 to '61 that this Continent was not broad enough nor long enough to contain the principles of liberty and the despotism of slavery for any great length of time together; and that one or the other must go to the wall and die there—not only cease to be a faction of power in the political world, but that one or the other—liberty or slavery—must die. I said to Mr Lincoln often and often that ill gotten gain did no man any good and that this applied to nations as well as individuals—that God would snatch from this American all the wrath of the nations unjustly wrung from the slave; and that God would put us back to that point where we earned the last honest dollar. I said to Mr. Lincoln pretty much in all of our conversations that a war on a large scale would come, because of the antagonism of ideas—That I felt it in the air and in my bones, and so I did. In looking over the whole country I did not see the great men—the *greatest man* who was able to control things—events if you please; and was on this account somewhat in despair of freedom. One morning during the time of these conversations between us Mr. Lincoln came into our office looking sadly: he and I were moved by a common—a like idea. The idea of war between the North and the South came up and was somewhat discussed by us. I said to Mr. Lincoln that I feared the loyal people of the North could not find any great heads or some great head to lead the people safely through the war and control things—events, thus saving human liberty to the Earth. Mr. Lincoln scratched his head one moment and then made this reply—"I have a belief that whatever antagonisms, along the lines of the wrong exist between slavery and freedom that the antagonism along the lines of the right will control the events for the eternal right. I have confidence in the people and of the right." Mr. Lincoln said by way of the illustration of his ideas and of my doubts this—"If you will take one of the these large sieves—coarse ones—to be found in any hard ware store and go to some beach and fill it nearly half full of gravel of different sizes and well and thoroughly shake the sieve hard & often and the harder and oftener the better, you will find the small pebbles slip through the sieve, and sink out of view and go to the ground. The next larger size will be unable to creep through the sieve and will rest on them. By thorough and repeated shakings you will find, on your own observation, that the larger pebbles have all climed on the top" "Now" said Mr Lincoln "if, as you say, the war is inevitable and will terribly shake up the country from circumference to the center, you will find by your own observation that the little men will fall out of view in the shaking. The mass of men will rest on some solid foundation; and at the same time you will find that the big men have climed to the top by the shaking". "Just so," said Mr Lincoln, "the big men will come to the surface—the big man too will come to the top and carry us safely through the war, controlling opposing forces—crush wrong and establish justice. "This" said Mr Lincoln "is my idea—my prediction & note it".

Little did I know how great our people are as a mass of men—how little did I know of the vast number of great men in the country who were wise leaders & brave ones in the terrible war; and how much less did I know that the great big man was touching my shoulder at the moment.

This figure Mr Lincoln actually used just as I have told it to you. I remember the conversation well—just as well as if it had happened on yesterday. Occasionally I remember some of our conversations on philosophy—science—art—law &c &c which have never been made public. I would send them to you, but what's the use? The Book is fixed like the law of the Medes & Persians, cast ironed.

Your Friend
W. H. Herndon

LC: HW3529–30; Exp 4:10:2444–47

242. To Jesse W. Weik

Springfield Ills. Jany 5th '89

Friend Weik—

Mr. Speed told me this story of Lincoln. Speed about 1839-'40 was keeping a pretty woman in this City and Lincoln desirous to have *a little* said to Speed— "Speed, do you know where I can get *some*; and in reply Speed said—"Yes I do, & if you will wait a moment or so I'll send you to the place with a note. You cant get *it* without a note or by my appearance". Speed wrote the note and Lincoln took it and went to see the girl—handed her the note after a short "how do you do &c.", Lincoln told his business and the girl, after some protestations, agreed to satisfy him. Things went on right—Lincoln and the girl stript off and went to bed. Before any thing was done Lincoln said to the girl—"How much do you charge". "Five dollars, Mr. Lincoln". Mr. Lincoln said—"I've only got $3." Well said the girl—"I'll trust you, Mr Lincoln, for $2. Lincoln thought a moment or so and said—"I do not wish to go on credit—I'm poor & don't know where my next dollar will come from and I cannot afford to Cheat you." Lincoln after some words of encouragement from the girl got up out of bed,—buttoned up his pants and offered the girl the $3.00, which she would not take, saying—Mr Lincoln—"You are the most Conscientious man I ever saw." Lincoln went out of the house, bidding the girl good evening and went to the store of Speed, saying nothing. Speed asked no questions and so the matter rested a day or so. Speed had occasion to go and see the girl in a few days and she told him just what was said and done between herself & Lincoln; and Speed told me the story and I have no doubt of its truthfulness.

Again—Mr. Lincoln told the following story of himself to Judge Matheny—Milton Hay and myself, all of us recollecting the story alike.—Mr. Lincoln went up to Bloomington Court, and was gone from home some two weeks & was desirous to get home to attend to our own court. This was about 1850, '51. Lincoln started home from Bloomington late on Saturday evening—got to Salt Creek about twenty miles north of this city and put up for the night with a Mr. Cottenbarger—an old friend of Lincoln.[1] The house was a log one and had but one room in it, Cottenbarger having just settled in a wild place. There were three beds in the room and some curtains between the beds. The bedsteads were arranged so that the foot of one bed was close up against the head of the other. The old man in the south east corner—the grown daughter in the middle and Lincoln's north. The people all went to bed, and [way?] in the night the girl's feet, by accident & when asleep, fell on Lincoln's pillow. Occasionally in her sleep she moved her feet about. This put the *devil* into Lincoln at once, thinking that the girl did this of a purpose. Lincoln reached up his hand and put it where it ought not to be. The girl awoke—got up and went to her mother's bed and told what had happened. Possibly Lincoln had tried to repeat what he had done just before. The mother said to the girl to pacify "For God's sake say no more and go to bed, the man means nothing. If the old man hears of this the deuce will be to pay". Lincoln heard the conversation between mother & daughter and thought that it might be possible that the old man was awake and not asleep. Lincoln knew Cottenbarger's physical power—a great big burly strong man with great courage and he therefore fixed his eye on a large heavy hickory chair in view with which to defend himself, if Cottenbarger should attack him. However all things settled down calmly & all went to sleep again, except Lincoln, now mortified to death at what he or *the devil in him* had done. Early in the morning Cottenbarger got up—got a long keen butcher knife—and whetted it on the rocky jamb—reached up the chimney and

---

1. According to the Federal Census and histories of DeWitt County, a number of early settlers in the Salt Creek area were named Coppenbarger. See, for example, *History of DeWitt County, Illinois: With Illustrations Descriptive of the Scenery, and Biographical Sketches of Some of the Prominent Men and Pioneers* (Philadelphia: Brink, 1882), 241–45.

cut down a piece of dried venison—took a piece of bread and went off into the woods. Lincoln in the mean while shivering kept his eye on the old man and on the chair. Lincoln heard some whispering between the old man and his wife and was convinced that the old man had heard all, and Lincoln really expected the devil was to pay. As soon as the old man had gone the old woman got up—made the fire and in a hurry got breakfast and hustled Lincoln off as quick as possible. Lincoln, glad to get off jumped quickly into his buggy & was off for home, a deeply and thoroughly mortified man. Cottenbarger had great discretion and hurried off to avoid a terrible fight with Lincoln. This hurt L so badly that he had to tell it to his friends for relief.

Your Friend
W. H Herndon

PS. You are a very modest *young* man and how does this suit you? Would the stories do "to point a moral or adorn a tale"? Would they not do for riders? H[2]

LC: HW3531–32; Exp 4:10:2448–51

243. To Jesse W. Weik

Springfield Ills Jany 8th '89

Friend Jesse—

. . .

How did Lincoln's figure in my letter of the 4th strike you?[1] It is a good thing and a true one. That letter tells nothing but the truth. How did Lincoln's vulgar stories about wanting a *little*. &c &c strike you? They are as true as holy writ & truer too.

Let what I now say be *private*—sacredly so. When Matheny—Stuart &c. &c were running the Conservative—getting up procession &c &c ostensibly for Filmore Lincoln said to me—"These men are stool pigeons for the democracy—bought up like cattle & hogs in the market. The Conservative is run by the democrats in fact. &c. &c."[2] Lincoln was very bitter over them & I guess he probably had some evidence of the truth of what he said, though he did not say so to me. This will account for his saying & doings about the Conservative as in pge. about 311 in the proofs. This shows his implied interest in crushing the influence of the Conservative by scattering the fact of its democratic & pro-slavery tendencies &c.

---

2. It may be doubted that WHH was serious about including these salacious anecdotes in the impending new edition of their biography. A more likely possibility, suggested by his considerable frustration at this stage, is that he offered such obviously objectionable anecdotes as a taunt to protest his collaborator's unwillingness to accept most of the changes or additions WHH had requested in the course of reading proof.

---

1. See the figure of the sieve in §241.
2. The *Conservative* was a Springfield newspaper intended ostensibly to promote the American Party presidential candidacy of Millard Fillmore in 1856. See §245, §246, §282, and *Herndon's Lincoln*, 228–29.

&c. Matheny did run with the Know Nothings in the social world and probably was somewhat sympathetic with them, though he pledged his honor to me that he was never a Know Nothing.[3]

Your proofs read well—suggest a thousand old facts to me and among them the above.

Your Friend

W. H Herndon

P.S—I see that you fall into the false idea that envy is a degrading passion. It is no more degrading than the passion for women. Envy is a spur—a whip, a nettle to drive us upward and onward. No quality that God has given us is degrading unless we make it so by abuse. I would erase the word *degrading* H

LC: *HW3533–34; Exp 4:10:2452–55*

244. To Jesse W. Weik

Springfield Ills Jany 11th '89

Friend Jesse—

. . .

In the last proofs you, in speaking of Stuart et al, say that *envy* is a *degrading* passion. I wish to say a word in order to put you right in your views of human nature. Every organ of the body and every faculty of the mind is for some good purpose in the providence of God. Envy is a feeling and whether it springs from the mind or body it is [inwrought?] in human nature and runs down through all the animal world. Envy has its divine purposes and *what* is it, for example? If I see a man in some high position—has wealth—has a pretty woman, and I envy the man's possesions it is an evidence that I want the position—want the wealth—want the pretty creature; and this *want* makes me struggle to get what I want. Envy is a spur—a whip—a nettle—a stimulant, driving my ambition to get what I do want. Envy to fret at another's sucess is a degrading passion when abused, or rather it is the abuse of envy—the [*illegible*] fret—that makes the *abuse* degrading. Jealousy is a good thing unless abused—so is appetite—so is the divine passion for woman—and so let no man say that God has given to nature, embodied in man, a degrading passion. It is poor imperfect man that abuses the divine in him. Lincoln was *envious* and he manifested it in many of his speeches: he wanted Douglas' position and his envy free from hate made him struggle for it, and that struggle gave him, not only Douglas' position but a higher one and satisfied his *wants* and gratified his *ambition*. Lincoln did not abuse that divine quality of his nature to get what he wanted. Lincoln in his speeches—various ones, tells on himself—proclaims it to the world—unwittingly—unconsciously—You do not like this kind of stuff, and yet it is necessary to think and get right. Your

---

3. For Know-Nothings, see §3, n. 2.

friend likes to get at the bottom of things by analysis, and induction, by synthesis and deduction, and so pardon his follies & his weaknesses. You, I think, are a worshiper of the pure narrative style—a good thing by the way, and I forgive you for the worship of it. Will you be as generous to your friend? I gave you my ideas of envy once before in a piece on Lincoln which you have in your possession. Good friend, pardon me for this repetition of ideas.

The more I think of Mrs Francis—Mary Todd and Mr. Lincoln the more am I convinced that Mary Todd helped Mrs. Francis in the conspiracy to yoke Lincoln. Miss Todd wanted L terribly and worked—played her cards through Mrs Francis' hands. By the way I now *think* that Speed told me a part [if not the whole?] of the conspiracy. Speed and [*manuscript torn*]sations about Lincoln and it [*manuscript torn*] he told me the story at a day—long before I commenced thoroughly taking notes in 1865—

Again the more I think of the Ann Rutledge story the more do I think that the girl had two engagements—ie that she was engaged to two men at one and the same. I do not recollect that she ever got a release from McNamar, though she tried to get one. Lincoln jumped in when Ann was ready to receive his jumps—. I do not think that Abm acted badly. I shall change my opinion of events & things on the coming of new facts and in more mature reflection in all cases—and so excuse me, for "sorter" wabbling around. I reserve the right to change when I am wrong in fact or opinion. I do not by this wish that the text of the book be changed because it is substantially correct anyhow. I have no suggestions to make & no pieces now to put in the book futher than you know of &c. Ugly weather here. How is it in Indiana?

LC: HW3535–36; Exp 4:10:2456–59

245. To Jesse W. Weik

Springfield Ills Jany 15th '89

Friend Weik:

. . . In the last chapter of our book please say *in a note* that the lectures which are the foundation of this chapter were delivered & published in '66—Decr.[1] Those lectures were the first analysis of Lincoln given to the country & are as true as the gospel. For Heaven's sake do fail to put the *Conservative* Know Nothing Matheny paper story &c &c on the true ground—*based on the facts*. If you will turn to Rosett's story & Matheny's you will find the facts. You have the evidence in our possession, and for Heavens' sake do not forget to erase the words—"*Lincoln told me so*" in the long armed ape Stanton story. I cannot swear at this late date where I got the story. I want to be on the safe side.[2] You will find what I refer to in the last corrected proof sent you and I think near the Conclusion of the

---

1. These lectures were delivered in December 1865.
2. WHH's disclaimer was ignored. See *Herndon's Lincoln*, 220.

last chapter. Friend, will you correct the Errors? Please answer. The *Conservative* was supposed to be a Democratic thing in *disguise* with a pro slavery tendency as interpreted—as seen out of Republican eyes.[3] I hope that you have made & will make all corrections of all the Errors which I will or have pointed out. I pray that there will be no mistakes. I do not fear the Critics, but I do fear myself.

. . .

Your Friend
W. H Herndon

LC: HW3537–38; Exp 4:10:2460–63

246. To Jesse W. Weik

Spfgd Ills Jany 19th '89

Friend Weik—

. . .

Your Friend
W H Herndon

P.S I now begin to think that when the *Conservative* was first started, under the care of Rosette[1] &c that it was a Filmore and a *Know Nothing* paper.[2] This was in 1856—. After this the paper fell into the hands of Stuart—Matheny & Co.; and it was then that it ceased to be *Know Nothing* and became a Bell & Everett paper in 1860. Whitehurst,[3] Matheny's brother in law was editor &c: it was at this time that I got in the Conservative the Richmond Enquirer article that created such a shaking in the dry bones. I simply state my opinion—see Rosett's and Matheny's evidence which I sent you about the time that I returned from Greencastle. In '60, if I am right, the Conservative was a democratic paper as thought by the Republicans, in disguise. Excuse me, won't you my good friend. H

LC: HW3539–40; Exp 4:10:2464–67

---

3. For the *Conservative*, see §243, §246, §282, and *Herndon's Lincoln*, 228–29.

---

1. John Rosette was a Springfield attorney.
2. For the *Conservative*, see §243, §245, §282, and *Herndon's Lincoln*, 228–29.
3. Stephen Whitehurst was a Springfield editor and politician.

247. To Jesse W. Weik

Spfgd Ills. Jany 20th '89

Friend Jesse:

. . .

Your Friend
W. H. Herndon

P.S Lincoln came out of the great Douglas race in 1858 after speaking probably 50 or 60 times a new man, vigorous—healthy—fresh as a young man, better colored—more elastic, more cheerful—less sad, stronger and improved every way. Douglas was worn out—voice gone—broken down—a wreck as it were. Saw both men during and just before and just after the race & state what I saw and know. Lincoln's voice was less husky—broken—wheezy—it improved all the time H

LC: HW3541–42; Exp 4:10:2469–71

248. To Jesse W. Weik

Spfgd Ills Jany. 28th '89

Friend Weik:

. . .

Your Friend
W. H Herndon

Second reading of the proofs. *Read carefully* the last half of pge 3 and the whole of 4th.

On pge about 351. where Lincoln put questions to Douglas you have left out a *good—Excellent* thing. The friends of Lincoln did not want him to put the questions to Douglas—see Lamon—Lincoln wanted to kill Douglas &c and said "I am fighting for bigger game &c."—see Lamon—Lincoln killed Douglas by those questions: he contemplated the consequences in this case just as he did Seward. . . . On page about 386 it is stated that L. went to Ohio and had his speeches printed &c. Not long since—say 2 years—saw a paragraph in the papers that Lincoln while in Ohio and while his speeches were being corrected &c published &c that he changed & altered parts of his speeches in material points. Lincoln only corrected typographical errors—& nothing more. Lincoln stated this to me: he changed no ideas—no sentiments—general language or the like. The speeches now stand exactly as he delivered them—Lincoln would not be guilty of changing his speeches.[1] I'll write out in full the whole story, as I got it from Lincoln, some time in the future. I recollect the story distinctly

---

1. For the changes AL made to the newspaper versions of his speeches in his 1858 debates with Douglas, see *Lincoln-Douglas Debates*, xxvii–xlvi.

The story in short is this—soon after Lincoln applied to Bradford to publish his speeches—Bradford refusing—he either wrote to Ohio or had application from the Ohio publishers Messrs _____² to publish his speeches; and things being understood between Lincoln & his Ohio publishers he went on to Ohio—Corrected his speeches in mere typographical errors—in mere wrong words—changing no ideas—sentiments nor opinions—thus making them exactly correspond to what he said on the stump though charged by some persons with material alterations some two or three years ago.³ Just before the speeches were published or a little before the publishers applied to Douglas for his consent to have speeches published with Lincoln, Douglas agreed to this upon the condition that he should have the privilege of writing an article somewhat after the order of the Harper article at Harpers Magazine⁴ to be inserted in the book with his speeches. To this the publishers—probably with Lincolns ideas of nonconsent refused the privilege. The publishers took the bull by the horns and published or commenced to publish Douglas' speeches. Douglas or his friends issued or threatened to get out an injunction stopping the publication of Douglas' speeches. The publishers in point of law thought that Douglas or his friends in the injunction could not succeed or Douglas thinking it wrong in public men to stop the publication of the speeches sent broadcast over the land are with their contents and not copy righted the publishers did publish the speeches in spite of the threatened injunction or the injunction in fact issued. Somehow the injunction was never carried out and the Lincoln Douglas speeches are the result. see the book. You know the balance H

LC: HW3543, [?]; Exp 4:10:2472–73; 4:11:2826–27

249. To Jesse W. Weik

Spfgd. Feby 5th '89

. . .

P.S No. 2

Is it your idea, your clear cut idea, that Mr. Lincoln's sadness—gloom and melancholy were caused *only* by domestic troubles & by a knowledge of his family history—his own descent &c.? If this is your idea let me say that you are, in my opinion, a little mistaken. My idea is that Lincoln's sadness &c were caused by prenatalism possibly—certainly by heredity—and his organism; and *intensified* by a knowledge of his family history—his descent &c resting on his sensative soul. I base my views on the evidences in your possession and to which I refer and make part of this. In reading the preface and judging—just now for the first time—from

2. John S. Bradford was a Springfield printer and politician. Follett, Foster, and Company of Columbus published the speeches made by AL and Stephen Douglas in their 1858 debates.

3. WHH's conception of AL's editorial method and results is far from the mark. See *Lincoln-Douglas Debates*, pp. xxvii–xlvi.

4. Stephen A. Douglas, "The Dividing Line between Federal and Local Authority: Popular Sovereignty in the Territories," *Harper's Magazine* 19 (September 1859), 519–37.

the silence of our book on the question and the preface I fear that you in part have formed a wrong opinion on this point. Please shape your ideas according to this before it is too late. I cannot ~~go over~~ in this letter go over the evidences proving my position.

[*In margin*: Lincoln's mother was a sad woman: she was disappointed in Thomas Lincoln—& doubted & grieved over it & lastly L's organism with the knowledge &c. &c did the business as I think. I include domestic troubles too.]

Again—you remember that in our book we speak of the principles of slavery covering—*according to Southern ideas from 1858* to '61, the white race as well as the black and refer to the Richmond Enquirer—Charleston Mercury &c to prove it. We do this when we speak of the Matheny & Stuart Conservative paper, published in this city about '58.[1] what I want to get at is this—Mr. Lincoln himself saw the trend and tendency of this southern opinion and gave it some hard licks in a message to Congress in Decr. 3d 1861. He said of this southern opinion this—"Monarchy itself is sometimes (in the southern Confederacy) hinted at as a possible refuge from the power of the people." See the message. (1861. Decr)[2] about 8th paragraph from the end of the message. Quote the whole paragraph if you can: it is a terrible denunciation of southern ideas, legislation &c. &c. . Please read the paragraph.

Again—Remember that it was announced by Stephens of Georgia that the new government of the southern confederacy was founded on the principles of slavery—that slavery was its grand & enduring corner stone.[3] See Arnold's life of Lincoln pge. 214. Keeping these things in mind you will well understand that the Richmond Enquirer &c spoke prophetically of the trend & tendencies of southern ultimate intention to enslave the poor whites &c. I am hurried to go to the City

Your Friend
W. H Herndon

LC: HW [?]; Exp 4:10:2477–78

250. To Jesse W. Weik

Springfield Ills. Feby. 9th 89 [1]

Friend Weik:

. . . On pge about 474–5, [*of the Herndon's Lincoln page proofs*] Hay uses the words *intellectual arrogance* and *unconscious assumption* and applies these to L & if correct *in Washington* they are false as to L. *in Ills*, but as they are not my words let them stand as written. Again Hay says that Lincoln was not a modest man—no great man is modest &c says Hay. Here again Mr L must have changed his nature

---

1. See *Herndon's Lincoln*, 228–29.

2. See "Annual Message to Congress," December 3, 1861, *Collected Works*, 5:51.

3. For Alexander Stephen's "cornerstone" declaration, see Nicolay and Hay, 3:202–3. For Stephen's objections to this account, see *Recollections of Alexander H. Stephens*, edited by Myra Lockett Avary (Baton Rouge: Louisiana State University Press, 1998 [1910]), 173.

in Washington somewhat. Lincoln *here* was a sensative man and to a certain extent a modest man. Let Hay's words stand as written. Hay's kid glove idea is very correct and well said. Such men could not understand this great rugged real man—a solid big God's reality.[1] One more word about Hay's idea. Lincoln may have been forced to manifest his real greatness—superiority—intellectual arrogance &c unconscious assumptions &c. by his environment in Washington: it is quite likely that he was forced—driven to this & I expect that this is the case. On reflection he had to rise or be forever swamped: he had to float or sink.

I distinctly remember that when Mr. Lincoln was making his *mum* speeches from Springfield to Washington in 1861, that they were called foolish efforts of an idiot—insane ravings of a weak man &c. The people did not understand the wise silences—the shrewdness—the secretiveness of the man. He said frequently on the trip that *there was a time to keep silence* and he kept his secrets and said nothing. These speeches are now I think being understood. They were prudent—wise—most proper & sagacious efforts of a wise and a great man. Mr. L did not want to commit himself and did not. When he got to Washington he had nothing to repent of— nothing to retract. Mr. Lincoln said at Lancaster Pa a very wise thing. Remember he wished to keep silence so as not to misunderstood nor misrepresented. He did not wish to keep repeating the same thing. What he said was this—"*But it is well known that the more a man speaks the less he is understood—The more he says one thing the more his adversaries contend he meant some thing else*". How true—how wise—how prudent and how sagacious. This should be nailed up on every man's door. Can you not use it in these proofs—say at or in about pge. 417–18. I quote L's words exactly. See Lincoln Memorial Album pge. 206.[2]

. . .

Your Friend,
W. H Herndon

P. S Read over the proofs the 2d time & made other corrections. H

LC: HW3547, [?]; Exp 4:10:2480–81, 4:11:2923–24

251. To Jesse W. Weik

Spfgd Ills Feby 9th '89 [2]

Friend Jesse:

I desire to leave my ideas on Mr. Lincoln's sadness—gloom & melancholy on the record. I have studied Mr. Lincoln from 1834 to the year 1889, and I have come to the conclusion long since that his sadness &c were caused by *three things*

---

1. WHH is reacting to points made about AL in a long letter from John Hay, somewhat toned down, quoted in *Herndon's Lincoln*, 308–10. For the original letter, see John Hay to WHH, September 5, 1866, *Herndon's Informants*, 332.

2. Oldroyd.

principally—first his organization—secondly his knowledge of the low condition of his family and his descent—not including any idea of his illegitimacy resting in his own mind; and thirdly his domestic relations—the hell of his domesticity or his domestic life. In this opinion I waive any idea of prenatalism, the influence of his mother's mind on him during her pregnancy, and hereditary influence. I would risk my chances in heaven on this long settled opinion, founded in long years of observation—experience, and reason. You may reply—"Do not the letters from Boston from Bartlett, the artist and from physicians—able distinguished and learned from Boston settle that question—rather unsesttle it", and to which I reply - "Neither Mr Bartlett nor any physician from Boston gave his opinion on the precise question.[1] Their letters and opinions were on Mr. Lincolns *low* organization, and not on the causes of Lincoln's sadness—gloom & melancholy". Now you have my distinc—definite and clean cut ideas. Generally I write to you loosely—carelessly—and rapidly, not caring what I said as to manner or matter of expression, but sticking to the precise or substantial truth. This was all I cared for, knowing that you would polish up things to suit yourself. I once talked about miasmatic influences on Lincoln in answer, as it were, to Nicolay & Hay's opinion on miasma.[2] You have the letters and I stick to them in substance, but they are not on the precise questions in this letter, though they bear on them somewhat. I need not say to you that I have studied the sciences somewhat relating to these questions, and think that I am fully supported by them. In conclusion let me say to you this—The world will never rest till it knows all about Lincoln, inside & outside.

Your Friend
W. H. Herndon

LC: HW3549; Exp 4:10:2484–85

252. To James H. Wilson[1]

Springfield Ills. Aug. 28 '89.

My Dear Sir:
   Your very kind and complimentary letter dated the 19th inst. is at hand for which I thank you. It pleases me to know that I please others. The only thing that I pride myself on about my life of Lincoln is the fact that I tried to tell the truth as I saw it.[2] In your letter you ask me some sharp and searching questions. It is true that I might have said much about myself and my very intimate knowledge

---

1. See §203.
2. See §180 and §181.

---

1. This is a document, presumably typewritten by JWW, headed: "(Copy of letter by W. H. Herndon to Gen. James H. Wilson. [handwritten appendage: "Wilmington Dela."])."
2. *Herndon's Lincoln.*

of Lincoln but I despise egotism so much that I preferred to say as little as possible about myself and my knowledge of Lincoln's inner life. I may say that I am sorry that I cannot answer your letter on knowledge. Mr. Lincoln was one of those peculiar men that are born into the world who have the genius of silence itself. Reticence was one of the man's attirbutes and a leading one—so much so that he seemed never to acknowledge assistance or favors. This man had no intuition about his nature and hence he had to reason things out—saw things through his brain—not through his soul. On the other hand, pardon me, I was intuitive and to that extent I was prophetic. I am a natural reformer—enthusiastic, hopeful and possibly have some moral courage about me. Lincoln was a natural conservative and I a natural radical. Mr. Lincoln has said in one or more of his letters that I was more learned than he was and had more advantages than he had. I therefore was the reader of the firm of "Lincoln & Herndon" and he the thinker. I read history, philosophy etc. and hence knew some of the experiences of the world. I told Mr. Lincoln as early as 1850–3 that Freedom and Slavery were antagonistic and that they could not co-exist on the same soil—that one or the other must perish soon—must go to the wall. I state these things to you in order to enable you to draw your own conclusions of my influence over Lincoln if I had any. I do not I do not know that I had any influence over the man and yet it is my opinion if that will help you along that I could not help but have more or less influence over my friend. In 1849—50 the world deserted Lincoln for his course on the Mexican war and yet I stood firm to my good friend, I was always as occasion would permit throwing out to Lincoln my Abolition ideas—what I thought and why I thought, Many of these doubtless were absorbed by the man. Our relations were always those of a close friendship. He had great confidence in my intuitions—my "bones philosophy" as he called it. I would not state these things to you or to any man had you not asked them. You wish to know Lincoln and I am trying to aid you in your wish. Mr. Lincoln never told me that I had any influence over him, but remember that he was the genius of silence; he kept his own secrets in all the ways of life. Mr. Lincoln had the genius of high cunning too. This great man was as a child in his sympathies—hated oppression—hated slavery in his soul from the cradle to the grave. He always took sides with the under dog. I say this was his very nature and I think that no man—no man's ideas ever caused it—only developed it and made it glow—burn brightly. Mr. Lincoln in his conservatism bordered on the timid and enthusiastic friends pushed him upward to a courageous and lofty plain. This is all I can say on knowledge. I tried hard to educate Lincoln in this matter. I wanted him to see slavery and its consequences as I saw them and I pushed matters as fast as I could but do not know that I effected anything. My mere opinion is another thing. Again Mr. Lincoln's heart was tender—tender as a woman's—was sympathetic—had a keen and quick sense of justice and rudeness and wrong stung him to the quick. He saw things accurately and seeing that slavery was wrong his whole nature abhorred it: he saw it and hated it and his honest soul would express itself. Lincoln came out of the lowest dregs of the poor white trash of the south but he had a healthy soul—nearly a perfect manhood at nature or by nature. This my friend is all that I can say to you just now—have been hard at work on my farm—have been working all morning and am somewhat tired. I may write to you again if the spirit moves me.

I have been in Illinois since 1820—was from Ky. and from Virginia parents, my father being a pro-slavery man and my mother an Abolitionist by nature; and I suppose I caught the hate of slavery from her and now good by for the present at least.

Your Friend
W. H. Herndon.

LC: HW3579–81; Exp 4:10:2541–43

253. To James H. Wilson[1]

Sep 23 1889.

X X X I now say to you that Mr Lincoln had a strong if not a terrible passion for women; he could ~~not~~ hardly keep his hands off from woman and yet much to his credit he lived a pure and virtuous life while married. His idea was that a woman had as much right to violate the marriage vow as the man—no more and no less His sense of right—his sense of justice—his honor forbade his violating his marriage vow. Judge Davis said to me in 1865 "Mr Lincoln's honor saved many a woman from ruin" and this is true to the spirit. This I know on my own knowledge. I have seen Lincoln tempted and I have seen him reject the approach of women.

LC: HW3594; Exp 4:10:2564

254. To James H. Wilson[1]

Oct. 1 1889

X X X X
"The Hanks family are or were a lecherous family—a family low even among the poor whites of the South. Lincoln as a matter of course knew all about them This hurt Lincoln in the extreme being very sensitive. I was careful never to say Hanks in his presence. Mr. Lincoln ordered a monument put over his fathers remains but never did over his mother's ashes. The whole Hanks family and Thomas Lincoln give a humble history. I have some evidences in my possession that old Thomas Lincoln, Abrahams father, was castrated—cut about the time that Abraham was begotten or

---

1. This document written in JWW's hand, headed: "Copy of letter by Herndon to Gen James H. Wilson." This and others of its kind presumably represent JWW's excerpts from letters he has returned to their owner.

---

1. This document written in JWW's hand, headed: "Copy of letter Oct. 1 1889 by Herndon to Gen James Wilson marked 'Private.'"

it may be before. Thomas Lincoln had no life—had no force—a mere animal; he simply vegetated; he simply crawled along breathing now and then. One story is that there was but one Nancy Hanks. If that is so she was Dennis Hanks mother and Dennis is a bastard. The whole history of this affair is a curious one and a shocking one. The Hanks people were a clever people—a social people and at heart a good people but unfortunately circumstances controlled them—made them what they were. The new generation of the Hanks are all right, honest—virtuous social and generous excellent citizens. I said as little of the Hanks in the life of Lincoln as I could because they are—the new generation among us. The Lincoln family were of the middle class. All this Hanks history I think stung Mr. Lincoln to the quick. From all that is in the book and from what I say to you made me say that Lincoln was of unknown origin—see page 182. I can say no more to you now x x x Lincoln was in mere meanness involving no principles rather supple [twisty?] and in this he did [doge?] less than any man I ever saw and I have grown up among politicians[2]

LC: HW3601; Exp 4:10:2575

255. To James H. Wilson[1]

Springfield Oct 15 '89.

My Dear Sir:

In answer to your last letter dated the 4th inst let me say that soon after the death of Mr. Lincoln I determined to write his life. Following up this idea I went up to Chicago and examined Dennis Hanks. This was about 1866–67.[2] He told me that Thomas Lincoln was castrated but refused to tell me when or for what. I inferred from Dennis' conversation that he knew the fact. In that examination he said that some soldiers during the war of 1812 came along and here he stopped and I inferred that Thomas had a fight and that he was injured in that fight. I have the words of men—probably founded in reputation that they or those from whom they received the information had seen the evidences of Thomas' castration—saw him in swimming. Now for some other facts. Thomas Lincoln married Nancy Hanks in 1806 and had a child by her in eight months less two days following the date of the marriage. Abraham was the second child and was born in about three years after the first child and the third child was born in about three years after Abram. The births followed regularly. This would bring the begetting of the last child about 1812. Now at this date Nancy ceased to bear any more children though she was in the prime of life and a buxom and well-developed woman.

I said to you in a former letter that Thomas Lincoln just vegetated up. He was devoid of energy—had no get up and go—was lazy, shiftless and of no force—was

---

2. This sentence is squeezed into the remaining space at the bottom of the page and probably accounts for the difficulty of deciphering certain words, as well as for its lack of coherence.

---

1. This document written in JWW's hand, headed: "Letter to Gen J H Wilson Oct 15 1889 by Herndon / Private."

2. WHH interviewed Dennis Hanks in Chicago on June 13, 1865. See Herndon's Informants, 35.

a worthless but rather good fellow. I suppose that the castration, if any, took all energy and life out of the man. Now put this and that together and the inference follows that Thomas L. was castrated but the when and for which I cannot exactly say, not wishing to go outside of my records evidences—proofs. Again Dennis told me that Thomas Lincoln found one Inlow in his house under peculiar circumstances and that they had a terrible fight about the matter Thomas biting off Inlow's nose. I have tried to get Dennis to tell all he knows but he refuses to state more. I have letters from persons in Kentucky that state that there was but one Nancy Hanks—that this Nancy bore Dennis—an illegitimate. Now if this be true than this Nancy is the mother of our Abraham and not above suspicion. Dennis says there were two Nancy Hanks and if this is so then Abraham probably is all right. A Mr. Friend in Ky says that there was but one Nancy Hanks and that no two were ever seen.[3] This man belongs to the Hanks family somehow. This man's father, or grandfather was the father of Dennis. There were many Hanks girls but no two Nancys. Abraham Lincoln once wrote to an inquirer this: "You are mistaken in my mother" but how mistaken he did not say. I never have heard that Lincoln ever went to his mothers' grave. He never put nor had put up a foot or head board to his mother's grave though he had one put over his father's. Mr Lincoln was always "mum" about his mother. I have always thought that Lincoln knew the various stories—rather the births of his mother—father and other relatives. I never dared to ask him any question about the Hanks family

I have written to Dennis asking to know if his mother was Abraham's mother but he will not answer. I have had others try to get out the fact but they too fail. Dennis was driven from his mother's home by the man who married his mother whoever that was

LC: HW3610–12; Exp 4:10:2578–80

256. To James H. Wilson[1]

Oct 22 1889

"I from the facts disclosed in my last letter inferred that Thomas Lincoln was castrated sometime near '12 during the war. There is another state of averred facts, namely that some people often saw Thomas Lincoln in swimming and saw that he was castrated or so born. We must now to get at the thing draw another inference from the facts so averred by others to me. The question is this—Is it usual for a grown-up man to go in swimming and expose his misfortune—show that he has lost somehow his manhood? From my knowledge I would say that a sensative person and the defect would on this ground make him sensitive, would almost stand crucifixion before he would expose to the gaze of men the loss of

---

3. See *Herndon's Informants*, 178.

---

1. This document written in JWW's hand, headed: "Copy of letter by Herndon to J. H. Wilson Wilmington Del / *Private*."

his manhood. I am trying to talk about *men*, not boys. Mere boys on the other hand would not care so much as men—at least until they approached manhood and felt the shame of it. From this state of averred facts I infer that for some unknown reason to me that Thomas lost his manhood during his boyhood days. I am informed by correspondents that for a money consideration Thomas L. married Nancy Hanks and that she had a child, her first born, in eight months less two days after marriage. I understand that physicians as well as medical books hold that no eight month child ever lived to manhood or womanhood. This is certainly a general rule. It is asserted to me that there was but one Nancy Hanks. If this is so then Thomas married Dennis Hanks mother who had one child before marriage. I am informed that Dennis Hanks says that there were two Nancys but of this there is a doubt. You will remember that Thomas had a terrible fight with Inlow. Dennis told me in person that he was an illegitimate and that the fight between Thomas and Inlow grew out of a peculiar state of circumstances. Keep in mind the worthlessness, laziness, and want of vim and vigor of Thomas. I am not asserting to you anything. I am stating to you only what I am told and you must form your own opinion. Consider my two letters in this special subject One and read over and over as Lincoln would say "till you get the hang of the school house." The reason I cannot be more positive in my opinions is because the facts are denied me in which to be more positive. Dennis Hanks refuses to tell me more or reveal more. I have written to him and have got others to do so but he remains mum. I would clear Lincoln and his whole family from this state of facts if I could do so. I almost worship Lincoln to tell you the naked truth; and what I have said about him apparently disparagingly was to show the power of the man in overcoming or greatly modifying the terrible environments that surrounded him in youth or rather in bending or controlling them to his own purposes or ends.

X X X X

You will please keep these two letters because they may be of some importance in the great future Other facts may come to light and with these two letters all will be made plain to the world. These letters are *private* except as herein stated and are not to be published under any circumstances till I cross the great river. I am abused enough without drawing out more

LC: HW3617–18; Exp 4:10:2589–90

257. To Jesse W. Weik

Spfgd Ills Jany 23d '90

Friend Weik—

. . .

I wish you would write out a Short eulogy on Lincoln's virtue during his married life. Lincoln I know, as well as I know anything, was true to his wife—to his marriage vow. His idea was that a woman had the same right to play with her tail that a man had and no more nor less and that he had no moral or other right to violate the sacred marriage vow. I have heard him say it a dozen or more times.

"Lincoln's honor" as Judge Davis said, "saved many a woman". This is true to my own knowledge. I have seen woman make advances & I have seen Lincoln reject or refuse them. Lincoln had terribly strong passions for woman—could scarcely keep his hands off them and yet he had honor and a strong will and these enabled him to put out the fires of his terrible passion. It is a physiological truth that most male consumptives have goatish passions. This eulogistic piece should have gone in the 1st ed of our book but was somehow overlooked. Don't fail to put it in the 2d ed.[1] It would have done us good then & will now.

. . .

Your Friend
W. H Herndon

LC: HW3643–44; Exp 4:10, 2629–2632

258. To Jesse W. Weik

Spfgd Ills. Mch. 7th '90

Friend Weik—

. . .

Mr White thinks that the story &c. of the Chronicals of Reuben or the Grigsby Episode ought to be stricken out in the 3d Edit, as it cannot be in the 2d Edit.[1] If it had never gone in the 1st Edit *possibly* I would say—don't put it in, but as it has gone before the world I am, as I now feel, opposed to modifying—changing or wholy omitting it in the 3d Edit. The whole story only goes to show the condition of society in Indiana—Lincoln's home from 1816 to 1831—that Lincoln was effected by his environments, but that in after life he was strong and great enough, through his struggles, to cast it off and rise above his early environments, which not one man in a million can do. The Episode is a part of his history—explains the *germs of his wit & his humor*. I admire the good tastes of life as well as any man or woman and cannot be made to defend the nasty—obscene or vulgar under any circumstances, but I *do* fail to see why the Episode causes a blush on any man's or woman's cheek. Some people are too nice for this material sphere—this muddy globe of ours. I'll think about this matter further. You know that I am Easily managed—want our book to be a glourious success.

Your Friend
W. H Herndon

Make no kind of a reply to what Nicolay & Hay say of our book. H

LC: HW3654; Exp 4:10:2650–51

---

1. By "2d ed." WHH means "second printing." The publisher of their biography had gone bankrupt shortly after publication in June of the previous year, and the authors were awaiting the publisher's reorganization and a promised second printing, which came a few months later with few changes.

1. Horace White greatly admired *Herndon's Lincoln* and was advising WHH and JWW on revisions. The "2d Edit." refers to the second printing of their biography, which was already in press. The "3d Edit" refers to a proposed revised and augmented edition. For the "Chronicles of Reuben," see §176.

259. To Cyrus O. Poole

Springfield, Ill., March 14 [1890].

Friend Poole:

Your clever note, dated the 3d inst., enclosing a slip from *The Sun*, is before me. I thank you for both. You are very correct when you say that I am interested in whatever is said of Lincoln, the great American *thinker*, king of men in the noblest sense. I have read the article with pleasure.

What Douglas said is very true Lincoln's heart was tender, but it was the feeblest organ of the man It is true, too, that Lincoln had a "high cunning" about him—shrewdness, tact, sagacity in the management of men: it was akin to genius, there being nothing low about it. He never tried to rule events but was governed by them. He keenly watched the flow of the great events of his time, and governed himself according to the forces that moved the world of man around him.

His philosophy was a fatalistic one, rather, his idea was that the universe is governed by law. Hence he waited on the results of those laws. He saw in the distance quicker than other men the results of the play or the forces, and seized his opportunity. As to men, he knew that they acted *alone* from motive, and he touched that spring adroitly.

You know there is a great deal of nonsense going around in the world about Lincoln, and men who did not know the man had better go slow in their beliefs of him, of what he thought and what he said and did. I think I understand Mr. Lincoln tolerably well, and hence I cast aside many floating rumors of and about him. Lincoln was slow to think, slow to act, and very cautious—wisely cautious His caution was sometimes regarded as overcaution. It seemed to some a species of timidity. Mr Lincoln was not going to be caught napping when he wrote that Weitzel letter.[1] He determined that no one should misinterpret his ideas or infer from his language, directly or indirectly, that he acknowledged the lawful existence of the Southern Confederacy. Hence the great caution of it, and the time it took him to write it.

One or two other words, and I'll quit this subject. You now know that Mr. Lincoln was a broad-minded, liberal-souled man. His philosophy made him so, in part at least. He believed that the present man was made by his environments—the thousand mental, moral, and physical facts around him—and was a mere child of circumstances. This he has often said to me in our office speculations. Hence he could say, "With malice toward none and charity for all." His philosophy was broad and his religion grand. To a certain extent he was a child of destiny, and yet it was his intellectual power that enabled him to see, away in advance, the play of the general forces that give man his opportunities, which he seized, and made himself, to that extent, a child of destiny.

---

1. See *Herndon's Informants*, 413.

In my "Life of Lincoln" I tried to stick to facts without giving my opinions about them or the man, leaving each person to form his own opinions. If I had commenced eulogizing I would have gone too far and been called a blind hero worshipper, a mere fool—which I would have been in that particular.

Your friend,
W. H. Herndon

New York Sun, *March 24, 1890.*[2]

260. To Jesse W. Weik

Springfield Ills April 4th '90

Friend Weik—

Inclosed you will find a letter of mine written to C. O. Poole, my old friend, which was published in the N.Y. Sun of the 24th Mch. '90.[1] The little slip accompanying the letter will explain why it was written. It was a hasty letter, not written for publication, but I suppose it struck Poole & possibly the Editor of the Sun. Please read the letter over & over & get the spirit of it. Jesse—there is a good chance for you to write out an eloquent note. In the first place Lincoln placed his administrative abilities in his power *to rule men*: he said this to Swett—see our life of. L. pg. 533. Read carefully from the words—"In his conduct of the war" down to & including—"I have kept these discordant elements together as well as any one could."[2] When this is done read his farewell Springfield speech wherein he—Lincoln—appeals to the Christians invokes their power & winds them around his finger see life of L 486.[3] Then think a little. When this is done look at his cabinet &c. &c. and why they—the members of it, were so appointed—men who opposed him in the Chicago Convention. Lincoln was a shrewd—sagacious long headed man—a cunning fox. From the time of his farewell Springfield speech he was at long head work reconciling antagonistic elements—discordant elements with which he had to deal: he used all just as he wished. I say he used all and made all his tools; he was the superior of all and governed all by his intellectual superiority. By appointing these Cabinet men he made the friends of each his friends Now read Swett's letter as above refered to and you will catch the idea of the note or piece which I want you to write out fully & eloquently. Read my letter to Poole over & over; it will help you. Can't such a piece go in the text of the book. Lincoln was a long headed old fox—a shrewd manipulator of men—a man full of practical political sagacities. As Swett says he was the great American trimmer when men

2. Printed under the headline "LINCOLN'S HIGH CUNNING / His Mental Habits and Philosophy Described by his Former Law Partner." Retrieved from the Library of Congress website, "Chronicling America" (http://chroniclingamerica.loc.gov).

1. See §259.
2. *Herndon's Lincoln*, 319.
3. Ibid., 291.

had to be used.[4] [*In margin*: Lincoln's idea was, how to make the North *one*—a solid & united *one*]

What I have said in the Poole letter and in this letter is true of Lincoln—true to the letter and the spirit.

. . .

Your Friend
W. H Herndon

P.S The note can best come in on pge 541. after the words "bargained for"

LC: HW3657; Exp 4:10:2656–57

261. To Horace White

Springfield Ills. April 28th '90

Friend White—[1]

Your letter of the 22d inst, requesting information, is before me; and in reply let me say that I never wrote a page—paragraph—sentence or word for Lamon's life of Lincoln, and never suggested to him any course or method to be pursued in his book. I sold to Lamon for $2000[2] a *copy* of my manuscripts—evidences &c of the Lincoln records, facts which I had gathered up to 1870–1 Lamon used my name, as I suppose to, give his book some popularity. If what facts—opinions— speculations &c &c. which he got of me were stricken from his book there would not be much left of it, as I think. The reason why Lamon did not finish his 2d vol—complete the life of Lincoln was because of a three cornered fight. Lamon & Black had a quarrel between themselves about the book and about the sum paid for the copy of the MSS. Lamon made to Black some statement as to the sum paid for the MSS which was not true as I am told. Lamon is a stubborn devil & would have nothing further to do in the matter. Lamon & Black had a kind of a quarrel with their publishers & lastly Holland's review of the book, which was a mean thing, squelched things completely. Black lost his money & his time through this mess.

In your letter you refer me to Lamon Pge 396 and ask me whether the paragraph referred to is true or false. In reply let me state that it is in all things substantially correct. In speaking of the democracy—of Douglas & the Charleston Convention; and the divided State of the democracy in '59 '60 Lincoln has said to me—often said to me and to others in my presence *substantially* this—"The end is not yet, but an explosion must come in the near future. Douglas is a great man in his way and has quite unlimited power over the great mass of his party,

---

4. See Leonard Swett to WHH, January 17, 1866, in *Herndon's Informants*, 165.

---

1. In top margin: "Private as to Lamon, Black &c including publishers."
2. For a statement by WHH giving the price as $4,000, see §84.

especially in the North. If he goes to the Charleston Convention, which he will do, he, in a kind of Spirit of revenge, will split the Convention wide open and give it the devil; & right here is our future success or rather the glad hope of it". By the way Lincoln prayed for this state of affairs: he saw in it his opportunity and wisely played his line. Lincoln studied the tendency & trend of political affairs and wisely drew his scientific—*yes scientific* conclusion as to general results and bided calmly his time. Lincoln was the great American *thinker* & *the unknown*—at least to the mass of men in America.

Your Friend
W. H. Herndon

P.S—Lincoln felt that Douglas was *the* strong man and that he must be put out of the way politically. He did not fear any man in the South and so L acted for 5 or 6 years: he was after Douglas—always scheming & planning H

ALPL: Horace White Papers

262. To Horace White

Springfield Ills May 9th '90

Friend White—[1]

. . .

Your Friend
W. H Herndon

In addition to what I have said to you about Lincoln & Douglas—I have heard L say in '59 that the Southern Slave holder throughout the South has treated & is treating Douglas badly, for has not D taught the people of the North that there is no difference between right & wrong on this question of slavery; he has said in the Senate Chamber that he did not care whether slavery was voted up or voted down. This indifference he has taught to the Northern Democracy—for years. H
Lincoln in his office conversations grew eloquent often—prophetic too.

ALPL: Horace White Papers

263. To Caroline H. Dall

Springfield Ills. July 19th '90

My Dear Friend:
. . . In your letter you state that Lincoln was an illegitimate and that I should have so stated. I did not think that the conflicting evidences before me justified

---

1. In top margin: "Private The notes of Lincoln & Douglas are not intended for your guide but to interest you in the by gone days—nothing more. H"

the bold assertion in a book whatever my private opinion was. Had I been certain
of the supposed fact I should have so asserted. Possibly I may have softened some
things but you will please remember that 20 or 25 years change our opinions of
men—measures and policies. In this book business I had no other policy than to
speak the truth, as I saw or remembered it. I thank you for your good opinion of
my book. I am willing that you shall leave the notes spoken of by you to posterity.
. . .

Your good friend as ever
W. H. Herndon

MHS: Caroline Healey Dall Papers

264. To Jesse W. Weik

Spfgd Ills. July 23d 90

Friend Jesse
. . .
I told you once that Lincoln had a terrible sexual passion, but that his sense of
justice—honor &c controlled. You know what Davis said about L's passion namely
that "L's honor saved a many a woman." Now, Jesse, give Lincoln a good note on
this question: he richly deserves it. I have seen pretty women make advances to
L which were rejected & you probably know one of 'em. Lincoln, after marriage,
was pure in this particular. All honor to him for that! Lincoln & I have talked
over this matter often and his idea was that a *woman* had in this particular just
the same rights as the man, but neither had the right to violate the marriage vow.
. . .

Your Friend
W H Herndon

LC: HW3673–74; Exp 4:10:2688–91

265. To Jesse W. Weik

Spfgd Ills July 25th 90

Friend Jesse
. . . I am quite intuitive about men as well as coming events. Lincoln used
to pay great attention or had respect rather to that peculiarity of my nature; &
in coming to the office of a morning, during the exciting years form '54 to '60
he would always say—"Billy—how is your bones philosophy this morning": he
said this, because I frequently told him that this or that would *inevitably* take
place because I feel it *in* my *bones*. This I told him often. Lincoln was entirely

logical—had no intuition at all. [*In margin*: You will see this better told in the every day life of Lincoln[1]]

. . .

Your Friend

W. H Herndon

LC: HW3675–76; Exp 4:10:2692–95

266. *To Jesse W. Weik*

Spfgd Ills. July 29th '90

Friend Jesse—

I refer to or send you some of the sayings—maxims—thoughts—short things of Lincon, showing his philosophy—nature & the like. Some of them ought to be put in gold and hung up in every mans house who looks to the future.[1]

		page
"That truth"	see Lincoln Mem Album[2]	page 231–2
Faith in the people	" " "	231–2
Events controlled him—Lincoln	" " "	312.
Fatalism see Arnold life of L.[3]		81
Keep silence.	see Mem Album[4]	158
Shifting scenes—see it all up	" "	192–3
The more a man speaks &c	" "	206
Keep silence	" "	192
Waited on events	" "	170–192
God's Decree—can't be reversed	" "	87
Right makes might	" "	141.
Hit at theology—Christianity"	" "	100
Hit at Christianity—miracles[5]	" "	228
God's will I'll do	" "	228
Must study the plain facts however	" "	228
Wait to know what Providence designs Lincoln Mem Album		pge 228
Motives rule men see our life of L[6]		pge. 554
No mortal could &c Lincoln Mem Album	" "	338
God's purposes—absolute—perfect	" "	338.

---

1. *Every-Day Life*, 260.

---

1. Alongside the entries, on both pages of the document: "suggestive & use those which you like".
2. Oldroyd.
3. Arnold.
4. Oldroyd.
5. In margin: "Miracles played out & God has quit revealing and closed up shop."
6. Original 1889 edition.

Invented a word see Barrett's life of L[7]			262
Constitution perfect—one bite	"	"	98
Reverence for law & order	"	"	98
Bad bargain, brake	"	"	782
Keep promise	"	"	456–7
Held the discordant elements see our Life[8]			533
Chief gem of my character	our life		223
Bad promises broken	Bartlett[9]		782
New state founded in slavery	"		786
Women of America	"		478
Constitution sacred, hands off	"		98
Monarchy South	"		309
Keep promises	our life of L223		

Could send you many more such things but I'll tire you out. These things—some of 'em will prove the text and assist you very much in forming your final opinion of L's philosophy and ideas. I hope that I've got the right pages put down. If there are mistakes hunt 'em up—ie find the correct page, book &c.

LC: HW3677–78; Exp 4:10:2696–97

267. *To Jesse W. Weik*

Spfgd Ills. Aug 3d '90

Friend Jesse—

Inclosed you will find "my piece".[1] Please read & reread it carefully—copy it & correct it. In it I say that Mr. Lincoln in '56–8 wrote a letter to Mr Wallace.[2] You have a copy of Wallace's letter, if not lost. If you can't find it among our papers you will find it in Lamon's Lincoln. In "my piece" I state the substance of one part of the letter. Please turn to Lamon & read the letter and if I am wrong modify. I haven't seen the letters for 20 or 25 years. I do not know what *page* it is in Lamon, having given away my Lamon to Remsburg. When you have done all this fix the proper *page* in "my piece" where the letter is to be found. I have left a blank for it. Fix the *date* of the Wallace letter in "my piece" if I am wrong, which I may be—guessed at the date. I remember what Lincoln said—read the letter to me before he sent it to Wallace.

None of Mr. Lincoln's biographers so far as I remember seem to understand the purposes—objects & interests of his little *non committal* speeches. He, as was the custom on such occassions, had to show himself on his journey to Washing-

---

7. Barrett.
8. *Herndon's Lincoln* (1889 edition).
9. Barrett.

---

1. This refers to "Lincoln's Silence—Sayings and Wisdom," LC: Exp 4:11, 2921–22, 2943–44.
2. See AL to Edward Wallace, Oct. 11,1859, *Collected Works*, 3:486–87.

ton—say something and be polite to the people: he purposely said nothing that would bind him or his administration in the future—did not wish to irritate the South—was himself *somewhat* ignorant of the feelings of the ruling class north and had to feel his way slowly—cautiously In one or more of his little journey speeches he implored the people to keep quiet and say nothing & do nothing that would further increase bad feeling—north as well as south. The future will give Lincoln—unbounded credit for his silence &c. A good many of the American news papers called these little & uncomprehended speeches—"Abes last jokes" & some of the English press joined in the loud guffaw. Please, put this in substance in "my note" when you correct and finish it. Write a good note on this whole subject as stated &c in "my piece". I would rewrite it but, Jesse, I am 2/3ds sick & 1/3 worn out with work on my farm—have to gather up things and peddle 'em out in the city. It's hot & dry here.

Your Friend
W. H Herndon

P.S Let us push Lincolns nature out to public view & defend him. H

LC: HW3679; Exp 4:10:2698–99

268. To Jesse W. Weik

Spfgd Ills. Aug 8th '90

Friend Jesse—

If you will turn to your Lincoln Memorial Album[1] at pge 72 and read from the 9th line—top—to "*love him*" on the same page you will get a kind of an idea that prompts me to send you a thousand little things, more or less.[2] The reading world loves to read of those delicate touches of life—heart pulses & thought flashes: they open the door wide of this our individual life and give us a glimpse of the dreams & speculations of the soul. All men love to get a full view of the good & the great. You know my tastes. I want and crave the sweet *&* gentle side of life—things that are pleasant as a general rule.

I send you some of Lincoln's *thoughts* in addition to the many heretofore sent you.[3]

170.	Lincoln Mem Album—development of the last fact[4]			
170.	"	"	"	speak only officially when &c[5]
180	"	"	"	Hear & see everything to the last idea[6]

1. Oldroyd.
2. The passage referred to reads in part: "When we see the gentler feelings of the human heart combined in a prominent man with a rigid sense of duty and the intellectual power and perseverance necessary to fulfill that duty, we not only admire that man but revere and love him."
3. Note alongside the items listed: "Suggestions only / May assist you."
4. Oldroyd "Speech at Buffalo, N.Y."; *Collected Works*, 4:220–21
5. Ibid.
6. Oldroyd, "Speech at Albany"; *Collected Works*, 4:226.

180 & 192	"	"	"	Silence now as to national policies[7]
180	"	"	"	Have patience—restrain ourselves
192.	"	"	"	Want to see all up before I act
264	Holland's life of L—Keep cool—no crisis &c[8]
196	Lincoln Mem Album—Preserve the union[9]
158	"	"	"	Get the exact idea & definition[10]

You will perceive in one of the above references (180) that Mr Lincoln pleads for patience & to put all restraints on our passion—ill temper—hot acts &c. Strange as it may appear to you it is nevertheless a fact, *in my opinion*, that Mr Lincoln never fully comprehended the situation; he talks of patience when treason has done its work; he should have talked of, "to arms" or kept his silence. In a speech made at Columbus Ohio he said, "It is a good thing that there is *no more than anxiety* for there is nothing going wrong &c &c". What!—Nothing going wrong?. Why, seven of the Southern states had seceded before that speech was made and he knew it. The speech was made the 13th Feby '61. The seven states had seceded in the fall & winter before. See Lincolns speech at Columbus Ohio Holland 262.[11] Again at Steubenville he said—"In plain words there is really *no crisis*, except an artificial one".[12] This was spoken on the 14th Feby '61 & 7 of the seceded states had gone out so far as they could—see Arnold 178.[13] When we consider that only 75000 men were called out to subdue 12 or 14 millions of brave people does it not appear that Lincoln did not comprehend the situation at all or begin to. He did not comprehend the situation or he *did* and concealed his ideas which was a crime under the circumstances, as I think. I prefer to think that L did not fully comprehend the state of affairs. You know that L had not good judgements and did love the truth. What think you? I said to you in a former late letter that none of the biographers of Lincoln explained the intents & purposes of those little speeches. Holland at pge. 254 does somewhat understand them. Barrett does not and I do not think that Lamon does. Arnold does not as I can find in his life of L. Jesse, explain the intents—purposes—objects &c of these little efforts of Lincoln. Lincoln said these little speeches were hard to make—see Barrett 533. I now shall say no more on the little speeches or their purposes &c.

Let me give you an idea of what I mean by saying I love *heart touches*—&c as a general rule. I have a lady neighbor by the name of Vannattin; she & her sister when young & residing in Spfgd were sent out to get up the cows & on returning home the girls were playfully running at a rapid rate backwards on the pavement,

7. Oldroyd, "Speech at Albany" and "Speech to Various Republican Associations"; *Collected Works*, 4:226 and 4:230–31.

8. Holland, "Speech at Pittsburgh, Pennsylvania"; *Collected Works*, 4:211.

9. Oldroyd, "Speech in the Senate Chamber. Trenton, New Jersey"; *Collected Works*, 4:235–36.

10. Oldroyd, "Speech to the Members of the Legislature of Indiana Who Waited upon Him at His Hotel"; *Collected Works*, 4:195–96 (citing a different report and text of the same speech).

11. *Collected Works*, 4:204.

12. Ibid., 4:211. These words were spoken not at Steubenville but at Pittsburgh, Pennsylvania.

13. Arnold.

when, through a hole in the pavement or its bad condition, her foot was caught and she was falling—she going west & Lincoln going east, when on seeing the girls situation Lincoln was moved to run quickly to her in order to prevent the fall and as she fell he caught her in his long & giant arms, saying to her as he gently and sweetly looked down in her face, after the girls fears had passed off, "Now you can say—you have been in Abraham's bosom." Mrs. Vannattin is truthful & remembers the words—is not genius enough to make up such a story.[14] The many references to books in this & former letters are not on the above line. The books have reference to L's *thoughts*—ideas &c.

If you will look at the last Century you will see that Nicolay & Hay's life of L is to be in 10 vols & to be ready for sale by Novr. '90—this fall. When can we get out our 3d Edit? Whoop it up—whoop it up, Jesse. I am on my way to the city and am somewhat in a hurry.

Your Friend
W. H Herndon

LC: HW3680–81; Exp 4:10:2700–03

269. To Jesse W. Weik

Spfgd Ills. Aug 19th '90

My good Friend—

You will see by the papers that Harrison & Wanamaker have excluded from the mails Tolstoi's Kreutzer Sonata. This act is despotic & tyranical, and will bring up eventually the whole question the rights of the free press—free speech—free mails &c. When Douglas in 1853–4 introduced the Kansas—Nebraska bill I distinctly recollect of telling Lincoln that though I deprecated the introduction of the bill, yet I thanked God that it opened for discussion the whole question of human liberty—free press—free men—free mail, &c. This question of free mails for the people will in time stalk into Congress: it will not down. The above—what I told Lincoln is not for our book—*nor* is what I said to you about my bones philosophy as expressed by Lincoln—nor is what I said to Lincoln about the co-existence of freedom & slavery on the same soil—. These sayings of mine to Lincoln nor Lincoln's expression—"How is your bones philosophy &c" to me to go in our book, because I am not egotistical nor do I wish to be so considered. I simply state these things to you as a friend.

. . .

Your Friend on the Road to the city
W. H Herndon

LC: HW3682; Exp 4:10:2704–05

---

14. Another version of this story is in *Herndon's Informants*, 721–22.

270. To Jesse W. Weik

Spfgd Ills. Septr 24th '90

Friend Weik—

Inclosed is a letter from McArthur which you may wish to see. I have had it a long time and should have sent it to you before this. Read it and file it away, if you wish. I send you likewise a letter from Mr King—an old abolitionist—friend of mine—is truthful. He says that Alsop[1]—an other old abolitionist and friend of mine and himself got the anti slavery men *generally* to vote for Lincoln in *'46* in this then Lincoln's district. I have no doubt of the truth of this—none at all. This will account for Lincoln's overwhelming majority over Peter Cartwright. I think Erastus Wright—the pension man[2] opposed Lincoln. You can make a note of these facts—or fact. Read King's letter—particular passage referred to marked by me. The note will fit in our book at pge. 273–4. Kings letter I have answered giving him & Alsop great credit for what they & friends did in the matter. They increased Lincoln's majority greatly. This I know of my own knowledge. King and Alsop were strong leaders of the anti slavery cause in Lincolns district in '46.

About the year '56 a gentleman from Chicago by the name of Z Eastman— Editor of an anti slavery paper in Chicago, came into my office & introduced himself to me.[3] After some general & running conversation on *this* subject & *that* Mr Eastman said to me, "Herndon I know you as a firm & true anti slavery man, but we anti-slavery men North don't know Mr Lincoln so well. What are his ideas on slavery and can we trust him?" I said to Mr Eastman in reply—"Mr Lincoln is a natural born anti slavery man and now you go home and use the influence of your paper for Lincoln". (This paper was the predecessor of the Chicago Tribune or the Press & Tribune, I forget exactly which—think it was the Tribune).[4] "Can you trust yourself", I said further to Mr Eastman "& if you can then you can trust Lincoln, for God will keep him right. Now you keep the people right and as to Lincoln you can trust. Tell our friends in Chicago & elsewhere to *trust*". Mr Eastman was a committee man from Chicago who was appointed to investigate &c. He went home to Chicago & opened his paper, as far as he could, for Lincoln. This is how the anti slavery men in Illinois were such strong friends of Mr. Lincoln. Eastman was appointed by Mr. Lincoln U. S. Consul for Great Britain as I remember it. Mr Eastman & myself have written to each other since this matter transpired. In this conversation Mr Eastman asked me if it would not be wise for the anti slavery men to go into the Know Nothing lodges & rile them. I said to him—"No—never do this wrong to our cause. We are all for the broadest liberty for all men." I have cut things short. Our conversation in '56 was probably two or three hours long & much was said of Lincoln—slavery—the anti-slavery cause—the progress of it—hopes &c. &c. I have forgotten the name of Eastman's

---

1. Thomas Alsop and Franklin T. King.
2. See §129.
3. For an earlier version, see §41.
4. Eastman published two anti-slavery newspapers in Chicago: the *Western Citizen* and *Free West*. The latter merged with the *Chicago Tribune* in 1856.

paper—have once or twice called or said it was the *Star*, but I think I was wrong in this. The Tribune men can tell you.

Let me tell you something else which I distinctly remember—see our life of Lincoln pges. 367–8, & read what I said as Editorial in the Journal. You will perceive in the piece that Douglas frequently interrupted Lincoln & now as to the why of it.[5] Lincoln in opening his speech said this—"I willingly give Senator Douglas, who now sits in front of me, the privilege of correcting me where I am wrong in the facts about the whole matter of the Kansas Nebraska bill, which was introduced by the Senator himself and which is the offspring of the ambition and greed of slavery. I say that I extend to him the privilege of correcting me in my facts & not in my inferences as they are subject of dispute among men and would cause too many collateral issues to be raised and no value to the main subject." Mr. Douglas was irritated and thoroughly aroused: he made statements often and irrelevant ones under the privilege of correcting facts. This was about to interrupt Mr. Lincolns speech and break the thread of it as a whole & set speech, when Mr. Lincoln said—"I revoke—I withdraw what I have said to the Hon Senator as to privilege and shall assert what I do assert as my own respectfully". This ended the annoyance to Lincoln and to the vast crowd in the hall. Douglas saw & took a mean advantage of the privilege granted to him by Lincoln: he made statements about things not in dispute nor bearing on the issues in dispute nor debate. In my opinion he did so to interrupt Lincoln and fret him and thus destroy the effect of L's speech. All this I saw and heard and distinctly remember it.

Your Friend

W. H. Herndon

LC: HW3689–90; Exp 4:10:2717–20

271. To Jesse W. Weik

Spfgd Ills Octr 2d '90

Friend Jesse—

. . .

I wish to relate to you an important fact. Soon after the assassination of Mr. Lincoln I interviewed Mr. Judd, two or three times, in relation to his knowledge of Lincoln *generally* and particularly about what L said in reference to the questions he intended to ask Douglas at Freeport. Turn to our life of L. 410. Douglas put

---

5. WHH's testimony about Douglas abusing Lincoln's invitation to correct any errors in his Oct. 4, 1854, speech conforms to what he told J. G. Holland in 1865 (Holland, 137–38), but it is not fully confirmed by any known contemporary account, including his own. The "Editorial" WHH quoted in his biography and refers to here, which consisted of several excerpts from what he had published in the *Illinois Journal*, October 10, 1854, reported only that Douglas "frequently interrupted Mr. Lincoln." For these passages, printed as a single excerpt, see *Herndon's Lincoln*, 227–28.

Two marginal notes on this passage: "This note if you write one can come in at pge 367–8.—date Octr '54" and "This was Lincoln's meeting only i e anti Nebraska."

7 questions to L. at Ottowa. Lincoln went to Chicago and had a meeting of his friends and told them that he intended to put 4 questions to Douglas at Freeport and among those questions was the 2d one which was substantially this "Can a territory exclude slavery from its limits while in a territorial condition or state". At the meeting of Lincoln's friends at Dixon or Chicago were Peck—Judd—Ray et al. All of them, after Lincoln had read the 4 questions to be put to Douglas at Freeport objected to them and said in substance that Douglas would not positively answer the question directly and that if he did it would be in the affirmative and that would elect him to the Senate again. "It is none of your business Mr Lincoln particularly to put the question because you are the candidate for the U.S. Senate and that is your particular business" said Lincoln's friends. Lincoln replied "Douglas will answer the question as soon as asked & if he does not I will push him to the wall at every joint debate or wherever I shall speak otherwise than in joint debate; and the sooner Douglas answers the better for him. The people demand a direct answer". "Douglas will answer in some glittering generalities and evade the question" said Peck—Ray et al. "Yes, he will answer directly" said Lincoln; and to which Lincoln's friends said, "to put the question is none of your business Mr. Lincoln and to which Mr Lincoln said—"yes it is my business, and if Douglas answers the question, which he will, either way he is a dead cock in the pit." Mr. Lincoln here went into a kind of argument to convince his friends that he was right and concluded by saying—"I am after larger game. The battle of 1860 is worth a hundred of this—". See Arnold pge. 150–1 and see Holland 189–193. Lincoln evidently wanted to kill Douglas politically and did it effectually. I say that Judd told me what Lincoln said in the meeting of friends at Dixon or Chicago, I think Chicago, though White says the meeting was at Dixon. Probably he is correct. Though Peck—Ray—Judd et all say that Lincoln uttered the above words still I doubt the *exact words*, because, as you well know that Mr. Lincoln was one of the most secretive men that ever lived. The expression means that, "I am a candidate for the Presidency of the U.S. of America. That is what I am fighting for". I do not think that Mr. Lincoln ever uttered the words as stated, though he looked at the time for the office. I think at most that the words as above are inferences, legitimate ones. Lincoln never told mortal man his purposes and plans—never. Evidently L beat around the bush. As I think of things I'll write you.

Your Friend
W. H. Herndon

P.S—When you come to this sphere of man and mud you will please write to me.

LC: HW3691–92; Exp 4:10:2721–24

272. To Jesse W. Weik

Spfgd Ills. Octr 5th '90

Friend Jesse—

Your two letters—one of the 30th inst & the other—are before me and in reply to the—wherein is stated the Lincoln & Duff Green story,[1] let me say that the story *as told* is untrue—1st Because it is contrary to Lincoln's nature & 2dly because Lincoln never uttered the foolish, pompous, self important expression—"Go before I forget myself and *the high position I hold*". Lincoln would not have listened to Green, but would have turned away from the "Cuss", paying no attention to the poor devil. Lincoln was not educated in invectives: his heart was too good—too kind and too charitable. As you are aware of the fact that Mr Lincoln was a fatalist I can say to you that he took his election as a fact written in the book of fate; he was not elevated to pride or pomp in his election nor depressed in defeat; his election did not in his opinion lift him up at all. I saw L in '61 and he was the same man that he was in 1840—when young & poor. This Duff Green as I remember him was a South Carolinian and was never in Ills to my knowledge—was no kin to our Greens of Menard Co. Green, if Lincoln knew him, was in Congress or a loafer about the House when Lincoln was in Congress. Green was once quite a man, but I suppose fell like Lucifer through his ambition. I think that I remember Green as a kind of free trader in '37–'46 or about those years. I have no doubt that there is a ground for the Duff Green story, but it never happened *as told*. There are thousands of such stories floating about through the world in relation to what Lincoln said—did and dreamed, but when put to the touch stone of Lincoln's nature—his constant mode of action—his sagacity—his prudence—his wisdom &c. &c they fade away like the mists of the morning before the blazing sun. Jesse, keep Lincoln's nature before you and your judgments will be correct.

. . .

Your Friend
W. H. Herndon

LC: HW3693–94; Exp 4:10:2725–28

273. To Jesse W. Weik

Spfgd Ills Octr 21st '90

My Dearest Jesse—

In your present fix you forget things now & then. Read our life of L at pgs 592–3 and you will see that we expressly say that L was *not* the master of the English language. On column 2 of the gal which you sent me last you say that L *was* the master of language.[1] You will find the expression used by you about 35

---

1. See Fehrenbacher, 367.

---

1. The galley proof that WHH refers to would not seem to be connected to any impending printing of their biography; it most likely was galley proof for something JWW had written.

lines above "Whig meeting". 2d col paragraph 2d. Please say that he used strong language to express his clear cut ideas. L was deficient in language: ~~or~~ Say that he was ~~quite~~ somewhat master of language. Any words will do except the words used by you. Modify the expression—say he used good language—. He was in a degree—to a certain extent master of language will do.

. . .

Your friend as Ever
W H Herndon

P.S Cant you select—pick out & insert by way of notes under Swetts letter what Swett said but suppressed by him in his last letter to me. I mean those parts which Swett said that no one would believe him &c[2]

LC: HW3696; Exp 4:10:2731–32

274. To James H. Wilson[1]

Nov 22 '90

X X X

"The reason why I asked you to burn my Lincoln letters I will explain to you sometime if I live. I cannot now. I know that Lincoln's greatness—for he was the great among the great of the world would well stand the whole truth—the whole naked truth. That all men from the truth could see him as I knew him was my motive. My sole motive in telling what I did and yet it is true that some men do not like, nor approve of it.

X X X X X

You ask me if Lincoln delivered the speech which Downing speaks about. I can only answer in this way—If you will turn to my life of Lincoln 1st vol pg 104 you will see what he did say in 1832.[2] The speech in the book is correct. I got it from two intelligent men who heard it shot off in a hurry. Possibly you may wish to know L's later views on the tariff & if you do let me knowingly say that he followed Clay in his ideas—i. e. L was, in after life a revenue tariff man affording incidental protection & that is 'all'

LC: HW3704; Exp 4:10:2747

---

2. WHH refers to Leonard Swett's January 17, 1866 letter about AL that was printed in *Herndon's Lincoln* (316–22) with changes Swett was allowed to make in 1887. For an account of the changes, see *Herndon's Informants*, 162–68.

---

1. Document written in JWW's hand, headed: "Letter Nov 22 '90 Herndon to J H Wilson."
2. See *Herndon's Lincoln*, 75.

275. *To Horace White*

Springfield Ills. Decr 4th '90

Friend White—[1]

In my last letter to you I stated that I had something to tell you about Lincoln which took place in '54—Octr I think. I will now state it & as you were present you may remember it, and if you do not this may refresh your memory. If you will turn to my life of Lincoln & read a short piece of Editorial for our Journal written by me—pge 368 on the evening of the speech, you will see that I stated that Douglas frequently interrupted Mr. Lincoln during his speech.[2] In reading your Excellent letter to me of the 27th Feby '90 and at the beginning of it you speak—to me at least, feelingly & eloquently of Lincoln and his speech in '54. Your remarks in that letter to me—the one which constitutes a chapter in the life of Lincoln & spoken of above, caused me to be put in the same state—condition—consciousness that I was in on the moment of the debate, and I saw everything—heard everything, as in the moment of the speech, after reading your remarks in the letter spoken of. We are curious creatures & the mind and its laws are a riddle to me. Is it not true that we remember things once supposed to be lost forever by being put in the same *state* as we were when we saw or heard the thing?

Mr. Lincoln after opening his speech and clearing away the under brush so that he might have a clear & open view of things said substantially this—"I give Senator Douglas the privilege of correcting me in any facts which I shall state, but not the inferences which I shall draw from them as they are the nib of the whole question and would open too broad a field of debate now & here". Douglas sat right under Lincoln and was a little "cocked" at the time. For some time Douglas made no corrections nor suggestions, but as Lincoln proceeded Douglas got hot & a little vexed, if not angry. Lincoln began to get warmer and struck harder & heavier blows and then it was that Douglas quite every moment made some side show so called corrections of unimportant things—collateral ones not in issue at all in anyway. The large audience saw & felt that Douglas was taking a mean advantage of Lincoln's granted privilege to him. The crowd at last got angry and showed its feelings in different ways though not inappropriately—not boisterously generally. Lincoln himself began to *feel* and I could see in his eyes a little ill feeling. You know that I understood Lincoln, I think, inside and outside. The crowd got madder & madder at the foolish corrections so called made by Douglas. Men were uneasy and restless & the women—God bless 'em—said by their acts—"Sit down, Mr. Douglas". Lincoln got more angry every moment and at last in self defence—rising to his full height cooly—calmly said—"Senator Douglas I withdraw the privilege of correcting me which I gave you a moment ago" "and now friends the facts which I shall hereafter state I shall state on my own responsibility". When

---

1. Top margin: "[If you] do not want this please send it to Mr Jesse Weik, Greencastle Indiana so that it may go in the record sometime H."

2. For WHH's "short piece," on AL's October 4, 1854, speech, see *Herndon's Lincoln*, 227–28. For another version of this episode, see §270.

this was said I could see smiles of approbation run over the faces of the crow and all was calm—peaceful & pleasant after that Before this things looked a little "scary"—"flighty' in one corner of the Hall.[3] I took notes of his—L's—speech and loaned them to Govr Yates who made in '56 & '8 many good speeches from them. I was up in the gallery and you on the little Elevation near the speaker. My piece in the Journal shows my honest opinion of Lincoln's speech and of the appearance and actions of Douglas.[4] The reason why I have written this to you is that you may wish to make a *note* of it sometime for your letter to me.

I wish now to make another Statement. If you remember you once asked me if the text in Lamon's life of Lincoln was correct—pge 396 as I remember it, and in answer to which question I said "it was substantially correct" & I say so now.[5] Our Judge J. H. Matheny said to me, only a month or so before he died which was some two months since, that he heard Lincoln say in substance—"If Douglas can draw off such & such men from the cause of republicanism and be made to support him, who says he does not care whether Slavery is voted up or voted down—if he can get strong & influential leading republican papers to laud him—& if he can attack and partly crush Buchannan's administration & can get in Illinois so many votes to Buchannan's none, then he will play the *devil* at Charleston. From a letter of yours written to me a good while ago I infer that you did not get mine fully explaining—or confirming Lamon. Excuse a friend, won't you?

Your Friend

W. H. Herndon

H

Exp 4:10:2753–56

276. To John E. Remsburg[1]

EXTRACTS FROM LETTERS WRITTEN 1880–1890

"I was the personal friend of Mr. Lincoln from 1834 to the day of his death. In 1843 we entered into a partnership which was never formally dissolved. When he became unpopular in this Congressional district because of his speeches on the

---

3. For other versions of this episode, see §30 and §270.
4. WHH's piece on AL's October 4, 1854, speech appeared in the *Illinois Journal* on October 10, 1854. Excerpts from this article are reprinted as a single excerpt in *Herndon's Lincoln*, 227–28.
5. See Lamon, 396. See also §261.

---

1. These extracts from WHH's letters to John E. Remsburg were first published in his book, *Abraham Lincoln: Was He a Christian?* (New York: Truth Seeker, 1893), 113–23, and later reprinted in Remsburg's *Six Historic Americans: Paine, Jefferson, Washington, Franklin, Lincoln, Grant, the Fathers and Saviors of our Republic* (New York: Truth Seeker [pref. 1906]), 113–23.

Mexican war, I was faithful to him. When he espoused the antislavery cause and in the eyes of most men had hopelessly ruined his political prospects, I stood by him, and through the press defended his course. In these dark hours, by our unity of sentiment and by political ostracism we were driven to a close and enduring friendship. You should take it for granted, then, that I knew Mr. Lincoln well. During all this time, from 1834 to 1862, when I last saw him, he never intimated to me, either directly or indirectly, that he had changed his religious opinions. Had he done so—had he let drop one word or look in that direction, I should have detected it.

"I had an excellent private library, probably the best in the city for admired books. To this library Mr. Lincoln had, as a matter of course, full and free access at all times. I purchased such books as Locke, Kant, Fichte, Lewes; Sir Wm. Hamilton's 'Discussions on Philosophy;' Spencer's 'First Principles,' 'Social Statics,' etc.; Buckle's 'History of Civilization,' and Lecky's 'History of Rationalism.' I also possessed the works of Parker, Paine, Emerson, and Strauss; Gregg's 'Creed of Christendom,' McNaught on Inspiration, Volney's 'Ruins,' Feuerbach's 'Essence of Christianity,' and other works on Infidelity. Mr. Lincoln read some of these works. About the year 1843 he borrowed 'The Vestiges of Creation' of Mr. James W. Keys, of this city, and read it carefully. He subsequently read the sixth edition of this work, which I loaned him. Mr. Lincoln had always denied special creation, but from his want of education he did not know just what to believe. He adopted the progressive and development theory as taught more or less directly in that work.[2] He despised speculation, especially in the metaphysical world. He was purely a practical man. He adopted Locke's notions as his system of mental philosophy, with some modifications to suit his own views. He held that reason drew her inferences as to law, etc., from observation, experience, and reflection on the facts and phenomena of nature. He was a pure sensationalist, except as above. He was a materialist in his philosophy. He denied dualism, and at times immortality in any sense.

"Before I wrote my Abbot letter[3] I diligently searched through Lincoln's letters, speeches, state papers, etc., to find the word *immortality*, and I could not find it anywhere except in his letter to his father. The word *immortality* appears but once in his writings."

"If he had been asked the plain question, 'Do you *know* that a God exists?' he would have said: 'I do *not know* that a God exists.'"

"At one moment in his life I know that he was an Atheist. I was preparing a speech on Kansas, and in it, like nearly all reformers, I invoked *God*. He made me wipe out that word and substitute the word *Maker*, affirming that said Maker was a principle of the universe. When he went to Washington he did the same to a friend there."

---

2. What WHH here calls "the progressive and development theory" became better known as the theory of evolution.

3. See §89.

"Mr. Lincoln told me, over and over, that man has no freedom of will, or, as he termed it, 'No man has a freedom of mind.' He was in one sense a fatalist, and so died. He believed that he was under the thumb of Providence (which to him was but another name for fate). The longer he lived the more firmly he believed it, and hence his oft invocations of God. But these invocations are no evidence to a rational mind that he adopted the blasphemy that God seduced his own daughter, begat a son on purpose to have mankind kill him, in order that he, God, might become reconciled to his own mistakes, according to the Christian view."

"Lincoln would wait patiently on the flow and logic of events. He believed that conditions make the man and not man the conditions. Under his own hand he says: 'I attempt no compliment to my own sagacity. I claim not to have controled events, but confess plainly that events have controled me.' He believed in the supreme reign of law. This law *fated* things, as he would express it. Now, how could a man be a Christian—could believe that Jesus Christ was God—could believe in the efficacy of prayer—and entertain such a belief?"

"He did not believe in the efficacy of prayer, although he used that conventional language. He said in Washington, 'God has his own purposes.' If God has his own purposes, then prayer will not change God's purposes."

"I have often said to you, and now repeat it, that Lincoln was a scientific Materialist, *i.e.*, that this was his tendency as opposed to the Spiritualistic idea. Lincoln always contended that general and universal laws ruled the universe—always did—do now—and ever will. He was an Agnostic generally, sometimes an Atheist."

"That Mr. Lincoln was an Infidel from 1834 to 1861, I know, and that he remained one to the day of his death, I honestly believe. I always understood that he was an Infidel, sometimes bordering on Atheism. I never saw any change in the man, and the change could not have escaped my observation had it happened."

"Lincoln's task was a terrible one. When he took the oath of office his soul was bent on securing harmony among all the people of the North, and so he chose for his Cabinet officers his opponents for the Presidential candidacy in order and as a means of creating a united North. He let all parties, professions, and callings have their way where their wishes did not cut across his own. He was apparently pliant and supple. He ruled men when men thought they were ruling him. He often said to me that the Christian religion was a dangerous element to deal with when aroused. He saw in the Kansas affairs—in the whole history of slavery, in fact—its rigor and encroachments, that Christianity was aroused. It must be controled, and that in the right direction. Hence he bent to it, fed it, and kept it within bounds, well knowing that it would crush his administration to atoms unless appeased. His oft and oft invocations of God, his conversations with Christians, his apparent respect for Christianity, etc., were all means to an end. And yet sometimes he showed that he hated its nasal whines."

"A gentleman of veracity in Washington told me this story and vouched for its truthfulness: 'A tall saddle-faced man,' said he, 'came to Washington to pray with Lincoln, having declared this to be his intention at the hotel. About 10 o'clock

A.M. the bloodless man, dressed in black with white cravat, went to the White House, sent in his card, and was admitted. Lincoln glanced at the man and knew his motives in an instant. He said to him angrily: "What, have you, too, come to torment me with your prayers?" The man was squelched—said, "No, Mr. Lincoln"—lied out and out. Lincoln spoiled those prayers.'"

"Mr. Lincoln was thought to be understood by the mob. But what a delusion! He was one of the most reticent men that ever lived. All of us—Stuart, Speed, Logan, Matheny, myself, and others, had to guess at much of the man. He was a mystery to the world—a sphinx to most men. One peculiarity of Mr. Lincoln was his irritability when anyone tried to peep into his own mind's laboratory. Considering all this, what can be thought of the stories about what he said to have confided to strangers in regard to his religion?"

"Not one of Lincoln's old acquaintances in this city ever heard of his conversion to Christianity by Dr. Smith or anyone else. It was never suggested nor thought of here until after his death."

"I never saw him read a second of time in Dr. Smith's book on Infidelity. He threw it down upon our table—spit upon as it were—and never opened it to my knowledge."

"My opinion is, from what I have heard and know, that these men—Gurley and Simpson—refused to be a party to a fraud on the public touching Lincoln's religion. I think that they understood each other the day that the remains of Lincoln were put to rest."

"Holland came into my office, in 1865, and asked me this question: 'What about Mr. Lincoln's Christianity?' To this, I replied: 'The less said about it the better.' Holland then said to me, 'Oh, never mind, I'll fix that,' and went over to Bateman and had it fixed."[4]

"Lincoln never revealed to Judge Davis, Judge Matheny, Joshua F. Speed, Joseph Gillespie, nor myself that he was a Christian, or that he had a change of heart, or anything like it, at any time. Now, taking into consideration the fact that he was one of the most non-communicative of men—that Bateman was, as it were, a mere stranger to him—that Bateman was frightened, excited, conscience-smitten when I approached him on the subject, and that in after years he confessed to me that his notes in Holland's 'Life of Lincoln' were colored—taking all this into consideration, I say, can you believe Bateman's story to be true?"

"I see quoted frequently a supposed speech made by Mr. Lincoln to the colored people of Baltimore, on the presentation of the Bible to him. This supposed speech contains the following: 'All the good from the Savior of the world is communicated to us through this book.' This idea is false and foolish. What becomes of nine-tenths of the life of Jesus of which we have no history—nine-tenths of the great facts of this grand man's life not recorded in this book? Mr. Lincoln was full and exact in his language. He never used the word Savior, unless in a conventional sense; in

---

4. For WHH's dispute with Newton Bateman over what the latter told J. G. Holland about AL's religion, see §43, §89, p.80, §92, p.116, §118.

fact, he never used the word at all. Again, he is made to say: 'But for this book we could not know right from wrong.' The lowest organized life, I was about to say, knows right from wrong in its particular sphere. Every good dog that comes into possession of a bone, knows that that bone belongs to him, and he knows that it is wrong for another dog to rob him of it. He protests with bristling hair and glistening teeth against such dog robbery. It requires no revelation to teach him right from wrong in the dog world; yet it requires a special revelation from God to teach us right from wrong in the human world. According to his speech, the dog has the advantage. But Mr. Lincoln never uttered such nonsense."

"I do think that anyone who knew Mr. Lincoln—his history—his philosophy—his opinions—and still asserts that he was a Christian, is an unbounded falsifier. I hate to speak thus plainly, but I cannot respect an untruthful man."

"Let me ask the Christian claimant a few questions. Do you mean to say, when you assert that Mr. Lincoln was a Christian, that he believed that Jesus was the Christ of God, as the evangelical world contends? If so, where do you get your information? Do you mean to say that Mr. Lincoln was a converted man and that he so declared? If so, where, when, and before whom did he declare or reveal it? Do you mean to say that Mr. Lincoln joined a church? If so, what church did he join, and when did he join it? Do you mean to say that Mr. Lincoln was a secret Christian, acting under the cloak of the devil to advance Christianity? If so, what is your authority? If you will tell me when it was that the Creator caught with his almighty arms, Abraham, and held him fast while he poured the oil of grace on his rebellious soul, then I will know when it was that he was converted from his Infidel views to Christianity."

"The best evidence this side of Lincoln's own written statement that he was an Infidel, if not an Atheist, as claimed by some, is the fact that he never mentions the name of Jesus. If he was a Christian it could be proved by his letters and speeches. That man is a poor defender of a principle, of a person, or of a thing, who never mentions that principle, person, or thing. I have never seen the name of Jesus mentioned by Mr. Lincoln."

"Mr. Lincoln never mentioned the name of Christ in his letters and speeches as a Christian. I have searched for such evidence, but could not find it. I have had others search, but they could not find it. This dead silence on the part of Mr. Lincoln is overwhelming proof that he was an unbeliever."

"While Lincoln frequently, in a conventional way, appeals to God, he never appeals to Christ nor mentions him. I know that he at first maintained that Jesus was a bastard, and later that he was the son of Joseph and not of God."

"Lincoln was not a Christian in any sense other than that he lived a good life and was a noble man. If a good life constitutes one a Christian, then Mill and a million other men who repudiated and denied Christianity were Christians, for they lived good and noble lives."

"If Mr. Lincoln changed his religious views he owed it to me to warn me, as he above all other men caused me to be an unbeliever. He said nothing to me, intimated nothing to me, either directly or indirectly. He owed this debt to many young men whom he had led astray, if astray the Christian calls it. I know of two young men of promise, now dead and gone—gone into endless misery, according to the evangelical creed—caused by Mr. Lincoln's teachings. I know some living here, men in prominent positions of life, who were made unbelievers by him."

"One by one, these apocryphal stories go by the board. Courageous and remorseless criticism will wipe out all these things. There will not be a vestige of them in fifty years to laugh at or to weep at."

Six Historic Americans, *113–23*

277. To Jesse W. Weik

Springfield Ills Jany 30th '91

LINCOLN'S MATERIALISM—"EXPLAINED"—A NOTE—

In our life of Lincoln, Jesse—I said, scientifically speaking, that Mr Lincoln was a materialist as opposed to a Spiritualist. The word materialist has so many definitions & inferences drawn from it that no one knows what a man means by that word till those who use it define and explain it. It can best be understood by the use and definition of the word spiritualism. Spiritualism means, in one sense, and that is the sense in which I use it, that this world is ruled, governed and guided by spirits distinct—outside of—separate from & above matter—the world. I said that Lincoln believed in materialism, as *opposed* to spiritualism—was inclined to that belief by his nature and now is materialism opposed—adverse, hostile to spiritualism? The sense in which I use the word is contrary & adverse to spritualism in this—that the word materialism means that the world is ruled, governed & guided, as well as controlled, by general—unvarying, irrefragable & irresistible laws, and not by spirits. These two words are opposites—adverse—contrary—different & repugnant to each other. Mr Lincoln believed that the world was governed by and guided by universal—unvarying, & irresistible irrefragable mechanical laws and not by spirits above—distinct and separate from matter—the world. These two words are the pivots around which the world's great debates have turned or whirled. Because a man believes in materialism as above used and intended to mean, it does not follow that he denies God—spirits—soul—immortality. Mr. Lincoln firmly believed in God & immortality as strongly as any Christian or thoroughly religious man. However Mr Lincoln had the world, its laws & its facts for scientific study: he believed in laws—general principles—was a sensationalist—a realist—a fatalist—a purely practical man & not a speculative one—was a thorough skeptic in all things—demanded evidence as foundations of his beliefs and was scientifically speaking a materialist as opposed to spiritualist. He lived a pure, chaste, virtuous life—a lofty one and this I well *know* from my observations & experiances of the man. In his practice of life he was quite spiritual. I do not now refer to that phase of spiritualism which teaches or believes that the spirits of the dead hold communion with the living. That is an other & a different question & not now before us.

W. H Herndon

Exp 4:10:2774–75

278. To Jesse W. Weik

Springfield Ills. Jany '91

Friend Weik—[1]

When I was in Greencastle in '87 I said to you that Lincoln had, *when a mere boy*, the Syphilis and now let me explain the matter in full which I have never done before. About the year 1835–6 Mr. Lincoln went to Beardstown and during a devilish passion had connection with a girl and caught the disease. Lincoln told me this and in a moment of folly I made a note of it in my mind and afterwards I transferred it as it were to a little memorandum book which I loaned to Lamon, not, as I should have done, erasing that note. About the year '36–7 Lincoln moved to Springfield and took up his quarters with Speed: they became very intimate. At this time I suppose that the disease hung to him and not wishing to trust our physicians wrote a note to Doct Drake,[2] the latter part of which he would not let Speed see, not wishing Speed to know it. Speed said to me that Lincoln would not let him see a part of the note. Speed wrote to me a letter saying that he supposed that L's letter to Dr Drake had reference to his—L's—crazy spell about the Ann Rutledge love affair &c and her death. You will find Speed's letter to me in our life of Lincoln. The note to Dr Drake in part had reference to his disease and not to his crazy spell, as Speed supposes. The note spoken of in the memorandum book was a loose affair, and I never intended that the world should see or hear of it. I now wish & for years have wished that that note was blotted out or burned to ashes. I write this to you fearing that at some future time the note—a loose thing as to date, place and circumstances, will come to light and be misunderstood. Lincoln was a man of terribly strong passions, but was true as steel to his wife during his whole marriage life: his honor, as Judge Davis, has said saved many a woman & it is most emphatically true as I know. I write this to you to explain the whole matter for the future if it should become necessary to do so. I deeply regret my part of the affair in every particular.

Your Friend
W. H. Herndon

P.S—Mrs. Dall was my guest for several days—say in '71 and she saw that memorandum book & took some notes of its contents & it may sometime come to light from that quarter, and so you have this as my defence. H

LC: HW3722; Exp 4:10:2776–77

---

1. In top margin: "Keep this Carefully if you please—May need it in defence—H"
2. Dr. Daniel Drake.

279. To Jesse W. Weik

Springfield Ills. Feby 5th '91

Friend Jesse—

I want to give you a kind of bribery story about Mr & Mrs Lincoln which took place soon after Lincoln was elected Presdnt. The story comes through Hermann Kreisman, who was appointed by Lincoln secretary of Legation, when Judd was appointed Minister to Germany.[1] Kreisman is a gentleman & can be relied on. The story is as follows—One Henderson of N.Y wished to be appointed to some office in the Custom House of New York.[2] To get the office he sent to Mrs. Lincon, in care of some jewelry house in this City, a diamond broach to be given to her upon the condition that he could get the promise of the office from Mrs L. Kreisman & Judd came to Springfield on some important business and were to meet Lincoln at some place by appointment, but he did not come as agreed, Mrs. Lincoln having cornered him & he could not get away. Mrs Lincoln got the diamond broach, having promised Henderson to get the office for him. Kreisman was dispatched to hunt up Lincoln. He went to Lincoln's house and was ushered in, in a hurry & probably by the servant, she not telling Mr & Mrs L. Kreisman found Mrs L in a hysterical fit cutting up like a crazy woman. She was begging Lincoln to appoint Henderson. Lincoln refused several time but Mrs L kept up her yells—her hysterical fit till Lincoln, in order to get rid of the woman & quiet the fit, did promise Mrs L that Henderson should have the office & Henderson got it according to the promise. Henderson was subsequently indicted in the U.S Court for defrauding the government but was acquitted on some technical point. Henderson knew how to reach Mrs L. & did reach her in Henderson's way. Lincoln to keep quiet in his house & to get this woman's fingers out of his hair did a wrong thing, if he knew why Mrs Lincoln was so anxious for Henderson's appointment. Such is woman & such is man the world over—weak creatures indeed. Lincoln must have had an idea of his motives & the cause of them that prompted Mrs Lincoln to want Henderson appointed. By the way Lincoln had no true notions of the propriety of things, as a general rule. I suppose that in this case Lincoln did not know what to do. The devil was after him & he stumbled.

Poor bedeviled fellow—unfortunate man!

. . .

Your Friend
W. H. Herndon

LC: HW3723–24; Exp 4:10:2778–79, 4:11:2881–82

---

1. WHH had recently learned of this story from Horace White. See §281.

2. Isaac Henderson, publisher of the *New York Post,* was appointed naval agent in the New York customhouse in 1861 and was later "dismissed when accused of misconduct." Michael Burlingame, "Mary Todd Lincoln's Unethical Conduct as First Lady," in *At Lincoln's Side: John Hay's Civil War Correspondence and Selected Writings,* edited by Michael Burlingame (Carbondale: Southern Illinois University Press, 2000), 189.

280. To Jesse W. Weik[1]

[c. February 1891]

One day I asked him why he was so careful: his reply was substantially this—"I have your money often & often and if I were to die, who would know that I had your money collected as fees away off in the circuit? No one and to prevent accidents I thus mark your share—"Herndon's". I never use any man's money under any circumstances—this I have determined". I may have given you this before & if so excuse me, won't you. It is so much like Lincoln that I couldn't help telling it again.[2]

. . .

Once you asked me, while speaking of Mr. Lincoln's religion, this question—"Did Stuart & Matheny deny what you state they said in Lamon";? and to which I answered—"No". You have in your possession a letter, [backed?] to "The Truth Seeker", as I remember it, which states what I did write to the Truth Seeker in substance and by that letter I stand. The letter to the T. S. is a corrected rather a substantial copy of the one in your hands—both letters are substantially the same however. Matheny acknowledged under his own hands that what was said in Lamon—what he purported to utter there was his "sayings." Stuart never denied what he is made to say, but goes off on an other track, not in issue &c. I have been extremely careful in this whole matter & I stand by what is said in Lamon in relation to Stuart and Matheny, as well as all other persons. I took notes at or near the moment of utterance.

Your Friend as Ever
W H Herndon

P.S I said in a letter to you that the stories of Lincoln walking so far were pure fiction. I wish to modify that expression by saying that I do not believe them, though they may be true. H

LC: HW3798–99; Exp 4:10:2782–83

281. To Horace White

Springfield Ills. Febry 13th '91

Friend White—

I thank you for your letter of the 26th ult. The story about Mrs Lincoln & her Henderson brouch rings like one of Mrs. Lincolns fits of rage. I have seen her often in just such spells of frenzy & I will venture all that I have that the story is

---

1. This document has been filed as pp. 3–4 of a letter to JWW dated February 13, 1891, but the lack of continuity between pages 2 and 3 indicates that these pages probably belong to another letter. The editors believe it likely that the actual date of the unlocated letter these pages belong to is close to February 13, 1891.

2. For an earlier but fuller account, see §221.

correct. Unfortunate woman! Miserable man! Lincoln had to do things which he knew were out of place in order to keep his wife's fingers out of his hair.

. . . I am still diligently gathering well authenticated facts of Lincoln. Many I reject, because they are not in harmony with the fundamental elements of L's nature and because they come to me in a most questionable shape. I expect to continue gathering facts about L as long as I live, & when I go hence the reading world shall have my MSS unchanged—unaltered & just as I took them down in writing. I think that they will be of value to mankind sometime. I have been at this business since '65. Every day or so I think of some fact or facts & they suggest to me some other fact or facts which wake in me a conscious state, as if the thing—conditions & time were just present. The human mind is a curious thing & is not understood thoroughly by any man.

. . .

Your Friend
W. H. Herndon

ALPL: Horace White Papers

282. To Jesse W. Weik

Springfield Ills Feby 21st '91

Friend Jesse—

In your letter of the 8th inst you ask me if I remember Mr. Lincoln's lecture here in '58–9 and in an answer to your question let me say, *I do distinctly remember it*. It was delivered here in Myer's Hall on the North side of the square, nearly mid way between 5 & 6 st & sometime, I think, in Febry—probably Jany '59. I heard the lecture *&* remember the subject of it very well. The title of it was substantially—"The time of the different inventions", mostly those mentioned in the Bible. Probably the word "discoveries" would suit the title as well. Knowing Mr. L as well as I did I was anxious to hear him, and did listen to him well—thoroughly—attentively—& curiously too. I know that Mr L was not fitted—qualified in any way to deliver a lecture to our people who were intelligent—well read—and well educated. I was not mistaken in the lecture which Mr. L read: it was a lifeless thing—a dull dead thing, "died a bornin." It fell on the ears of the audience as a cold flat thing. There was no life—imagination or fancy in it—no spirit & no life. The whole thing was a kind of farce and injured Mr L's reputation as a man of sense among his friends and enemies.[1]

Mr. Lincoln was a peculiar—mysterious man. I wrote to you once that Mr L had *a double Consciousness*—a double life. The two States, never in the normal man, Co-exist in Equal & vigorous activities though they succeed each other quickly. One state predominates & while it so rules, the other state is somewhat

1. On AL as a lecturer, see §96, p. 102 and §153.

quiescent—shadoway, yet being—a real thing. This is the sole reason why L so quickly passed from one State of consciousness to an other & a different State. In one moment he was in a state of abstraction & then quickly in an other state when he was a social, talkative & a communicative fellow. In our office on the west side of the Square we had a long office table running north & south.[2] Mr L always took his seat on the East side of the table, looking outward; and I sat on the west side of the table looking eastward; & thus we sat face. About one o'clock in the day time the sun, especially in the summer, streamed through the western windows of our office & flooded Lincoln's face, so that I could see the very back parts of his eyes. When thus situated and in one of his abstract moods I studied the man & think that I could read his thoughts clearly—distinctly—certainly *in a general way*. You know my love of reading men—mind—moods—characteristics &c. You are aware that I love the science of the mind quite over all studies & I had the very best of opportunites to do so. On looking at the man under the above conditions speculatively—critically, he would to the observer's surprise without warning burst out in a loud laugh or quickly spring up and run down stairs as if his house were on fire, saying nothing. Sometimes it took a strong effort on his part to awake—arouse himself from the condition on purpose or with intent to live in another state of consciousness. To do this he would tell a story or read a Chapter in such a book as Jack Downing—Nasby—Mark Twain—Bill Nye—or Josh Billings.[3] The sharp parts of one state of Consciousness touched the other state, & it was therefore easy for him to pass from one state to an other and a different state. Such was the man always. This [law of?] the man may spring out of the double brain each part lying close together, touch to touch, one life in one hemisphere of the brain and the other life in the other. Jesse, you don't like this kind of stuff, I know and will quit it, cutting it short for your sake—yes for your sake.

. . .

I said to you while I was in Greencastle that Lincoln told me that Jno T Stuart—Matheny—& the leading Filmore men in this section were bribed by the Buchanan Corruption fund—said that he believed that the Filmore party—i e leaders of it through the state were bought & sold like hogs are sold in the mark. That induced me to kill the *Conservative* published here.[4] I had two ideas in getting in the Richmond Enquirer article[5]—1st I wanted it published in the *Conservative* so as to show the rank & file of the Filmore boys the course they were expected to move—vote & act and in the end shout for Slavery; & in the 2d place I wanted

2. Presumably in reference to the anecdote that follows, WHH wrote in the margin: "Jesse—you can make an interesting note of this where in our book we speak of Mr L's sadness, gloom—&c. characteristics &c. It can come in at pge 590 of our book unless you (590) can find a better place."

3. For Jack Downing and Petroleum V. Nasby, see §133. Josh Billings (Henry Wheeler Shaw) was also dispensing slangy wit and wisdom in the 1860s. Mark Twain and Bill Nye were yet to be heard from during AL's lifetime.

4. For the *Conservative*, see §208, §243, §245, §246, §247, §282, and *Herndon's Lincoln*, 228–29.

5. In margin: "The Richmond Enquirer's article maintained that slavery was right in principle & that it covered the white race as well as the black. It was a long piece & a well written one." See §243 and §246.

to kill the *Conservative* out & out. It did soon die, possibly for want of funds or because of the Richmond Enquirer piece. Here then is a full explanation of what I told you when I was in your city. I remember too of writing to you some general words about this matter, but I repeat in order to make the matter full & plain. Lincoln *knew* what he was talking about, let me assure you. This cannot now go in print but it can go to the world if needed, in the great future.

. . .

Your Friend
W. H. Herndon

LC: HW3729–31; Exp 4:10:2788–93

283. To Jesse W. Weik

Springfield Ills. Feby. 26th '91

Friend Jesse—

I wish to say a word or two about Mr. Lincolns fatalism—First he believed that both matter & mind are governed by certain irrefragable & irresistible laws, & that no prayers of ours could arrest their operation in the least—2dly That what was to be would be inevitably—3dly That the laws of human nature are persistent & permanent and could not be reversed: he said this in his printed speech in '42,[1] & 4thly he said, while he was president, that he did not rule events, during any time in his administration, but that events ruled him.[2] All these things are of record and there is no mistake about it. It follows that Mr Lincoln was a fatalist, as he himself has said, though his fatalism was not of the extreme order like the Mahometan idea of fate, because he believed firmly in the power of human effort to modify the environments which surround us. He made efforts at all times to modify & change public opinion and to climb to the presidential heights: he toiled & struggled in in this line as scarcely any man ever did. As to free will, he said that that which was governed by a power *outside* itself was not self governed & that which was not self governed was not free, though he admitted that the will to a very limited extent, in some fields of operation, was somewhat free. The laws of the universe are, except as to human nature, *outside* of the will and governed it. The will, in addition, had to act along the lines of human nature including the laws of motive, thus giving the will only a small field of action for the exercise of its freedom, so called.

I wish to use the above statement of facts for an end—namely to show that Mr. Lincoln believed that men are the children of Conditions—of circumstances *&* of their environments which surrounds them, including a hundred thousand years or more of education with acquired habits & the tendency to heredity, moulding them as they are & will forever be. His whole philosophy made him free from

---

1. "Temperance Address," February 22, 1842, *Collected Works*, 1:273.
2. AL to Albert G. Hodges, April 4, 1864, *Collected Works*, 7:282.

hate—free from love, intense & free from malice. No man was responsible for what he was—thought or did, because he was a child of conditions. No man was censured by him or ought to be by others he was, by his philosophy, full of charity for his fellow man—No man was to be eulogized for what he did or censured for what he did not do or did do. Hence Lincoln could well exclaim—"With malice toward none & charity for all". I never heard him censure any one but slightly nor eulogize any, probably with two milk & cider efforts—one of which was on Thomas Jefferson & the other on Henry Clay.[3] He himself said—"I am not accustomed to deal in eulogies". I have often thought that he did not care anything for men—thought that he looked through them for or at the principles behind them, and of which they were the representatives. He worshipped principles—laws.

You once sent me a bitter invective said to be spoken by Lincoln to one Duff Green, a southern nullifier & free trader, who had spoken to L harshly about the war & its cruelties.[4] The invective was found, as you told me, in Belfords Magazine.[5] Now from the above, my friend Jesse, do you not see that the Belford piece is an absurdity—"a bald lie made out of whole cloth". So are all such invectives said to be from Lincoln. An other invective said to be pronounced by L against an African Slave driver will be found in Arnold's *romantic* life of L at pges 433–4.[6] This is all "bosh—a lie". Again there is an other piece though not of the same kind as the above, to be found the Independent—year '59–'60, N.Y. The article was written by a Mr. *Gulliver* for the N.Y Independent—[7] Gulliver, eh! I counted 9 or more bare faced errors in the article. Gulliver said that Lincoln opened to him his methods of Education in a free & easy style. Jesse, I could pick out a hundred, if not a thousand more things as the above now & then floating around in the news paper Sea. I have purposely written you this, so that, if you need it, which I do not think you do; you can be on your guard as to the correctness of what you see & read.

If Lincoln's limited fatalism leads to the banishment of malice—causes freedom from malice & vindictiveness—to his broad & living charity for the foibles of his fellow man—and to his *general* love for all men of all races & all religions, & to

---

3. For AL's praise of Jefferson, see AL to Henry L. Pierce and Others, April 6, 1859, *Collected Works*, 3: 374–76. For Clay, see "Eulogy on Henry Clay," July 6, 1852, *Collected Works*, 2: 121–32.

4. See §272.

5. See "Lincoln in Richmond: Admiral Porter's Mistakes," *Belford's Magazine* 6, no.33 (February 1891): 335–36.

6. Arnold.

7. The Rev. John P. Gulliver described a conversation with AL in *The Independent* (September 4, 1864), which was reprinted two years later in Carpenter, 308–17. Here and elsewhere WHH dismisses Gulliver's account because of its errors; but before publishing, Gulliver sent a proof of the article directly to AL for corrections, which were not forthcoming. See John P. Gulliver to AL, August 26 and September 12, 1864, Abraham Lincoln Papers at the Library of Congress, (memory.loc.gov). Purged of incidental errors, Gulliver's account is revealing.

his nobility of thoughts & *deed*, then the race had better adopt a limited fatalism as theory & practice of its daily life, rather than the so-called Christianity.

. . .

Friend Herndon

LC: HW3734–35; Exp 4:10:2797–800

284. To Jesse W. Weik

Home in the Country. Feby 27th '91

. . .[1]

Let me write out what Judge Matheny told me more in full than I did to White. Lincoln said the same thing to me in a half dozen times & different ways. Mr. Lincoln was speaking about the power of Douglas—Slavery—the Charleston Convention—the dissolution of it &c. He said this in substance "If Douglas could draw off such men as Washburn et al, such men good & true republicans & support Douglas & his Sham Squatter Sovreignty—if he could get such leading papers as the NY. Tribune & others to pat Douglas on the back while it was somewhat injuring the cause; & if Douglas could crush the whole of Buchanan's administration with its power & its patronage in Ills & get all the democratic votes in Illinois except about five thousand, *then* he would play the very devil at Charleston. The explosion is certain & will come & probably bust up the democratic party for good—for some time to come. The materials at Charleston will be of an explosive nature and explode they will. Mark my words " The reason why I did not write it out for Mr White was because he knew what Lincoln did say as appeared in Lamon's life of Lincon 396. Lincoln said much more than is said here or can now be said[2]

Your Friend
W H Herndon

LC: HW3736; Exp 4:10:2801–2

285. To Jesse W. Weik

Springfield Ills. 27th '91 Feby.

Jesse—

About the year 1857 I walked into our office with "The Annual of Science,"[1] which I had purchased of Bradford & Johnson, Lincoln then being in the office reading the news papers. On seeing me he said—"Hello, Billy, what book is that

---

1. Marginal note: "These letters & the ones heretofore sent you ought to fill you with unbounded hope. It does me. The book only wants a chance & that's all."

2. See §261 and §275.

---

1. Probably *The Annals of Science: Being a Record of Inventions and Improvements*, a serial publication appearing 1852–54. For another version of this story, see §141.

which you have under your arm" & to which I replied—"The Annual of Science". "Let me see it" said Lincoln. I handed it to him: he looked over it for some little time & then made the remark "It's got up on the right plan; because it gives the successes and failures of experiments. The history of the successes of life & experiment shows what can be done in art, science—philosophy; & economizes time and expense. The history of failures shows what cannot be done, as a general rule and puts the artist—scientist & philosopher on his guard & sets him a thinking on the right line. We always hear of the successes of life & experiment, but scarcely ever of the failures. Were the failures published to the world as well as the successes much brain work & pain work—as well as money & time would be saved." Continuing, Mr Lincoln said—"By jing I must go & buy a copy, it pleases me so well"; & so he did go and buy his copy—brought it to the office and then took it home as he went to dinner & put it in his library, as I suppose. I told you these facts when I was in Greencastle, but I suppose that you have forgotten them & this is the reason why I repeat.

About this time '57–8 Mr. Lincoln was engaged somewhat in mathematics & the study of rational philosophy. I say *somewhat*, because he was a fire with politics, they being his life—newspapers his food & office his ambition & his end. Well, he purchased a small compass—slate—pencils—heavy paper &c. &c and sat down in our office for a siege on the squaring of the circle: he sat for 3 or 4 days till nearly exhausted & starved, butting up against the squaring of the circle. I understand that the perfect squaring of the circle is an impossibility, but being green myself, shall not say that it can nor cannot be done. Mr Lincoln was a peculiar man—had an absolute confidence in his own powers, and that is the reason why he never asked any body for advice nor took any man's opinion for his pride—was self helping—& self reliant. He looked to himself & stood by himself with steadfastness & of idea & purpose & seemed to say—"Lincoln said so & that is my sole guide". I say & say it to you that Mr. Lincoln was a peculiar—mysterious & reticent minded man. You had to judge him by what he *did* & not so much as what *he said*, because he scarcely ever talked: he was honest & told the truth always *so far* as he talked, but in his talk he said just enough to say nothing at all. Profoundly secretive man! A wily man in mental reservations! He was [begotten?] by the eternal silences and was a very great man take him [round &?] round—& a very wise & true man take him all in all—such was Lincoln as I saw him.

Inclosed you will find a letter of mine written to the Religio-Philisophical Journal of Chicago, touching some of Lincoln's peculiarities, the letter being dated Decr '85, about the time you and I saw each other, as I now remember it.[2] You will perceive that I keep to the track. Truth is always harmonious—at all time agreeing with itself. Read it. One more word—Mr. Poole or Mr Bundy sent me the Religio-P. Journal in which was Mr. Poole's speech on Lincon, and in which it was strongly intimated that L was a Spiritualist. This excited—called my attention to the fact, if it was so, & so I commenced a thorough investigation of the subject and

---

2. See §139.

in such thorough investigation I found out that there was *no foundation*—not in the least for the idea that he was a Spiritualist, though there were some peculiarities in Lincon that lead one to believe that he was touched with it on some occasions. I then wrote—that is, a soon I received the paper, to the editor the inclosed letter. After I wrote the letters I commenced the investigation as stated above and landed at the Conclusion above. File it & this letter away and keep them.   . . .

Your Friend

Wm. H. Herndon

LC: HW3739–40; Exp 4:10:2803–06

286. To Truman Bartlett

Springfield, Ills Feby 27th '91

Friend Bartlett—[1]

. . .

To help you *somewhat*, I hope, in your conceptions—ideas about Mr Lincoln, let me say to you that he had *a double consciousness*—if not a treble consciousness. First he was a terribly gloomy—sad man at times—2dly he was at times full of humor—"joky"—witty & happy. Gloom & sadness were his predominant state—3dly at times he was neither sad nor humorous, but was simply in a pleasant mood—i e he was not in a gloomy nor a mirthful fit—*was kindly thoughful,* not serious ever—a state of thought & good feeling united for the moment. This state appeared in him when in a pleasant conversation with friends. This last state was not of long duration. Lincoln was a curious—mysterious—quite an incomprehensible man. Do not think that I exaggerate. These states—double or treble are the causes why the phos are a little different as to likeness. The moment Lincoln took his seat at the pho machine & looked down the barrel of it he became sad—rather serious, as all business with him was serious, life included. . . .

Your Friend

W. H. Herndon

MHS: Truman Bartlett Papers

---

1. Note in top margin in Bartlett's hand: "Last letter from Mr. Herndon. He died 18 Mar, '91."

UNDATED LETTERS

287. To John M. Keyes and Samuel B. Munson[1]

[1886–87?]

Mesrs. Keys & Munson—

It was distinctly understood between Lincoln & myself that I wanted to hold no office under his administration, as I held the Bank Commissioners office under Govr Bissel who appointed me at the solicitation and request of Mr Lincoln.

Your Friend
W H. Herndon

Lincoln Memorial Shrine

288. To John C. Henderson[1]

Springfield, Ill.

You request me to state to you what were the feelings, sentiments and ideas of Mr. Lincoln touching the great subject of public—universal—education of the people, especially in America. I became acquainted with Mr. Lincoln in 1834, while he lived in New Salem, in Sangamon County, in this State (Illinois), and knew him well from '34 to the day of his death; and I ought to know his feelings, sentiments and ideas on this subject. I know what he has really said on the question of education, and I know what he has written on it; he has said to me, and to others in my presence and hearing, that "universal education should go along with and accompany the universal ballot in America; that the very best, firmest and most enduring basis of our Republic was the education, the thorough and the universal education of the great American people; and that the intelligence of the mass of our people was the light and the life of the Republic." This I have heard him say in *substance* over and over, again and again. Mr. Lincoln was conscientiously just, truthful and honest, and hence thought that every other person was just, truthful and honest; but in this belief he was often sorely disappointed. He had an infinite faith—trust—in the people, and in their instinct of, and mental insight into, the fundamentals of government. He trusted the people, and saw no creature made purposely to rule them without their consent. He looked to the great mass of men for the right, and had full faith in the honesty and capability of the people

---

1. Written on a slip of paper, possibly for inclusion in the "Lincoln Memorial Collection" that Keyes and Munson were establishing, with WHH's help, in 1886 and 1887.

---

1. Published in a New York magazine in 1895 with the following headline and headnote: AN UNPUBLISHED LETTER FROM LINCOLN'S /LAW PARTNER. / *LINCOLN ON EDUCATION—HIS VIEW OF WOMAN'S / RIGHTS—AN EARLY REFORMER.* / BY W.H. HERNDON, ESQ.

[The venerable W. H. Herndon, who for twenty-five years was Abraham Lincoln's law partner, and knew him better than perhaps any man now living, wrote the following—a letter to Mr. John C. Henderson, of this city, giving facts which are an interesting and valuable contribution to the history of one of America's most celebrated statesman.]

for self-government. As a politician and a statesman he took no steps in advance of the great mass of our people. Before he acted on any great political or other question touching the people's interest, he took notes, made observations, felt the public pulse; and when he thought that the people were ready he acted, and not before. At times I thought he was timid, overcautious; but in the end he was right and I was wrong. Mr. Lincoln's ideas were that men do not of themselves make events, but that events make men. Hence he waited with a cautious patience, a philosophic judgment, on the constant and regular flow and logic of them.

Give Mr. Lincoln his own time and he was a man of great common sense, which he applied to the daily and practical affairs of men; he was not a genius, but was better; he was a good man, an honest man, a sound man, and an upright and downright one. When he once formed an opinion he never took a backward step. What I have said to you herein marked him somewhat as a politician and a statesman. Mr. Lincoln trusted in the people and appealed to them, and they in their turn trusted and appealed to him. Neither was disappointed.

If what I have stated to you is correct, *truthful*, then Mr. Lincoln must have written something on the subject of education. If he had faith in the people—if he thought that universal education should go along with and accompany the universal ballot; and if he thought that the strongest, firmest and most enduring basis of a Republic was the thorough and universal education of the great mass of our people, then he must have taken a firm stand on this great question, and so he did. Let me explain. Mr. Lincoln became a candidate in this State (Illinois) in 1832, for the Legislature. It was then and continued for years to be a custom for the respective candidates to issue a handbill—a program of the principles which they would advocate if elected to the honorable position. According to that universal and long-settled custom here in this State, Mr. Lincoln did on the ninth day of March, 1832, issue his handbill, containing the things—subjects and laws which he would advocate in the Legislature, if elected. Mr. Lincoln traveled around the country, saw the people, and asked them to support him for the causes which he advocated on the stump and in his handbill. In that handbill he uses these exact words:

> "Upon the subject of education, not promising to dictate any plan or system respecting it, I can only say that I view it as *the* most important subject which we as a people can be engaged in. That every man may receive at least a moderate education and thereby be enabled to read the histories of his own and other countries, by which he may duly appreciate the value of our free institutions, appears to be an object of vital importance even on this account alone, to say nothing of the advantages and satisfaction to be derived from all being able to read the Scriptures and other works, both of a religious and moral nature, for themselves.
>
> "For my part, I desire to see the time when education—and by its means, morality, sobriety, enterprise and industry—shall become much more general than at present, and should be gratified to have it in my power to contribute

something to the advancement of any measure which might have a tendency to accelerate the happy period."[2]

Mr. Lincoln was defeated in 1832, but was elected in 1834 to the Legislature. I have been informed, but do not know of my own knowledge, that Mr. Lincoln most heartily supported every measure which came before the Legislature touching the question of the people's education and common schools. I have been told this by a member of the Legislature of this State in 1834-'35. I believe it. In short, on this question, Mr. Lincoln's ideas of the education of the people were practical; he wished the people educated and enlightened on practical questions for a practical life and an immediate, practical end. He was a practical man in all the ways and walks of life. Mr. Lincoln was not a great general reader, but was a special one. When he wished to know anything he hunted it up and dug it out to the small, fibrous end of the very taproot. I say that Mr. Lincoln was a practical man, and hence he was a special man; that is, he worked for a practical and paying end. He did not much care to know anything that he would have no use for. Politics was his constant study and newspapers his ever-present library. Mr. Lincoln was the great practical—the embodiment of caution and prudence. "Take him all in all, and we shall not soon see his like again."

As remarked, many, many times before, Mr. Lincoln had a keen, quick sense of the eternal right and just. Seeing that Woman was denied in *free* America her right to the elective franchise, being the equal but the other side—the other and better half of man—he always advocated her rights—*yes, rights*. In the year 1836 Mr. Lincoln issued a kind of handbill, making a declaration of some things which he wished and would advocate, and among them were these—I quote his words:

"I go for *all* sharing the privileges of the Government *who assist in bearing its burdens*. Consequently, I go for admitting *all* whites to the right of suffrage *who pay taxes* or bear arms, by no means excluding *females*.

"If elected I shall consider the *whole* people of Sangamon my constituents, as well those who oppose as those that support me."[3]

Mr. Lincoln was twenty-three years of age when he issued his first handbill in '32, and twenty-seven when he issued the one in '36. When Mr. Lincoln once, as said before, on due consideration, took a step forward, he never took one backward. He would at any time have supported and advocated and voted for woman's rights. Tho he believed in woman's rights, he thought the time probably had not yet come to openly advocate the idea before the people. He said: "This question is one simply of time."

New York Independent, *April 4, 1895.*

---

2. From "Communication to the People of Sangamo County," March 9, 1832, *Collected Works*, 1:8.
3. "To the Editor of the *Sangamo Journal*," June 13, 1836, *Collected Works*, 1:48.

289. To Jesse W. Weik[1]

CORY

"Springfield Ills Oct. 10th 1860

Dear William:

I cannot give you details, but it is entirely certain that Pennsylvania and Indiana have gone Republican very largely, Penn 25,000 & Indiana 5 to 10. Ohio of course is safe.

Yours as Ever

A. Lincoln"

The history of the letter is as follows. I was making a speech for Lincoln in Petersburg on the evening of Oct. 10th and had fairly got into the spirit of the hour when some one rushed into the court room and handed me the letter. I, at first, thought that it might contain sad news from my family. I opened the letter and read it over to myself before reading to the people and then I read it aloud to the crowd. I never finished that speech. The crowd yelled—screamed—threw up their hats—ran out of doors—made bonfires—&c. &c. and so the speech was never finished so joyous were we all. The hand writing was a little tremulous showing that L was excited—nervous. I gave the letter in '81 to a Mr. Parker, President of the Englewood Soldiers Memorial association near Chicago. You will find an account of the letter &c in a book recently published in Chicago by Rhodes & McClure, publishing company. The book seems to be a pretty good one in a certain time & is called "Lincoln Stories".[2] It is somewhat after the order of "The every day life of Lincoln",[3] which you have.

Your Friend

W. H Herndon

LC: Exp 4:7:27–28

1. This is from the second and third page of a letter whose first page has not been identified. The letter dates from the late 1880s.

2. Probably *Anecdotes of Abraham Lincoln and Lincoln's Stories: Including Early Life Stories, Professional Life Stories, White House Stories, War Stories, Miscellaneous Stories* (Chicago: Rhodes and McClure, 1879).

3. *Every-Day Life.*

Register of Correspondents

ABBOT, FRANCIS E. (1836–1903)

Editor of *The Index*, the publication of the Free Religious Association, an organization founded in 1867 to promote the scientific study of theology and to encourage liberty of religious thought.

ARNOLD, ISAAC N. (1815–1884)

A Chicago attorney and politician, and contemporary of AL's. Arnold was a member of Congress for two terms (1860–64) and was the author of two of the earliest biographies of AL, *History of Abraham Lincoln and the Overthrow of Slavery* (Chicago: 1866) and *The Life of Abraham Lincoln* (Chicago: 1885).

ANDREW, JOHN A. (1818–1867)

Republican governor of Massachusetts during the Civil War and an early advocate of the recruitment of African Americans into the Union Army. He became increasingly critical of AL as the war progressed.

BARTLETT, TRUMAN H. (1835–1922)

An American sculptor and instructor in the Art Department of the Massachusetts Institute of Technology. Long fascinated by AL's physical appearance, he professed to see in him "a deep harmony between the outer and inner man."

BOYD, ANDREW H. (FL. 1870)

One of the very earliest collectors of Lincoln bibliography and memorabilia. He joined forces with bibliographer Charles H. Hart to publish the *Memorial Lincoln Bibliography* (1870), a book that for many years was the manual for other collectors of Lincolniana.

CARPENTER, FRANCIS B. (1830–1900)

An American painter best known as the author of *Six Months in the White House with Abraham Lincoln*, an informative memoir of his life in the executive mansion while working on his most famous painting, *First Reading of the Emancipation Proclamation*.

CRITTENDEN, JOHN J. (1787–1863)

An influential Whig senator from Kentucky in favor of compromising the sectional crisis who earlier sided with Stephen A. Douglas over AL in the 1858 Illinois Senate race because of Douglas's opposition to the Lecompton Constitution.

CRONYN, DAVID (1839–1911)

A student at Meadville (Pennsylvania) Theological School who wrote to WHH to ask if AL had once said that he would join a church "which made the simple love of God and man the condition of membership," and whether he had been acquainted with the Unitarian Church.

DALL, CAROLINE HEALEY (1822–1912)

A Boston-based teacher, lecturer, and women's rights activist who supported AL's presidency and later considered writing his biography.

DAVIS, DAVID (1815–1886)

The presiding judge of the Illinois Eighth Circuit, before whom AL practiced for more than ten years. Davis also managed the campaign to secure AL's nomination at the Republican convention in Chicago in 1860 and was subsequently appointed to the U.S. Supreme Court.

DWIGHT, THEODORE F. (1846–1917)

A librarian and chief of the Bureau of Rolls and Library at the U.S. Department of State—and not, as WHH suspected, the son of Theodore Dwight (1764–1846), the author of *The Character of Thomas Jefferson, as Exhibited in His Own Writings* (1839).

EASTMAN, ZEBINA (1815–1883)

An anti-slavery journalist, first in Hennepin, Illinois, and then Chicago, who supported AL's 1860 presidential campaign and was subsequently appointed U.S. consul at Bristol, England.

FLAGG, WILLARD C. (1829–1878)

A prominent horticulturalist and political activist in Madison County, Illinois, who served two terms in the Illinois senate and was a leader in the organization of the Granger Movement in Illinois. Undoubtedly the recipient of WHH's letter of December 22, 1868, Flagg appears a less likely candidate for the letters of October and December of 1875.

FOWLER, JOSEPH (1820–1902)

A Tennessee Unionist who served in his state's military government during the Civil War and was named a U.S. senator after Tennessee's readmission to the Union.

GAY, SYDNEY HOWARD (1814–1888)

An early lecturer for the American Anti-Slavery Society, Gay later edited that association's newspaper, the *Anti-Slavery Standard*, and was managing editor of the *New York Tribune* during the Civil War.

GILLESPIE, JOSEPH (1809–1885)

A close legal and political friend whom AL had known since the Black Hawk War. Gillespie was an active promoter of the Republican Party and AL's role in it.

GOODRICH, CHAUNCEY (1817–1868)

A member of Connecticut's great Goodrich family who was involved with his father, Chauncey A. Goodrich, in the revision of Webster's unabridged dictionary. Related to Noah Webster and probably the recipient of WHH's letter of November 17, 1866.

HALL, JOHN J. (1829–1909)

The son of AL's stepsister Matilda Johnston Hall. After Thomas Lincoln's death in 1851, Hall purchased his farm in Coles County, Illinois, where he and his family then lived with AL's stepmother, Sarah Bush Lincoln.

HARDIN, JOHN J. (1810–1847)

A fellow Whig and early political rival of AL's in the Illinois Seventh Congressional District, where he, AL, and Edward D. Baker took turns representing that district in Congress in the 1840s. Hardin was killed in the Mexican War at Buena Vista on February 23, 1847.

HART, CHARLES H. (1847–1918)

As a young Philadelphia law student, Hart prepared a bibliography of eulogies and memorial addresses prompted by AL's death, which was jointly published with Andrew Boyd as *Memorial Lincoln Bibliography* (1870).

HENDERSON, JOHN C.

Not identified.

HICKMAN, MR.

Not identified.

HOLLAND, JOSIAH G. (1819–1881)

A prominent New England journalist and early AL biographer who was associated with the *Springfield (Mass.) Republican* and a co-founder of *Scribner's Monthly.*

KEYES, JOHN M. (FL. 1886–87)

Having purchased a number of Lincoln items from WHH, Keyes and Samuel B. Munson opened an exhibit of AL memorabilia in Chicago late in 1886, for which WHH acted as onsite curator and interpreter from late November 1886 to January 1887.

KLINE, MR.

Not identified.

LAMON, WARD HILL (1828–1893)

An Illinois lawyer friend of AL's, Lamon accompanied AL to Washington, where he served as marshal of the District of Columbia. In 1869 Lamon purchased from WHH the three-volume copy of his "Lincoln Record," which served as the principal source for the controversial biography of AL ghostwritten by Chauncey F. Black and published under Lamon's name in 1872.

LINDMAN, J. J. (FL. 1887)

Possibly John J. Lindman, who is listed as a commission merchant in the Chicago city directory for 1886.

MACDONALD, EUGENE M. (?–1909)

Editor of the freethought publication *The Truth Seeker*, Macdonald succeeded its founder, D. M. Bennett, at his death in 1882.

MAIN, MR.

Not identified.

MCPHERSON, EDWARD (1830–1895)

Originally a Gettysburg, Pennsylvania, attorney and journalist, McPherson was a two-term Republican congressman after 1859 and then served as clerk of the U.S. House of Representatives until 1875.

MILES, GEORGE U. (1796–1882)

The father of WHH's second wife, Anna, Miles assisted WHH in collecting information about AL's life in the New Salem neighborhood.

MUNSON, SAMUEL B. (FL. 1886–1887)

In partnership with John M. Keyes, Munson established the Lincoln Memorial Collection, which featured many Lincoln-related items acquired from WHH in 1886–87.

NICOLAY, JOHN G. (1832–1901)

A native of Germany, Nicolay was AL's private secretary in the White House, later U.S. consul in Paris and marshal of the U.S. Supreme Court, and with John Hay, the co-author of a ten-volume biography of AL, first serialized in *The Century* (1886–90).

NOYES, MR.

Not identified.

OGLESBY, RICHARD J. (1825–1899)

A legal and political colleague of AL's from central Illinois who was elected governor of Illinois three times and also served in the U.S. Senate.

PARKER, THEODORE (1810–1860)

A prominent Unitarian minister and orator in Massachusetts, critical of orthodox Christian theology, and perhaps best known as an outspoken abolitionist who carried on a substantial correspondence with WHH.

PHILLIPS, WENDELL (1811–1884)

One of the most prominent and vehement New England abolitionists who at first favored acceptance of the Confederacy as ending the slave power's dominance of the Federal government; Phillips was a sharp critic of AL's administration.

PIERCE, EDWARD L. (1829–1897)

A Massachusetts lawyer and author perhaps best known for organizing the plantations and freedmen of the Sea Islands of South Carolina after their occupation by Union forces in 1861. Also an important informant for WHH about AL's visit to New England in 1848.

POOLE, CYRUS O. (1821–1901)

A New York City attorney and spiritualist who published "The Religious Convictions of Abraham Lincoln: A Study" in the *Religio-Philosophical Journal* on November 28, 1885.

REMSBURG, JOHN E. (1848–1919)

A religious skeptic from Kansas who wrote and lectured widely on free thought.

SEWALL, SAMUEL E. (1799–1888)

An attorney and state legislator who was a prominent Boston abolitionist. Probably the recipient of WHH's letter of February 1, 1861.

SEWARD, WILLIAM H. (1801–1872)

As governor of New York and U.S. senator, Seward was a prominent opponent of slavery and the leading contender for the 1860 Republican presidential nomination; he served as AL's secretary of state.

SMITH, MR.

Not identified.

SWANSON, J. H. (FL. 1888)

In 1888, he was a citizen of the new town of Herington, Kansas.

TRUMBULL, LYMAN (1813–1896)

Originally a Jacksonian Democrat who opposed slavery, Trumbull was elected to the U.S. Senate as an Anti-Nebraska Democrat in 1855, a seat for which AL also contended. Trumbull became a Republican a year later and supported AL's presidential candidacy and his wartime policies.

WEIK, JESSE W. (1857–1930)

As WHH's collaborator, Weik was the recipient of hundreds of letters from WHH, many of which were about AL. A relatively young aspiring writer, Weik composed most of the text of *Herndon's Lincoln*, their jointly authored biography, working mainly from WHH's letters and his collection of reminiscences of AL by others who knew him.

WHITE, HORACE (1834–1916)

A journalist who covered AL's pre-presidential career in Illinois approvingly and who criticized AL's apparent slowness on the slavery issue during the Civil War. He admired *Herndon's Lincoln* and helped WHH and JWW find a second publisher for their biography of AL.

WHITNEY, HENRY CLAY (1831–1905)

A lawyer with AL on the Eighth Circuit and campaigner for AL in 1858 and 1860. Whitney's *Life on the Circuit with Lincoln* is a memoir of legal circuit-riding in Illinois, and he made important contributions to WHH's collection of informant materials.

WILSON, JAMES H. (1837–1925)

A West Point graduate and an accomplished commander during the Civil War, Wilson was active after the war in business, public affairs, and in writing.

YATES, RICHARD (1815–1873)

Politically associated with AL, first as a Whig and later as a Republican, Yates was the embattled Civil War governor of Illinois who frequently criticized AL for his slowness to act.

Acknowledgments

This volume, the fourth in the Lincoln Studies Center Publication Series, has had a long gestation. This was partly due to the need, initially, to conduct a national survey of repositories where letters written by William H. Herndon might possibly be held, followed by the evaluation necessary to determine which letters, or parts thereof, should be included in this edition, and finally the time required for transcription, proofing, and annotation. Over the extended period involved in this process, the editors have incurred many obligations to persons and institutions whose assistance and cooperation were invaluable and are gratefully acknowledged in what follows.

By far the largest portion of the known letters about Lincoln written by Herndon is in the Herndon-Weik Collection at the Manuscript Division of the Library of Congress. In our many visits to the library in the service of this project, we have enjoyed splendid cooperation from John R. Sellers, longtime specialist in charge of Lincoln-era manuscripts, and his very helpful and accommodating successor, Michelle Knowl. For generous cooperation and assistance in the Manuscript Reading Room, we are particularly indebted to the late Mary Wolfskill and her very cooperative successor, Jeffrey Flannery. In the Library's Rare Book Division, we have enjoyed the valuable assistance of Clark Evans.

The second-largest number of selections in this volume come from the rich Lincoln holdings of the Huntington Library, the Ward Hill Lamon and Charles H. Hart Collections in particular. We are pleased to acknowledge the kind assistance received at the Huntington from Robert Skotheim, Virginia Renner, John Rhodhamel, Martin Ridge, and Paul Zall. We should also note that fellowships at the Huntington helped lay the groundwork for the editorial enterprise of which this volume is a part.

At the Abraham Lincoln Presidential Library (formerly the Illinois State Historical Library) in Springfield, Illinois, we were welcomed and assisted by Janice Petterchak, Katherine Harris, Kim Bauer, Thomas Schwartz, Cheryl Schnirring, Glenna Schoeder-Lein, and James Cornelius.

Among the many other librarians who have assisted us, we are pleased to acknowledge the following: at Allegheny College, Connie Thorson; at the Boston Public Library, Jean Nadhege; at the John Hay Library, Brown University, Mary-Jo Kline and Holly Snyder; at the Chicago History Museum (formerly the Chicago Historical Society), Russell Lewis and Lesley Martin; at the Butler Library, Columbia University, Bernard R. Crystal; at the Kroch Library, Cornell University, Lorna Knight; at the Houghton Library of Harvard College, Jennie

Rathbun; at the University Library, University of Illinois at Urbana-Champaign, John M. Hoffmann and Ryan Ross; at the Indiana Historical Society, Glen L. McMullen; at the Lincoln Memorial Shrine in California, Nathan Gonzales; at Lincoln Memorial University, Steve Wilson and Charles Hubbard; at the New York Historical Society, T. K.; at the New York Public Library, Jim Noske; at the Massachusetts Historical Society, Nicholas Graham; at the Historical Society of Pennsylvania, Sandra Rayser Ragonese; at the Yale University Library, Christine Weideman.

We gratefully acknowledge also the contributions of private collectors Bob G. Field, Joseph L. Rembusch, and David Swanson, who kindly shared their holdings. Kenneth L. Tabb, county clerk of Hardin County, Kentucky, answered some pertinent questions about nineteenth-century office holding. Candace O'Connor kindly performed specialized research for which she was uniquely qualified.

We have benefited in this long project from the advice and contribution of many scholars but perhaps from none more than Michael Burlingame. John M. Hoffman has generously gone out of his way to help us on several occasions. Others who have encouraged and assisted us include John Sellers, Michelle Krowl, Clark Evans, Matthew Norman, Elizabeth Brown Pryor, Richard Carwardine.

As always, we have been blest with the assistance that we invariably receive from members of the Knox College Library staff: Jeffrey Douglas, Anne Giffey, Carley Robison, Bonnie Niehus, and Kay Vander Meulen, and especially from Sharon Clayton, Laurie Sauer, and Irene Ponce.

We take great pleasure in acknowledging the invaluable contribution of Meredith Witherell to the groundwork for this project in its early stages. She served as office manager, chief correspondent, file coordinator, manuscript detective, as well as hawkeyed transcriber and proofreader. Her energy and enthusiasm for bringing a large set of manuscripts and records under control helped to jump-start the project.

Knox College students have assisted us in all our projects and were involved in this enterprise from its very beginning. Accordingly, we are pleased to recognize the efforts of Suellen Riley, Matt Waldren, Derek Papp, Joel Ward, Marie Hawn, and Todd Trainor. Jessa Kennedy Dahl, Claire Healy, and Ai Miller have been especially helpful for extended stints as student office assistants.

At Knox College, Dean Lawrence Breitborde was a constant and indispensable source of support for the Lincoln Studies Center, first as a concept and then for more than a dozen years as a working enterprise. President Roger Taylor generously offered encouragement and moral support on a regular basis for this and, indeed, for all the activities of the Lincoln Studies Center. The editors consider that such support reflects yet another dimension of the longstanding institutional commitment to scholarship that has prevailed throughout their long tenure at Knox College.

And finally, the editors once again thank our wives, Sharon E. Wilson and Norma G. Davis, for their sterling support and for enduring, ungrudgingly, the trials and inconveniences of a failed retirement project.

Index

WILLIAM H. HERNDON (1818–1891) was Abraham Lincoln's law partner from 1844 until Lincoln became president in 1861. In 1889, he published a biography of the late president called *Herndon's Lincoln: The True Story of a Great Life*.

RODNEY O. DAVIS and DOUGLAS L. WILSON are co-directors of the Lincoln Studies Center at Knox College, in Galesburg, Illinois, and the co-editors of *Herndon's Informants, Herndon's Lincoln*, and *The Lincoln-Douglas Debates*.

THE KNOX COLLEGE LINCOLN
STUDIES CENTER SERIES

Herndon's Lincoln
   William H. Herndon and Jesse W. Weik;
   edited by Douglas L. Wilson and Rodney O. Davis

The Lincoln-Douglas Debates
   The Lincoln Studies Center Edition
   Edited by Rodney O. Davis and Douglas L. Wilson

The Civil War Diary of Gideon Welles, Lincoln's Secretary of the Navy
   The Original Manuscript Edition
   Edited by William E. Gienapp and Erica L. Gienapp

Herndon on Lincoln: Letters
   William H. Herndon;
   edited by Douglas L. Wilson and Rodney O. Davis

The University of Illinois Press
is a founding member of the
Association of American University Presses.

Composed in 10.5/12 Adobe Garamond
by Jim Proefrock
at the University of Illinois Press
Manufactured by Sheridan Books, Inc.

University of Illinois Press
1325 South Oak Street
Champaign, IL 61820-6903
www.press.uillinois.edu